Pop Goes the Decade

Pop Goes the Decade

The Fifties

RALPH G. GIORDANO

**With Essay Contributions by
Matthew R. Giordano,
Jeff Benjamin, and
Omar Swartz**

GREENWOOD™

An Imprint of ABC-CLIO, LLC
Santa Barbara, California • Denver, Colorado

Library of Congress Cataloging-in-Publication Data

Names: Giordano, Ralph G., author.
Title: Pop goes the decade : the fifties / Ralph G. Giordano.
Description: Santa Barbara, California : Greenwood, an imprint of ABC-CLIO,
    LLC, 2017. | Includes bibliographical references and index.
Identifiers: LCCN 2016048960 (print) | LCCN 2017007833 (ebook) |
    ISBN 9781440844713 (hard copy : acid-free paper) | ISBN 9781440844720 (ebook)
Subjects: LCSH: Popular culture—United States—History—20th century | United
    States—Civilization—1945– | United States—Social life and
    customs—1945–1970. | United States—Intellectual life—20th century.
Classification: LCC E169.12 .G556 2017 (print) | LCC E169.12 (ebook) | DDC
    306.0973—dc23
LC record available at https://lccn.loc.gov/2016048960

ISBN: 978-1-4408-4471-3
EISBN: 978-1-4408-4472-0

21 20 19 18 17   1 2 3 4 5

This book is also available as an eBook.

Greenwood
An Imprint of ABC-CLIO, LLC

ABC-CLIO, LLC
130 Cremona Drive, P.O. Box 1911
Santa Barbara, California 93116-1911
www.abc-clio.com

This book is printed on acid-free paper ∞

Manufactured in the United States of America

Dedicated
to
Madison Paige Giordano

Contents

Timeline

1950 (U.S. CENSUS: 150.7 MILLION PEOPLE)

- World War II-era G.I. Bill of Rights (1947 to 1956).
- First modern credit card introduced.
- January 27: Klaus Fuchs confession of spying for the Soviets implicates his sister-in-law and her husband, Ethel and Julius Rosenberg.
- January 31: President Harry Truman announces development of the hydrogen bomb.
- February 9: Senator Joseph McCarthy gives Wheeling, West Virginia, speech claiming Communist infiltration in U.S. government.
- June: Korean War begins and military advisors sent to South Vietnam.

1951

- Color television introduced to market.
- March 29: Julius and Ethel Rosenberg convicted of espionage.
- September 4: Truman speaks in first coast-to-coast live television broadcast.
- December: Buckminster Fuller patents "Geodesic Dome."

1952

- Mr. Potato Head is the first toy advertised on television.
- July 25: Puerto Rico becomes a U.S. Commonwealth.
- November 1: The United States explodes first hydrogen bomb at Eniwetok Atoll in the Marshall Islands in the South Pacific.
- November 4: Dwight D. Eisenhower elected president over Adlai Stevenson.

1953

- March 5: Soviet Premier Josef Stalin dies.
- Alfred Kinsey's *Sexual Behavior in the Human Female* is published.
- June 19: Julius and Ethel Rosenberg executed for espionage.
- July 27: Korean War cease-fire.
- December: Color television available for consumer purchase.

1954

- January 21: First atomic submarine U.S.S. *Nautilus* launched.
- April 22: Televised hearings of Senator McCarthy's allegation of Communist infiltration of the United States Army.
- May 17: Segregation ruled illegal in Supreme Court decision of *Brown v. The Board of Education of Topeka, Kansas*.
- Disney's television show *Davy Crockett* creates a consumer fad of purchasing products associated with the title character.

1955

- Cleveland disc jockey Alan Freed coins the phrase "Rock 'n' Roll."
- March 26: Polio vaccine is announced.
- May 31: U.S. Supreme Court orders nationwide desegregation of public schools.
- July 17: Disneyland opens in California.
- September 30: James Dean dies in car accident.
- December 1: Rosa Parks refuses to give up her seat on a bus.

1956

- Television, Rock 'n' Roll, and teenage dancing displayed on *American Bandstand*, a show hosted by Dick Clark in Philadelphia.
- Elvis Presley appears on the *Ed Sullivan Show*.
- Television remote control is invented.
- June 29: Federal Interstate Highway Act passed.
- October: New York Yankees' Don Larsen pitches first perfect game in World Series history. The Yankees would dominate World Series play during the decade.
- November: Eisenhower re-elected over Adlai Stevenson.

1957

- January: Wham-O releases the first Frisbee.
- October 4: Soviet satellite *Sputnik* launches the Space Age.

- September 24: Governor Orval Faubus calls out National Guard to stop nine black students from entering Central High School in Little Rock, Arkansas.
- December: America's first attempt at a satellite launch fails.

1958

- Hula Hoops become popular.
- January 31: First successful launch of a U.S. space satellite, *Explorer I.*
- March 24: Elvis Presley drafted into the U.S. Army.
- December 10: Beginning of passenger jet service between New York and Miami.

1959

- January 3: Alaska admitted as the 49th state of the union.
- January: The United States recognizes Fidel Castro as leader of new Cuban government.
- February 22: First NASCAR Daytona 500 race on a "Super Speedway" in Daytona Beach, Florida.
- April: NASA announces the "Mercury Seven" as the first astronauts for manned space missions.
- August 21: Hawaii admitted as the 50th state of the union.

1960 (U.S. CENSUS: 176 MILLION PEOPLE)

Background and Introduction

Prior to entering into the Second World War, President Franklin D. Roosevelt addressed the 77th Congress as he spoke to the American people about the need to shift from neutrality to helping Europe fight back against fascism. On January 6, 1941, Roosevelt stated that all nations of the world were entitled to the same four essential freedoms shared by Americans. He said:

> We look forward to a world founded upon four essential freedoms. The first is freedom of speech and expression everywhere in the world. The second is freedom of every person to worship God in his own way. . . . The third is freedom from want. . . . The fourth is freedom from fear. (77th Congress, 6 January 1941: 44–45)

Roosevelt spoke about the "four freedoms" on numerous occasions throughout the war and continuously stressed the fact that the world could not "exist half slave and half free."

The premise of Freedom of Speech, Freedom of Worship, Freedom from Want, and Freedom from Fear was fully supported by his 1940 political opponent Wendell Wilkie (1892–1944). Wilkie's influence upon American public opinion was considered by most to be second only to that of Roosevelt. But unlike the ambiguity of Roosevelt's proclamation, Wilkie was much more specific about the situation in the United States. In his publication *One World* (1943), Wilkie stated, "If we want to talk about freedom, we must mean freedom for others as well as ourselves, and we must mean freedom for everyone inside our frontiers." Inspired by both Wilkie and Roosevelt, the *Pittsburgh Courier,* an African-American newspaper, coined the phrase "Double-V," which meant victory over fascism abroad and victory over segregation at home (Foner, 243–246).

The United States prevailed in World War II, and its ideals of liberty and democracy inspired many other nations to seek the same. Yet the problem was that those same freedoms offered to the rest of the world were not prevalent at home. During the 1950s, those so-called "freedoms" were routinely suppressed, often by legal means. Freedom of speech was only allowed when expressing blind patriotic loyalty. The House Un-American Activities Committee (HUAC) and Senator Joseph McCarthy routinely invoked fear as a political tool. Worship was limited to white Christian values, which in the South used hate and violence to suppress equality for African Americans. And affluence, such as access to suburbia, was only accessible to white Americans.

The fog of nostalgia has clouded the actual reality. The 1950s were rampant with falsehoods and fake threats. The nostalgia can easily be traced to the lingering images that remain not of reality, but rather the portrayal of an idyllic American society as seen on television. The reality at the time was that the nation was in the midst of believing in the existence of internal subversion by Communists, living in fear of an imminent nuclear attack, outright rejecting human integration, legally lynching African Americans, denying women equal opportunities, and jailing gays and lesbians, all in the name of preserving traditional 1950s American family values. Noted *New York Times* film critic Stephen Holden properly described the 1950s as

> An oppressive, puritanical conformism dominated white America . . . anti-Semitism was pervasive; and the fear of Communism was epidemic. Teenage culture had yet to flower. The early murmurings of rock 'n' roll were distant stirrings on black R&B radio, and racial segregation held sway. The tone of everyday life was circumspect and grimly proper. (Holden, "Back to the 1950s," p. C11)

For the most part, the summation could read that Communist infiltration and Rock 'n' Roll were contributing to the ruination of the United States. Racial segregation was legal. Gay and lesbian people were non-existent, marijuana made people insane, sexual activity was taboo, and tobacco was viewed as healthy and associated with intelligence. The decade could easily be promoted by snapshot bookend headlines with many new items in between, such as the following:

AMERICANS WORRY about COMMUNISTS and NUCLEAR ATTACK
Interstate highways / G.I. Bill of Rights / Suburban Transformation
Television's "Uncle Miltie" / Automobiles / Vacations / Disneyland
Everybody Loved Lucy and Liked Ike / Conformity was the Norm
Rock 'n' Roll and Elvis Presley go against the norm.
Goods were plentiful / Americans could afford to buy them.
Marilyn Monroe / Julius and Ethel Rosenberg / Rocky Marciano.
Korean War / New York Yankees Win Six World Series / Rock Around the Clock
Violent Segregation / School Desegregation / Rosa Parks / Emmett Till
Satellites / Sputnik
BABY BOOM—76 MILLION BABIES BORN

Chart B.1   United States Population, 1950–1960

Year	Population	Plus Change
1950	152,271,417	3,083,287
1951	154,877,889	2,606,472
1952	157,552,740	2,674,851
1953	160,184,192	2,631,452
1954	163,025,854	2,841,662
1955	165,931,202	2,905,348
1956	168,903,031	2,971,829
1957	171,984,130	3,081,099
1958	174,881,904	2,897,774
1959	177,829,628	2,947,724
1960	180,671,158	2,841,530

Source: Demographia.com (www.demographia.com/
db-uspop1900.htm). Chart compiled by author.

INTRODUCTION

In August 1945, World War II ended dramatically with the dropping of atomic bombs on Hiroshima and Nagasaki. (The war in Europe had ended a few months earlier.) Although much of the world was literally in ruins, the United States mainland was relatively intact. At the time, the United States also was the world's most powerful nation as it controlled the world's supply of nuclear weapons. Americans might have been worried about the threat of atomic warfare and nuclear annihilation, but economically, many were better off than ever. Within a short time, over 12 million American servicemen and women were shipped back to the United States hoping to live in post-war peace and prosperity. For many, the G.I. Bill gave veterans the opportunity for college educational waivers and job training, thereby easing the reintroduction of military personnel back into civilian life. Prompted by a Veterans Administration G.I. loan for a 30-year home mortgage (with a mortgage tax deduction) to purchase one's own home, among other benefits, a massive migration to suburbia occurred. New industries, consumer products, and middle-class suburban neighborhoods permeated the United States. Goods were plentiful and most Americans could afford to buy them. The 1950s introduced the development of massive federal funded interstate highways, which allowed easy access not only to the new suburban tract developments, but also throughout the United States itself. Vacation travel, with an abundance of automobiles, was more commonplace than ever. With that also came the creation of an American "middle class." The Immigration and Nationality Act of 1952 was passed by Congress over a presidential veto, allowing immigration as well as ending an almost century-old exclusion of Asians into the country. Despite relaxation on immigration policies, prosperity and advantage were mainly confined to white, non-ethnic Americans (Giordano 2003, 33–34).

For white Americans, the financial possibilities seemed limitless. Within the first year of the end of the war, more than three million women left the workforce and were newly married or reunited with their soldier husbands. Birth rates increased dramatically and the baby boom began as about 4.4 million babies were born each year. The Baby Boom era was defined as an overlapping period of decades from 1947 to 1964. During that time, more than 76 million babies were born. Young parents at the forefront of the Baby Boom could at least allay the fears of their parents' generation by the availability of the polio vaccine. (Prior to the vaccine, about one-third of the population was born with some type of polio affliction, either very mild or very severe.) By mid-decade, the vaccine was made available to the American public at almost no cost, thereby eliminating the possibly of contracting the disease.

The trend in the new economically powerful United States was consumerism and conformity. Unlike both previous and later decades, Americans were working fewer hours while making a living wage. Those wages were attributed to a rise in labor unions, as over 36 percent of the workforce was unionized. Leisure time was promoted throughout the country, led by President Eisenhower. As a result, adults, teens, and children had more leisure time than ever before. New toys and games were produced including the Frisbee, Silly Putty, Mr. Potato Head, Lego Toy Bricks, and Hula Hoops. The 1955 opening of the Disneyland amusement park in California epitomized middle-class vacation affordability. By the end of the decade, the nation added two new stars to its flag as both Alaska and Hawaii joined the union as the 49th and 50th states of the United States of America.

During the post-war period, many strived for a new idealized "American Dream" of home ownership, marriage, family, and consumerism that were continually seen on televisions and in other mass-market media such as magazines and newspapers. The idea was driven by a consumer culture and idealized suburban life. But that life was often unattainable and soon created a new dilemma. As American society was carefully reconstructed, specific gender roles were required. The feminine role of the 1940s was changed from the self-sufficient "Rosie the Riveter" who helped win World War II to that of a "Happy Homemaker." During the 1950s and early 1960s, magazines and television continually portrayed and advertised the glory and happiness of middle-class motherhood and marriage. On the surface, and for nostalgia-driven Americans of the 21st century who confused conformity for utopia, the 1950s were a great time for American history. Yet many people might mistake a yearning for "living in the good old days" as forgetting the innocence of youth for any time period. In turn, the actual reality of a time period such as the 1950s is often regulated to a non-existent memory.

CONFORMITY SURFACE CONTROL

On the surface, American society appeared well under control. However, it was the slow change and resistance to the suppressive "normality" that eventually caused an explosion in society during the mid-to-late 1960s. Many of the later progressive movements such as gender equality (feminism), racial equality, and any public display of human sexuality, among many others were mostly non-existent during the 1950s. One approach viewed as innocent by the 21st-century generation was Elvis Presley and Rock 'n' Roll. All of the previously mentioned critiques of suppression were rolled into one person: "Elvis the Pelvis." It is hard for later generations to understand the massive and sometimes violent suppression against both the music and the man. One social critic termed the period "subversive." A similar critique, although mainly upon white corporate America, was provided in 1950 by sociologist David Riesman's *The Lonely Crowd.*

Within a politically and socially charged climate, Rock 'n' Roll music exploded across the United States. Many artists, such as Chuck Berry, Little Richard, and Fats Domino, had roots in rhythm and blues. Others, including Elvis Presley, Buddy Holly, Jerry Lee Lewis, Carl Perkins, and Bill Haley and the Comets, had their roots in country and western music. By the late 1940s, a square dance movement throughout the United States overshadowed traditional country and western music and dancing. Many of the nation's schools provided square dancing in physical education programs as well as community centers, and others promoted it as a healthy recreational activity. Square dance festivals and barn dances were held in towns and cities of every size, including New York City, that attracted between 5,000 and 10,000 participants. Hollywood capitalized on that popularity with *Hollywood Barn Dance* (1947), *Square Dance Jubilee* (1949), *The Arkansas Swing* (1949), and *Square Dance Katy* (1950). There was also a proliferation of Hollywood westerns dating back to a trend that began in the 1930s. Two of the most famous westerns from the period were *High Noon* (1952) starring Gary Cooper and *The Searchers* (1956) starring John Wayne. Hundreds of others were made quickly and without much of a plot. They were known as "B Westerns" and were often included as part of a matinee double feature. A sampling from 1950 included *Arizona Territory; Bonanza Town; Broken Arrow; Canyon Riders; Colt .45; Fort Worth; In Old Amarillo;* and *Salt Lake Raiders*. Two from 1952 included *Apache Country* and *Apache War Smoke*. Among the dozens of "B Westerns" released in 1956, similar titles included *Gun Battle at Monterey; Gun Duel in Durango; Gun for a Coward; Gun Glory; Gunfight at the O.K. Corral; Gunfire at Indian Gap; The Guns of Fort Petticoat;* and *Gunsight Ridge;* as well as dozens of other western-themed titles. Another popular movie format featured a "singing cowboy," with stars such as Gene Autry and Roy Rogers. The combination of the singing cowboy, barn dances, and western swing music was a popular trend in post-war Hollywood movies.

Teenagers and young adults continued the 1940s tradition of gathering at roller-skating rinks, bowling alleys, drive-in burger joints, and at malt shops (sometimes known as "soda fountains" or "ice cream parlors"). Many of these establishments provided music by means of a jukebox. A new jukebox addition was the installation of "wall boxes," which could access the music selection from a remote location within the establishment. The wall box was a compact, tableside selection device that allowed individuals to select songs controlled by the jukebox. In many of these locations, teenagers would dance to music played on the jukebox, often the newly emerging Rock 'n' Roll.

Dancing at proms, "record hops," and "sock-hops" were a common teenage activity. A sock-hop was termed after the practice of teens dancing without shoes and only their socks. The reason for this was that community-organized teen dances were often held in gymnasiums. Therefore, in order not to damage the gym floor, teens were asked to remove their shoes. Music was supplied sometimes by a band composed of fellow high school students or an individual who played records on a turntable, sometimes wired into the available public address system. The events were carefully chaperoned by concerned adults, as were high school proms. Sometimes the high school dances featured a local celebrity radio disc jockey. One of the most recognized among teenagers was *American Bandstand* host Dick Clark. In 1957 alone, he made well over 180 personal appearances at such dances (Jackson, 127).

The overt portrayal of the new American "normal" was strict conformity and financial comfort in a suburban home filled with consumer items. The pervasive idea, as previously mentioned, was continually portrayed in mainstream media outlets such as magazines and newspapers. But nowhere was the "normal" hammered home stronger than on television. The visual images seen on such TV shows as *Father Knows Best* and *Leave It to Beaver* lingered on for generations. The fictional images and accompanying news accounts often praised the fulfillment of the "American Dream." Despite the overall appearance of an affluent, white, middle-class society, the United States was strictly segregated. Although not seen on television, either fictionally or editorially, poverty, racism, and immigrant alienation were prevalent. Prior to a massive demographic restructuring on immigration reform in 1965 known as the Hart-Celler Act, the country was basically divided along racial lines. Society was also divided as severe poverty among African Americans was often double that of white citizens. (In the 1950s, neither the term "African American" nor "Black" was used. The reference was either "Colored" or "Negro.")

Poverty was not prevalent among all African Americans. In many cases, prominence and financial gains were achieved, but solely within their own segregated communities. In 1957, E. Franklin Frazier noted in *Black Bourgeoisie* that African Americans maintained a social life often replicating the white population of America. They included fraternal organizations, churches, and community groups, but were completely separated from white society. Events such as elite debutante balls and cotillions were held in fashionable, although segregated hotels. Frazier noted that the ability to enjoy a social life similar to the white population "became identified with the condition of freedom" (203). One newfound freedom was driving an automobile throughout the nation's growing highway system.

Vacationing was not without dangers for non-whites. Strict segregation laws in the southern states required careful planning when traveling by car. A helpful and sometimes life-saving aid was *The Negro Travelers' Green Book* (first published in 1936 as *The Negro Motorist Green Book*), written and published by Victor H. Green (1892–1960). Green, who lived in the segregated neighborhood of Harlem in New York City, was employed as a federal postal worker.

He became active in civic affairs and recognized the need for such a book as vacations were becoming commonplace for all Americans.

The automobile travel guide was not unique to American travelers. As early as 1902, the American Automobile Association of America (known as the "AAA" or "Triple A") had published a similar guide for motorists. Throughout the 20th century, the AAA Motor Guide provided valuable travel aid and service for millions of American motorists. The AAA, however, did not accept membership nor offer service for blacks. Therefore, Green's publication filled a necessary void.

Similar to the AAA guides, Green provided a listing of businesses such as hotels and diners as well as gas stations and vehicle repair shops that would offer service to African Americans. In many areas of the country, white-owned businesses regularly refused service to black customers. Additional notes were provided for the listing of "sundown towns." A "sundown town" was a town or city that had legal laws requiring all non-whites to leave the area after the sun went down. The guide included most of North America and the Caribbean Islands and allowed "Negro" travelers the ability to plot out a safe course along the nation's highways while being able to arrange for a hotel accommodation, refuel the car, and purchase a meal.

By 1956, as the 20th anniversary edition was published, the danger was as prevalent as ever. Yet the need for safe travel knowledge for African Americans was still not widely available. In his introduction, Green noted the continued need to travel "without encountering embarrassing situations." He reminded his fellow travelers, "The White traveler has had no problem in getting accommodations, but with the Negro it has been different" (3). As an activist, he did not give up hope for a safer future. Green added a proclamation that he along with all African Americans "look forward to the day when as a racial group, we will enjoy the rights and privileges guaranteed us, but as of now withheld in certain areas of these United States" (5).

A main reason for the widespread inequality was legal segregation of society both in neighborhoods as well as places of public accommodation and schools. For the most part, blacks were denied access to the voting booths and often had little or no representation in legal affairs pertaining to their status in society. Those civil rights for African Americans did not become the law of the land until President Lyndon Johnson enacted the Federal Civil Rights Act of 1964 and the Voting Rights Act of 1965. Even then, the barriers were slowly removed often through long and tiring Supreme Court cases such as the marriage equality granted by the 1967 U.S. Supreme Court decision in *Loving v. Virginia* (388 U.S. 1).

INVISIBLE ETHNIC GROUPS

The situation was not unique to African Americans; Hispanics and Native American Indians also endured oppression at the hands of the government. In both instances, President Eisenhower issued restrictive legislation. One 1953 action labeled with the derogatory title of "Operation Wetback" sought to deport millions of Mexican Americans. For American Indians, they were subjected to a policy known as "Termination." This policy eliminated any federal financial support, including job placement off of reservations and housing relocation assistance to accommodating cities.

The overt reasoning for the termination action was the belief that Indians would be better served by assimilating into mainstream American society. The policy, which was in place from the 1940s throughout the 1960s, effectively increased poverty on the reservations. Unbeknownst to the public, the Bureau of Indian Affairs, an agency dating to the 19th century, was mismanaging funds at the time. But because they covered up the corruption, the blame was placed on the Indians themselves. As a result, sovereign nation status was slowly removed from tribes, and by the mid 1960s, more than 100 tribes were officially terminated as individual sovereign nations and cut off from federal aid (Boundless, "Indian Relocation"). Other ethnic groups such as Italians, Jews, Asians, and especially women also suffered discrimination, including common derogatory language and mainstream jokes.

NOSTALGIA AND FORGOTTEN REALITY

After World War II, many Americans wanted to put the war behind them and move on with their lives. However, the post-war period was not without hostilities. The beginning of the decade saw the United States involved in another foreign war in Korea. The "war" was not officially declared by the U.S. Congress—it was considered a "police action" sanctioned by the United Nations. Often termed "The Forgotten War" in history books, the unofficial "war" resulted in significant American military casualties. In a source released by the Department of Defense in 2015, the total amount of U.S. deaths was 36,574, and another 103,284 were wounded in action. But for many Americans, Korea did not have the same effect upon their daily lives as did World War II ("Korean War Fast Facts," n.p.).

Often, when Americans think back upon the 1950s, it is with forlorn nostalgia for an innocent time gone by. But most of that was driven by a 1950s resurgence of music during the 1970s. Many of the negative aspects surrounding Rock 'n' Roll were lost to later generations due to movies made with 1950s themes such as *American Graffiti* (1973), *Grease* (1978), and a top-rated TV show *Happy Days* (1974–1984). For the most part, the mainstream American public was totally unaware or had just simply forgotten about the controversy over the so-called "obscene" message of Rock 'n' Roll and its founder, Alan Freed.

American Graffiti, written and directed by the legendary George Lucas, represents a good case in point. Although the fictional movie was set in 1962, it is in essence a movie reflective of 1950s-era teenagers. The events were based on a foundational cultural suppression during the 1950s. The following decade was almost equally divided between those who held onto the ways of the past who were often termed "hawks" and those who sought progressive change, sometimes called "doves." The "hawks" were made up mainly of white adults opposed to changing conformist 1950s attitudes. They had grown up in an era with legalized segregation and were falsely informed about the threat of Communism and the American need to "contain it." As a result, they openly supported segregation as well as the war in Vietnam in order to contain the spread of Communism. At the same time, they defiantly defended patriotic conformity while supporting the spread of American hegemony worldwide. The "doves" opposed American military intervention anywhere in the world—especially Vietnam. They also represented the disenchanted youth growing out of the rebellious 1950s Rock 'n' Roll generation who rebelled against authority and lost faith in a country that they thought continued to suppress equality and individual liberty.

Within this double-decade cultural climate, Lucas realized that many of the movies of the 1950s left audiences pessimistic about the future. Regarding the making of *American Graffiti*, he said, "I decided it was time to make a movie where people felt better coming out of the theater than when they went in." But, according to Lucas, the message was "about teenagers moving forward and making decisions about what they want to do in life. But it is also about the fact that you can't live in the past." The movie did in fact make people feel "better coming out of the theater." And that is exactly what happened. The movie was a surprise hit in 1973, jumping to the top of the box office and often placing in the Top Ten list of greatest American movies. However, just the reverse of not living "in the past" happened. The success of the movie launched a wide-ranging nostalgia of the 1950s, especially the music and the idea of teenage high school simplicity (Miller, *Flowers in the Dustbin*, 312–315).

Portrayals of the American teenager in popular culture during the 1950s centered on the "high school experience." One song that epitomized the idealism of the American teenager was Chuck Berry's "Hail, Hail Rock and Roll." Despite these nostalgic images, very few teenagers actually graduated from high school. According to the Statistical Abstract of the United States, by 1960, only 39.5 percent of males and 42.5 percent of females actually graduated high school. As for college, only 9.7 percent of males and 5.8 percent of females graduated with a degree. By comparison, in 2006, more than 85 percent of the population graduated high school. (That statistic remained fairly constant through 2016.) As for college, nearly 30 percent of the population attained a college degree with an almost equal division between males and females by the year 2016.

During the fledging television years of the 1950s, an abundance of original programming included dramas (often live), comedies, quiz shows, game shows, variety shows, and westerns. The variety shows, sometimes termed "Vaudeo," were a take-off on a combination of early 20th-century vaudeville stage acts and variety entertainment geared toward the mainstream television audience. Television was first and foremost a financial commercial venture intent on making money. Hence, other than the first news-related programming, all airings were accompanied by commercial advertising. During the early years, many of the shows had single sponsorship, such as Texaco gasoline for Milton Berle's #1-rated variety show the *Texaco Star Theatre*; however, these ad placements shaped a powerful image of popular culture. The popular television shows of the 1950s reflected the social conformity of the period and were careful to exclude stories and representations of minorities. They portrayed homogenous, white, non-ethnic suburban families in which the mother was a housewife and the father worked at some unnamed job and always came home for dinner.

During the late 1940s and 1950s, the American way of life went through a complete transition from an entire nation focused on the Second World War to settling into a post-war life of peace, prosperity, and conformity. And although many portrayals of the time cited a successful quiet transformation, nothing could be further from reality.

Americans had to contend with a new Cold War with the Soviet Union as containment of Communism was top-most in the minds of all Americans. By 1950, a widespread paranoia that engulfed the entire country became known as the "Red Scare." Senator Joseph McCarthy and the HUAC committee seized the newspaper headlines, falsely warning Americans that they were endangered by Communist infiltration in Hollywood and government. His false warnings were taken quite seriously and hundreds of thousands of adults built backyard, underground bomb shelters to protect themselves in case of a nuclear attack. School children were taught to "duck and cover" as they actively participated in Civil Defense drills.

The schools, as well as the nation, were also divided by legal segregation. However, almost every area of the nation resisted federally mandated segregation in one way or another. Resistance in the south, especially among the 11 former Confederate states, was often fierce, violent, and deadly. School desegregation rulings led to many southern white school councils to simply de-fund the public schools and open all-white "private academies." In 1956, the year after *Brown v. Board of Education,* more than 100 elected representatives of the U.S. Congress signed the *"Southern Manifesto."* The document protested and formed resistance against integration of any sort especially in places of public accommodation such as parks, swimming pools, and movies theaters. Southern whites often reacted violently without threat of criminal prosecution. The black response was non-violent resistance in the form of boycotts and legal action brought before the U.S. Supreme Court.

Racial segregation was evident in all aspects and areas of American society. Although it was not always clearly defined in the north, cities like New York had a clear distinction of ethnic neighborhoods, such as Harlem in Manhattan and Bedford-Stuyvesant in Brooklyn, almost exclusively for blacks. In the south, overt segregation was clearly defined by signs on water fountains, bus stations, movie theaters, and all other places of public accommodation. These signs simply read "COLORED ONLY" or "WHITE ONLY." The situation often applied to Italians, Jews, Polish, Hispanics, and women, among others. The eventual dismantling was slow but progressive as individuals, such as baseball players Jackie Robinson in the National League and Larry Doby in the American League, broke "the color barrier" in 1947. Rosa Parks' famous refusal to give up her seat on a bus in Montgomery, Alabama, occurred in 1955. The previous year, the U.S. Supreme Court in the *Brown v. the Board of Education* decision effectively ended nationwide school segregation.

Despite the historic 1955 Supreme Court decision of *Brown v. The Board of Education*, the rush to establish equality and civil rights legislation was not a major priority. In his seminal work *Lies My Teacher Told Me*, historian James Loewen noted:

> In those years white historians would hardly fault [former president Woodrow] Wilson for segregating the federal government, because no consensus held that racial segregation was wrong. The foremost public issue of that postwar era was not race relations but the containment of communism. (262)

As it was, all across the United States, minorities seemed to be shut out of the emerging American Dream.

IGNORANCE OF DEATH CAUSED BY SMOKING

Smoking was one of the most dominant and public displays of conformity during the 1950s. Despite the fact that we now know it to be one of the worst health hazards ever, smoking was prevalent just about everywhere. At the time just about every place of public accommodation allowed smoking, including airplanes, buses, taxi cabs, movie theaters, banks, offices, ballparks, supermarkets, and restaurants, to name just a few. In a Stanford University report from 2011, "The history of the discovery of the cigarette–lung cancer link," Dr. Robert N. Proctor noted that during the 1950s, almost 70 percent of all Americans over the age of 16 smoked at some point. Women, who smoked at a rate almost as high as men, were completely unaware of the dangers, especially smoking during pregnancy.

In 1954, researchers provided conclusive evidence "proven beyond a reasonable doubt" that the "odds of dying from lung cancer" increased dramatically for those who smoked. The high rate of lung cancer also increased among those individuals who lived or worked in areas where they were subjected to "second-hand smoke." That same year, the American Cancer Society announced to the public that "available evidence indicates an association between smoking, particularly cigarette smoking, and lung cancer." Despite the undeniable and credible evidence about the severity of the dangers of smoking, the tobacco manufacturers did not release the information to the public. The real dangers of smoking were completely masked by false dangers, especially the danger associated with the Red Menace.

JOSEPH STALIN, JOSEPH McCARTHY, AND THE RED MENACE

So much of what American life became after the war was predicated on the effects of the war itself. Major post-war concerns include the Soviet Union, Communism, and Joseph Stalin (1878–1953), as the Cold War that would last throughout the 1950s. It was during this uncertain era that Wisconsin Senator Joseph McCarthy (1908–1957) rose to prominence.

During the first third of the decade, Americans were besieged by the fear of the Communist "Red Menace." This Red Scare was led by Senator Joseph McCarthy. Much of that fear was directed towards the looming figure of the Soviet leader Joseph (sometimes "Josef") Stalin in the Union of Soviet Socialist Republics (USSR). Stalin's death on March 6, 1953, was major news and was printed in large headlines on daily newspapers and weekly news magazines all throughout the nation. Stalin as a world leader reigned over the Soviet Union for 29 years. During that time, Americans were reminded that his spreading Communist empire covered nearly one quarter of the earth and controlled at least one-third of the entire world's population. *Time* magazine characterized him as "the most powerful man of his time . . . the most feared and hated . . . just another human animal . . . more terrible than Ivan the Terrible." Overall, Americans responded to the news of Stalin's death with a resounding sense of joy. With the ongoing war in Korea, one U.S. Army unit made a sign proclaiming, "Joe's dead: so they said; hurray, hurray; that's one less Red." One Chicago tavern owner responded by placing a black funeral wreath in his window with the announcement "Joe's gone, vodka on the house" (*Time*, March 16, 1953, 23, 29, 42).

Apparently Americans had a short memory, as popular opinion of Stalin changed from pre-war villain to hero during the Second World War, and again back to villain. Just a few years earlier, Stalin was portrayed by the American media as a trusted ally in the fight against Nazi Germany. By 1941, however, the story began to change. In Europe, Adolph Hitler ordered an invasion of Russia. By December of that year, Germany appeared ready to take Moscow, and without warning, a Japanese attack occurred at Pearl Harbor in Hawaii. The United States was now unexpectedly in a global world war with an apparent defeat looming. Early in 1942, Russian soldiers managed a counterattack and appeared to be pushing the Germans back. Realizing that the United States and the Soviet Union were fighting a common enemy, the media portrayal of Stalin and the Russian people changed immediately. British Prime Minister Winston Churchill, during an NBC radio broadcast to the American people said, "the Russian danger is now the danger of the United States." The Russians appeared as the only adversary able to thwart the German onslaught. Americans often expressed gratitude for their valiant effort as the U.S. government instituted a policy of sending armaments and naval ships to Russia known as "Lend-Lease." The former villain Joseph Stalin was now an ally of both the United States and Great Britain. All media outlets including newspapers, radio, magazines, books and movies began to portray Stalin in a new and favorable light. These media sources were very influential in shaping America's views of U.S. foreign policy.

Time magazine also quickly changed its tune. The January 5, 1942, cover attempted to stress the importance of unity among the allied nations by picturing separate photos of the new "Big Three": Stalin, Roosevelt, and Churchill. The editors of *Time* also stated that Stalin was "the only leader who has yet to face a major German drive without a military disaster" (*Time*, 42). In the ensuing months, not only *Time* continued to praise Stalin, but other popular magazines such as the *Saturday Evening Post*, *Look*, *Life*, and *Reader's Digest* praised all that was Russian.

At the end of World War II, many Americans thought they would enter into a period of prosperous peaceful isolation. After all, the United States had the most destructive weapon in the history of humankind: the atomic bomb. Therefore, the United States could dictate world policy and live in peace. To the American public, however, the Soviet Union and Communism appeared to be gaining a foothold in much of the recently liberated free world. In 1948, to combat the potential threat of a war with the Soviet Union, peacetime Selective Service was reinstated. In 1949, the Soviet Union detonated its own atomic bomb and the United States was faced with the threat of a nuclear attack. The five-year period between the war and the new decade of the 1950s placed the wartime allies on opposite sides. Truman publicly announced that the world was divided, and outlined a policy known as "The Truman Doctrine." One side was guided by the "will of the majority." In direct opposition was the Soviet Union, based on the forced "will of a minority" and imposing Communism upon its people. Therefore, any notion that the United States would return to peacetime isolationism was officially abandoned. The U.S. Congress soon formed the House Un-American Activities Committee (HUAC) authorizing a search for Communist infiltrators within the United States. (The irony of this statement is that the United States promoted an international ideology that was not maintained within its own country. Throughout the 1950s, strict legal segregation and almost non-existent civil rights for women kept a strict division between an America that was literally "half free.")

By the time the HUAC was gaining publicity, the Soviet Union had detonated its first atomic bomb and Stalin had already sent troops into Prague in 1949. The media and the U.S. government, contributing to a widespread national surge of anti-Communist feelings, played up these events. Stalin was viewed as the "external devil" but there was also an "enemy within, as a new Red Scare fell upon the American people. With the groundwork set by HUAC, the situation was ripe to continue the paranoia. The Truman Doctrine abandoned the United States' policy of peacetime isolationism and committed itself to the point of no turning back in the new "Cold War" against the Soviet Union and Communism. The widespread and popular notion, many concluded, was that American Communists were conducting atomic espionage for the Soviet Union (McCormick, 69).

By 1950, Senator Joseph McCarthy seized the headlines, warning the American public of the dangers of Stalin and Communism. Sympathy or coercion of Stalin involved the risk of being labeled a "Red" or a "Communist." Many prominent figures who earlier, during the 1930s and 1940s, had praised Stalin were now "blacklisted" and publicly harassed. During later hearings of the HUAC in 1951, when McCarthy was in full gear, the "naming of names" became the watchwords. The fear of Communism resulted in a rise in patriotic, fraternal, and religious affiliations. Church membership of all denominations reached an all-time high. The question "Have you now or ever been a member of the Communist Party?" was routinely asked upon job applications and even fishing licenses. In 1954, as an affirmation against the atheistic beliefs of the Soviets, Congress added the words "under God" to the Pledge of Allegiance. The Red Scare was so pervasive that for the first time, the distinction between politics and culture was almost completely obliterated (Ernest R. May, "U.S. Government Legacy of the Cold War" in Hogan, 222–223).

The national paranoia was also fueled either directly or subliminally in Hollywood. Movies included titles such as *The Red Menace* (1949), *I Married a Communist* (1949), *Spy in the Sky* (1958), and *War of the Satellites* (1958), among dozens of others. Within the home, a family board game introduced in 1952 called

Victory Over Communism was advertised as an "Educational All-American Game." A children's card game *Satellite Space Race* (1958) awarded points for a "friendly satellite" card and deducted points for a Soviet "sputnik" card" (Barson, 13, 120–122).

THE KOREAN WAR: 1950 TO 1953

The early part of the decade was also tarnished by American involvement in another foreign war. This time it was in Korea, sometimes known as "The Forgotten War." The war lasted from June 1950 until July 1953. For some, the only public remembrance was that of the farewell speech given by General Douglas MacArthur (1880–1964). During a speech to the U.S. Congress on April 19, 1951, he made his famous statement, "Old soldiers never die, they just fade away." He made this statement after being relieved of duty as supreme commander of American forces in Korea (Chafe, 249).

For some, the Korean War was viewed as a necessary means to stop the spread of Communism. A 1951 *Time* magazine advertisement offered an informational booklet titled "How Stalin Hopes We Will Destroy America." It offered information on "ways to stop inflation" and to fight against the new Communist threat. One year later, *Time* told its readers, "Stalin's switch from accenting the enmity of Capitalism v. Communism to stressing intramural struggle between capitalistic countries—was a sharp turn, but not a new one. . . . his aim is clearly not to negotiate with the western coalition, but to smash it." (*Time*, June 11, 1951, 89; October 13, 1952, 32). At the time of Stalin's death (1953), the Korean War continued, Senator Joseph McCarthy was a national figure, and the Cold War was a permanent part of American life.

FURTHER READING

Eric Foner. *The Story of American Freedom.* New York: W. W. Norton & Company, 1998.

David Halberstam. *The Fifties.* New York: Metro Books, 2001.

Ken Hollings. *Welcome to Mars: Politics, Pop Culture, and Weird Science in 1950s America.* Berkeley, CA: North Atlantic Books, 2014.

Michael Kammen. *American Culture American Tastes: Social Change and the 20th Century.* New York: Basic Books, 1999.

Stephen J. Whitfield. *The Culture of the Cold War*, 2nd edition. Baltimore, MD: Johns Hopkins University Press, 1996.

Exploring Popular Culture

CHAPTER 1

Film

As with each of the preceding decades, movies were a popular form of American entertainment. Unlike the preceding years, the movies during the 1950s constituted a break from many of the long-standing Hollywood traditions. Professor Robert E. Yahnke of the University of Minnesota described the change:

> What begins to happen during the 1950s is a movement away from the big Studio Film to the little film about believable characters whose conflicts are more inward than outward. In some respects, the best films of the 1950s are the ones that forecast the great films on the 1960s. Examples include *On the Waterfront* (1954), *Rebel Without a Cause* (1954), *Marty* (1955), *Paths of Glory* (1957), *12 Angry Men* (1957), *Separate Tables* (1958), and *Wild River* (1960). These films have in common two important qualities—directors interested in telling small but important stories and fresh actors who bring new dimensions to characterization and emotional intensity. (Yahnke, 2010)

Some of those "fresh actors" included Marlon Brando, James Dean, and Marilyn Monroe. In an age dominated by television, each of these stars contributed in some of the most memorable classic American movies of all time.

With growing competition from television, Hollywood responded with a variety of films to attract audiences. For a short time after the war, there was a proliferation of films with a dark view of reality known as "film noir." The "noirs" were movies with themes of pessimism, fatalism, menace, and cynical characters. The term "film noir" (a French word that translates to "black film") was derived from the heavy use of shadows and low lighting within each scene. As a storyline, the "noirs" were mostly suspenseful crime dramas that were made from the end of the war to about the mid-1950s. Some of the noirs included a crime/heist film *The Asphalt Jungle* (1950) and a detective mystery *Dial M for Murder* (1954). Despite the popular appeal of "film noir," movie

themes quickly shifted to nonsensical, conformist, and anti-Communist rhetoric. Some of these genres included teen-inspired films such as *Rebel Without
a Cause* (1955) starring James Dean and *The Wild One* (1953) with Marlon
Brando. Others included animated children's films such as Disney's *The Lady
and the Tramp* (1955)—the largest-grossing film of the decade. Some of the
science fiction and horror themes were subtle responses to the Cold War paranoia, such as *The Day the Earth Stood Still* (1951) and *The Invasion of the Body
Snatchers* (1956). A significant new format of widescreen color movies of massive epics such as *The Ten Commandments* (1956) and *Ben Hur* (1959) provided
a visual experience that television could not match.

Throughout the 1950s (and for some, into the 1960s), the major movie stars
of the 1940s continued to star in significant movies. They included: Humphrey
Bogart in an Academy Award performance in *The African Queen* (1951) as well
as in *The Caine Mutiny* (1954); Gary Cooper and Grace Kelly in *High Noon*
(1952); and Bette Davis in *All About Eve* (1950). Jimmy Stewart starred in two
of the all-time best movies directed by Alfred Hitchcock: *Rear Window* (1954)
and *Vertigo* (1958). John Wayne, one of Hollywood's all-time superstars, continued his western-themed tradition with *The Searchers* (1956). Many of the
movie stars as well as the Hollywood film industry came under close scrutiny
during the Red Scare of the Cold War. Oftentimes Congress held meetings
on the supposed subversive nature of movie content such as the House Un-
American Activities Committee (HUAC) hearings.

THE HUAC, WALT DISNEY, AND RONALD REAGAN

During the 1930s and into the 1940s, a significant number of movie production tradespeople was affiliated with the Hollywood labor union called the
International Alliance of Theatrical and Stage Employees Union (IATSE). Often
accusations arose that the IATSE was controlled by organized crime as labor
leaders were often jailed for the crime of extortion. In turn, they viewed the
unions as "too powerful" because the unions set minimum wages for all of
the individuals hired to produce a film. The studio heads, and capitalists in
general, sought to increase profits for themselves and wanted to disband the
unions. In doing so, they insinuated that the unions were a "Communist plot."
To support the accusations, the overtly conservative HUAC held hearings about
the so-called subversive elements of Communist infiltration in Hollywood.

Two prominent witnesses in support of the studios were Walt Disney
(1901–1966) and Ronald Reagan (1911–2004). Both blamed the labor problems
at the Hollywood studios on Communist infiltration. Disney's personal interest was in reaction to a 1945 strike against Walt Disney Productions. He claimed
that the craft union representing Disney cartoonists were Communists. In
1947, another strike, marred by violence, was eventually settled by a coalition
led by Screen Actors Guild president Ronald Reagan. In October 1947, both
Disney and Reagan testified as "friendly witnesses" before the HUAC. Each cat-
egorized the strikes and labor struggles as a real-life battle between the forces of
Communism and American patriotism. When asked about the possibility of
inserting any Communist type of "propaganda" into his films, Disney replied:

We watch so that nothing gets into the films that would be harmful in any way to any group or any country. We have large audiences of children and different groups, and we try to keep them as free from anything that would offend anybody as possible. We work hard to see that nothing of that sort creeps in.

The conversation quickly came to the direct question as to whether Communists were in fact entrenched in the Hollywood studios. The conversation between Congressman H. Allen Smith and Walt Disney went as follows:

Mr. Smith: Do you have any people in your studio at the present time that you believe are Communist or Fascist employed there?

Mr. Disney: No, at the present time I feel that everybody in my studio is 100 percent American.

Mr. Smith: Have you had at any time, in your opinion, in the past, have you at any time in the past had any Communists employed at your studio?

Mr. Disney: Yes; in the past I had some people that I definitely feel were Communists.

Mr. Smith: As a matter of fact, Mr. Disney, you experienced a strike at your studio, did you not?

Mr. Disney: Yes.

Mr. Smith: And is it your opinion that [the] strike was instituted by members of the Communist Party to serve their purposes?

Mr. Disney: Well, it proved itself so with time, and I definitely feel it was a Communist group trying to take over my artists and they did take them over.

Reagan's testimony was in connection with whether any members of the guild union were Communists. His testimony in reply to HUAC Chief Investigator Robert E. Stripling went in part as follows:

Mr. Stripling: Has it ever been reported to you that certain members of the guild were Communists?

Mr. Reagan: Yes, sir; I have heard different discussions and some of them tagged as Communists.

Mr. Stripling: Would you say that this clique has attempted to dominate the guild?

Mr. Reagan: Well, sir, by attempting to put their own particular views on various issues, I guess in regard to that you would have to say that our side was attempting to dominate, too, because we were fighting just as hard to put over our views, in which we sincerely believed, and I think, we were proven correct by the figures.

(The full transcript is available at: House Committee on Un-American Activities, *Hearings Regarding the Communist Infiltration of the Motion Picture Industry*, 80th Congress, 1st Session, October 23–24, 1947 (Washington: Government Printing Office, 1947).)

The HUAC hearings contributed to the Cold War paranoia, effectively pitting American ideology against Soviet Communism. Reagan would later serve as

Governor of California from 1967 to 1975 and President of the United States from 1981 to 1989. The following essay provides a glimpse into Reagan's revival of similar rhetoric during the 1980s.

* * * * *

PRESIDENT RONALD REAGAN AND THE REVIVAL OF 1950s COLD WAR FILMS

By Matthew R. Giordano

Before the Cold War came to a close in the 1980s, a former actor turned politician named Ronald Reagan would enter the Oval Office after running a remarkable presidential campaign. In doing so, he revived the narrative set forth after World War II that the Soviet Union was in fact the biggest threat to peace and prosperity in the world. Additionally, as this rhetoric had simmered down over the years, thanks in large part to the fact that both nations never entered into a full-scale nuclear war, it was imperative for the president to remind the American people of the "Red Scare" of the 1950s. The revival was to get Americans to be fervent again in their commitment to the defeat of Communism, not only in the Soviet Union but also around the globe. Just like in 1950s America, Hollywood films would play a crucial role in getting the president's message across to the American people. This is not to say that Hollywood was being guided by the White House to make certain films, although the fact the President Reagan was a former actor (whose acting credits dated from 1937 to 1965) and a former member and president of the Screen Actors Guild should be mentioned. It is important to note that just as in the 1950s, certain filmmakers seemed anxious to express President Reagan's ideology in their films and thus help present a new, yet familiar narrative to the American people.

In the 1950s, Hollywood produced a plethora of films with notable Cold War themes such as *The Day the Earth Stood Still* (1951), *High Noon* (1952), *Invaders from Mars* (1953), *The Man Who Japed* (1956), and *Invasion of the Body Snatchers* (1956). This trend would begin to decrease in the following two decades. Even though movies portraying Communists as inhumane villains would still be present during these decades, especially in films like *The Manchurian Candidate* (1962) and in many of the James Bond films of the 1960s, it is undeniable that anti-Communist rhetoric had been toned down and Americans were beginning to lose their ever-present fear of a Communist invasion. Arguably, the genius of President Reagan's rise to political power involved the re-examination and exploitation of a Communist threat against America, even though it was clear by the 1980s that the Soviet Union was in a steep decline and that their days as an empire were numbered. Moreover, the ideological messages presented in certain Hollywood action films, particular in the 1980s, proved to be a great political tool for the president. It also helped to redisplay the masculinity and the toughness of the new American male in a uniquely individualistic and "American" way. As America was continuing to grow as an economic powerhouse and embrace modernity, the male "American" heroes stand out even more as being ready to embrace the future and this would arguably be the future of American Economic Imperialism. It is in this era of the 1980s that an overabundance of Hollywood action films permeated the market and revived 1950s anti-Communist rhetoric.

However, the 1980s action films were arguably less ideologically complex then 1950s science fiction films *The Day the Earth Stood Still* (1951), *Invasion of the Body Snatchers* (1956), or the western *High Noon* (1952), in which paranoia and fear were an ever-present source of evil as well as the Communists themselves. Action films of the 1980s like *Red Dawn* (1984), *War Games* (1982), *Rocky 4* (1985), *Top Gun* (1987), *Fire Fox* (1982), *The Fourth Protocol* (1987), *Invasion USA* (1985), *Rambo: First Blood Part 2* (1985), *Rambo 3* (1988), *Missing in Action* (1984), and *Iron Eagle* (1986) made it simple and clear that the Soviets and Communism were the enemy that needed to be defeated and were less ideologically complex than their predecessors. This is exactly the type of rhetoric that President Reagan openly embraced.

On an ideological level, there is arguably no greater way to get people to refocus on a singular emotional message better than having them watch Hollywood movies. The fictional film always holds the potential to manipulate people on an emotional level. This has been the case ever since Russian filmmaker Sergei Eisenstein figured out the use of the cinematic montage and the principles of editing. Of course Hollywood's ultimate goal is to make a profit. Therefore, Hollywood decided to embrace the ideology from the White House because it would prove to be profitable; movies like *Top Gun* (1987) and the others were exceptionally successful in box office dollars.

It is important to note that film can, and has been used to, disseminate ideological and sometimes propaganda messages. It is worth remembering that German filmmaker Leni Reifensthal made a film called *Triumph of the Will* (1935) with the sole purpose to gain support for the Nazi Party. This film was also made in conjunction with the propaganda arm of the Nazi Party. Hitler was fully aware of how important film was to promoting his horrendous messages of hate. So while obviously these previously mentioned 1980s American action films were not in any way, shape, or form attempts at propaganda, they still emitted some seriously strong ideological messages. Furthermore, the central ideological message of these 1980s action films seems to be that the American people could return to the prosperous and seemingly simplistic times of the 1950s, a nostalgic time when America was the beacon of hope in the world if we remembered that the Soviet Union was the greatest threat to our peace and prosperity. After all, in President Reagan's words that he borrowed from the classic *Star Wars* movie trilogy, he described the Soviet Empire as the "The Evil Empire."

Ultimately, these action films of the 1980s seemed to fail to account for the fact that tensions had died down dramatically between the Soviets and the Americans by this time. The Soviet Union was not nearly as strong during the 1980s as it had been in the 1950s, as President Reagan and many of these action films wanted you to think. This is clearly evident by the fall of the Soviet Union in 1989. The fact that the Soviets would never invade America and ultimately could not even handle their own internal problems only proved they were never any real threat to America. It should also be mentioned that despite the supposed military might of the Soviet Union at this time, once they entered into a long and particularly bloody war with Afghanistan in 1979, their own empire would never be the same. The Afghanistan war lasted for 10 years from 1979 to 1989 and it left both the Soviet Union and Afghanistan in extremely miserable states both socially and financially. Shortly after this war, the Soviet economy as well as their empire collapsed. The Soviet Union could no longer afford to keep pace with the United States in the nuclear arms race.

Watching certain Hollywood films, especially in the action genre in the 1980s, it is hard not to think that the Soviet Union was the source of all the "evil" in the world and that America was the source of all that was "good." A powerful narrative film is usually not interested in telling both sides of a story in any accurate detail. What is important to remember is that emotionally charged one-sided narrative films from Hollywood that reach many millions of people can influence the way that people view the world, at least on an ideological level. This cinematic ideological reconditioning seemed to be prevalent in the 1950s, but was even more so in the 1980s. As films tend to reflect the societal and ideological concepts of the day, looking back at Hollywood action films during the presidency of Ronald Reagan offers fascinating insight into how certain members of the American populace viewed the world at that time; obviously, it was not always in a completely accurate way.

Note: Matthew R. Giordano is an adjunct professor of film history and theory at St. John's University in New York City.

THE HOLLYWOOD TEN AND "THE BLACKLIST"

One month after Reagan and Disney testified before the HUAC, a "blacklist" was created, and on it were 10 Hollywood writers and directors. The reason cited was "Contempt of Congress" for their collective refusal to testify before the HUAC. Congress wanted "The Hollywood Ten" to answer the allegations that it was the screenwriters and directors who intentionally put Communist propaganda into American films. The accusations against these supposed "Communist sympathizers" started with a July 1946 trade publication *The Hollywood Reporter*. Shortly thereafter, studio executives such as Jack Warner started "naming names" of Communist infiltrators. The HUAC was fully satisfied with Warner's testimony and his continued promise that no Communist wrote for his studio. To further placate the HUAC, his Warner Bros. Studio produced and released a string of anti-Communist films. One example was *I Was a Communist for the FBI* (1951) that showed Soviet spies subverting the American steel unions (Culbert, 13).

Warner's statements and actions, combined with testimony provided by Disney and Reagan, solidified the HUAC's belief that Communist infiltration existed in the movie industry. Therefore, further testimony was demanded from the actual screenwriters and directors. The HUAC compiled a list of people whom they wanted to appear before the committee. Some of those on the list feared prosecution and fled the country. The remaining names on the list amounted to ten individuals, each of whom was prominent in the industry; they were subpoenaed by Congress. All ten, however, refused to testify. They were Alvah Bessie, Herbert Biberman, Lester Cole, Edward Dmytryk, Ring Lardner Jr., John Howard Lawson, Albert Maltz, Samuel Ornitz, Robert Adrian Scott, and Dalton Trumbo. All were eventually fired by Hollywood Studios, who collectively "blacklisted" all of them from working in the business. (At the time, the "studio system" that existed held a monopoly over employment and production of all Hollywood movies.)

Collectively, the Hollywood Ten paid a high price for their actions. In November 1947, they were cited for contempt of Congress. A trial in April 1948 found all 10 guilty, and sentenced each of them to one year in prison. They entered prison in 1950, as a "Red Scare" engulfed the country. The paranoia spread, not just in Hollywood, but also into all areas of American life. Many other individuals suffered similar blacklisting, many due to the mere accusation of being a Communist. Other times, the movie industry found itself the subject of the U.S. Supreme Court (Sklar, 262–266).

BLOCK BOOKING AND THE END OF THE STUDIO SYSTEM

In 1948, a U.S. Supreme Court case *U.S. v. Paramount Pictures, Inc., et al.* 334 US 131 (1948) (sometimes known as the "Hollywood Antitrust Case of 1948" or simply the "Paramount Case") affected all the major studios—Columbia, MGM, RKO, Paramount, 20th Century-Fox, United Artists, Universal, and Warner Bros. The ruling disbanded the long tradition of an "assembly line" method of making movies known as the "studio system." (The movie production studios had controlled all aspects of the business including production, distribution, and theater ownership.) The system also had the major studios working in collaboration with actors, actresses, directors, and technical staff under direct contract with a particular studio. The system known as "vertical integration" controlled almost 96 percent of all aspects of the business. In essence, it was a monopoly, and therefore contested under earlier conditions of the Sherman Anti-Trust Act. The system had existed from the earliest days of Hollywood, but became most prevalent and controlling throughout the 1930s and 1940s. The weakening of the studio system came a few years before the huge impact of television that drew audiences away from the movie theaters and further weakened the studios' power.

A small group of independent theater owners and non-contracted independent moviemakers brought forward the action that prompted the Paramount Case. Independent films were produced prior to the Supreme Court ruling; however, they had limited distribution access and attracted little media attention. A main reason for limited independent film distribution was due to the process known as "block booking." In essence, block booking meant that any particular major studio would "sell" a bulk package of movies to theaters. Considering that the studios were in the business of mass-producing movies, some were destined to be hits while many others were not, or in movie terms a "bomb." But if a theater owner wanted a particular movie such as an audience favorite like *Gone with the Wind* (1939), the studio would bundle it with a series of normally unwanted movies. If not, the "hit" movie was not available for purchase. For the theater owners, this meant having to buy an unwanted and often-unprofitable item. For an independent filmmaker it also was a formidable obstacle to having their films shown in a theater. The purchase of a "block" of movies meant that there were few, if any, time slots to show an independent film. That hit movie in turn would be coupled with a much lesser film from that same studio that became part of regularly scheduled "double features." Therefore, the theater owners had more than enough movies to show.

The practice of block booking started as early as 1915 by studio magnate Adolph Zukor of Paramount. By the 1930s and 1940s, often known as "The Studio Era," the practice of block booking was widely practiced within the industry. The booking extended beyond feature films to include shorts, cartoons, self-promotional studio advertisements, and newsreels. Some termed this added element "full-line forcing" because this practice forced the sale of unwanted products. The larger chain theaters could somewhat afford to just shelve a picture and leave it unshown, but for the lone theater owner, the forced sale of 15–20 unwanted feature films meant allocating six months to a year of unwanted films. Therefore, it could be a financial disaster. Some of the theater owners regulated themselves to becoming "B movie houses." This type of operation was able to purchase a feature film, without attachment to buy other movies, much later than its first-run release date. These types of movie theaters offered a reduced entry fee and stayed viable for a few decades, existing into the early 1980s.

During 1949 and 1950, regular movie attendance was about 90 million per week. Within one year however, attendance quickly dropped to 50 million per week, as television quickly became the main choice of entertainment. The drastic drop in paid attendance led to severe financial impact for movie theater owners. By 1953, more than 25 percent of the nation's theaters closed. In southern California, for example, 134 theaters closed, and in New York City,

Chart 1.1 American Movie Attendance and Movie Screens

Year	Average Weekly Movie Attendance	Number of Movie Screens (Indoor and Drive-In)
1920	38.0 Million	15.0 Thousand
1930	90.0 Million	23.0 Thousand
1940	80.0 Million	19.0 Thousand
1950	60.0 Million	19.1 Thousand
1960	25.1 Million	12.7 Thousand
1970	17.7 Million	13.8 Thousand
1980	19.6 Million	17.7 Thousand
1990	22.9 Million	23.8 Thousand

Source: Alex Ben Block and Lucy Autrey Wilson, *George Lucas's Blockbusting* (New York: It Books Harper Collins, 2010), p. 414.

55 theaters closed (Whitfield, 153). Ten years later, television was booming, the movie industry was restructuring, and attendance suffered a drastic drop to around 46 million per week. Estimates for free in-home television viewing were not accurately available, but could have ranged as high as 175 to 200 million people per week. It is without a doubt that television played a significant role in drawing away movie audiences, but even without the new medium, Hollywood had other troubles including the legal decision of the Supreme Court Paramount case.

Television was the overwhelming choice of entertainment, but movies were still viable. The actual number of movies produced was significantly lower than the previous decades of the 1930s and 1940s, but many of the 1950s movies attracted large audiences due to good stories and better visual enhancements such as color, 3D, and widescreen format. They included *Singing in the Rain* (1952), *The Band Wagon* (1953), *Peter Pan* (1953), *Lady and the Tramp* (1955), *The Bridge on the River Kwai* (1957), and biblical epics such as *Quo Vadis* (1951), *The Robe* (1953), *The Ten Commandments* (1956), and *Ben-Hur* (1959).

Disney released five full-length feature films during the 1950s, four of which placed in the top 12 highest earners. The 1955 release of *Lady and the Tramp* turned out to be the highest-grossing film of the entire decade. The second-highest earner of the decade was another Disney classic: *Peter Pan*, released in 1953. Not far behind was the 1959 feature *Sleeping Beauty*, which placed at number five. Another Disney movie, *Cinderella*, (1950) placed 12th on the list. The only Disney release not to make the top 30 was *Alice in Wonderland* (1951). Its first-run release brought in a disappointing $2.4 million at the box office. Walt Disney cited its non-success due to Alice "lacking warmth" as a character. After some reworking of the original film, an edited version was shown as part of *The Wonderful World of Disney* television series. Disney Studios also decided to make *Alice in Wonderland* its first ever re-release in the movie theaters. As a result of the re-release and subsequent re-releases over the following decades, *Alice* (as it was affectionately known) eventually pushed the lifetime movie gross to well over $1 billion.

A significant change, which led to these select but successful movies such as *Alice in Wonderland*, was that studios began to study audience demographics. In previous decades, the assumption was that immigrants and working-class people attended in larger numbers. This statistic did in fact bear out in the early, pre-World War I days of the Nickelodeons and the small storefront-type viewing halls. But throughout the post-World War I years and through the 1920s into the 1940s, movie producers often decided on film production purely on a whim or, as it was known, "by the seat of their pants." In contrast, after the Second World War, as noted by film historian Robert Sklar:

> The motion picture industry began to study its audience systematically, and what it discovered was both surprising and pleasing. Contrary to received wisdom researchers found that the more education a person had, the more often he or she went to the movies; people at higher income levels attended movies more frequently than the people in lower brackets; as many men went to the movies as did women; and (the least surprising revelation) young people went to movies more than older people. (Sklar, 269)

Chart 1.2   Top 30 Highest-Grossing Movies of the 1950s

Rank	Movie Title	Year	Gross in Millions
1.	*Lady and the Tramp* (Disney)	1955	$93.6
2.	*Peter Pan* (Disney)	1953	$87.4
3.	*The Ten Commandments*	1956	$80.0
4.	*Ben-Hur*	1959	$70.0
5.	*Sleeping Beauty* (Disney)	1959	$51.6
6.	*Around the World in Eighty Days*	1956	$42.0
7.	*This Is Cinerama*	1952	$41.6
8.	*South Pacific*	1958	$36.8
9.	*The Greatest Show on Earth*	1952	$36.0
10.	*The Robe*	1953	$36.0
11.	*Giant*	1956	$35.0
12.	*Cinderella* (Disney)	1950	$34.1
13.	*The Bridge on the River Kwai*	1957	$33.3
14.	*From Here to Eternity*	1953	$30.5
15.	*Quo Vadis*	1951	$30.0
16.	*Rear Window*	1954	$29.0
17.	*Sayonara*	1957	$26.3
18.	*Demetrius and the Gladiators*	1954	$26.0
19.	*Peyton Place*	1957	$25.6
20.	*Some Like It Hot*	1959	$25.0
21.	*House of Wax*	1953	$23.8
22.	*Operation Petticoat*	1959	$23.3
23.	*Auntie Mame*	1958	$23.3
24.	*The Caine Mutiny*	1954	$21.8
25.	*The King and I*	1956	$21.3
26.	*Mister Roberts*	1955	$21.2
27.	*Shane*	1953	$20.0
28.	*Pillow Talk*	1959	$18.8
29.	*Galapagos*	1955	$17.7
30.	*Cat on a Hot Tin Roof*	1958	$17.6

Source: Chart compiled by author.

The disbanding of the old studio system also opened the door for less restrictions upon filmmakers as the boundaries of censorship were tested. One example was director Otto Preminger. His movies often introduced audiences to such taboo subjects as rape in *Anatomy of a Murder* (1959) and drug addiction in *The Man with the Golden Arm* (1955). Later in 1962, the issue of homosexuality was brought forward in *Advise & Consent*. With the studio system disbanded, independent film producers could enter into new realms of marketing, production, and experimentation. One of the most unlikely films to benefit was the low-budget independent film the *Little Fugitive* (1953).

CONEY ISLAND AND *THE LITTLE FUGITIVE*

The *Little Fugitive* was exactly the type of film that would not have been made by a major studio. The reasons were many, including an experimental new technique by using non-professional actors and filming in an actual location without the knowledge of most of the participants. The basic storyline of *Little Fugitive*, directed by Morris Engel, is a simple tale of a seven-year-old Brooklyn boy named Joey (actor Richie Andrusco). During the course of a summer play day, he thinks he has mistakenly shot and killed his brother. Although his brother is playing a prank on his younger brother, Joey has decided to run away. He goes to Brooklyn's famous Coney Island where he wanders among the rides, amusements, the beach, and the famed boardwalk. The movie was filmed on location and serves as an excellent "time capsule" of what Coney Island was like during the 1950s. Movie critic Dennis Schwartz said, "It's an affecting lyrical comedy-drama that fully captures the flavor of urban childhood innocence of the 1950s" (Schwartz, "Little Fugitive Movie Review," n.p.). In 2006, a remake also titled *Little Fugitive* (director Joanna Lipper) was made with a similar storyline.

The Coney Island scenes were filmed with a concealed camera allowing much of the film to be as lifelike as possible. Only a few of the main actors were in character, whereas the beachgoers and those partaking in the attractions did not know they were being filmed. The unique camera technique was said to influence some of the great directors of the time, including the French New Wave director François Truffaut. Of the film technique, Truffaut wrote: "Our New Wave would never have come into being if it hadn't been for the young American [director] Morris Engel, who showed us the way to independent production with [this] fine movie" (Brody, "Talking with Truffaut," n.p.).

The *Little Fugitive* was written and directed by a trio of Ray Ashley, Morris Engel, and Ruth Orkin, who collectively received the 1954 Oscar nomination for Best Writing for a Motion Picture Story. The movie also played in Italy and won an Italian National Syndicate of Film Journalists Award for Best Foreign Film. Although not a top-grosser in terms of dollars at the box office, the USA National Board of Review (NBR) cited it as one of Top Ten films of 1953. In 1997, the National Film Preservation Board placed it among the National Film Registry. The low-budget, black-and-white *Little Fugitive* was an anomaly, but along with many new features, it added to the movie-going experience during the decade.

TV PARTNERSHIP AND WIDE-SCREEN FEATURE FILMS

As the 1948 *Paramount* case decision and the rise in the popularity of television caused a continuing decline in movie attendance, the major studios greatly reduced the number of new movie productions. In 1950, only 263 new feature films from the major studios were released. Throughout the next 10 years, the number of new productions dropped each year to a low of 184 released in 1960. Independent features also declined from a high of 359 in 1950 to 203 in 1960. Both the major studios and the independent filmmakers looked for ways to increase audience attendance at first-run movies in the theaters. The studios soon realized that television was not an enemy, but rather a similar format. Therefore, movie studios took to using the commercial airtime of television for advertising first-run movies. They also began a partnership of leasing some of the classic older movies such as *Gone with the Wind* and *The Wizard of Oz*, as well as the many B-movies for television viewing. In 1956, *Gone with the Wind* was first broadcast on television, and *The Wizard of Oz* aired for the first time on network television later that same year. (By the start of the 1960s, *The Wizard of Oz* was a yearly television event.) As the movie industry and television realized that a partnership could benefit both, MGM Studios released a *Wizard of Oz* film soundtrack album. The TV show was also preceded by an introduction by original cast member Bert Lahr (The Cowardly Lion) and Judy Garland's daughter, the 10-year-old Liza Minnelli. One aspect of the film that was not replicated on the small home television sets was the switch from brown sepia tone while in Kansas to the vivid Technicolor once Dorothy arrives in the Land of Oz. The television sets at the time broadcast almost exclusively in black and white; therefore, the movie was seen by home viewers in black and white. Some appliance stores advertised "in-store" color viewing of the program. (At the time, color TV sets were about two to three times the cost of an average set and very few programs broadcast in color.)

One major technological breakthrough, which television could not match, was the wide-screen movie. In early 1952, a wide-screen process known as "Cinerama" changed the way a theatrical movie was viewed. The Cinerama process placed three standard 35 mm projectors in tandem to project a wide image on the movie screen. The process later incorporated an anamorphic lens to "compress" a wide image onto a standard 35 mm film negative. The almost-square film negative had a superimposed rectangular image along the middle, leaving a black edge on both the top and the bottom. The Cinerama image was then projected on a curved screen to avoid distortion.

In September 1952, a demonstration film called *This Is Cinerama* was released by 20th Century Fox. The film was a surprise hit and later placed in the top-five money earners among all films released that year. The film used color images of a helicopter take-off, a ride on a roller coaster, and an aerial shot of raging waterfalls. It took viewers to St. Mark's Square, the Grand Canal of Venice, and the full span of the Golden Gate Bridge. The movie trailer noted that Cinerama adds "the full scope of normal vision of which you see so much out of the corner of your eye" ("Movie Trailer: *This Is Cinerama*," n.p.). *This Is Cinerama* was re-mastered for limited showing in 2014 and also was placed on the National Film Registry.

The term "aspect ratio" for a movie screen is the width of an image divided by its height. Most of the original movie screens had an aspect ratio of 1.33:1, which meant for every one-foot wide the height ratio was 1.33 feet. That standard screen size, first developed by Thomas Edison, is easily understood as four-foot wide by three-foot high. The 1.33 ratio was officially adopted as an industry standard in 1917 by the Society of Motion Picture Engineers. That

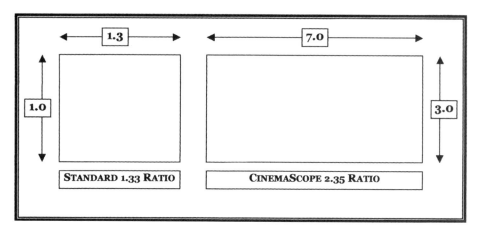

STANDARD 1.33 RATIO

CINEMASCOPE 2.35 RATIO

Chart 1.3

same aspect ratio remained the Hollywood movie standard until the early 1950s, and it was also the standard ratio of 1950s television sets. As the wider movie screens became the standard, Cinerama had an initial aspect ratio of 2.60:1. By the end of the decade the industry standard was CinemaScope at an aspect ratio of 2.35:1. In similar fashion, the Cinemascope ratio is more easily described as seven-foot wide by three-foot high (Block and Wilson, 330–331).

In 1953, a similar wide-screen format labeled CinemaScope was introduced by 20th Century Fox. Unlike the three-camera system for Cinerama, the CinemaScope process involved only one camera that compressed the image through one anamorphic lens into a long rectangle during filming. The same lens "unsqueezed" the image when projected on the movie screen. (When lenses manufactured by Panasonic were used, the process was known as "Panavision.") CinemaScope could also be projected upon a flat screen rather than a curved screen. In a short time, CinemaScope was adopted by almost all of the major studios including Columbia Pictures, Disney (under the title of Buena Vista), MGM, and United Artists. Paramount Studios also used a wide-screen format known as "Vista Vision." In essence, the 35 mm film and projection was now 70 mm. Later terminology often called any wide-screen process "letterbox." The wide-screen epics of CinemaScope were something television could not match with lavish color remakes of some old Hollywood moneymakers of Biblical tales. The massive epics were well-suited for the wider screens with thousands of extras and huge sets, such as *The Robe* (1953), *The Ten Commandments* (1956), and *Ben-Hur* (1959). Each epic tale amounted to financial success at the box office. CinemaScope remained the industry standard until 1967. Another innovation that could not be replicated in the home was a drive-in movie.

THE "DRIVE-IN" MOVIE THEATER AND 3D MOVIES

With the large migration to the suburbs and the success of television, traditional movie theaters within the cities closed at a rapid rate. But the overall number of movie screens did not drastically decline. The difference was due to the construction of drive-in movie theaters often located well outside the city limits, many near new suburban developments. The basic drive-in theater was a large, paved, open area parking lot with lined-out spaces with the cars facing an outdoor movie screen. An automobile and its occupants could drive up to a ticket window, purchase the required number of admission tickets, and pull into a designated space. Alongside the driver's side window was a pole on which was mounted a wired speaker box. The box was lifted from the pole and hooked on the car window to provide sound from the movie. Some of the drive-ins also provided seats for walk-ins and playgrounds for families with children.

The drive-in was not a new idea, as about 1,100 drive-ins existed in various areas across the country, dating back to before the war. Due to the mass migration to the suburbs and the overall decline and neglect of the inner cities, the construction of new drive-in theaters proved profitable. By 1950, more than 1,000 new theaters were built, bringing the total number to over 2,100. By 1960, more than 3,000 additional theaters were built for a total of more than 5,200. Every state across America had drive-in movie theaters, but the most numbered in the warm-all-year-round states. Texas, as one example, had the most with 475 locations. Most of the drive-ins had a capacity between 200 to 700 cars. Therefore, with an average of two to four people per car, attendance could easily number 800 to 2,000 people. The highest-capacity drive-in was in Copiague, New York, that covered an area of 28 acres. Parking capacity at Copiague was for 2,500 cars, with an added feature of indoor seating for an additional 1,200 people. The site also had a restaurant, cafeteria, and an outdoor playground for children. Owners of the drive-ins continually looked for new ways to attract customers by adding special attractions—cartoon festivals, special admission rates for children, a bulk price for an entire carload, and fireworks, among other novelties (Sanders, 35–37).

The search for technological advantages that television could not match led to the brief 1950s fad of 3D movies. (Some of the earliest 3D-type features dated to the 1920s.) The idea behind this format was to accomplish the illusion of three-dimensional reality for the movie audience. To accomplish the sensation, a unique projection technique basically overlapped two film negatives of the same shot, thereby creating a fuzzy appearance to the naked eye. In order to view the enhanced 3D effects, special glasses developed by Polaroid were worn. Most of the thin plastic lenses in cardboard frames were clear and "polarized." Some were made with a separate red and green lens.

The first popular 3D movie was *Bwana Devil* (1952), which advertised movie viewing in "natural vision." *Bwana Devil* featured three-dimensional effects such as lions that appeared to be leaping towards the audience. Three-dimension, however, was a short-lived fad in the 1950s as the wide-screen CinemaScope technique fared better. Others blamed the awkwardness of wearing the cardboard glasses, while others sometimes complained of headaches while viewing the 3-D movies (Block and Wilson, 334–35).

THE NEW "HOLLYWOOD ANGST" OF MARLON BRANDO AND JAMES DEAN

The idea of the "Hollywood Celebrity" was not new to the decade of the 1950s. In the past, the Hollywood studio machine produced not only films, but also stars. The old studio producers had actors and actresses under contract, and in doing so, trained them in acting, dancing, singing, poise, and whatever else was necessary. As early as the first days when feature films became popular, so did the actors and actresses who had starring roles. The 1910s and 1920s produced the likes of Charlie Chaplin, Buster Keaton, Harold Lloyd, Douglas Fairbanks, Mary Pickford, Clara Bow, Rudolph Valentino, Thelma Todd, Louise Brooks, and others. By the 1920s, celebrity movie star gossip was common in newspapers and mass-market magazines. More often than not, the stories of the on-stage and off-screen lives of the movie stars were just as fictitious as the movie plots. Nevertheless, the American public sought to emulate the movie stars for a standard of parties, cars, and fashion. The powerful images shown in the movies were often responsible for the way Americans dressed, talked, and lived. That same notion continued in the 1950s.

During the successful movie runs of Marlon Brando and James Dean, many other notable stars achieved success and acclaim. They included comedy duo Bud Abbott and Lou Costello, Gary Cooper, Doris Day, Susan Hayward, William Holden, Rock Hudson, Gene Kelly, the team of Dean Martin and Jerry Lewis, Debbie Reynolds, Randolph Scott, John Wayne, and others. Also included among the stars were the 1950s female "sex symbols" such as Brigitte Bardot, Jayne Mansfield, and Bettie Page.

Marlon Brando was one star who was not a product of the old studio system, nor did he spend years working at his craft before becoming a major star. During the late 1940s, he was part of a new school known as "method acting." Brando studied at the Dramatic Workshop (the name given to the acting studio at the New School for Social Research in New York City) with famed teachers Erwin Piscator, Lee Strasberg, and Stella Adler. For an individual such as Brando, who was born in Omaha, Nebraska, his path from midwestern farm boy to one of the top American movie actors of all time seems typical of the American success story. In his autobiography *Songs My Mother Taught Me*, Brando credited his acting knowledge to the teaching of Adler and director Elia Kazan. Adler is often credited with Brando's transformation from "an unsophisticated midwestern farm boy into a knowledgeable and cosmopolitan artist" (Mizruchi, 45–46).

During his rise to stardom, Brando secured a few stage appearances in New York. In October 1944, he made his Broadway debut in the play *I Remember Mama*. (He had been turned down for military service due to a bad knee.) As Hollywood agents raved over his on-stage vitality, Brando supposedly turned down offers for screen tests because he did not want to be locked into a long-term studio contract. In the binds of a studio contract, he would not have had any control over his career path, nor his choice of acting style. In 1946, he starred in the play *Candida*, of which he only did 24 performances. The following year, he was cast in the soon to be iconic role of Stanley Kowalski in Tennessee Williams' *A Streetcar Named Desire*. In all, Brando performed as Kowalski 855 times on the Broadway stage. A 2005 *Vanity Fair* article claimed, "No other actor has ever rocketed to overnight stardom on the Broadway stage as Marlon Brando did in 1947" (Schulberg, "The Man Who Would Be King").

In 1951, *A Streetcar Named Desire* was released on film, and Brando's performance was unlike anything people had seen before. He exuded raw sexuality and masculinity. He also earned an Academy Award nomination for Best Actor for his performance. (The award that year went to Humphrey Bogart for *The African Queen*.) Brando not only introduced a new method style of acting, he also personified a new "cool" in his movies. One such example was his character Johnny in *The Wild One* (1953). The plot centers on a motorcycle gang that terrorizes a small town. Many in America viewed this film as symbolic of an American youth out of control and cause for increased juvenile delinquency. In essence, *The Wild One* did evoke youthful rebellion. The rebellion was not against anything in particular, but rather everything that 1950s American society represented. One such example occurs during a brief exchange in a diner. At one point, Brando is asked, "Hey Johnny, what are you rebelling against?" His simple reply is, "Whadda you got?" This role as Johnny proved popular among teenagers and had an impact on a large segment of American youth. Many teenagers emulated Johnny's clothing style of denim jeans, white t-shirt, and a black leather jacket. Adam Bernstein, writing Brando's obituary for *The Washington Post*, described the influence:

> Brando also had a huge impact on public behavior. He was, at first, a strikingly muscular and vital figure who defined 1950s leather-jacketed masculinity. He wore jeans to swank parties, insulted star-making gossip columnists and flaunted his preference for dark-skinned women, then a social taboo—anything to pique the Hollywood system that tried to control his public image. (Bernstein, "Actor Marlon Brando, 80, Dies," n.p.)

Brando was not only a huge box office success, but in each succeeding role, he continued achieving wide critical acclaim. During the decade he made a total of 11 movies:

1950: *Come Out Fighting* (TV movie) and *The Men*

1951: *A Streetcar Named Desire*

1952: *Viva Zapata*

1953: *Julius Caesar* and *The Wild One*

1954: *On the Waterfront* and *Désirée*

1955: *Guys and Dolls*

1956: *The Teahouse of the August Moon*

1957: *Sayonara*

1958: *The Young Lions*

During the decade, he was nominated for a Best Actor Oscar five times, including four straight years for *A Streetcar Named Desire* (1951), *Viva Zapata* (1952), *Julius Caesar* (1953), a win in 1954 for *On the Waterfront*, and *Sayonara* (1957). His first Oscar came at the age of 30, which until that time was the youngest age of any Best Actor winner.

As applauded and revered as Brando was throughout the 1950s, his image was soon tarnished during the 1960s. He received a huge salary to star in *Mutiny on the Bounty* (1962). Although the MGM film was one of the year's top grossing movies and received an Oscar nomination for Best Picture, it did not return a profit over its extravagant budget and salary costs. Throughout the 1960s, other films followed with similar high production that did not bring in the profits sought by the Hollywood producers. As a result, movie producers soon labeled Brando as "box office poison." Some also say that his political activism in support of Native American Indians and his participation in the 1963 Martin Luther King march on Washington for civil rights alienated him from the Hollywood producers. However, his political activism did result in many theater owners in the southern states outright refusing to show his films.

Brando's legacy has lived on in movie history, but the tragedy surrounding the short career of James Dean (1931–1955) loomed larger in American popular culture. In sum, the entirety of the rebellious, non-conformist, 1950s teenager was fully epitomized by Dean. In September 2015, journalist Tim Gray noted in *Variety*:

Marlon Brando introduced a new "method style" of acting and personified a new "cool" in his movies. One such example was his character Johnny in *The Wild One* (1953). The story line follows a motorcycle gang that terrorizes a small town. Many in America viewed this film as symbolic of an American youth out of control and giving rise to increased juvenile delinquency. (Metro-Goldwyn-Mayer/Photofest)

Sixty years after these events, [James Dean] remains an icon, based on only three films. Dean hit a nerve because he was the right star in the right roles at the right time. After the Depression and World War II, many American adults wanted things to be "nice" and trouble-free. The affluent middle class moved into new suburban developments, while Madison Avenue started targeting teenagers as a distinct demographic with their own spending money. (Gray, "James Dean: After 60 Years")

Dean might have been the most unlikely actor to ever become such a legendary movie sensation. All told, he accumulated 31 acting credits, with only seven of those as movies. For the first half of the 1950s he was considered a complete unknown. He did have over 20 television acting credits from 1951 to 1955, mostly on live anthology dramas. Yet none of those roles provided any major leap to stardom.

Dean's first feature film as a lead actor was in *East of Eden* (1955). In the movie version of John Steinbeck's best-selling novel *East of Eden* (Viking Press, 1952),

Dean played a troubled young man conflicted about his family life. Typical of so many movie adaptations of novels, very little of Steinbeck's story was written into the movie screenplay. Movie critic Bosley Crowther complained of a "compressed" script that included only a small portion of Steinbeck's original story. He added, "It is questionable whether that part contains the best of the book." Despite the critique, Crowther did think that the film, under the direction of Elia Kazan, "in one respect, it is brilliant." He also praised the vivid color and technical use of CinemaScope (Crowther, "East of Eden").

At the time, the 50-year-old Crowther was considered the "dean of movie critics." But he might not have been totally fair in his assessment of Dean's film portrayal of Cal Task. Writing a movie review in the *New York Times* on March 10, 1955, Crowther claimed all of the actors' attempt at "anguish" was "perceptibly stylized and grotesque." Crowther was particular harsh on the young actor's major debut. He chided:

> Especially is this true of James Dean in the role of the confused and cranky Cal. This young actor, who is here doing his first big screen stint, is a mass of histrionic gingerbread. He scuffs his feet, he whirls, he pouts, he sputters, he leans against walls, he rolls his eyes, he swallows his words, he ambles slack-kneed—all like Marlon Brando used to do. Never have we seen a performer so clearly follow another's style. Mr. Kazan should be spanked for permitting him to do such a sophomoric thing. Whatever there might be of reasonable torment in this youngster is buried beneath the clumsy display. (Crowther, "The Screen: 'East of Eden' Has Debut," n.p.)

The official nationwide release of *East of Eden* was on April 10, 1955. (Bosley Crowther's review appeared one month earlier at a special screening in New York City.) Prior to the screening, there was significant "Hollywood buzz" about the forthcoming film. In a January 1955 article, *Look* magazine predicted the movie would make Dean a star. The article claimed the young actor was "the most dynamic discovery since Marlon Brando" (Nixon, "East of Eden," n.p.). In February, *Vogue* magazine proclaimed Dean as "intense, with such strong projection that he is always noticed" (Nixon, "East of Eden," n.p.). Also in February, the esteemed gossip columnist Louella Parsons (whose statements could either instantly "make" or "break" a celebrity's career) in *Cosmopolitan* magazine exalted, "It is what Dean projects on the screen that makes him my pick among the new actors for stardom in 1955. He is a great young actor. I predict a long and brilliant career" (quoted in Nixon, "East of Eden").

But the "long and brilliant career" never came to be. On September 30, 1955, just a few short months after the premier of *East of Eden*, Dean was killed in a car crash in California at the age of 24. At the time of his death, he had completed two other movies: *Rebel Without a Cause* and *Giant*. Each was later released to box office success—*Rebel* in October 1955, and *Giant* the following year in November. For each film, Dean received a posthumous Best Actor nomination for an Academy Award.

It was *Rebel Without a Cause* that secured James Dean's legendary fame among teenage worshippers and also propelled the film to become an instant Hollywood classic. Turner Classic Movies (TCM) provided a synopsis for *Rebel Without a Cause*:

> Teenager Jim Stark (James Dean) struggles to make sense of his middle class upbringing and the gnawing restlessness within himself, made worse by a mother and father completely out of touch with his problems and concerns. As the new kid at the local high school, Jim is treated like an outsider but he eventually finds a kindred spirit in fellow students Judy (Natalie Wood) and Plato (Sal Mineo). The three form an unconventional "family" of their own, but their strong bond only temporarily brings them love, acceptance, and security before outside forces tear them apart. ("*Rebel Without a Cause*," n.p.)

On October 25, 1955, *Rebel Without a Cause* opened in New York to mixed reviews. Bosley Crowther said the movie was "violent, brutal and disturbing." It was also not any surprise that Crowther once again panned Dean's acting. Crowther thought Dean should not have "been so intent on imitating Marlon Brando in varying degrees" (Crowther, "The Screen: Delinquency; Rebel Without Cause," n.p.). In stark contrast, *Time* magazine praised Dean's role "of unusual sensibility and charm." *Variety* said the movie was "exciting, suspenseful and provocative" (quoted in Feaster and McGee, "*Rebel Without a Cause*," n.p.). In later years, TCM movie critic Felicia Feaster called it, "One of the cinemas' most enduring, masterfully directed troubled-youth pictures" ("*Rebel Without a Cause*: The Essentials," n.p.). *Rebel Without a Cause* portrayed troubled youth and families torn right out of and in stark contrast to the idealized 1950s television sitcoms such as *The Adventures of Ozzie and Harriet, Leave It to Beaver*, and *The Donna Reed Show*.

With typical Hollywood bravado, some of the movie poster taglines read as a warning or impending disaster of the reality of a troubled American society. Some samples from *Rebel Without a Cause* included:

- Teenage terror torn from today's headlines.
- Warner Bros.' challenging drama of today's juvenile violence!
- Jim Stark . . . a kid from a "good" family—what makes him tick . . . like a bomb?
- The bad boy from a good family.
- Warner Bros. put all the force of the screen into a challenging drama of today's juvenile violence!

For the most part, Warner Bros. studio did not have to create a "buzz," because Dean had already achieved a cult-like following among teenage movie fans (Feaster and McGee, "*Rebel Without a Cause*: The Essentials," n.p.).

In August 1956, some newspapers and tabloids ran stories about a growing fan "cultism" for the deceased Dean. By the time *Giant* was released, between 5,000 and 6,000 fan letters each week were still being addressed to the deceased star. In 2015, Randal C. Archibold, trying to explain Dean's status as a "legend," asked why after 60 years a legion of newfound fans were drawn to James Dean. Archibold described Dean as "a young, sexy star who dangled his cigarettes just so, played misunderstood, rebellious characters struggling in the suburbs and practiced an eclectic range of hobbies, like racing fast cars." Archibold was "not clear" why the attraction remained after so many years. The answer might have been provided by one young 21st-century fan who replied, "What kind of kid doesn't want to do those things?" (Archibold, "Where a Young Actor Died and a Legend Was Born").

Of all James Dean's acting work, the most chilling was filmed for a pending TV commercial shot on September 15, 1955 (just two weeks before his own death). Dean was recruited for a public service announcement (PSA) to warn about the dangers of fast driving. The promotion was co-sponsored by Warner Bros. to promote the movie release of *Giant*. Dean appeared in his cowboy outfit as his Jett Rink character from the movie. In the commercial, actor Gig Young asked Dean to provide a few words about "safe driving."

James Dean's legendary fame among teenager worshipers was epitomized in *Rebel Without a Cause* (1955). He played a troubled youth among disrupted families that stood in stark contrast with the idealized 1950s TV families. The movie propelled Dean to stardom and the film as an instant Hollywood classic. (Warner Bros./Photofest)

Dean did say he drove his own racing car "going over 100 miles an hour." But he said that type of speed was only for the racetrack (of which Dean was a recent enthusiast and avid participant). Young asked for Dean's opinion about fast driving on the highway, asking, "Do you think it's a good idea?" Dean suggested that all drivers should be "very cautious," adding, "I don't have the urge to speed on the highway." Young concluded with the question, "Jimmy. Do you have any advice for the young drivers?" The PSA scripted line was supposed to be read as, "The life you save may be your own." But in typical Dean fashion, he paused and ad-libbed with "The life you might save might be mine" (Video: "James Dean warns kids of fast driving on the highway, 1955").

Due to his tragic death just a short time later, the commercial was not aired. (It is readily accessible to 21st-century audiences on YouTube.) In a twist of fate, the wreckage of Dean's 1955 Porsche Super Speedster car was placed on display in Los

Angeles. A placard was placed adjacent to the carnage that reads: "Los Angeles Safety Council *Presents* James Dean's Last Sports Car." In the ultimate irony to Dean's own words in his PSA, another sign was placed adjacent to the wreck that read: "This Accident Could Have Been Avoided." Dean was certainly one of the top male 1950s Hollywood icons and has lived on in legend. On the female side, there were many popular stars. But, none, male or female, was more famous, or has lived on as more legendary, than Marilyn Monroe.

THE BLONDE BOMBSHELL: MARILYN MONROE

Three of the so-called "classic pin-ups" and sex symbols of the 1950s were Jayne Mansfield, Bettie Page, and Marilyn Monroe. There were certainly many others, including Brigitte Bardot, Diana Dors, Anne Francis, Ava Garner, Susan Hayward, Rita Hayworth, Kim Novak, and Lana Turner. There were also pin-ups among burlesque queens such as Tempest Storm and Blaze Starr. Although Jayne Mansfield (1933–1967) and Marilyn Monroe (1926–1962) appeared in many popular films, it was their sexuality that perpetuated their fame throughout the decade. Bettie Page (1923–2008), on the other hand, achieved fame mainly through her popularity as a "pin-up" girl and burlesque queen, but not necessarily through mainstream movies.

Stars such as Mansfield and Monroe were often described as the quintessential "blonde bombshells." The original "blonde bombshell" is often attributed to 1930s actress Jean Harlow (1911–1937). During the 1950s, the term was often applied to any actress who exuded on-screen sex appeal. In addition, the constant media attention did not suggest any intelligence associated with the hair color. The degradation of women, especially those with blonde hair (often dyed or bleached), continued into the 21st century.

Marilyn Monroe was considered not only the greatest sex symbol of the decade, but quite possibly of all time. Monroe was born to Gladys Pearl Baker in Los Angeles, California, on June 1, 1926, with the birth name of Norma Jeane Mortenson. A short time after her birth, she was baptized under the name "Norma Jeane Baker" (sometimes noted as "Jean"). As a young girl, she never knew her father, and her mother was placed in a mental institution. She grew up in orphanages and was later placed in foster care. Only a few days after turning 16, she married James Dougherty. They divorced after four years of marriage. In Dougherty's 2005 *Los Angeles Times* obituary, he said the marriage was "years before she became the iconic sex symbol Marilyn Monroe." As Monroe became famous in later years, Dougherty often said "I never knew Marilyn Monroe . . . I knew and loved Norma Jean." After her divorce from Dougherty, she began using the name "Marilyn Monroe." She did not legally change her name until February 1956 through the City Court of the State of New York (McLellan, "James Dougherty, 84; Was Married to Marilyn Monroe Before She Became a Star," n.p.). By 1953, Monroe had become one of Hollywood's top stars with roles in three major money-making films that all focused on her on-screen sex appeal. They were *Niagara, Gentlemen Prefer Blondes*, and *How to Marry a Millionaire*, all released in 1953.

Niagara (1953) was a "film noir" suspense thriller with Monroe receiving top billing in the lead role of Rose Loomis. *Niagara* was slightly different from other film noirs in that the movie was filmed in Technicolor. The story and lighting was technically "noir," but seeing Marilyn Monroe in color was a sensation in itself. Her acting in the movie was quite good, but it was her character's overt sexuality that propelled her to stardom.

With Technicolor, moviegoers could see for themselves her bright red lips, milky white skin, and blonde hair. The movie trailer for *Niagara* described Monroe "as the tantalizing temptress whose kisses fired men's souls." The trailer showed Monroe in compromising positions such as in the bedroom, the shower, or in a romantic embrace. The promotional tagline added, "She sang of love, just as she lived for love. As she lured men on and on to their eternal destruction. And her own husband was no exception." A review published in the *New York Times* on January 22, 1953, made note of Monroe's on-screen sexuality:

> Perhaps Miss Monroe is not the perfect actress at this point. But neither the director nor the gentlemen who handled the cameras appeared to be concerned with this. They have caught every possible curve both in the intimacy of the boudoir and in equally revealing tight dresses. And they have illustrated pretty concretely that she can be seductive—even when she walks. (Weiler, "Niagara Falls Vies with Marilyn Monroe," n.p.)

Similar reviews focusing on her sensuality were written for the comedy *Gentlemen Prefer Blondes* (1953) as she played a similar but innocent temptress in search of a husband. In a July 16, 1953, review in the *New York Times*, Bosley Crowther said of the co-stars, "Miss [Jane] Russell and Miss [Marilyn] Monroe keep you looking at them even when they have little or nothing to do. Call it inherent magnetism. Call it luxurious coquetry. Call it whatever you fancy. It's what makes this a—well, buoyant show" (Crowther, "The Screen in Review: 'Gentlemen Prefer Blondes,' " n.p.). With those two movies, her "star image" was firmly established.

For the studios and producers, who only wanted box office moneymakers, they continually capitalized on Monroe's sex appeal. She was immediately cast in a similar comedy role in *How to Marry a Millionaire* (1953) with Hollywood starlets Betty Grable and Lauren Bacall. The studios called those type of movies "light-hearted fare," such as another Monroe role in *There's No Business Like Show Business* (1954). Another was *The Seven Year Itch* (1955) that Turner Classic Movies described the simple plot as, "A married man whose wife is on vacation falls for the blonde bombshell upstairs" ("The Seven Year Itch," n.p.). It was during the filming of that movie that the single-most famous of all Monroe's photo images emerged—and possibly the single-most famous Hollywood image of all time.

The scene in point from *The Seven Year Itch* features Monroe walking along a New York City street. As she looks down, she stands over a subway grate. As she waits for the eventual passing of an underground subway car, a sudden gush of air bellows from below the grate pushing her skirt upward like a parachute. The indelible image of Marilyn smiling innocently while attempting to hold down her skirt became an instant sensation. The wide CinemaScope on-screen scene image contained both Monroe and "wide-eyed" actor Tom Ewell looking on in fantasy. The release of a cropped photo of just Marilyn was quickly reproduced in 8×10 glossies and posters. The image lived on well into later decades; as TCM wrote, that one scene "entered the ranks of pop culture when Marilyn stepped on a subway grating wearing a billowy white skirt" ("The Seven Year Itch," n.p.).

She continued grabbing newspaper headline attention. Her wedding to New York Yankee baseball star Joe DiMaggio, on January 14, 1954, was heralded with much fanfare and constant media coverage. By October of that same year, after only 274 days of marriage, they filed for divorce. She married a third time in 1956 to famed playwright Arthur Miller, but the marriage also ended in divorce in 1961. Throughout her short life, all sorts of rumors linked her in romantic entanglements with celebrities and politicians. Her desire to earn serious dramatic roles led her to relocate to New York City to study at the famed Actor's Studio. Her later dramatic performance in *Bus Stop* (1956) was widely praised and she was nominated for a 1957 Golden Globe Award as Best Motion Picture Actress. Monroe was able to demonstrate her capable acting qualities when she was paired with quality directors. In 1959, she worked with director Billy Wilder in a comedy box office success *Some Like It Hot*, a film that eventually

Throughout the history of Hollywood, no actor or actress was either more famous or more legendary than Marilyn Monroe. It was this image (usually cropped to show only Marilyn), shot during the filming of *The Seven Year Itch* (1955), that became Monroe's most famous. Some might say that the photo is the single most famous Hollywood image of all time. (Twentieth Century Fox/Photofest)

placed at #14 on the American Film Institute's "100 Greatest Films of All Time"—
see Chart 1.4. Her role as the ukulele-playing singer Sugar Kane Kowalczyk in
an all-girl 1920s jazz band earned her a Golden Globe Award as "Best Actress in
a Comedy." But audiences and the media, and most importantly Hollywood
producers, continued to push the sex appeal. A woman's role in 1950s society
was not that of an independent career-woman; it was either as a sexual "play-
thing" for men or as a devoted housewife. In Monroe's case, it was as a play-
thing. During the height of her fame, she once admitted to a British journalist
that the secret of Hollywood was simply sex:

> You can't sleep your way into being a star . . . but it helps. A lot of actresses get
> their first chance that way. . . . In Hollywood a girl's virtue is much less impor-
> tant than her hair-do. You're judged on how you look, not by what you are . . .
> I've slept with producers. I'd be a liar if I said I didn't. . . . They wanted to sam-
> ple the merchandise, and if you didn't go along, there were 25 girls who would.
> (Steinem, 89–90)

Later in her short life she confessed to a friend, "I spent a great deal of time on
my knees." She was referring to the "old" and "powerful" male producers of
Hollywood, who were, as writer Gloria Steinem noted, "fond of degrading
women" (*Marilyn: Norma Jeane*, 87–90, 205). When Monroe moved to New York
to pursue her studies as a dramatic actress, she was not taken seriously. In later
years, writer Gloria Steinem often explained that the definition of success for a
1950s female was dependent upon marrying a "successful man." In sum, as
Gloria has often said, "You had to become the man you married." Steinem, who
recalled seeing her first Monroe film during the early 1950s, said, "It was not
easy for young women of the 1950s to resist the pressure to be mothers early."
Steinem noted, despite it all, Monroe was "a woman of the fifties" where men
needed to be strong and masculine and women frail and dainty. The simple fact
was that, "Men need women to be feminine" (*Marilyn: Norma Jeane*, 117–118).
It is that same image that has lingered in the mind, both during the 1950s and into
the present, of a voluptuous female body without any genuine intellectual
substance.

One of the most genuine and honest biographies of the famous Hollywood
star is the aforementioned *Marilyn: Norma Jeane* (Signet Classics, 1986), written
by Gloria Steinem. The Grand Rapids Press said that the biography provided
"empathy without sensationalism" (*Marilyn: Norma Jeane*, back cover). Steinem's
biography can easily draw a comparison between author and star, as both were
intricate to American popular culture during the 20th century. Steinem, along
with Betty Friedan and others (see Controversies chapter later in the book), was
instrumental in bringing forward the suppression, inequality, subjugation, and
degradation that women faced during the 1950s.

As Monroe is always known as "Marilyn," Steinem is always known to all as
simply "Gloria." She was instrumental in founding the first magazine devoted
solely to issues concerning women. The first issue of *Ms. Magazine* premiered
in December 1971 and quickly sold out. In 1972, during the "birth year of *Ms.*,"
one of the editors, Harriet Lyons, suggested a cover story on Marilyn Monroe
for the August issue to coincide with the 10-year anniversary of the star's

death. The subsequent issue ran a cover story with the title, "The Woman Who Died Too Soon." Gloria's summation in the article, as it applied to Marilyn, was: "Nothing is enough, if unreality is the measure" (Steinem, "The Woman Who Will Not Die," n.p.). It was *Ms.* and Gloria Steinem who revealed the human side of the famous icon whom the world knew as "Marilyn Monroe." In her bestseller, *Marilyn: Norma Jeane*, Steinem explored the "woman behind the myth." She revealed the real "Norma Jeane," who was vulnerable, compassionate, kind, intelligent, and, due to fame and media image, lonely. In her own unfinished autobiography, *My Story*, Marilyn explained, "Sometimes I've been to a party where no one spoke to me for a whole evening. The men frightened by their wives or sweeties, would give me a wide berth. And the ladies would gang up in a corner to discuss my dangerous character" (Steinem, *Marilyn: Norma Jeane*, 25).

A similar statement was provided by Dalia Leeds who befriended Monroe. Leeds was an Israeli woman who had recently married and moved to New York City. For the most part she was unaware of Marilyn's fame, which was instrumental to their close friendship. According to Leeds, Monroe was "vulnerable." Unlike the tabloid stories, Leeds described the famed celebrity as "an ordinary woman who was shy, curious, and lonely." After their meeting and growing friendship developed, Leeds concluded, "I decided I would never trust gossip magazines again—she was so different from her image" (Steinem, *Marilyn: Norma Jeane*, 109).

Her fame and popularity among the public never seemed to waiver. Although she never received or was ever nominated for an Academy Award, she was often recognized by the prestigious Golden Globes and the British Academy of Film and Television Arts (BAFTA). (She was twice nominated by BAFTA for Best Foreign Actress: in 1956 for *The Seven Year Itch*, and again in 1958 for *The Prince and the Showgirl*.) The Golden Globes awarded her the "World Film Favorite—Female" in 1956. She was honored with the same award again, on March 5, 1962, at the 19th Golden Globe Awards ceremony. That award was overshadowed a few months later, as she was found dead in her California home at the age of 36.

On August 5, 1962, a housekeeper found Monroe's body in a bedroom in her Los Angeles home. The news and photos of her death spread like wildfire. Her death was carried as front-page headlines in all the major newspapers and tabloids across America, with all sorts of speculation as to the cause of death. Some headlines included:

From the *Los Angeles Times:*

MARILYN MONROE
FOUND DEAD
Sleeping Pill Overdose Blamed

From the *New York Mirror:*

MARILYN MONROE
Kills Self Found Nude in Bed . . . Hand
On Phone . . . Took 40 Pills

From the *New York Daily News*:

MARILYN DEAD
[Her smiling photo filled almost the entire page]
The Monroe Saga: 7 Pages of Stories and Pictures

The fascination of Marilyn as tabloid fodder continued for many years after her death. Almost immediately, photos from the coroner's office were leaked to the press, as were other photos from her bedroom, and circulated among the tabloids.

The cause of her death was never fully confirmed, as all sorts of speculation, accusations, and conspiracy theories arose. Her death has remained a mystery, but her legend lives on. (See more detailed information in Legacy chapter later in the book.) Literally thousands of examples of memorabilia and news stories arose on the 50th anniversary of her death. *Playboy* magazine capitalized on the moment by republishing the nude photos as well as a facsimile of the original 1953 edition. The *New York Daily News* reprinted more than 50 past photographs from their files, showcasing a full range of her life, beginning with a "teenaged Norma Jeane Baker, future film star and sex symbol Marilyn Monroe, circa 1940." Another was a 1942 wedding day photograph of the 16-year-old Norma Jeane and James Dougherty. Other photos included promotional stills from movies and her famous marriages to DiMaggio and Miller. One 1955 photograph was of her and actor Marlon Brando (both at the height of their careers) attending a movie premier. In later years, Brando said about Monroe:

> Marilyn was a sensitive, misunderstood person, much more perceptive than was generally assumed. She had been beaten down, but had a strong emotional intelligence—a keen intuition for the feelings of others, the most refined type of intelligence. (Biography.com, "Marilyn Monroe Biography," n.p.).

Despite the praise from those who knew her well, during her lifetime and as a continuing legend, she was remembered and typecast in the media as purely a "sex symbol." During both her lifetime and continuing well into the 21st century, she became the physical benchmark against whom all other attractive female starlets were measured.

Monroe's image and popularity is truly a lasting legacy. In June 1999, she placed sixth in the American Film Institute's list of the top 25 female stars of all time. A more endearing remembrance was presented on January 22, 2016, as the Smithsonian Institute's National Portrait Gallery installed a portrait of her on its "Recognize Wall." In late 2014, the Smithsonian created the "Recognize Wall" as an opportunity to showcase specific individuals "who have influenced American politics, history and culture" ("And the Winner Is . . . Marilyn Monroe!" n.p.). As an ongoing, rotating, twice-a-year exhibit, the museum offered up three different portraits of famous Hollywood starlets. The final selection for the display was based on fan voting. The Monroe portrait was selected from a short list that also included actresses Rita Hayworth and Mae West. The online voting at smithsonianmag.com selected a 1952 photograph taken by Philippe Halsman for *Life* magazine. At the time of the *Life* photo shoot, Monroe was still an unknown. The portrait was kept in a prominent public space until March 6, 2016.

THE 21st-CENTURY LEGACY OF 1950s MOVIES

In 1998, the American Film Institute (AFI) listed the "100 Greatest American Films of All Time" compiled from more than 1,500 industry professionals. Among those who weighed in were actors, film critics, cinematographers, directors, editors, executives, film historians, producers, and screenwriters. The top movie of all time, and also at the top of most every other reputable list, was the 1941 classic *Citizen Kane*, directed by Orson Welles. The AFI listed 19 movies produced during the 1950s. The highest ranked on the list at #8 was *On the Waterfront*, directed by Elia Kazan in 1954. Others included #10 *Singin' in the Rain* (dir. Stanley Donen and Gene Kelly, 1952), #12 *Sunset Boulevard* (dir. Billy Wilder, 1950), #13 *The Bridge Over the River Kwai* (dir. David Lean, 1957), #14 *Some Like It Hot* (dir. Billy Wilder, 1959), #16 *All About Eve* (dir. Joseph L. Mankiewicz, 1950), #17 *The African Queen* (dir. John Huston, 1951), #40 *North by Northwest* (1959) and #42 *Rear Window* (1954) both by director Alfred Hitchcock, #45 *A Streetcar Named Desire* (dir. Elia Kazan, 1951), #52 *From Here to Eternity* (dir. Fred Zinnemann, 1953), #59 *Rebel Without A Cause* (dir. Nicholas Ray, 1955), #61 *Vertigo* (dir. Alfred Hitchcock, 1958), #68 *An American in Paris* (dir. Vincente Minnelli, 1951), and #69 *Shane*, #82 *Giant* (1956), and #92 *A Place in the Sun* (1951) were all directed by George Stevens. In between at #72 was *Ben-Hur* (dir. William Wyler, 1959), followed by #96 *The Searchers* (dir. John Ford, 1956) ("AFI's 100 Greatest American Movies of All Time," n.p.).

The revised AFI list for the 10th anniversary confirmed the lasting legacy of the movies during the 1950s. Although thousands of American movies were released during the 10-year period, *Singin' in the Rain* moved up from #10 to #5. Two others made large jumps as *Vertigo* moved into the top ten at #9 (from #61), as did *The Searchers* to #12 (from #96). *Shane* also moved up from #69 to #45. Surprisingly, the total number of 1950s movies increased with two more added to the new Top 100 list, *12 Angry Men* (1957) at #87 (dir. Sidney Lumet, 1957) and *High Noon* (1952) directed by Fred Zinnemann at # 27.

Six movies that did not repeat on the Top 100 list were *From Here to Eternity, Rebel Without a Cause, A Place in the Sun, An American in Paris,* and *Giant.* Eight others remained, but moved down. *On the Waterfront* dropped out of the top 10 from #8 to #19. *Sunset Boulevard* dropped from #12 to #16, as did *The Bridge Over the River Kwai* down to #36, *Some Like It Hot* to #22, *All About Eve* to #28; *The African Queen* went far down from #17 to #65, *North by Northwest* from #40 to #55. *Rear Window* moved down only slightly from #42 to #48, as did *A Streetcar Named Desire* from #45 to #47. *Ben-Hur* completed the list down from #72 to #100.

Some critics might point out that the AFI list was composed by a select group of individuals well-versed in movie history, with maybe an eye towards nostalgia. However, the legacy of American films reached beyond the physical borders of the United States. In 2015, the BBC of England sponsored "a poll of 62 film critics from around the world." Among the film critics included those from academia, the blogosphere, newspaper reviewers, and others. Each was asked

Chart 1.4   1950s Films on AFI's "100 Greatest Films of All Time" (1998)

AFI Rank	Movie Title	Director	Year
#8	*On the Waterfront*	Elia Kazan	1954
#10	*Singing in the Rain*	Stanley Donen/Gene Kelly	1952
#12	*Sunset Boulevard*	Billy Wilder	1950
#13	*Bridge on the River Kwai*	David Lean	1957
#14	*Some Like It Hot*	Billy Wilder	1959
#16	*All About Eve*	Joseph L. Mankiewicz	1950
#17	*The African Queen*	John Huston	1951
#40	*North by Northwest*	Alfred Hitchcock	1959
#42	*Rear Window*	Alfred Hitchcock	1954
#45	*A Streetcar Named Desire*	Elia Kazan	1951
#52	*From Here to Eternity*	Fred Zinnemann	1953
#59	*Rebel Without a Cause*	Nicholas Ray	1955
#61	*Vertigo*	Alfred Hitchcock	1958
#68	*An American in Paris*	Vincente Minnelli	1951
#69	*Shane*	George Stevens	1953
#72	*Ben-Hur*	William Wyler	1959
#82	*Giant*	George Stevens	1956
#92	*A Place in the Sun*	George Stevens	1951
#96	*The Searchers*	John Ford	1956

Source: American Film Institute: www.afi.com/100years/movies.aspx. Chart compiled by author.

1950s Films on AFI's "100 Greatest Films of All Time" (2008)

AFI Rank	Movie Title	Director	Year
#5	*Singin' in the Rain*	Stanley Donen/Gene Kelly	1952
#9	*Vertigo*	Alfred Hitchcock	1958
#12	*The Searchers*	John Ford	1956
#19	*On the Waterfront*	Elia Kazan	1954
#22	*Some Like It Hot*	Billy Wilder	1959
#27	*High Noon*	Fred Zinnemann	1952
#28	*All About Eve*	Joseph L. Mankiewicz	1950
#36	*The Bridge on the River Kwai*	David Lean	1957
#45	*Shane*	George Stevens	1953
#47	*A Streetcar Named Desire*	Elia Kazan	1951
#48	*Rear Window*	Alfred Hitchcock	1954
#55	*North by Northwest*	Alfred Hitchcock	1959
#65	*The African Queen*	John Huston	1951
#87	*12 Angry Men*	Sidney Lumet	1957
#100	*Ben-Hur*	William Wyler	1959

Source: American Film Institute: www.afi.com/100years/movies10.aspx . Chart compiled by author.

CHART 1.5   1950s Films on Screenrant's "The 100 Best American Films" (2015)

AFI Rank	Movie Title	Director	Year
#3	*Vertigo*	Alfred Hitchcock	1958
#5	*The Searchers*	John Ford	1956
#7	*Singin' in the Rain*	Stanley Donen/Gene Kelly	1952
#13	*North by Northwest*	Alfred Hitchcock	1959
#30	*Some Like It Hot*	Billy Wilder	1959
#37	***Imitation of Life***	**Douglas Sirk**	**1959**
#41	***Rio Bravo***	**Howard Hawks**	**1959**
#48	*A Place in the Sun*	George Stevens	1951
#51	***Touch of Evil***	**Orson Welles**	**1958**
#54	*Sunset Boulevard*	Billy Wilder	1950
#64	***Johnny Guitar***	**Nicholas Ray**	**1954**
#70	***The Band Wagon***	**Vincente Minnelli**	**1953**
#89	***In A Lonely Place***	**Nicholas Ray**	**1950**
#92	***Night of the Lonely Hunter***	**Charles Laughton**	**1955**
#100	*Ace in the Hole*	**Billy Wilder**	**1951**

Source: ScreenRant.com: screenrant.com/100-best-american-films/. Chart compiled by author.

to make a top 10 list. A value point system was added and a top 100 list compiled. The criteria were defined as: "In order to qualify as an American film, a title simply had to have been produced by an American studio or funded from an American source—the nationality of the director and the filming locations didn't matter" ("The 100 Best American Films [2015]," n.p.). The Orson Welles classic *Citizen Kane* (1941), known for its technical and cinema innovations, placed at the #1 spot. The Francis Ford Coppola epic *The Godfather* (1972) placed at #2, but Alfred Hitchcock's *Vertigo* (1958) placed high on the list at #3. In all, the BBC Top 100 Movies of All Time contained 15 that were produced during the 1950s (BBC, "The 100 Greatest American Films," n.p.).

Many other surveys, blogs, and trade publications have provided all sorts of lists for Hollywood movies. The lists are sometimes based on a particular genre such as horror, fantasy, science fiction, action, romance, comedy, or westerns. Those lists are usually based only on full-length feature films catering to a broad popular appeal. Movies, however, are not limited to just the features. Throughout the history of movie production, film has been used for a variety of techniques and subject matter. One source to catalog film of all kind is the National Film Preservation Board.

THE NATIONAL FILM REGISTRY

The National Film Preservation Board (NFP) under the auspices of the U.S. Library of Congress was established by the Congressional National Film

Chart 1.6   The National Film Registry—Films of the 1950s

All About Eve	1950	Carmen Jones	1954
The Asphalt Jungle	1950	The House in the Middle	1954
Born Yesterday	1950	Johnny Guitar	1954
D.O.A.	1950	On the Waterfront	1954
In a Lonely Place	1950	The Naked Spur	1953
Sunset Boulevard	1950	Rear Window	1954
Winchester '73	1950	Sabrina	1954
The African Queen	1951	Salt of the Earth	1954
An American in Paris	1951	Seven Brides for Seven Brothers	1954
The Day the Earth Stood Still	1951	A Star Is Born	1954
Duck and Cover	1951	A Time Out of War	1954
Gerald McBoing-Boing	1951	All That Heaven Allows	1955
Notes on the Port of St. Francis	1951	Kiss Me Deadly	1955
A Place in the Sun	1951	Marty	1955
A Streetcar Named Desire	1951	Night of the Hunter	1955
The Thing from Another World	1951	Oklahoma!	1955
The Bad and the Beautiful	1952	Rebel Without Cause	1955
High Noon	1952	The Court Jester	1956
Magical Maestro	1952	Disneyland Dream	1956
The Quiet Man	1952	Forbidden Planet	1956
Singin' in the Rain	1952	Giant	1956
This Is Cinerama	1952	Invasion of the Body Snatchers	1956
All My Babies	1953	Modesta	1956
The Band Wagon	1953	One Froggy Evening	1956
The Big Heat	1953	The Searchers	1956
Duck Amuck	1953	The Ten Commandments	1956
Eaux d'Artifice	1953	3:10 to Yuma	1957
From Here to Eternity	1953	12 Angry Men	1957
The Hitch-Hiker	1953	The Bridge on the River Kwai	1957
House of Wax	1953	A Face in the Crowd	1957
Little Fugitive	1953	Glimpse of the Garden	1957
The Living Desert	1953	The Hunters	1957
The Naked Spur	1953	The Incredible Shrinking Man	1957
Roman Holiday	1953	Jailhouse Rock	1957
Shane	1953	Let's All Go to the Lobby	1957
The Tell-Tale Heart	1953	On the Bowery	1957
The War of the Worlds	1953	Paths of Glory	1957

(continued)

Chart 1.6   The National Film Registry—Films of the 1950s

Sweet Smell of Success	1957	The Cry of Jazz	1959
The Tall T	1957	Imitation of Life	1959
What's Opera, Doc?	1957	Jazz on a Summer's Day	1959
Will Success Spoil Rock Hunter?	1957	North by Northwest	1959
The 7th Voyage of Sinbad	1958	Pillow Talk	1959
Gigi	1958	Porgy and Bess	1959
A Movie	1958	Pull My Daisy	1959
Touch of Evil	1958	Rio Bravo	1959
Vertigo	1958	Shadows	1959
Anatomy of Murder	1959	Some Like It Hot	1959
Ben-Hur	1959		

Source: Library of Congress National Film Registry, loc.gov/programs/national-film
-preservation-board/film-registry/complete-national-film-registry-listing. Chart compiled by
author.

Preservation Act of 1988. It was established "to ensure the survival, conservation and increased public availability of America's film heritage" ("National Film Preservation Board (NFP)," n.p.). The requirement for preservation is for "culturally, historically, or aesthetically significant films." Each year the National Film Registry selects 25 films to add to the collection. Many of the films are easily recognizable as Hollywood classics, but that is not the sole requirement or reason for inclusion. Other important additions include documentaries, newsreels, animated shorts, and orphan films. "Orphan films" are typically out of copyright, or not within the commercial market of typical distribution of Hollywood films. A January 12, 2001, PBS broadcast titled *Saving Orphan Films* listed such designations as home movies, educational documentaries, outtakes, experimental, amateur work, student productions, and surveillance tapes, to name a few. A typical example was the educational *Duck and Cover* (1951) in which Bert the Turtle happily informed American schoolchildren what to do during a nuclear attack (more in Technology chapter).

FURTHER READING

Alex Ben Block and Lucy Autrey Wilson, editors. *George Lucas's Blockbusting: A Decade-by-Decade Survey of Timeless Movies Including Untold Secrets of Their Financial and Cultural Success.* New York: It Books Harper Collins, 2010.

Ralph G. Giordano. *Fun and Games in Twentieth Century America: A Historical Guide to Leisure.* Westport, CT: Greenwood, 2003.

David Halberstam. *The Fifties.* New York: Metro Books, 2001.

Susan L. Mizruchi. *Brando's Smile: His Life, Thought, and Work.* New York: W. W. Norton & Company, 2014.

Don and Susan Sanders. *Drive-in Movie Memories.* New Hampshire: Carriage House Publishing, 2000.

Robert Sklar. *Movie-Made America: A Cultural History of American Movies*. New York: Vintage Books, 1994.

Gloria Steinem. *Marilyn: Norma Jeane*. New York: Signet Classics, 1986.

Stephen J. Whitfield. *The Culture of the Cold War*. 2nd ed. Baltimore, MD: Johns Hopkins University Press, 1996.

CHAPTER 2

Television

Television was the predominant factor that shaped American life in the 1950s. More than any other technological development of the 20th century, it was television that drastically changed American social and leisure habits (leisure was a new concept for much of the population). In 1948, television was still in development, as radio was the dominant entertainment medium. That would all change quickly as television overtook radio in popularity. Radio did not disappear as the format changed from drama, musical variety, comedy, and the like to mostly musical formats. Television on the other hand provided visual enhancement to the former radio formats.

THE GOLDEN AGE OF TELEVISION

By the end of the 1950s, television would become firmly rooted in American culture as an abundance of sets were purchased nationwide. In 1947, only 9,000 or so television sets existed nationwide, but television was "catching on like a case of high-toned scarlet fever," according to a March 1948 edition of *Newsweek* magazine (Panati, 240). By 1960, more than 45.8 million households had at least one television set; some were even purchasing two or three. By 1960, more than two-thirds of the American population watched television on a regular basis. Almost immediately, studies revealed that the average individual (with a television) was watching more than five hours a day. The immense popularity contributed to a decline in other forms of "going out" entertainment such as to a restaurant or to the movies. The effective beginning of television programming was during the 1948 fall season. Many historians and scholars cite the time period that ran roughly between 1948 and 1959 as the "Golden Age of Television." At that time, there were four major networks: ABC, CBS, NBC, and DuMont (Panati, 240).

Chart 2.1   TV History "Quick Facts"

1949

- 2 million TV sets in United States (720,000 in New York City).
- TV sales up 600 percent (DuMont 20-inch set cost $999).
- *Howdy Doody* merchandising tops $11 million for the year.

1950

- April: 5.3 million TV sets in American homes.
- October: 8 million TV sets—107 stations.

1951

- Milton Berle offered 30-year "lifetime" contract.
- June: 13 million TV sets in the United States.
- September: President Truman speaks in first coast-to-coast telecast.
- October: *I Love Lucy* premieres on CBS.

1952

- January: *Today Show* begins with Dave Garroway.
- April: Additional UHF Channels (14 through 83) approved by FCC.

1953

- TV sets in 25.2 million homes (50 percent of all Americans have a television).
- November: *The Colgate Comedy Hour* first color broadcast.

1954

- March: 370 TV stations operating in the United States.
- March: First color commercial.
- April: RCA model CT-100 offers color television capability at $1,000.

1955

- June: *The $64,000 Question* premieres.
- September: *Gunsmoke* begins 20-year run.
- October: *The Honeymooners* premieres with Jackie Gleason.
- October: *The Mickey Mouse Club* first telecast on ABC.
- October: *Captain Kangaroo* begins on CBS.

1956

- April: *As The World Turns* premieres as a daytime serial.
- November: CBS begins videotape to replaces Kinescopes.
- November: TV sets in 41,000,000 homes.

1957

- October: *Leave It to Beaver* premieres on CBS.
- RCA sells 85,000 color model CT-5 TV sets.

1958

- RCA sells 80,000 color model CT-7 TV sets.
- Total sales of all brands of color TV sets tops 150,000.

Chart 2.1   TV History "Quick Facts" (continued)

1959

- TV sets in 42 million homes.
- September: *Bonanza*, first Western broadcast in color.
- October: *The Twilight Zone* premieres on CBS.
- RCA sells 90,000 color model CT-9 TV sets.

Source: www.tvhistory.tv/1950-1959.htm. Chart compiled by author.

In 1948, only about 2 percent of American homes had a television. The cost of a basic TV set was about $400, which was often beyond the means of an average American family. As a comparison, the average yearly family income was $3,500, an average car cost a little over $1,700, and a Levittown suburban home sold for $7,990. By 1950, more than 3.9 million households had television sets (about 9 percent of the total population), as the costs were a bit lower with some smaller models at less than $300. In 1956, as television increased in popularity and some sets dipped below $200, more than 70 percent of American homes had TV sets. By 1959, that figure had increased to 85.9 percent ("TV Selling Prices," TVHistory.com, n.p.).

But the Golden Age of Television was more than just lowering the cost of a basic television set. Famed TV celebrity Steve Allen, writing in 2014, noted:

> One aspect of early television that can never be recaptured is the combined sense of astonishment and glamour that greeted the medium during its infancy. At the midpoint of the 20th century, the public was properly agog about being able to see and hear actual events that were happening across town or hundreds of miles away. Relatively few people had sets in their homes, but popular fascination with TV was so pronounced that crowds would gather on the sidewalks in front of stores that displayed a working television set or two. (Allen, "Television in the United States," n.p.)

During the 10-year span of the 1950s, television production changed dramatically. The production quality in 1950 was best described by one theater professional as "amateurs playing at home movies." But in a relatively short time, the production value was continually perfected (Allen, "Television in the United States," n.p.).

THE BIRTH OF TELEVISION

In 1948, television was still considered to be in an experimental stage. At the start of the 1950s, radio was a very profitable commercial venture and maintained an aura of respectability. At that time, the American people still relied on radio for their news, sports, and entertainment. With the quick growth of television, radio did not so much disappear as it went through a transition into a music market dominated by popular songs and later in the decade Rock 'n' Roll (see Music chapter later in the book). A new design of transistors provided for smaller portable radios that a person could easily carry, but also allowed for a basic radio installation in automobiles.

Most of the contemporary big name entertainers of radio such as Jack Benny, Bob Hope, and the team of George Burns and Gracie Allen were at first reluctant to risk their lucrative radio careers on an untested venture such as television. The easiest format switch came from network news and popular entertainment. The *Archive of American Television* noted one of the first prime examples of a radio show adapted for television was *Your Hit Parade* (on radio from 1935 to 1955 and on TV from 1950 to 1959). The show was a weekly countdown of the top 10 popular song hits of the previous week. The *Archive of American Television* further described the radio format for *Your Hit Parade* as having six or seven of the songs sung by a regular cast of vocalists. The format remained basically the same in the new transition from radio to television (even during a revival attempt in 1974). The major difference from radio was that with television the American public could actually see their favorite entertainers singing the hits rather than just hear them. Another such program that made the changeover from radio to television was *This Is Your Life* (on radio from 1948 to 1952 and on television from 1952 to 1961). The simple format featured host Ralph Edwards interviewing a celebrity and surprising that individual with a reunion of family, long-lost childhood friends, or a high school teacher, among others. The *Archive of American Television* described it this way:

> Each week, an unsuspecting celebrity would be lured by some ruse to a location near the studio. The celebrity would then be surprised with the news that they are to be the featured guest. Next, the celebrity was escorted into the studio, and one by one, people who were significant in the guest's life would be brought out to offer anecdotes. At the end of the show, family members and friends would surround the guest, who would then be presented with gifts. These usually included jewelry, a scrapbook of memories, a home 16 mm projector and a camera. ("TV History," n.p.)

Prior to the reunion, an off-screen voice would reveal something from that person's past. The individual would then come on screen offering the viewing audience a happy and emotional reunion. On radio, the surprise reaction could not be seen, but on television, the audience loved the spontaneous facial expressions of surprise. In a short time, the switch also occurred for *The Jack Benny Program* and *Burns and Allen,* among dozens of others ("TV History," n.p.).

THE JACK BENNY PROGRAM AND THE "LAUGH TRACK"

Jack Benny's transition from radio to television was almost seamless. One reason might have been that his show did not have a set format over an entire season. This allowed for an easy transition from radio to television, not just for Benny but also others, during the early days from 1948 to about 1951. Benny's program ran for more than 30 years: first on NBC radio from 1932 to 1948, switched to CBS radio from 1949 to 1955, and on TV from 1950 to 1965. The self-titled television comedy sitcom *The Jack Benny Program* that began in 1950 was just an extension of his popular radio program that dated from 1932.

At the time, the vast majority of television shows were filmed in New York City. Similar to the days of radio programing, the television comedies were often filmed in front of a live audience in order to record spontaneous laughter. Benny, as one of the best-known entertainers from the 20th century, set the tone for many of the situational comedies (known as "sitcoms") that were to follow, especially for those that were filmed before a live audience. In contrast, *The Jack Benny Program* was filmed and produced in Hollywood at the Desilu Studios. Benny combined a few unique concepts regarding audience response. He first performed both an opening and closing monologue in front of a live audience. The remainder of the episode was filmed without an audience. After the episode was completed, an audience was brought in to view the program and their laughter was recorded. The advantage of film for a comedy allowed the engineers to control an appropriate, consistent volume of the laughter. In some cases, the audience laughed too loud, thereby drowning out the actor's lines. At other times, the laughter did not occur at the appropriate response time to the joke. By the late 1950s, Benny's show was instrumental in the introduction of an overdub technique known as the "laugh track," pre-recorded laughter that was inserted into the program at the appropriate time to respond to a specific situation (Dunning, 355–356).

During the filming of Benny's shows, sound engineer Charley Douglass noticed that the live audience response was more often than not inconsistent. Douglass had the idea to insert pre-recorded laughter at the appropriate moment. At other times he also chose to temper the live audience response so as not to drown out the performers. The trade industry term was "sweetening," but became commonly known as the laugh track. (Sometimes it was referred to as the "applause track," but Douglass called it the "Laff Box.") The idea for the first network show to use a laugh track might well have come from *The Hank McCune Show* (1950–1953). Some, such as Dunning, cite it as the first network program to use a tape of prerecorded laughter. *The Hank McCune Show* premiered in 1949 as a regional Los Angeles variety series and was added to the weekly NBC-TV national lineup in 1950. The lasting legacy of the show remains a footnote for adding prerecorded laughter, as it was cancelled almost immediately. The difference with *The Jack Benny Show* is that Douglass tempered the laughter in the appropriate situation rather than insert a constant din of laughter (Dunning, 356–357).

One of the many television stories that might be fact or simply legend, but most appropriately fitting, is a story about comedian Milton Berle previewing a pre-recorded situation that did not receive a laugh. Berle asked Douglass to insert audience laughter after a particular joke. After viewing and listening to the finished product, Berle reportedly ad-libbed, "See, I told you it was funny." The story in itself might be funny, but in television history, Berle was one legendary performer who very rarely failed at making his audience laugh (Dunning, 357).

MILTON BERLE: "UNCLE MILTIE" AND "MR. TELEVISION"

By all accounts, it was *The Texaco Star Theater* airing on NBC-TV from 1948 to 1953 starring Milton Berle (1908–2002) that was the first "smash hit" television show. At the time, it was the most popular program in the history of televi-sion. Writing in *The New York Times*, Lawrence Van Gelder credited Berle with "igniting a national craze for the new medium [of television]":

> Mr. Berle almost single-handedly led the entertainment revolution that addicted the nation to the small screen by wobbling on his ankles while wearing high heels, flouncing in evening gowns, grinning to reveal blacked-out teeth, braying, "What the hey," being whacked silly with sacks of flour after shouting "Makeup!" and invariably thrusting himself into the routines of his guests. (Van Gelder, "Milton Berle, TV's First Star as 'Uncle Miltie,' Dies at 93," p. A29)

Berle's popularity was also attributed as a main reason why the purchase of television sets increased dramatically from 1947 to 1951. An article in the prom-inent national *LIFE* magazine reported a total of only 17 television stations broadcasting to about 136,000 American homes in 1947. The following year the number increased to 50 broadcast stations and 700,000 TV homes. The quick accession of the television broadcast industry was often attributed to audiences' desire to watch Milton Berle. His audience share was often more than 60 percent of the viewing audience and, at one time, more than 80 percent. The audience waited in anticipation, because Berle's entrance was usually in some type of out-rageous costume. He followed with his trademark welcome, "Good evening, ladies and germs." When Berle left the air in 1956, television was in almost 70 percent of American homes and Berle had acquired the nickname "Mr. Tele-vision" (Van Gelder, p. A29).

Berle's television presence became so endeared as a fixture in American homes that he came to be known as their "Uncle Miltie." In a four-hour inter-view by Dan Pasternack, conducted in 1995 and preserved by the *Archive of American Television*, Berle revealed how he attained the moniker of "Uncle Miltie." Berl explained:

Chart 2.2   American Households with a TV Set

Year	Number of Households with a TV Set	Percent of Households with a TV Set
1940	0	0%
1946	8	0%
1947	14	0%
1948	172	0%
1949	940,000	2%
1950	3.88 million	8%
1955	30.70 million	67%
1960	45.75 million	88%

Source: Alex Ben Block and Lucy Autrey Wilson, *George Lucas's Blockbusting*. New York: It Books Harper Collins, 2010, p. 320. Chart compiled by author.

One Tuesday night, we had four minutes to go and I had to stall. I had to start ad-libbing. I said, "I want to thank you, especially the boys and girls, and my little nephews and nieces that are watching, this is your Uncle Miltie saying good night." I said it once. The next day, I went to Boston and passed two hardhat workers. One of them said, "Hi, Uncle Miltie!" First person that ever called me Uncle Miltie. I told this story to my mother. She said, "That's a very good moniker for you." From then on, I said Uncle Miltie. (Pasternak, "Milton Berle Interview," n.p.)

Berle and his *Texaco Star Theater* not only dominated Tuesday evening prime time, it was rated as the overall number-one television program. Oftentimes the Nielsen ratings claimed Berle's audience share topped 80 percent of all television viewers, a number often placed at more than 44 million people. Berle's dominance of the new medium also caused an adverse effect on other activities. In what is often termed "collateral damage," theater owners reported lower ticket sales on Tuesday evenings, and restaurants and other businesses also reported lower income. At the same time, appliance stores reported the demand for TV sets nearly doubled (Pasternak, "Milton Berle Interview," and Panati, 257).

In early 1948, Berle's radio program was cancelled, but he received a call from an advertising agent about hosting another program. The agent represented Texaco gasoline, which sought to sponsor a radio show on Wednesday evenings between 9 and 10 P.M. The show did well and the ad exec Mr. Kirk from the Kuder Agency said Texaco wanted to explore a similar type show on television. As for the transition to a brand new and still experimental medium, Berle recalled:

Maybe it was because I had been around when the so-called brains of vaudeville had been laughing at silent movies as just a fad that the public would soon tire of, or maybe it was because I saw that television could give a visual entertainer the exposure he could never get from radio. Whatever it was about television, it appealed to me. (Van Gelder, "TV's First Star," n.p.)

Milton Berle, known affectionately to his viewers as "Uncle Miltie," though many cultural historians called him "Mr. Television." By all accounts it was *The Texaco Star Theater* airing on NBC-TV from 1948 to 1953 starring Milton Berle that was the first "smash hit" TV show. At the time, it was the most popular program in the short history of television. (NBC/Photofest)

Berle accepted the format change from radio to television, but not a change. Prior to accepting the job, he said to himself, "Don't go looking for something new. Do what you have done best, what got you your big break." Berle recounted speaking about the format to Texaco and the Kuder Agency,

> So I suggested to the powers at Texaco a show in which I would serve as host, do some of my routines and introduce guest stars, who would do their specialties, and then I would mix it up with them for some comedy—in other words, what I had been doing for years in vaudeville and nightclubs. (Van Gelder, "TV's First Star," n.p.)

Doing continuous live television and radio took a toll on Berle. To alleviate the situation, he negotiated a deal to allow him every fourth week off. But in the television world, the viewing audiences proved fickle. Americans set their lifestyles around the regular weekly programs. Without the reliability of having "Uncle Miltie" available each and every week, the ratings slipped to #20. He later conceded that taking the time off "was a big mistake." As the sole sponsor, Texaco was worried and was in a position to demand format changes. Berle complied, dropping the familiar vaudeville format. He introduced a new fictional character named after himself. The idea was to portray "the problems of putting on a weekly television show." The cast included his "agent" (actor Fred Clark), a "secretary" (actress Ruth Gilbert), and an assistant (actor Arnold Stang). In an age long before the advent of reality television, Berle might have been a pioneer. Prior to the change in sponsors, he continually surprised his audience with all sorts of "wild" freewheeling antics, as the show seemed utterly spontaneous. With live television, some of it was, yet a talented team of writers and production assistants developed each show. With the new format, the old spontaneous feeling disappeared. Berle was not the center of the humor, but rather as he recalled, "I was everybody's straight man" (Pasternak, n.p.). His initial ratings climbed back up and were high (placing #5 behind *I Love Lucy, Dragnet, The Colgate Comedy Hour,* and *Racket Squad*) but the audience soon began to fall off.

Berle's sponsorship changed again in 1955 and renamed the program the *Milton Berle Show*. Ratings were respectable, but near the end of the 1955–1956 season, he was informed that the show was cancelled. Some sources claimed that because he was already cancelled, he had nothing to lose with booking a controversial new entertainer named Elvis Presley. At the time, Presley was still unknown to the national adult audiences. When Berle was contacted by Presley's manager, an audition was arranged. With nothing to lose, he booked Presley for two appearances. Although very few American households had sets capable of color viewing, that show was one of the early shows broadcast in color. The entire show of April 3, 1956, was set upon the U.S. Navy ship U.S.S. *Hancock*. During the live broadcast, Elvis sang two of his hits, "Heartbreak Hotel" and "Blue Suede Shoes." After the latter song, Berle was introduced as "twin brother Melvin Presley" and the two sang a comedic reprise of "Blue Suede Shoes" (It was not public knowledge that Elvis had a real twin brother that died in childbirth.) ("Elvis Presley: The Milton Berle Show: April 3, 1955," n.p.).

For the second appearance on June 5, 1956, Berle played up on Presley's rising popularity. In one skit Berle, acting as a record store owner, stood behind a counter with a sign that announced: "Today Only in Person Elvis Presley with Autographed Records." A long line of excited young female fans was already formed. The routine went as follows:

Excited fan asks Berle: "Hey man, do you really know Elvis Presley?"

Berle replied: "Do I know Elvis Presley. I remember when he was a kid and he used to sing on the farm."

(Some other banter followed.)

Berle told the fans: "You'll get him. You'll get the whole thing. Now stand in line."

(Elvis walks out. Berle is oblivious in recognizing Presley, revealing the previous embellishment as to actually "knowing" the young singer.)

Berle says to Elvis: "Hey young man, if you want an autograph will you stand in the back there. I don't care who you are."

Elvis replied: "I'mma Elvis Presley."

(The screaming fans, not sure who is who, mistakenly tear off Berle's clothes! Berle looking tired, quickly smiled and ended the charade/skit.)

Berle says: "Elvis, sing your hit song."

Elvis sings: "I Want You, I Need You, I Love You."
(YouTube: "Presley, *The Milton Berle Show,* June 5, 1956," n.p.)

The full skit is available to 21st-century audiences on YouTube. Later in the same show, the introduction was simple as Berle proclaimed, "Here he is, the biggest singing sensation all over the country, Elvis Presley!" The song Elvis performed is the best-preserved video version of his massive hit song "Hound Dog." After the song, Presley engaged with Berle in a bit of comedy banter. Through it all, it was obvious by the big smile on Berle's face that he actually enjoyed and was sincere in his praise for Elvis.

EVERYBODY LOVES LUCY

During the early age of television, it was Milton Berle who was the dominant leader in the new medium. He was loved as "Uncle Miltie" but audiences also came to love a woman named "Lucy." *I Love Lucy* was an immediate hit right from the start with its premiere in October 1951. In all the episodes, it was actress Lucille Ball (1911–1989) in the role of "Lucy Ricardo" who was the comedic center of the show. Without Lucy, the series did not have much. In a 1989 obituary that appeared in both the *Los Angeles Times* and *The New York Times,* Roxanne Arnold described Ball as "the leggy showgirl, model and B-grade movie queen whose pumpkin hair and genius for comedy made her an icon of television" (Arnold, "Lucille Ball Dies," n.p.).

I Love Lucy was a 30-minute comedy that aired at 9 P.M. on Monday nights. From its premiere in 1951 to its final episode in 1957, *I Love Lucy* was not only the dominant family comedy, it was also the #1 rated broadcast of the time. Over the course of their six primetime Monday night seasons on CBS-TV, *I Love*

Beginning with its premier in October 1951, *I Love Lucy* was an immediate hit and soon became the top rated TV program. The episodes focused on the life of two married couples: the comedic housewife Lucy and her husband bandleader Ricky Ricardo and their landlords and best friends Fred and Ethel Mertz. Pictured left to right Lucy (actress Lucille Ball standing), Fred and Ethel Mertz (actor William Frawley and actress Vivian Vance seated) and husband Ricky (actor Desi Arnaz seated far right). (CBS/Photofest)

Lucy was the #1 show outright in four of its six seasons. The lowest rating was only at #3. When production ceased in 1957, it was still the #1 rated TV program. Similar to other sitcoms of the time, Lucy was a stay-at-home wife. Unlike the other female portrayals, Lucy had ambitions for establishing a show business career or sometimes an entrepreneurial activity. Yet, typical of the 1950s female portrayal, Lucy was always bumbling and stumbling in all her endeavors. Her on-screen husband "Ricky," played by her real-life husband Desi Arnaz (1917–1986), was a bandleader who worked for a fictional nightclub known as The Tropicana. He eventually bought the club and renamed it Club Babalu. Fred and Ethel Mertz, played by actor William Frawley (1887–1966) and actress Vivian Vance (1909–1979), were both best friends of the Ricardos and their landlords (Anderson, "I Love Lucy," n.p.).

In Ball's obituary, Roxanne Arnold said, "The show was a weekly dash into absurdity that boasted the biggest television audience of its time—of almost any time" ("Lucille Ball Dies," n.p.). There were all sorts of quirky, but always funny, situations depicting Lucy scheming to obtain either some kind of financial reward or a show business opportunity. The situations ranged from the

Chart 2.3   Top-Rated TV Show of Each Season, Nielsen Media Research

Season	Program	Rating	TV-Owning Households (in millions)
1950–1951	*Texaco Star Theater*	61.6	10.32
1951–1952	*Godfrey's Talent Scouts*	53.8	15.30
1952–1953	*I Love Lucy*	67.3	20.40
1953–1954	*I Love Lucy*	58.8	26.00
1953–1955	*I Love Lucy*	49.3	30.70
1955–1956	*$64,000 Question*	47.5	34.90
1956–1957	*I Love Lucy*	43.7	38.90
1957–1958	*Gunsmoke*	43.1	41.92
1958–1959	*Gunsmoke*	39.6	43.95
1959–1960	*Gunsmoke*	40.3	45.75

Source: www.tvhistory.tv/Top_Shows_Each_Season_50-00.JPG. Chart compiled by author.

often quoted "Vitameatavegamin" commercial to the chocolate assembly line gone awry, performed with Vance. The weekly antics truly gave credence to the term "situation comedy." In a 1981 interview with *The New York Times,* Ball offered her own description of the series. Of her Lucy Ricardo character, she said:

> There were two key qualities to her. She was always in financial trouble—if she wanted a fur collar, a ratty little fur collar, she had to figure out a way to make some extra money to get it . . . And she always had a domineering figure over her . . . I wanted our characters to have problems. I wanted to be an average housewife. A very nosy but very average housewife. And I wanted my husband to love me. (Arnold, "Lucille Ball Dies," n.p.)

Each episode usually ended with the apparent notion that Lucy would be best suited for staying within the home and therefore happy with the household domestic duties. In real life, however, she was just the opposite.

I Love Lucy was such a dominant mainstay on Monday nights that many stores and other businesses often conceded their evening hours to the popularity of Lucy. Television viewing in itself created an environment for many American families to stay at home, but watching *I Love Lucy* kept many home specifically on Monday evenings. As Richard Christansen reported in *The Chicago Tribune,* the Marshall Field & Co. store in Chicago could not compete with the series and placed a sign in their window, "We love Lucy too, so from now on we will be open on Thursday night instead of Monday." Ball was so popular that when the HUAC accused her of being a Communist at a time when the mere accusation was enough to ruin a person's career, her fans were unfazed. The charges were quickly dropped after one commentator said, "The only thing red about her is her hair. And even that isn't real" (Christiansen, "Why Love Lucy?").

During the 1953 season, Lucille Ball became pregnant in real life with the couple's first child. Rather than hide the fact that she was with child, TV historian Michael Logan claimed that both Lucy and Desi fully understood the publicity value and worked the pregnancy into the script. At the time, the irony of the situation was that the actual word "pregnant" could not be spoken on television. The word used most often was "expecting." In addition, if a mother was expecting, camera angles were careful not to show too much of anything that portrayed a bulging belly. Later, analysts also questioned with an amusing twist how the pregnancy could have actually occurred, because any shots within the couple's bedroom (not just *Lucy*, but all television shows) showed twin beds. The obvious indication was that the couple did not actually sleep together.

Nonetheless, in preparation for the birth episode, the on-air show for the viewing audience was filmed two months earlier than her actual delivery date. In the months leading up to the show, Lucy and Desi took full advantage of the publicity value. On January 19, 1953, "Lucy" not only delivered the fictional baby on television, she also delivered her real baby a few hours before the broadcast. In what might be the ultimate publicity stunt in television history, a Cesarean birth was scheduled for the same date of the broadcast. The anticipation and connection to both the real-life and fictional Lucy proved quite profitable. The birth episode of "Lucy Goes to the Hospital," which introduced the viewers to their son "Little Ricky," was seen by over 44 million people, a number that represented more than 72 percent of all American homes (Arnold, "Lucille Ball Dies," n.p.).

In a 1981 interview with *The New York Times*, Ball recalled her excitement over the birth. She said, "I was so damned happy, just floating on a cloud, and I think the way I felt came across on the film. I loved doing all those pregnant shows." As a side note to the show's popularity, an address to the nation by President Eisenhower did not preempt the show. TV historian Dan Logan reported that the president's staff was careful not to schedule the address on the same night as *I Love Lucy*. Therefore, Eisenhower's address was scheduled for the previous evening and drew a respectable audience of 29 million (Logan, "TV Guide Magazine's 60th Anniversary," n.p.).

Americans were certainly in "love" with Lucy and her family. Twenty-first-century high school textbooks, such as *The American Journey*, often portrayed Lucille Ball and Desi Arnaz as "An American Story." The "story" factually reported the huge popularity of the television sitcom and listed it as the highest-rated television series. The textbook used *I Love Lucy* to promote the domestic nature of a happy marriage and birthing of children during the 1950s. But the series represented much more. In contrast, the storyline for high school students does not mention the fact that Lucille Ball was one of the very first (if not the first) female to be directly involved in the production of her own series.

Similar to other early sitcoms, *I Love Lucy* had its origins as a radio program. During the late 1940s, Lucille Ball had a somewhat successful radio comedy for the CBS network titled *My Favorite Husband*. At the time, an actor named Richard Denning played her "husband." When CBS asked Ball to develop a television series based on the radio program, she opted for an actor change for her television husband. The selection of her real-life husband Desi Arnaz was not the first choice by the network to play Lucy's on-screen husband "Ricky Ricardo." The executives at CBS-TV felt the public would not "believe" the marriage. But most accounts claim the networks did not want to portray a Hispanic character. Arnaz's heritage was in fact Cuban.

Arnaz was not an unknown; he was a somewhat popular Latin bandleader and Hollywood actor. It was only through the insistence of Ball that Arnaz would be cast in the role of her sitcom husband that the network agreed. Despite the reluctance by the network, the casting of a real-life married couple was not unusual for the time. Other real-life married couples included *The George Burns and Gracie Allen Show* (1950–58) and the Nelsons in *The Adventures of Ozzie and Harriet* (1952–57). For all the shows, the prevalent theme was domesticity. According to television historian Christopher Anderson, "Television in the 1950s was an insistently domestic medium, abundant with images of marriage and family" (Anderson, "I Love Lucy: U.S. Situation Comedy," n.p.).

The TV portrayal of the happily married Ricardo couple was so persuasive that Lucille Ball and Desi Arnaz totally surprised an unsuspecting public when their own real-life marital discord was made public. In 1960, as the husband and wife duo were starring in a new CBS series *The Lucy-Desi Comedy Hour*, Ball filed for divorce, a result of Desi's numerous extramarital affairs. Despite the marital discord, the couple maintained a business relationship and an on-air persona that hid the truth from the American public. During the 1950s, Lucy and Ricky along with their friendly neighbors Fred and Ethel Mertz were the darlings of television.

Unlike the late 1950s when the popular comedy family sitcoms such as *The Donna Reed Show, Leave It to Beaver*, and *Father Knows Best* were set in a fictitious suburbia, the early popular comedies were located in urban settings, mainly New York City. They included *The Goldbergs* (1949–1957) and *The Honeymooners* (1955–1956), who lived in New York City apartment buildings. The Ricardos lived in an apartment on Manhattan's Upper East Side at the fictitious address of 623 East 68th Street for the first three seasons. By season four, the Ricardos and Mertzs traveled to Hollywood as "Ricky" was offered a movie deal. Upon their return and in their sixth season, the Ricardos moved from their city apartment to the suburbs of Connecticut. The fictional TV move coincided with the real-life massive migration of Americans into the newly built suburbs such as Levittown in Long Island.

The reason for the city setting was as simple as the audience connection. Most of the televisions purchased were in the New York City area. Another factor was reception of the TV signal itself that was sent out from a broadcast tower with a limited range. The reception for a television set was similar to that of a radio through wireless airwaves. A television set required a special metal antenna to receive the signals. There were two basic types. The first was an indoor metal version that was placed directly on top the television box, also known as "rabbit ears." The second most common option was a larger metal outdoor version located on the roof of either a residential home or apartment building. The common attachment was to a protruding chimney or vertical pipe penetration. It was easy to see the rapid growth of television as antennas sprouted up like trees in a forest on the roofs in both cities and nearby suburbia. By the

TV signals were sent out from a broadcast tower and received in the home through either an indoor antenna known as "rabbit ears" or a rooftop metal antenna (pictured here). The antenna was a common option located on the roof of either a residential home or apartment building. The common attachment was to a protruding chimney or vertical pipe penetration. (Photo by Ralph G. Giordano)

21st century many (but not all) of the antennae's disappeared due to the widespread use of pay cable television.

During negotiations for the production of the series, CBS-TV and the sponsor insisted that the program be broadcast live from New York City. At the time, the studio maintained its network production facilities in the bustling metropolis. In a foresight that proved not only lucrative to Lucy and Desi, but eventually the entire television industry, the couple persuaded the executives at CBS-TV to switch the production to Hollywood in California. They also had the foresight to record the episodes on film, similar to movie production. Along with the new television series, Arnaz and Ball had recently launched a new production company known as Desilu (a combination of the first names of Desi and Lucy). They also had an idea to take advantage of movie industry production facilities and to ensure the long-term value of their series by capturing it on film (Anderson, "I Love Lucy, n.p.).

Similar to other television shows at the time, including comedy, variety, and drama, each episode was performed before a live studio audience. Most of the shows employed a camera feed that broadcast live without any taping of the actual show. A technique known as "Kinescope" preserved a fair number of early programs. In its simplest terms, the technique placed a film camera aimed at the television set. The lens resembled a small telescope and a film copy was made directly from the live broadcast. The technique was primitive and did

not provide for quality reproduction. The Kinescope idea was eventually eliminated as Desilu studios revolutionized the industry with a different but age-
old format. Lucy and Desi insisted on filming each episode just as they would a
Hollywood movie. Ball was later quoted as saying: "CBS thought we were out
of our minds to want to do it on film" (Arnold, "Lucille Ball Dies," n.p.). Knowing the limitations of a film camera, yet at the same time knowing that some of
Ball's best comedy evolved often from spontaneity, a different technique was
needed. Therefore, Desilu Productions implemented a three-camera system,
which was able to film continuous action from three different angles, and the
film could be edited at a later date. The system was not new, but was perfected
during the series production. The technique basically remained within the forte
of Desilu Studios throughout the 1950s and into the 1960s. By the 1970s, the
three-camera film technique became a mainstay of just about every TV sitcom.

The main idea of using film was not just for better visual quality, but also for
later use of the episodes for syndicated reruns. For the most part, studio executives dismissed the idea of preserving television episodes for posterity. As preposterous as it sounds to contemporary audiences, the CBS-TV executives did not
think anyone would want to watch any of the episodes more than once. During
the early 1950s, syndication was not part of any of the networks standard prac-
tices. As an exchange, the network demanded a concession for Desilu to pick
up the additional cost of film production. The cost was not in actual fees paid
to CBS-TV, but rather a reduced fee for Lucy and Desi. The network thought it
had negotiated a great bargain deal with the reduced production costs, but the
financial rewards were soon reaped by Desilu Studios. As a result, Desilu had
distribution rights to the previously filmed episodes. In essence, after the first
broadcast, Lucy and Desi could make any deal to sell the episodes as they saw
fit. Therefore, Lucy and Desi offered smaller regional television networks looking to fill up their broadcast day syndicated reruns of I Love Lucy.

Lucille Ball has the distinction of being the first female to both lead and, most
important, "own" a production studio. Initially, both she and Desi Arnaz partnered to form Desilu Productions. Mainly under the direction of Ball (Desi was
bought out after the divorce and Lucy held majority ownership), Desilu Studios branched out into other television productions in both the networks and
syndication. By the time she sold the production studio in the mid-1960s, she
was listed as the highest-earning female in the entertainment business. A significant sum was attained by the sale of first-run episodes of I Love Lucy to the network and through the profits of syndicated reruns. (In fact, her earnings also
placed her among the top within the wholly dominated male echelon.) At its
peak, Desilu employed more than 2,000 people on 62 acres of land and 36 sound
stages. After the sale, Ball was listed as "the richest woman in television" (Anderson, "I Love Lucy: U.S. Situation Comedy," n.p.).

In 1984, as the world's best-known television star, Lucille Ball was one of the
first seven inductees into the Television Hall of Fame. The others included
Milton Berle, Paddy Chayefsky, Norman Lear, Edward R. Murrow, William
Paley, and David Sarnoff. In accepting her award, Ball gave credit to the "talented
and creative people" who helped her career. Ball's public persona provided
humility as she would always credit her success to a good supporting cast of

characters. In a 1983 interview with *Rolling Stone* magazine, she asserted, "I am *not* funny. My writers were funny. My directors were funny. The situations were funny. . . . What I am is *brave*. I have never been scared. Not when I did movies, certainly not when I was a model and not when I did *I Love Lucy*." But the humility does reveal a very truthful statement, any success story is dependent upon a good, if not excellent, supporting cast. Yet, without the vehicle of a show such as *I Love Lucy* combined with Ball's impeccable delivery, facial antics, and comedic body movements, the show just would not have worked as well as it did (Arnold, "Lucille Ball Dies," n.p.).

FAMILY COMEDIES AND *THE HONEYMOONERS*

Many other of the half-hour sitcoms also lived on in reruns in the later decades. Unlike *I Love Lucy,* almost all the other popular sitcoms of the late 1950s portrayed homogenous white, non-ethnic, middle-class suburban families in which the mother was a housewife and the father worked at some unnamed job and always came home for dinner. The most notable included the long-running *The Adventures of Ozzie and Harriet* (1952–1965), *Father Knows Best* (1954–1960), and *Leave It to Beaver* (1957–1963). One notable exception to the "unnamed profession" was *The Donna Reed Show* (1958–1966), as her husband "Dr. Stone" was a pediatrician. These popular television shows mirrored and also influenced the social conformity of the time. One particular show that also lived on in reruns was *Mister Ed* (1958–1966). It portrayed a white homogenous family and neighbors. However, rather than children, this comedy was about an architect who owned a mischievous talking horse. Despite the subtle differences, they all excluded stories of sexual promiscuity or unpatriotic behavior.

Television also remained segregated and excluded the faces of minorities from any corporate advertising or as the focus of any show. In addition, almost all the television shows did not show any evidence of a family struggling financially. One exception from the 1950s was the short-lived *The Honeymooners,* which portrayed two city municipal workers: bus driver Ralph Kramden (actor Jackie Gleason) and sewer worker Ed Norton (actor Art Carney) along with their wives Alice Kramden (actress Audrey Meadows) and Trixie Norton (actress Joyce Randolph). In developing the series, Gleason wanted a realistic portrayal of the life of a poor husband and wife living in Brooklyn, New York. In fact, it began as a sketch comedy in 1951 on the DuMont network show *Cavalcade of Stars* (1949–1952) and also reprised on an earlier version of a Gleason variety show from 1952 to 1955. Similar to other shows of the time, *The Honeymooners* was filmed before a live audience. It debuted as a half-hour series on October 1, 1955, and during its first season was the #2 rated TV show.

The simple plot often had Ralph Kramden and Ed Norton thinking up get-rich-quick schemes in hopes of a better life. The patient wives stood by and usually the Kramdens would argue over the various failures of Ralph and Ed. During the ensuing arguments, which seemed to occur in every episode, Ralph threatened Alice with a wary fist, saying, "One of these days, Alice, I'm gonna send you straight to the moon." Sometimes the line was, "One of these days, Alice. Pow, right in the kisser." He never did hit her, but the arguing and threat of violence reflective of a real-life situation was universally unlike any other sitcom of the time. Ultimately their devout love for each other would end each episode on a happy note (which was the theme of 1950s family sitcoms). Many an episode ended with Ralph apologizing to Alice, giving her a hug and proclaiming: "Baby, you're the greatest."

The immediate success of *The Honeymooners* did not last. In a short time, the ratings dropped to #19, as it came in direct competition from the popular singer Perry Como whose long-running musical variety show ran from 1948 to 1967. In the legacy of TV history, Como's show was long forgotten, but not *The Honeymooners*. The final episode of *The Honeymooners* as a weekly series aired on September 22, 1956, after only 39 episodes. Although it ended as a weekly series, the cast often appeared in a recurring segment on the later CBS-TV *The Jackie Gleason Show* (1957–59; 1964–70). Due to reruns, "The Classic 39 Episodes," as they became known, were watched over and over again well into the 21st century.

LIVE ANTHOLOGY TV DRAMAS

Comedy sitcoms of the 1950s were conducive to reruns for later generations, and as a result remained as the best-remembered shows from the time. But the early years did produce a significant amount of program variety. A significant format of the late 1940s and early 1950s was the live anthology dramas. The difference from the sitcoms such as *I Love Lucy* was that almost all of them were aired live and many were not preserved on film or tape. The Museum of Broadcast Communications described them as "an early American television series format or genre in which each episode was a discrete story/play rather than a weekly return to the same setting, characters, and stars" (Ritrosky-Winslow, "Anthology Dramas," n.p.).

At a time when most of the sitcoms did not have any deep intrigue, many of the drama programs provided stories that received wide critical acclaim. This is not to say that all of the anthologies were well received by critics. As an overall genre they were very good, but not every feature was outstanding. In fact, the time allotted was a critical factor in developing a quality story. The wide offering of anthologies varied in different broadcast length ranging from 30-, 60-, or sometimes a 90-minute variation such as *Playhouse 90*. Included within the allotted time was, of course, commercials, which limited the actual story time to about 22, 44, and 66 minutes, respectively.

In the late 1940s, drama programming on television was scheduled about once a month. The first regularly scheduled once-a-week drama series began with NBC's *Kraft Television Theatre* (1947–1955). The following year others appeared that included the *Actors Studio* (1948–1950 on both CBS and ABC), *Philco Television Playhouse* (1948–1955), *Westinghouse Studio One* (1948–1958), *Mr. Black* (ABC, 1949), and *The Ford Television Theater* (1952–1957). Most were patterned as Broadway-style dramas, often presenting literary classic work as the central theme. The dramas were broadcast live from New York City, which provided an instant connection with the prestige of Broadway Theater. The popularity caused a ripple effect as many others were soon put on the air. Anna Everett noted, "This rotating system of anthology drama production resulted in a creative firmament for television that many television historians consider as yet unsurpassed" ("Golden Age of Television Drama," n.p.).

Everett cited the first of the "Golden Age" dramas as the *Kraft Television Theater*. This show, which ran from May 1947 through 1955, was originally broadcast over NBC-TV. In 1953, the hour-long *Kraft Television Theater* had a unique distinction to air the same program on two different networks. It aired Wednesdays on NBC-TV at 9 P.M. and also Thursdays on ABC-TV at 9:30 P.M. The critically acclaimed drama *The Ford Theater* (1948–1957) had the unique distinction of airing on each of the three networks of CBS, NBC, and ABC during its run. Others included the *Goodyear Television Playhouses* (NBC, 1948–1955), *Studio One* (CBS, 1948–1958), *Tele-Theatre* (NBC, 1948–1950), the *Actors Studio* (ABC and CBS, 1948–1949), and *Four Star Playhouse* (CBS, 1952–1956). At the time, each of the drama anthologies had a single sponsor, and therefore the sponsors had great control over influencing the content. The term often applied was "dead-centerism," referring to the fact that the sponsors dictated avoidance of any socially unacceptable or politically charged themes (Everett, "Golden Age of Television Drama," n.p.).

By 1950, a significant amount of the dramas aired as a half-hour format. They included *Lights Out* (on radio 1934–1947 and television 1946–1952), *Colgate Theater* (1949–1958), *Danger* (1950–1955), and *Lux Video Theatre* (1950–1954, extended to 60 minutes in 1954–1957). Unlike the longer dramas filmed in New York, most of the 30-minute dramas were broadcast from Hollywood. At that time, Hollywood was also entering the television business and many of the 30-minute dramas were produced in California staffed with movie production people. The dramas coincided with a time when the Hollywood studio system had disbanded due to a Supreme Court decision (see Film chapter). These formats offered actors, directors, and technical people the opportunity to work in a craft similar to the film industry. The shortened 30-minute timeframe did not allow for either character or story development and usually did not receive the same praise as the hour-long shows.

Offshoot genres, but still considered drama, were the suspense and mystery anthologies. They included *Kraft Suspense Theater* (NBC, 1963–1965), *The Clock* (NBC, ABC, 1949–1951), *Mr. Arsenic* (ABC, 1952,) and *Alfred Hitchcock Presents* (CBS, NBC, 1955–65) and *The Twilight Zone* (CBS, 1959–64). Both *The Twilight Zone* and *Alfred Hitchcock Presents* provided successful 30-minute dramas as weekly, unrelated short-story episodes, sometimes comedic, science fiction, or horrific, but always suspenseful. The crime drama *Dragnet* (1951–1959) was one of many involving police detectives. It was set in Los Angeles with the methodical detective Sgt. Friday and partners solving crimes all within the allotted 30 minutes of airtime—including commercials. Ongoing dramatic series also included lovable animals such as *Lassie* (1954–1974), which was an ongoing saga of a family and their dog. The family would often find themselves in some sort of danger, for which Lassie would either come to the rescue or alert authorities.

Despite the popularity of television in general, the anthologies, which became known as "teledramas," were a major factor for television replacing radio as the dominant in-home entertainment choice. The Museum of Broadcast

Communication in Chicago says "live teledramas helped television to displace radio, the stage and film as the favorite leisure-time activities for the nation's burgeoning suburban families." By 1960, the anthology drama faded out as station owners were tied into a national syndication network of safe "middle-of-the-road"-type of television shows (Everett, "Golden Age of Television Drama," n.p.).

TV WESTERNS AND DAVY CROCKETT

Westerns, more than any other genre, reinforced the American mythical idea of conquering the frontier. Stephen Kiss, writing "On TV Westerns of the 1950s and '60s," for the New York Public Library, defined them as "a nostalgic eulogy to the early days of the expansive, untamed American frontier . . . glorifying the past-fading values and aspirations of the mythical by-gone age of the West." Before their popularity on television, they were a popular recurring movie genre. The first full-length Hollywood western, *The Great Train Robbery* (1903), was also the first full-length movie in Hollywood history. They continued throughout the decades in film and also on radio. The basic premise of each was the idea of a lone individual standing up in the face of adversity and overcoming the odds against him (very rarely, if ever, "her"). They might include fighting off invading hordes (Indians), overcoming nature (the frontier), or simply fighting off a "gunslinger" or arresting the "bad guys." This format played perfectly into the 1950s ideal of American conformity and patriotism. The themes always professed hard work, the determination to succeed against all odds, and that justice always triumphs over evil (Kiss, "On TV Westerns of the 1950s and '60s," n.p.).

The TV westerns, cast on a much smaller scale than their movie counterparts, were nonetheless not conducive to filming on a New York or Hollywood soundstage. But almost all were filmed (just like many of their early movie counterparts) just outside Los Angeles. The terrain offered a setting that could easily pass for the old American frontier. Film-like sets were constructed in the outer areas of Hollywood to accommodate the filming of the television western series. The settings would typically include the local jail, saloon, horse stable, blacksmith shop, store, and the like. Many of the 1950s westerns continued on in reruns in the 21st century on cable channels such as TVLand, Me-TV, and RTV, among others.

Throughout the years and continuing into the 1950s the western genre (sometimes called a "cowboy movie") continually brought audiences into the theaters. By the mid-1950s, television was no different. At the end of the decade, westerns reigned supreme. *Gunsmoke* (1955–1975), as a prime example, was the #1 rated show for the last three television seasons of the decade. It also was the longest-running western in television series history. Dozens of other popular television westerns also filled the airwaves. They included *The Lone Ranger, Wanted Dead or Alive, Maverick, Have Gun Will Travel, Bat Masterson, The Roy Rogers Show,* and *Bonanza*. By 1959, seven of the top ten Nielsen-rated shows were westerns. In all, 30 westerns occupied weekly prime-time slots. Others, such as *The Roy Rogers Show* and *Rin Tin Tin*, were Saturday morning features geared towards children. According to the archives at TVHistory.com, "Westerns reinforced the 1950s notion that everything was OK in America. . . . [M]ost programs of the early 1950s drew a clear line between the good guys and the bad guys. There was very little danger of injury or death, and good always triumphed in the end" ("TV History," n.p.).

One of the proposed limited Disney television features was *The Adventures of Davy Crockett*, with Fess Parker (1924–2010) hired to play the lead role. The show was loosely based on the historical American frontiersman Davy Crockett, who became a mythical hero after his real-life death at the Alamo in 1836. The "frontier" theme was to align with one of the themes in Disney's new California theme park. The series sparked a high popularity among its young audience, launching an unexpected merchandising craze. In quick succession, all sorts of products such as coonskin caps, toy rifles, and comic books flooded the stores. The popularity also included a hit record of the theme song "The Ballad of Davy Crockett." The title song was recorded by a few different singers including Bill Hayes, Tennessee Ernie Ford, and even actor Fess Parker. In 1955, it rated among the top songs of the entire year. The Bill Hayes version was the most successful placing #6 on the prestigious *Billboard* chart. It also charted at #1 on *Your Hit Parade*, # 7 on *Variety*, and #1 on *Cash Box*. Parker's version also spent some time at #1 and finished the year at #31 overall, as did Ford's version at #37.

CHILDREN'S TELEVISION: *ROMPER ROOM*, BOZO, AND HOWDY DOODY

Television continued expanding its variety of program offerings, including those shows especially for children. Throughout the nation, local television stations produced television shows specifically for children. All types of children's programming sprang up with all sorts of characters and puppets. Almost all featured a live audience of local youngsters. The selection process for a child audience member was often as simple as writing a letter to the local television station. Some of the more popular programs had long waiting lists, some in excess of six months. One long-running 1950s regional favorite was *Wallace and Ladmo* (1954–1989) in Phoenix, Arizona. *Wallace and Ladmo* had its own clown named Boffo, among other characters such as Aunt Maud and Captain Super ("Local Kids' TV," n.p.).

One of the longest-running children's show was *Romper Room* (1953–1994), an educational program created by Bert and Nancy Claster. Unlike the regional programs, *Romper Room* was franchised out to other regional markets. Many of the major cities aired their own *Romper Room* with a local host who had been trained by the Clasters. Each of the shows offered games, songs, and activities aimed at a preschool audience. Yet each show maintained a regional atmosphere by incorporating local community events. Other children's programs also franchised into local television markets.

One of the most memorable franchises was Bozo the Clown, who greeted the children with the opening line, "Hey, boys and girls! It's Bozo." In fact, Bozo as a "franchise" eventually had more than 200 different actors playing "Bozo" appearing at one time or another on regional TV programs. (The original Bozo the Clown was a character created in 1949 specifically for television by actor Pinto Colvig.) In 1956, Larry Harmon bought the rights to Bozo from Colvig and quickly built a training base to franchise the clown character. The character was not only a television personality, but also franchised to make live appearances at schools, stores, community events, or car dealerships, among others with the sole purpose to attract customers. According to a PBS documentary *Pioneers of Television*, the most successful of all children's programs, *Sesame Street* (1969–present day), "was built, in part, from lessons learned from the original, quirky local kids' television programming that was blooming in the 1950s" ("Local Kids' TV," n.p.).

In the midst of the diverse 1950s television programing emerged one of the most endearing children's shows of all time—*Howdy Doody*. The show, as one of the first nationally syndicated children's shows, was aimed at the children, but its advertising focused on their parents, mainly for the purchase of TV sets for the home. The idea for *Howdy Doody* began on an NBC radio affiliate in 1947 as *The Triple B Ranch* with host "Big Brother Bob Smith." Smith (1917–1998) began each show as he greeted the listening audience by saying, "Oh, ho, ho, howdy doody." Smith's agent convinced NBC to try the radio program as a children's TV show called *Puppet Playhouse*. One week after the first broadcast of December 17, 1947, the title was changed to *The Howdy Doody Show*. The star became known as "Buffalo Bob Smith" who presided over "Doodyville" with the studio audience of children known as the "Kids of the Peanut Gallery." The show was considered an immediate success and became the first NBC-TV show to air five days a week in prime time. It was also duplicated in Canada with a host known as "Timber Tom," played by actor and singer Robert Goulet (Rautiolla-Williams, "Howdy Doody," n.p.).

Buffalo Bob opened each show with the question, "Hey kids, what time is it?" The peanut gallery responded (and presumably, the kids watching at home) with a resounding, "It's Howdy Doody Time!" Howdy Doody was a much-loved marionette that first appeared in 1948 and was part of every show. Television historian Suzanne Rautiolla-Williams described him as "an all-American boy with red hair, forty-eight freckles (one for each state in the Union), and a permanent smile." Buffalo Bob spoke to Howdy Doody as he would have to a real-life child, which transferred over to the live children's audience both in the studio and watching at home. Howdy Doody was not the only puppet on the show; others included Phineas T. Bluster, Dilly Dally, and Flub-a-Dub. Other live actors appeared as the regular characters on the show. Actor Bill LeCornec (1915–1997) played Chief Thunderthud and actress Judy Tyler (1932–1957) appeared as Princess Summerfall Winterspring. But the most lovable of all the characters who joined Buffalo Bob and Howdy Doody was Clarabell Hornblower the Clown (Rautiolla-Williams, "Howdy Doody," n.p.).

Clarabell Hornblower was born in the fictitious "Clown Town" and was widely known as "Clarabell the Clown." When *Howdy Doody* premiered, Clarabell was played by Bob Keeshan (1927–2004). In 1952, Keeshan left the show and was replaced by Nick Nicholson, who two years later was replaced by Lew Anderson. Regardless who played the clown, Clarabell was always silent, only

In the midst of the diverse 1950s television programming emerged one of the most endearing children's shows of all time: *Howdy Doody*. Shown from left: "Buffalo Bob" Smith, Howdy Doody, and "Clarabell the Clown." (NBC/Photofest)

communicating by honking a horn for simple replies of "yes" or "no." Keeshan, who left the show in 1952, went on to host his own widely popular children's television show, *Captain Kangaroo*. Keeshan maintained that role for a 30-year run, from 1955 to 1984.

Advertising dollars, however, eventually proved to be the downfall of the *Howdy Doody* series. To make room for the more lucrative prime-time programing aimed at adults, *The Howdy Doody Show* was moved in 1956 from its five-day-a-week time slot to only Saturday mornings. In that new time slot, the show was just as popular, but eventually was cancelled in late 1960. The final show on September 24, 1960, was the 2,343rd episode. In fact, that final episode was the only time when Clarabell spoke. Fittingly in its final moments—Clarabell simply said, "Good-bye, kids" (Rautiolla-Williams, "Howdy Doody," n.p.).

TELEVISION DANCE SHOWS

Most American households had only one television set; therefore, all members of the family watched many of the same programs together. As the decade progressed, teenagers became a major market in purchasing commercial products, especially music. Teenagers not only listened to music, they also bought it. In addition to listening to the new breakthrough Rock 'n' Roll music on the radio; teenagers also had access to watching the songs performed on television, although in a much sanitized form. In turn, television shows geared to the teenage audience were produced.

TV-Teen Club (1949) was considered the first television show to feature teenagers dancing. The show was broadcast locally over WFIL-TV in Philadelphia and later nationally by ABC-TV as a television series from 1949 to 1954. The host for *TV-Teen Club* was the famed "King of Jazz" bandleader Paul Whiteman (1890–1967), who was one of America's most famous musicians during the 1920s. On the show, teenagers were shown dancing to a live band playing music, mostly for the jitterbug. For the most part, the other contemporary television shows featured music and dances from the big band era. In 1951, the first national television show featuring a dance band was *The Freddy Martin Show*. It was an all-band show without any dancing and lasted only two seasons (Jackson, 12–13).

In all likelihood, Marge and Gower Champion were the first dance couple to achieve notoriety directly from the medium of television. In 1949, the couple appeared as regulars on an early television variety show, *The Admiral Broadway Revue*. The exposure offered by the TV show brought them offers to dance in Hollywood movies. They soon danced their way through many 1950s Hollywood musicals including *Showboat* (1951), *Lovely to Look At* (1952), *Give a Girl a Break* (1953), *Three for the Show* (1955), and *Jupiter's Darling* (1955). Their popularity in movies brought them an offer to star in their own television series. In 1957, they hosted the NBC-TV primetime *The Marge and Gower Champion Show*. It was not a show about dance instruction although the theme song was "Let's Dance, Let's Dance, Let's Dance." Actually, it was a situation comedy with Gower playing the role of a choreographer and Marge a dancer. The television show always featured at least one scene with the Champions dancing. At the time, Rock 'n' Roll music and dancing were about to explode upon America and create a new wave of dance hysteria throughout the American public (Dannett and Rachel, 184; Thomas, 45).

American Bandstand

At about the same time that television dance shows such as *The Lawrence Welk Show* (1953–1982) and the *Arthur Murray Dance Party* (1950–1961) focused on adults, *American Bandstand* focused solely on teenagers. The simple format of not only *Bandstand* but also many other regional teenage dance shows had featured the TV/DJ host playing records or introducing live acts. The kids danced as the cameras followed their actions. The most popular of the period was the nationally broadcast *American Bandstand* (1952–1988). Prior to the dance show going national, it was broadcast regionally in Philadelphia as *Bandstand*. In an attempt to capitalize on the success of broadcast legends Grady and Hurst, WFIL-TV contracted with Bob Horn (1916–1966), a local Philadelphia radio disc jockey to move his popular radio show to television. The television version of *Bandstand* debuted on October 6, 1952. The show aired on Monday to Friday afternoons from 3:30 P.M. to 4:45 P.M. from the WFIL-TV studios located on 46th and Market Streets in West Philadelphia.

A large part of the growing appeal of *Bandstand* was due to its new host Dick Clark, who replaced Bob Horn in 1956. With Clark as host, the show went national over ABC-TV and was renamed *American Bandstand*. Clark's youthful appeal and good-natured, comfortable on-air personality regularly attracted more than 20 million teenagers to its TV viewing audience. As a national program, it aired from 3 P.M. until 4:30 P.M. The Philadelphia region could watch the live show from 2:30 P.M. to 5 P.M. With national exposure, teens across the nation soon copied Philadelphia youth culture. They also were treated to the new and upcoming acts providing music for teenagers. As a result of the mass audience of millions of teens who could learn in their own living room, a new dance could sweep the nation literally overnight (Jackson, 18–19, 65).

Of the many teenage television dance shows, Dick Clark was the only one to host a national broadcast. Other similar regional shows included former bandleader Ted Steele's *Teen Bandstand* in New York; *Bandstand Matinee* hosted by Jim Lounsberry in Chicago; *Detroit Bandstand*; *Connecticut Bandstand*; *Milt Grant's Record Hop* in Washington, D.C.; *The Art Laboe Show* in Los Angeles; George Edick's *Party Time* in St. Louis, Missouri; The *Grady and Hurst Show* from Wilmington, Delaware; and *The Buddy Deane Show* from Baltimore, Maryland. In 1957, *The Buddy Deane Show* was the top-rated regional program in the United States. In a sad tribute to American society, Deane, as did almost all the other television dance shows, maintained a strictly segregated "whites only" teenage dance program. Their answer to the race situation was to have a "Negro day" once a month (Jackson, 141–142).

American Bandstand was not officially segregated, but despite Philadelphia's large African American population, very few were allowed into the studio. In some limited instances, African Americans were allowed onto the set, but could not engage in interracial dancing. In contrast, many of the featured musical guests were often African American or distinctively ethnic. Almost all of the dancers were white between the ages of 14 and 18 who came from four local high schools. The reality of legal segregation and animosity towards Rock 'n' Roll was always a concern. As a national commercial television program, *American Bandstand* was in no position to change the TV image of an idealized version of a non-ethnic, homogenous white environment.

With the nationwide network, an artist could make one appearance on *Bandstand* and have their recording become a hit almost overnight. Yet with the "shift" to a national audience there was also the *Bandstand* image of a shift to "clean-cut" white groups and teen idols such as Frankie Avalon, Bobby Rydell, Fabian Forte, Annette Funicello, and Connie Francis. *American Bandstand* historian John A. Jackson claims, "By using *Bandstand* to introduce young white singers less offensive than 'Elvis the Pelvis,' the show's host [Dick Clark] did more than any other non-performer to change the face of rock 'n' roll—and amassed a personal fortune in the process" (41).

In reviewing the first nationwide show, noted television critic J.P. Shanley of *The New York Times* did not offer much praise: "Viewers who are beyond voting age are not likely to derive much pleasure from *American Bandstand*" (Shanley, "TV: Teen-Agers Only," n.p.). His adult perspective placed the entertainment value below that of other variety television shows of the time. He cautioned that watching the 90-minute show "of music and dancing to be something of an ordeal." Clark's choice of Presley's "Teddy Bear" to open the show did not go without Shanley providing an opportunity to express his disapproval of Rock 'n' Roll and Elvis Presley. Shanley added sarcastically, "After 'Teddy Bear,' some of the subsequent records were less atrocious." In contrast, Shanley did approve of the clean-cut image of both the host and the teenagers ("TV: Teen-Agers Only," n.p.).

Despite the criticism from the adult world, *American Bandstand* was a sensation among the youth. Dick Clark and *American Bandstand* soon became features of the 1950s as well as an indelible part of American culture. With an average viewing audience of more than 20 million teenagers, commercial advertisers took notice, which was more than enough to keep *American Bandstand* on the air. As with any successful endeavor, corporate advertisers yearned for more. Therefore, a Monday night hour-long version was started in 1957. On February 15, 1958, the show moved to the prestigious Saturday evening prime-time slot of 7:30 P.M. to 8:30 P.M., where it stayed on the air for two years. The daytime feature was later moved to only once a week on Saturday afternoons and ran until 1988 (Jackson, 41–42).

The significance of both the show and the broadcast building was recognized as an American historical landmark. The building itself, as the broadcast studios of WFIL-TV, was placed on the National Register of Historic Buildings. Its distinction is that when it was built in 1947–48, it was one of the first of its kind in America designed and constructed specifically to be a television studio. A historical marker plaque set directly outside the building and which is still there today, placed *American Bandstand* first in order over the building's architectural significance. It reads as follows:

> The television program had a major impact on the music, dance, and lifestyles of American teenagers. "Bandstand," a local show, began in 1952. Dick Clark became host in 1956, and on August 5, 1957, "American Bandstand" debuted on the nationwide ABC network. Until 1964 the show was broadcast from WFIL-TV here. This 1947 building was one of the first designed and constructed exclusively for television productions.

The marker location at 4601 Market Street in Philadelphia was dedicated on August 5, 1997, on the 40th anniversary of the national broadcast.

TELEVISION NEWS

From its inception, television, as did the World Wide Web in the 21st century, offered a promise for journalistic truth and educational opportunities. With the networks beholden to federal government oversight, specific time slots for non-commercial editorial programing was required. In sum, journalistic news shows without commercial advertising were required by federal decree. As the decade progressed and moved into the 1960s, newscasts sought commercial advertisers as they began competing for ratings. The loss was the journalistic integrity of uninterrupted editorial content. With commercial advertising, a delicate, compromised balance was inadvertently created as news reports needed to be careful not to provide adverse information that might discredit a sponsor's product. Eventually the news programs became profitable commercial ventures, but some questioned the content as moving from the factual to the fictional. (For more, see Media and Advertising chapter.)

THE QUIZ SHOW SCANDAL

One of the most popular of all the types of 1950s programming were the "quiz shows," airing both during the daytime and also in the prime-time evening hours. The format pitted non-celebrity contestants against each other, usually in a test of knowledge to answer questions delivered by an on-air celebrity host. A few, such as *What's My Line* (1950–1967) offered a celebrity panel trying to guess the occupation of a "mystery guest." Regardless of the format, each of the quiz shows provided cash awards (some quite large) for answering questions. A few, such as *Tic-Tac-Dough* (1956–1959) and *Twenty-One* (1956–1958), averaged more than 25 million viewers per week and placed in the top 20 of all television programs. During their peak years of 1955 and 1956, at least 16 quiz shows aired in prime time, with six rated in the top 30. As quickly as the quiz shows became popular, so was their demise when they were rocked by a major scandal ("TV History," n.p.).

The $64,000 Question was a prime example of the massive popularity of quiz shows. During the 1955–1956 season, *The $64,000 Question* was the #1 rated prime-time television program. It attained a 47.5 percent weekly share of the audience, a number that represented 34.9 million households with an estimated total viewing audience of more than 55 million people. (In 1955, the entire U.S. population numbered 165.9 million.) *The $64,000 Question* (1955–1958) was not an oddity, as all sorts of quiz shows did well in the ratings ("TV History," n.p.).

On *Twenty-One*, host Jack Barry was at a podium between two contestants, each in a soundproof glass "isolation" booth. The premise was that one challenger was pitted against the previous week's champion. (A contestant continued as "champion" until dethroned by a new contestant.) Each was asked questions based on various point totals selected by the contestant. A 1-point question was the easiest with the difficulty rising up to 11 points. The idea was to accumulate points similar to the casino game of blackjack. After each question, the contestants alternated back and forth. Communication was through headphones, which each contestant wore to hear Barry. While one spoke, the other was cut off from hearing anything. Sources at Television and Radio Industry History Resources claim that the first few episodes were an "honest" attempt for contestants to provide answers on their own. The producers, however, were not impressed by the limited knowledge of the contestants, nor was the viewing audience. Facing subsequent pressure from their single sponsor Geritol to turn around the "dismal failure," they decided to fix the problem by "fixing" the show ("The Quiz Show Scandal," n.p.).

In future episodes, the producers decided that certain contestants would fare better with audiences and therefore provided answers to the questions beforehand. With only the producers and the contestants aware that the game was fixed, the American public began a fascination with a college professor from Columbia University named Charles Van Doren. He came into major media attention as he played on *Twenty-One* to a series of ties against the previous champion, a municipal worker from Queens, New York, named Herb Stempel. In previous weeks, Stempel had won about $50,000, an amazing sum for the time. Van Doren eventually won more than $140,000 during a series of months as he garnered national media attention. (Van Doren's first appearance was on November 28, 1956; he defeated Stempel on December 5, 1956. Van Doren's run came to an end on March 11, 1957.) In essence, his continued appearance proved popular and he became a celebrity. In turn, ratings went up and the sponsors made money. Therefore, it was decided to continue providing him with answers so that he (and the show) remained in the public's attention. As a result, Van Doren was featured on the cover of the national *Time* magazine and in many newspapers. When his run ended he was offered an on-air spot on the popular morning *Today Show* (1952–present day) on NBC-TV ("The Quiz Show Scandal," n.p.).

Shortly after Van Doren's debut on the *Today Show,* Stempel made public accusations that the show was fixed. He claimed that he and Van Doren, as well as other contestants, had been coached and given answers prior to each show. At first, very few believed Stempel, including the American public. After the initial accusations, other evidence was found of providing answers in a notebook for a daytime CBS-TV game show *Dotto.* That particular show was cancelled immediately. With the information going public, another former *Twenty-One* contestant, James Snodgrass, came forward. His evidence was substantiated by sealed postal envelopes that he had mailed to himself before each appearance. Within each envelope were the answers to his upcoming show, thereby providing solid evidence that the quiz show was fixed. Despite it all, the viewing public did not believe the accusations against Van Doren until he admitted his own guilt before a congressional hearing. He read a statement admitting that he was coached and had received answers prior to the show. The executives at NBC-TV opted to cancel both *Twenty-One* and also Van Doren's contract with the *Today Show* ("The Quiz Show Scandal," n.p.).

Television historians place the incidents involving the quiz shows as the defining end of the Golden Age of Television. This act reflected the lost trust of the viewing public that translated into fewer viewers, resulting in a ratings drop and subsequent loss of commercial sponsors. The decline in the number of quiz shows also contributed in part to a decline in live TV. Whereas 80 percent of network television was broadcast live in 1953, by 1960 that number was down to 36 percent. Almost all of the television genres of situation comedies, westerns, soap operas, adventures, police dramas, and medical dramas began filming episodes rather than airing live. The vast majority of live television was regulated were to sports, some news programs, and a few daytime soap operas ("Television in the United States," n.p.).

THE NIELSEN RATING SYSTEM

The overall rating of a particular television show and its placement on a numerical list is determined by an intricate rating system. The Nielsen Company, which is a global information gathering company, determined the overall ratings for the individual television shows. One division of the company, Nielsen Media

Chart 2.4   Top 10 Television Programs, April 1950

No.	Nielsen Top 10 Program	Rating
1.	*Texaco Star Theater (The Milton Berle Show)*	77.7
2.	*Arthur Godfrey's Talent Scouts*	70.6
3.	*Star Spangled Revue (Bob Hope Special)*	57.6
4.	*Arthur Godfrey and Friends*	57.4
5.	*Toast of the Town*	55.1
6.	*Stop the Music* (1st half)	51.6
7.	*Stop the Music* (2nd half)	48.6
8.	*Cavalcade of Sports*	45.1
9.	*Lone Ranger*	44.8
10.	*Television Playhouse*	44.5

No.	Videodex Top 10 Program	Rating
1.	*Texaco Star Theatre (The Milton Berle Show)*	65.3
2.	*Arthur Godfrey's Talent Scouts*	53.5
3.	*Arthur Godfrey and Friends*	47.8
4.	*Toast of the Town*	44.6
5.	*Stop the Music*	39.5
6.	*Fireside Theater*	38.9
7.	*Television Theater*	38.8
8.	*TV Playhouse*	36.5
9.	*Martin Kane*	36.0
10.	*Lights Out*	36.0

No.	The Pulse Top 10 Program	Rating
1.	*Texaco Star Theater (The Milton Berle Show)*	55.2
2.	*Arthur Godfrey's Talent Scouts*	42.6
3.	*Arthur Godfrey and Friends*	40.8
4.	*Toast of the Ton*	40.2
5.	*Stop the Music*	34.5
6.	*The Goldbergs*	33.0
7.	*Television Theater*	31.8
8.	*Saturday Night Revue*	31.6
9.	*Fireside Theater*	29.3
10.	*Studio One*	28.2

Source: The Chicago Daily Tribune, May 31, 1950 article in "National Nielsen, Videodex and Pulse Ratings, April 1950," *Television Obscurities.* Chart compiled by the author.

Research (NMR), began measuring audience responses with radio in 1947. Other divisions of the company monitored theater, movies, and newspapers. In 1950, they began measuring television viewing and soon became the industry standard. In the words of the Nielsen Company, the ratings system became the "Holy Grail of audience measurement and helps media companies and brands make the right planning and programming decisions." Simply known as the "Nielsens," they are usually the determining factor in canceling or renewing a particular show. Of most importance, the ratings determine the viability of how much an advertiser would pay for a commercial slot. Therefore, the highest-rated shows charge more for an advertisement slot than a low-rated show ("Nielsen: About Us," n.p.).

In 1950, three companies tracked television: Nielsen, Videodex, and Pulse. All three listed *Texaco Star Theater* as the #1 rated show. In subsequent years, the NMR Nielsen Ratings was the main source for television ratings ("National Nielsen, Videodex and Pulse Ratings, April 1950," n.p.).

During the 1950s and for most of the remainder of the century, NMR placed an item called an "audimeter" in about 1,700 various American households. Another 850 households or so were picked to keep a "diary" of their viewing habits. (In later years, the number was set at 2,300 individuals from about 800 households.) The "audimeter," known simply as the "People Meter," provided weekly statistics, whereas the "diary" provided quarterly results ("Nielsen: About Us," n.p.). The sampling was supposed to represent a typical cross-section of the American demographic population. A mathematical extrapolation based on the total number of households with television sets was applied for the final calculations. Later advancements in technology, such as cable and satellite access, allowed for computer user monitoring.

According to the company's website, "Nielsen is synonymous with television audience measurement. We invented it. Since day one, we've offered the media industry the expertise it needs to make the best marketing decisions possible" ("Television," Nielsen.com). The data collection system was applied to market research by advertisers who sought to place specific products geared towards the specific individuals. A televised sporting event, for example, such as football would not advertise female cosmetic items. Instead those particular items would be placed as commercials on programs such as daytime soap operas that would most likely be viewed by a larger female audience. As the Nielsen Company explained:

> Our capabilities provide relevant metrics that are necessary to inform successful marketing and programming and drive continued growth. . . . This measurement breadth allows clients to plan programming and advertising for their ideal audience. That great lipstick ad you saw during your favorite reality show—that was no accident—it was informed by big data. ("Television," Nielsen.com)

On a page called "How we do it" on their website, the Nielson company explains the individuals were "chosen at random through proven methodology [determined by] housing types, household sizes, and geographical locations" ("Television," Nielsen.com).

THE BIRTH OF THE TELEVISION CRITIC

The Nielsen ratings were not the only way to gauge the success of a television show. Another method was a review by a television critic. Newspaper journalist Jack Gould (1914–1993) is credited as being the first television critic. As a staff writer for the *New York Times* beginning in 1937, Gould often wrote about the entertainment industry. By 1944, he was the main radio critic for the newspaper. But by the end of the 1940s and all through the 1950s, he was the paper's main television critic. He held that position while managing a staff of eight until 1972. Writing Gould's obituary, Glenn Collins noted:

> Mr. Gould is widely believed to have been the most influential television critic in the industry's formative years. His skeptical, often moralistic reviews and news analyses led others in the industry to label him "the conscience of the industry." (Collins, "Jack Gould," p. B6)

Many reports noted that when Gould wrote a review, the network executives paid very close attention. Gould's work earned him numerous awards and continuous critical acclaim for his integrity. For example, in 1956 he outright criticized the networks for avoiding televised news information on the international crisis in Egypt and the Suez Canal. The shame was heightened by the fact that the networks deemed the airing of "game shows" of more commercial importance. Gould's power was evident as the major networks soon preempted all the shows and televised the United Nations Security Council proceedings of the Suez event. (In 1957, Gould received the prestigious Peabody Award.) Special praise was offered for his support of Edward R. Murrow's exposé of the Red Baiting tactics of Senator Joseph R. McCarthy. He was often credited with breaking exclusive numerous news stories; the best remembered was the "Quiz Show Scandal" (Collins, "Jack Gould," p. B6).

TELEVISION'S IMPACT ON EVERYDAY LIFE

Although the term "Golden Age of Television" was sometimes applied in the early 21st century as the "Second Golden Age," the 1950s were a golden age for vastly different reasons. Television changed Americans' leisure pursuits in the same manner that the automobile had in previous decades. Unlike the automobile, which allowed the freedom to roam far away from the home, with television people were actually staying home. Many accounts indicate that the entire family and sometimes neighbors all gathered together to watch television. Studies reported, however, that the moment the television was turned on, family conversations stopped and that television also interfered with the traditional family dinner hour.

It would be hard to argue any factor other than television as the predominant element that shaped American life in the 1950s. It was television, more than any other technological development of the 20th century, that drastically changed American social and leisure habits (leisure being a newfound concept for much of the population). In 1950, a TV set was an expensive novelty, but it was quickly mass-produced; millions of sets were soon readily affordable and came to dominate the home life of a large majority of the population. The widespread access to television was aided by mid-1950s extension of coaxial cables throughout the nation. Congressional action allowed the issuances of a greater number of station licenses for new regional broadcast stations. U.S. Congress licensing also increased the allotted airtime allowed to the four major broadcast networks of ABC, CBS, NBC, and DuMont. Television was also aided by the demographic shift and large-scale development in suburbia. With the mass migration of middle-class Americans from the cities to suburbia, there was also a shift in television content. If one was to judge the 1950s only by the television shows alone, a summation could easily be formed that no segregation, racial discrimination, poverty, homosexuality, divorce, gambling, drug addictions, alcoholism, or any societal problem ever existed (Everett, "Golden Age of Television Drama," n.p.). Television provided a non-factual image of a father attired in a drab, often gray suit, white shirt, and dark tie as he (not she) happily left for work at a 9-to-5 job after a similarly happy breakfast with the wife and family. The kids went off to school and the mom stayed home and kept house. The daily television programming paralleled that non-reality. By 1959, television had reached far into the lives of all Americans.

With an entirely new medium available for consumer consumption, the need to fill up the broadcast day increased. The televised programming day settled into niche time schedules matched to the perceived workday and home life of the suburban American family. The morning slots provided light-hearted newscasts such as *The Today Show*. The daytime slots contained original programming such as game shows, children's programs, and soap operas for the stay-at-home mother. The "soaps," a favorite from radio days, were live dramas combining romantic intrigue and personal trauma. The term is often attributed to the advertising of detergent soaps during the broadcasts. The afternoon slot coincided with children and teens returning home from school as they settled in to watch shows such as *The Mickey Mouse Club* and *Howdy Doody*. Teenagers embraced dance shows like *American Bandstand*. The dinner hour, sometimes supplemented by a frozen "TV dinner," offered daily doses of a recap of the day's news events, while the evening prime-time hours offered programming geared to family viewing. The late evening hours slotted old movies and talk shows. The entire focus was on conformity and American patriotism. Many a 1950s American remembers "sign-off," as most television stations went off-air from around midnight to 6 A.M. The sign-off usually pictured an American flag waving in the wind while prerecorded music of the "Star-Spangled Banner" played. With no on-air programming, the message was that most Americans were asleep.

FURTHER READING

Milton Berle and Haskel Frankel. *Milton Berle: An Autobiography*, New York: Delacorte Press, 1974.

Tim Brooks and Earle Marsh, eds. *The Complete Directory to Prime Time Network TV Shows: 1946–Present*, 5th edition. New York: Ballantine, 1992.

Bill Cotter. *The Wonderful World of Disney Television*. New York: Hyperion Books, 1997.

John Dunning. *On the Air: The Encyclopedia of Old-Time Radio*. New York: Oxford University Press, 1998.

Fred J. MacDonald. *One Nation Under Television: The Rise and Decline of Network TV*. New York: Pantheon, 1990.

Michael Shore with Dick Clark. *The History of American Bandstand: It's Got a Great Beat and You Can Dance to It!* New York: Ballantine Books, 1985.

Stephen J. Whitfield. *The Culture of the Cold War*, 2nd edition. Baltimore, MD: Johns Hopkins University Press, 1996.

CHAPTER 3

Technology

The 1950s, just like any other time in history, provided its share of technological advancements. One of those advancements was the helicopter. Although it was not invented during the decade, it did evolve from the 1940s with significant advancements during the 1950s from a mere curiosity to serving many practical advantages. As the decade opened, the first trans continental flight of a rotor-driven helicopter was accomplished. During the Korean War, the helicopter was employed as a medical air evacuation platform. Other technological innovations occurred in many other areas such as radio transistors and musical instruments.

TRANSISTORS, LP's, 45's, AND FENDER'S *STRATOCASTER*

In 1953, Texas Instruments Corporation released a new, smaller type of transistor. (The invention of the transistor is credited to a research team at Bell Labs in late 1947.) The transistor led to a billion-dollar industry, laying the groundwork for later wide-scale development in computers and electronics. A leader in transistor research was General Electric (GE), located in Schenectady, New York. That work at GE led to significant advancements in the semiconductor (the essential component of almost all electronics). GE remained as the leading research institution in that field throughout the 1950s and into the 1960s.

At the same time, a new development in smaller, inexpensive transistors produced radios that were portable. As a result, radios were adapted for automobiles, and smaller radios were literally in the hands of teenagers. Unlike a television, which was bulky, expensive, and rarely one to a home, a teenager could retreat to an out-of-the-way place and listen to a radio program of choice. Youngsters could take the small hand-held transistor radio out of earshot of overly restrictive or segregationist adults and listen to late-night DJs, playing the scandalous music of rhythm and blues or Rock 'n' Roll. Listening to the music combined with post-war prosperity and mass-market production led to a significant amount of recorded music purchased for in-home personal use.

In the post-war period, more than 400 new record labels produced records at an amazing rate. In 1950, Americans purchased more than 190 million records; by mid-decade, the number doubled. It continued growing and by 1960, the number of records sold each year was over 600 million. An astounding 70 percent of those purchases were by teenagers. A significant factor in those numbers was the widening appeal of the music that was commonly being called "Rock 'n' Roll" (Kammen, 180).

To stay viable, radio programming offered more music and also a wider market for Rock 'n' Roll and rhythm and blues. Unlike swing and jazz, which used drums and bass to play rhythm, Rock 'n' Roll made use of those same instruments to play a heavy beat that "drove" the sound of the music. (Similar to rhythm and blues, the accent was on the second and fourth beats of music.) The most prominent addition to the Rock 'n' Roll sound was the solid body electric guitar. In 1950, Leo Fender introduced the solid-body *Telecaster* Electric Guitar (revised in 1954 as the *Stratocaster*). Prior to Fender's solid-body design, guitars were deep bodied with a hole under the strings to allow the music to resonate. The Fender solid body enabled the music to be picked up electronically and transferred to an amplifier, thereby allowing a heavier downbeat and louder sound. The solid-body guitar would become the trademark of the Rock 'n' Roll bands.

A major technological innovation for television was the 1951 addition of coaxial cable. The demographic shift of many families to the far-reaching suburbs, as well as those in rural areas, were sometimes out of reach of antennae reception to view their favorite television programs. Widespread nationwide access was aided by the extension of coaxial cables throughout the nation. Subsequent Congressional legislation allowed more stations to be able to achieve a television broadcast license. This effectively provided the East Coast, the West Coast, and the middle part of America simultaneous coverage. The coaxial cables meant that rather than transmitting through the airwaves, the images could be transmitted electronically. The addition of videotape and video recorders also helped for newscasts to show prerecorded footage of a news event that might have occurred earlier in the day.

Of more than just a passing note was the technological innovations from a very popular children's television show. The *Howdy Doody Show* often provided a fictional fantasy tool such as the "Electromindomizer" that purportedly read the minds of the children of Doodyville. Another was in the hands of Clarabell the Clown, who only communicated via a honking horn. But Clarabell had access to a "Honkadoodle" that translated the honking horn of Mother Goose nursery rhymes into audible English for the children to hear. The fictionalized features were not all that farfetched, yet one real-life innovation that was incorporated into many other television broadcasts was the use of a split screen. In June 1949, with Howdy Doody in a Chicago studio and Buffalo Bob Smith in a New York studio, both appeared on the split screen at the same time. This was most likely the first time a cross-country link was televised. The technique would be used many times throughout the 1950s, especially for a newscaster in the studio and a live reporter on the street. The technical innovations at the *Howdy*

Doody Show did not stop there. In 1955, the popular program was the first show on NBC-TV to broadcast in color (Rautiolla-Williams, "Howdy Doody," n.p.).

Other technological firsts during the 1950s that had much more of an impact in later decades was the oral contraceptive Enovid (commonly known as "The Pill"); the modern credit card introduced in 1950; a working robot in 1954; and the photovoltaic solar cell in that same year. Television programs were recorded on videotape in 1956. Two years later in 1958, the both the computer modem and the microchip were introduced. Among the many other technological advancements were advancements and discoveries such as rockets, air travel, jet engines, atomic bombs, hydrogen bombs, nuclear power, satellites, and the polio vaccine.

ROCKETS, SABRE JETS, AND THE J-47 ENGINE

By the end of World War II, America had a monopoly on the atomic bomb, but the country had lagged far behind in jet and rocket technology. During the war, the Germans developed two effective rockets: the V-1 Buzz Bomb and the V-2 Rocket. Each was capable of launching attacks against England. The Germans also had learned the technology to put the swept wing jet fighter Messerschmitt ME-262 into effective combat operation. In the years immediately after the war, the National Advisory Committee for Aeronautics (NACA) was under heavy military pressure to develop similar military jets and swept-wing aircraft for the United States. The post-war research and effectiveness of NACA produced a program that would eventually benefit both the military and civilian air transportation.

Rocket- and jet-powered engines were envisioned in some of the earlier 1930s Hollywood movies featuring action heroes, such as *Buck Rogers* and *The Rocketeer*. During the early 1940s, coming on the heels of the pure imagination from the preceding decade, aircraft engineers envisioned actual jet-powered aircraft. They applied these ideas in wind tunnel tests, but problems revealed non-stability in traditional straight-wing aircraft. The standard arrangement of airplane wings placed perpendicular to the fuselage proved highly unstable as aircraft speed exceeded 600 miles per hour (mph). At those speeds, the wings fluttered drastically and sometimes caused separation from the fuselage or loss of the horizontal stabilizer. Each situation resulted in the loss of the aircraft and often the life of the pilot. To counteract turbulence, designers implemented a swept-wing design, in which the wings were at an angle (variable from 30 to 45 degrees) towards the back of the fuselage. (In later years, the wings were sometimes swept forward.) To increase airspeed, the propeller-driven engines also needed an alternative power source. At first scientists recommended rocket engines similar to the German V-2. At the time, rocket engine advancements provided the necessary amount of power, or "thrust," that contemporary jet engines could not provide.

Increasing the speed of aircraft to reach the "speed of sound" was attained with a rocket engine. The speed of sound was termed Mach 1 or 761.2 mph at sea level. According to information provided by the Smithsonian Air & Space Museum, the speed of sound varies in relation to altitude related to sea level. The actual speed of sound "Mach 1" also varies with the ambient air temperature. Therefore, as altitude increases, the temperature decreases, and so does the speed of sound. From an altitude between 36,000 to 60,000 feet, the speed of sound remains stable at about 661 mph ("How Things Fly," n.p.). In 1947, the "sound barrier" was broken by Air Force pilot Chuck Yeager, in a Bell Aircraft Company "Bell X-1."

To increase both production and further the research of rocket design, the United States enlisted the aid of former German scientist Wernher von Braun and other wartime scientists who had worked on the original V-2 rockets. The collaborative effort produced an American version of the V-2 that was built and launched at a military proving ground at White Sands, New Mexico. The group eventually designed a series of missiles for military warfare. In addition, von Braun's later work led to the development of rockets capable of exploring space. To proceed with the space program, on July 29, 1958, Congress authorized the formation of the National Aeronautics and Space Administration (NASA). The new government program was responsible for implementing aeronautical and aerospace research for the foundation of a civilian space program. Most of the future rocket design centered on possible NASA-type space missions. The American military temporarily settled upon some smaller rocket versions for battlefield use and stepped up research on jet engines for military aircraft.

The Boeing B-47 Stratojet bomber is often credited as the first operational jet aircraft flown by the United States. As a swept-wing multiengine bomber, it also represented a milestone in both aviation history and a revolution in aircraft design. The Boeing Aviation website claims, "Every large jet aircraft today is a descendant of the B-47" ("History," Boeing.com, n.p.). Prior to the development of the B-47, Boeing engineers had envisioned a jet-powered plane as early as 1943. Wind tunnel tests of straight-wing jet aircraft indicated that the wing design did not employ the full potential of jet-engine power. To continue the research, Boeing engineers were sent to Europe after the war to learn what the Germans had done in jet experimentation. As the engineers toured some of the captured aeronautics facilities, a secret wind tunnel was discovered that contained valuable data on swept-wing design. The information was soon applied to an experimental XB-47 by adding a swept-back wing design at a 35-degree angle. Six prototype turbojet engines from the General Electric Company known as the "J-35" were encased in under-wing nacelles of the XB-47. Information on Boeing's website listed December 17, 1947 as the date of the XB-47's first flight as the jet-powered aircraft attained a top speed of 607 mph. The success led to a large-scale military production order with improvements made on the engine now known as the GE J-47 and the aircraft designated as the B-47. From 1947 to 1956, more than 2,000 of the B-47 type jet aircraft were built with the GE J-47 jet engines. The B-47 became the backbone of the newly founded U.S. Air Force Strategic Air Command ("GE Aviation: Powering a Century of Flight," n.p.).

Before, during, and after World War II, the General Electric Company (GE) was contracted to build most of the military supply of propeller-driven aircraft engines. At the time, the aircraft engines were powered by gasoline, which contained three basic elements of carbon, hydrogen, and oxygen. Propeller-driven engines required different air intake than a conventional automobile engine,

The swept wing design is seen here on the single-seat fighter North American F-86 Sabre jet. The first test flight was on October 1, 1947, and was used extensively in the Korean War that began on June 25, 1950, and ended on July 27, 1953. Wartime need produced an improved Sabre with a top speed of 650 mph. The fighter was put into large-scale production with more than 6,000 made. (This photo is of a 1/48 scale plastic model assembled and painted by Ralph G. Giordano.)

which also burned gasoline. For the proper combustion to take place within either the automobile or aircraft engine, certain fixed chemical laws had to occur. To provide either engine with the maximum amount of power, the correct mixture of both fuel and air is required. An insufficient combination of these elements results in a loss of engine combustion. This combination was not as critical for an automobile engine as it was for an aircraft engine. For an aircraft engine to operate at maximum efficiency flying at altitudes where the air was thin, special attention to "fuel-air ratios" was needed. As it was described in a 1943 GE technical manual, the "gasoline engine is as dependent upon the weight of air it receives as it is upon the amount or fuel supplied to it." In order to maintain the same amount of horsepower for an aircraft engine the amount of air intake was increased through a manifold. As this type of mechanical process was applied to the aircraft it was known as "supercharging." In a technical manual TM 1-404, December 30, 1943, GE engineers described the supercharging as it "puts more pounds of air in the same cylinder volume and, therefore, more power is developed."

CIVILIAN AIR TRANSPORTATION

In 1958, standard travel on passenger jets began with the introduction of the Boeing 707 and Douglas DC-8 jet-powered airliners. (Each was capable of traveling at least twice as fast as their propeller-driven predecessors.) Both the Boeing 707 and Douglas DC-8 were faster and proved to be more economical in fuel costs than their propeller-driven predecessors. The lower operating cost and higher speed allowed airlines to offer lower passenger rates, thereby increasing the number of passengers traveling for leisure and vacation. By late 1958, all the major airlines made the switch to jet-powered passenger aircraft for long-distance flights (Kaplan, 212–13).

The economical advantage of jet aircraft had everything to do with the engine. The J-47 was a revolutionary engine for the military jet age, but the civilian commercial airliners such as the reliable Boeing 707 relied on a Pratt & Whitney JT3 engine. (The JT-3 was a commercial variant of the U.S. Air Force's J53.) In comparison to the propeller-type piston engines, the jet engines had far fewer moving parts. Less moving parts meant more reliability; of utmost concern was an advantage of less costly maintenance. Unlike the radial propeller-driven engines that burned gasoline, jet engines used a cheaper variant of kerosene. The kerosene offered a dual advantage of not only being less expensive than gasoline, but produced tremendous thrust for its weight.

The first generation of jet airliners, such as the four-engine Boeing 707, were designed for both transcontinental and transatlantic flights. Many different versions of the swept-wing 707 were produced from 1958 to 1979. Notable improvements included an increased passenger capacity from 140 to 219, and the non-stop flight range improved from 2,500 to 5,750 miles. Another example was the Douglas DC-8 four-engine jet airliner that replaced the piston-engine DC-7 for long-distance flights. The DC-8 had an advantage over other similar jet aircraft with a larger passenger capacity of 259. Production totals for all variants of the DC-8 eventually numbered more than 550 in active flight service. By 1995, more than 300 of the Douglas DC-8's making daily scheduled flights were still in regular service. A report in *Aviation Week* discovered that at least 36 DC-8s were still flying in the year 2013 ("History," Boeing.com, n.p.).

In October 1958, Pan American Airlines (Pan Am) began transatlantic service carrying more than 100 passengers between New York and London in the Boeing 707. (The flight had only one stopover. A later Boeing version, the 707-320, was capable of crossing the Atlantic non-stop.) In quick succession, other competing airlines offered similar service. National Airlines also started domestic jet service in 1958 with a fleet of Boeing 707s, acquired through a loan arrangement with Pan Am. In January 1959, American Airlines also purchased a significant amount of 707s for domestic service. In September 1959, both United Airlines and Delta Air Lines began jet service with the Douglas DC-8 airliner. Continental Airlines also announced its "golden jet service" would begin in 1959 via a colorful advertising brochure. Other jet aircraft types were also in service such as the British de Havilland D.H. 106 Comet and Soviet Tupolev Tu-104. But it was the Boeing 707s and Douglas DC-8s that provided faster speeds and greater range than the others. In 1959, American Airlines set the standard for a transcontinental airliner as a regularly scheduled Boeing 707 flight crossed non-stop from New York to San Francisco in five hours. In comparison, the fastest propeller-driven DC-7 took about eight hours ("GE Aviation: Powering a Century of Flight," n.p.).

AIRLINE DEATHS, SAFETY, AND THE FEDERAL AVIATION AGENCY

With the increase in air travel also came greater concern for safety. Mid-air collisions and crashes, although rare, were cause for sensational tragedies. Unlike an automobile, with a limited number of passengers (about two to six), airplanes carried a larger number of passengers. In addition, safety concerns arose for people on the ground and those living near airports. During the early part of the decade, air fatalities were not as numerous, mainly due to a limited daily flight schedule of propeller-driven passenger aircraft. In later years, as the amount of air traffic dramatically increased, so did the amount of fatalities. As a result, public concern arose for municipal and federal safety regulations.

Over one 58-day period, in late 1951 and into early 1952, three air crashes occurred over Elizabeth, New Jersey, involving Newark Airport.

December 16, 1951: A Curtiss C-46 leaving Newark crashed into an Elizabeth warehouse, killing all 56 people onboard.

January 22, 1952: A Convair CV-240 en route to Newark from Syracuse in a storm crashed into a row of homes on Williamson Street in Elizabeth, killing all 23 on the airplane and seven people on the ground.

February 11, 1952: Shortly after takeoff, a Miami-bound DC-6 crashed into a four-story apartment building in Elizabeth. Twenty-nine of the 63 on-board passengers died, another four people were killed on the ground.

Of morbid coincidence, a congressional subcommittee was scheduled to meet on the same February morning as the third crash. In response to the first two crashes, residents of Elizabeth, New Jersey, were set to testify, asking for the closure of Newark Airport. The Port Authority, which owned and operated the airport, resisted closure and was ready with a prepared statement calling "the airport one of the safest in the nation." Upon hearing of the crash, Port Authority officials asked newspapers not to print the statement.

Newark Airport was immediately closed to all commercial air traffic until a new runway was constructed directing air traffic away from the city of Elizabeth. (The airport reopened in November 1952.) In response to the triple tragedy, President Truman announced the formation of an airport safety commission. Truman named the famous General James Doolittle to head the commission. (Doolittle had achieved fame during World War II for leading a bombing raid against Tokyo. He was also an early proponent of airpower for military use in warfare.) A report was issued in May 1954 by the Doolittle Commission recommending a coordinated effort between airport design and municipal building to keep clear paths of aircraft approach free of residential dwellings. Some other recommendations included a "fan-shaped" safety zone "prohibiting hospitals, schools and houses of worship." The plan did not involve existing airports, but was required for new airport design and construction. As the recommendations were being considered, other tragedies involving American air travel still happened (Hyman, "How Three Planes Crashed in Three Months in Elizabeth in '50s," n.p.).

The 1951–1952 outcry from the residents of Elizabeth, New Jersey, was not the only instance of public citizens demanding airline safety regulations. As air fatalities mounted, the Congressional response was almost non-existent. Yet the number of individuals and aircraft continued to fill the sky at an amazing rate. By mid-decade, more than 1,700 commercial aircraft filled the skies compared to only about 300 or so in 1950. Of note, no nationwide radar coverage existed as airplane takeoff and landing was monitored visually from an airport control tower. Air-to-ground radio communication existed only when and if a pilot reported its location to a ground station. Despite the ad hoc attempt at coordinating air travel it took another tragedy to regulate nationwide safety measures. The incident that finally prompted the United States government to intervene occurred over one the most famous tourist attractions in America— the Grand Canyon.

On June 30, 1956, a mid-air collision over the Grand Canyon involving a United Airlines DC-7 with 58 people onboard and a Trans World Airlines (TWA) Lockheed Constellation with 70 onboard killed all the passengers and crew from both aircraft. Newspapers across the country carried the story as front page headlines. A banner two-line headline of *The New York Times* dated July 1, 1956, read:

TWO AIRLINERS CARRYING 128 VANISH IN WEST;
WRECKAGE OF ONE SIGHTED IN GRAND CANYON

During the investigation of the crash, it was revealed that each pilot was operating under visual flight rules. This meant that the pilot looked out the cockpit window to see if any other aircraft were in the vicinity. The remote location of the accident only added to the sensational nature of the crash due to the limited amount of air traffic over Grand Canyon National Park. The cause of the crash turned out to be the simple error that the pilots just did not see each other. In 2006, Elaine Jarvik writing in the Salt Lake City *Deseret News* revisited the incident. (As the article appeared, 50 years after the tragic event, remnants of the crash were still evident at the remote crash site.) She wrote:

> It was, at the time, the most stunning aviation disaster in U.S. history: 128 deaths, compounded by the breathtaking coincidence of the crash itself. Not only had two commercial airliners ended up at the same exact point in space at the exact same time, they had fallen from the sky into one of the most scenic spots on Earth. (Jarvik, "Vestiges of '56 Collision Still Imbedded in Grand Canyon," n.p.)

At the time of the crash, a proposal sat before Congress for the creation of a regulatory Federal Aviation Administration. That proposal, as did many other proposed safety regulations for a national air traffic control system, was denied funding.

The outpouring of national attention caused Congress to finally act by passing "The Federal Aviation Act of 1958." The legislation created a federally funded oversight authority known as the Federal Aviation Agency (FAA) to regulate air space. The act also established passenger safety regulations and national air traffic control. One result of the accident was the FAA mandate to install a "Black Box" in all passenger aircraft. The device monitored all onboard communication and provided valuable information for future accident investigations. (Jarvik, "Vestiges of '56 Collision," n.p.)

The new FAA regulations did not eliminate all traffic accidents or even deaths, but the regulations did improve overall safety. During the first half of the 1950s, accidents and air fatalities were about five times greater than comparable times. The fatality rate was about five people killed for every 100,000 hours of scheduled flight time. With FAA regulations in place that rate dropped to an average of only one death for every 100,000 hours of flying. By the year 2000, flying was the safest way of travel in America. The reduction in fatalities was, no pun intended, not by accident.

Regardless of safety regulations, not all accidents could be avoided, but surviving a crash was more likely. One of the most notable air accidents of the time occurred on February 3, 1959. A private Beechcraft Bonanza crashed after takeoff in Clear Lake, Iowa, killing three famous Rock 'n' Roll stars: Buddy Holly, Ritchie Valens, J.P. Richardson, and its pilot Roger Peterson.

The plane crash came to be known as "The Day the Music Died," and lived on in legend and song well into the 21st century. The accident garnered a major share of the national headlines as the incident overshadowed the passenger airline crash in New York City on that same day. On that day, a Lockheed L-188 crashed into New York's East River, and 65 of 73 were killed. (Some reports list 72 onboard, which did not count an infant.) On the New York flight was producer Beulah Zaca of the popular TV children's show *Kukla, Fran and Ollie*, who died in the crash. Also on board was an American Airlines director of facility planning, Richard Winn. The sensational accidents did generate headlines but overall the FAA regulations made air travel safer and more reliable. Airfare prices were also becoming affordable for middle-class individuals seeking vacation and leisure destinations, some in faraway places and different time zones.

The speed of delivering a passenger across time zones was not without newfound complications. The disruption of daily schedules led to a discomfort known as "jet lag." Air travelers would sometimes experience symptoms that included malaise, insomnia, lightheadedness, and disorientation. There was no medical cure other than allowing a few days for the body to adjust to the new time zone. Another malady was "airsickness," which sometimes caused a passenger to vomit. Both of these situations were not overly publicized, but the airlines did attempt to provide comfort by hiring flight attendants known as "stewardesses."

JACKIE COCHRAN AND THE SEXUALIZATION OF STEWARDESSES

With the increase in air travel also came amenities in air service. In competition for travel and business customers, airlines provided in-flight service attendants to aid in customer comfort. At the time, they were called "stewardesses," an association with another service position but gender different from a male "steward." A steward was a familiar term to railroad and cruise ship passengers, meaning a man who was employed to serve the needs of the passengers. Unlike the all-male stewards on trains and ships the in-flight air service employees were all women. In contrast, the pilots were all men. As advertisers promoted the new "friendly skies," the stewardesses were sought after by the all-too-friendly male business passengers seeking more than just air service.

Despite the fact that female air legends such as Amelia Earhart (1897–1931) and Jacqueline "Jackie" Cochran (1906–1980) were examples of outstanding pilots, the airlines did not hire or train women for that role. The airlines often relied on hiring male pilots who were trained in the military. During the 1950s, many of the civilian airline pilots had received their air training during World War II. Often forgotten is that a branch of the U.S. Army Air Corp included the Women's Auxiliary Army Corps (WAACs) and Women Airforce Service Pilots (WASPs). Both the WAACs and WASPs were trained as pilots for ferrying fighter aircraft and bombers into war zones.

During World War II, Cochran supervised both the WAAC and WASP programs and oversaw the training of hundreds of female pilots. She also earned the distinction as the first female to fly a war-ready bomber across the Atlantic Ocean. (That new program was known as the Women's Auxiliary Ferrying Squadron, or the WAFS.) In recognition of her service to her country she earned the U.S. Distinguished Service Medal (the first awarded to a woman). Of interest is that many of her official biographies list her achievements preceded by "as the first woman to." Her "female" achievements during that time included being the first woman to fly a jet across the Atlantic and also the first to break through the sound barrier. In reality, many of her air records and achievements were outright aviation records for any pilot, male or female. She continued a notable aviation career throughout the 1950s and beyond. In 1971, Cochran was enshrined in the National Aviation Hall of Fame. Her biography noted, "when she died in 1980, she held more speed, altitude, and distance records than anyone in the world—male or female." After the war, almost all of the achievements of females in wartime, were quickly forgotten ("Jacqueline Cochran, Record Setter," n.p.).

Unknown by the public was that the stewardesses were highly trained in all sorts of emergency rescue procedures and various other safety skills. To the almost all male business-class travelers, the female stewardess served moreso as an idealized fabrication of sexual pleasure. The airlines were as much to fault as society itself. In Victoria Vantoch's *The Jet Sex: Airline Stewardesses and the Making of an American Icon* (University of Pennsylvania Press, 2013), she provides historical insight into the gender discrimination of the profession. Vantoch writes:

> Airline ads of the era portrayed the stewardess as the consummate 1950s woman—a quintessential wife-to-be, who knew how to apply lipstick, pamper men, and mix [mingle]. Stewardess supervisors were instructed to nix [not hire] applicants with particular nose shapes, lip shapes, and hair textures. (Vantoch, 29)

Airline executives prided themselves on hiring just the "right kind of girl" for the job. The "right kind" was an unmarried woman under the age of 30. In keeping with the overall expectations of the role of women in 1950s society, she only worked until she could find a husband and become a homemaker. One airline executive noted, "If a flight attendant was still on the job after three years . . . I'd know we were getting the wrong kind of girl. She's not getting married" (quoted in Steinem, 2015, 90).

Keeping with the overall cult of domesticity of the 1950s also went hand-in-hand with the overt racial segregation of the time. Vantoch explains, "While masquerading as objective beauty standards, these requirements were, in fact, used to exclude minorities from this iconic position." Vantoch recalled one incident in 1956 when an African-American woman named Patricia Banks applied to Capitol Airlines to work as a stewardess. She was denied employment and filed suit in court based on racial discrimination. After four years, a court ruled in her favor. Although Capitol Airlines eventually hired Banks in 1960, she was still subjected to overt gender discrimination (Vantoch, 58–61). In addition, strict limitations were placed upon the female body shape that included height, weight, hairstyle, makeup, and skirt length, among other nuances. If a flight attendant deviated from any of the prescribed requirements, such as getting married, she was immediately fired from her job. Another unique requirement was that the women under 30 did not have a "broad nose." The reference was to restrict the hiring of any Jewish women. As Gloria Steinem wrote in her book *My Life on the Road*, this was only one requirement of the "many racist reasons why stewardesses were overwhelmingly white" (89–90).

A BIGGER AND BETTER ATOMIC BOMB—INTO THE NUCLEAR AGE

In the years immediately following World War II, the United States and the Soviet Union (USSR) engaged in a tense ideological, political, and military rivalry that became known as the Cold War. (Some say the name came from journalist Walter Lippman [1889–1974], who wrote a series of articles in 1947 titled *The Cold War*. Some others attribute the phrase of the "Cold War," as used by Bernard Baruch [1870–1965] during a Congressional debate in April 1945.) During the Cold War, both nations tried to extend influence and promote their own systems of government around the world. A number of Americans fueled by intense paranoia created by the media and the likes of Senator Joe McCarthy believed that the nation's security depended on preventing the spread of Communism. A major "defense" weapon that was promoted in America to fight Communism was atomic energy. Of major consequence were advanced weapons such as thermonuclear bombs ("Timeline of the Nuclear Age," n.p.).

With the outbreak of WWII, Germany experimented with the possibility of transforming nuclear energy into a weapon such as an atomic bomb. An important ingredient to produce the weapon was "heavy water." The first production plant of its kind was built in Norway in 1934 as scientists came across heavy water as an accidental by-product during an ammonia production process. Therefore, the 1940 German invasion and subsequent occupation of

Norway had multiple military objectives. One was the natural geographic position for launching air raids against northern England. The other was to secure the necessary ingredient for constructing an atomic weapon.

Germany was not the only country trying to build such a weapon. In early 1941 (prior to American entry into the war), an American chemist named Glenn Seaborg discovered plutonium. American physicists confirmed that plutonium was "fissionable" and could be made into a bomb. (An atomic bomb is detonated by a fission chain reaction process of breaking up atoms of either uranium or plutonium.) On December 6, 1941, President Roosevelt issued an executive order to secretly fund the "Manhattan Project" with the authorization to "build an atomic bomb." The following day Japan attacked the U.S. military base at Pearl Harbor in Hawaii, forcing American entry into World War II. The ultimate end of the war would end with the use of two atomic bombs dropped over the Japanese homeland ("Timeline of the Nuclear Age," n.p.).

The physical construction and testing of the atomic bomb was located in Los Alamos, New Mexico, but production and lab science work took place in other facilities throughout the country. The production of fissionable material took place in Hanford, Washington, and a science lab was located at Columbia University in the borough of Manhattan in New York City (hence the code name "The Manhattan Project"). After years of testing, a bomb was successfully developed and a test explosion verified that the bomb would actually work. During a secret test on July 16, 1945, a nuclear device was detonated at a site in New Mexico. That area where the world's first nuclear explosion took place at the White Sands Missile Range was known as the "Trinity Site." The U.S. National Parks Service erected an obelisk in 1965 to denote the exact location, which was later designated as a national historic landmark. A bronze plaque was attached to an obelisk made of coarse stone that sits within a chainlink

Trinity Site Obelisk. The black plaque on top reads: *Trinity Site Where the World's First Nuclear Device Was Exploded On July 16, 1945 Erected 1965 White Sands Missile Range J. Frederick Thorlin Major General U.S. Army Commanding.* The gold plaque below it declares the site a national historic landmark and reads: *Trinity Site has been designated a National Historical Landmark.* (National Parks Service) fenced in an area topped with barbed wire within the barren wasteland site in New Mexico.

At the time, military and government officials became aware that any type of atomic warfare caused horrific death and possible worldwide contamination. Yet that knowledge did not deter the United States from actively pursuing the all-out production of previously unimaginable types of nuclear weapons during the post-war years. The push forward for even more powerful and destructive weapons did not seem to take into account the after effects of nuclear fallout (Yamazaki, "Hiroshima and Nagasaki Death Toll," n.p.).

The arguments both for and against the use of nuclear weapons to end the Second World War have continued to the present day. Yet the actual use of atomic weapons is often consigned to the history books as isolated only to the two Japanese cities. Often forgotten is that it was not the only time the United States government authorized the use of atomic devices for atmospheric explosions. In response to a successful Soviet test of an atomic weapon in 1949, the race for nuclear military supremacy accelerated. In an effort to outpace the Soviets and qualm the fear that the Soviets might have an edge, President Truman announced the commitment to build a "superbomb." The first tests for the more powerful weapon began on January 27, 1951, in Nevada. At the time, England also authorized the development and testing of an atomic device at the Monte Bello Islands off the coast of Western Australia. Both the British and Soviets accelerated their testing throughout the 1950s.

YUCCA FLAT: "A FRIGHTENING SIGHT THAT ONE SHOULD NEVER FORGET"

The Nevada desert became a common place for the United States government testing of atomic bombs. According to official government records, at least 100 "above-ground nuclear tests" were conducted between 1951 and 1962. (The term "atmospheric testing" is more accurate because the bombs and nuclear devices were exploded at various heights above the ground.) The Nevada test site located in Nye County about 65 miles northwest of Las Vegas was established as a 680-square-mile area by a presidential decree on December 18, 1950. (Truman was also president in August 1945, and it was he who gave the final go-ahead to drop the bombs on Hiroshima and Nagasaki.) The atmospheric test was only a small part of the total 928 nuclear detonations at the military site known as the Nevada Proving Grounds. The other 828 nuclear tests were conducted at sites located underground. Some of tests contained multiple explosions causing some sources to place the actual number at more than 1,000 total nuclear tests at the site. Regardless, the number of tests were so numerous that the atomic explosions became commonplace. With the aid of quite a few of the tests broadcast live on television, the American public also became familiar with the common sight of a "mushroom cloud."

An atomic bomb explosion was not easy to hide. Mushroom clouds that appeared after detonation could be seen from more than 100 miles away, some as far away as San Francisco. The sight of the cloud was not as unnerving as the rumbling and vibrations that shook buildings and rattled windows in nearby downtown Las Vegas. The public became a bit unnerved with the secrecy and the unknown of what was causing the explosions. Therefore, the newly formed Atomic Energy Commission (AEC) was under public pressure to release information. On January 11, 1951, the U.S. Atomic Energy Commission distributed a handbill providing some limited information regarding future testing at the Nevada Proving Ground. The complete text of the letter was as follows:

<u>WARNING</u>

January 11, 1951

From this day forward the U.S. Atomic Energy Commission has been authorized to use part of the Las Vegas Bombing and Gunnery Range for test work necessary to the atomic weapons development program.

Test activities will include experimental nuclear detonations for the development of atomic bombs—so-called "A-Bombs"—carried out under controlled conditions.

<u>NO PUBLIC ANNOUNCEMENT OF THE TIME OF
ANY TEST WILL BE MADE</u>

Unauthorized persons who pass inside the limits of the Las Vegas Bombing Gunnery Range may be subject to injury from or as a result of the AEC test activities.

Health and safety authorities have determined that no danger from or as a result of AEC testing activities may be expected outside the limits of the Las Vegas Bombing and Gunnery Range. All necessary precautions, including radiological surveys and patrolling of the surrounding territory, will be undertaken to insure that safety conditions are maintained.

Full security restrictions of the Atomic Energy Act will apply to the work in this area.

RALPH P. JOHNSON, Project Manager
Las Vegas Project Office
U.S. Atomic Energy Commission

(*Note*: Capitalization, indenting, and underlining is as it appeared on the original handbill. Source: "Nevada Test Site Guide, DOE/NV-715 Federal Government of the United States.")

A few weeks after the unannounced test of January 27, 1951, the AEC decided to announce the date of future testing. The AEC invited news journalists to witness an explosion scheduled for April 22, 1952, which would be the 17th overall to date. The test with the code name "Operation Open Shot" was scheduled at the Yucca Flat site one of four areas at the Nevada Proving Grounds. A special area was set up for the journalists about 45 miles away atop the 9,000-foot Mt. Charleston. The area was dubbed "News Nob" as dozens of reporters and photographers camped out at the site in anticipation of the event. One Los Angeles TV station KTLA had the intrepid idea to provide television viewers with the first-ever live broadcast of an atomic explosion. In 2013, journalist Richard Wirth, recalling the event wrote: "[A]ccording to *Broadcasting* magazine [Issue of April 28th, 1952], an estimated 5,000,000 viewers across the United States witnessed the awesome power of the detonation of an Atomic Bomb live in their living rooms" ("KTLA & the Atomic Bomb, Live," n.p.). With more than 5 million viewers looking on from the comfort of their living rooms, the atomic age was now a reality for all Americans.

Prior to the detonation, the media was given an advance countdown of 36 seconds as the bomb was released from an Air Force bomber at 9:30 A.M. (Pacific Time). As the KTLA TV camera focused on the explosion area, newscaster Gil Martyn began a calm count up starting with "1, 2, 3, . . ." Before reaching 36, the explosion happened at about 20 seconds. As the bright white flash was seen on the screen, Martyn went from calm to an excited, chilling, on-air professional description of the events unfolding before him. The television audience saw the live image in black and white while Martyn saw a vivid colorful reality and voiced over the following:

> There it is, that brilliant flash, that white light that precedes the explosion of the atomic bomb number seventeen. Forty miles away a brilliant white flash, almost blinding, with those rocket trails coming out of it, the fire is dying now, it is turning to a dull red, not quite the vivid orange and purple and green of past atomic bombs, but a beautiful sight. The typical funnel shaped rising into that giant mushroom cloud and now blossoming out [brief pause] like a big ball of cotton. An amazing sight even from forty miles away here as I adjust my glasses [binoculars]. It's taking on now a purplish hue as I'm bringing it into focus. There's still fire in the top of it, that Dante inferno red that I described before. And now the purple tinges are coming up, but this, ah this is different. This is not the typical giant mushroom shape of atomic bombs before. It has a typical mushroom shape, slightly, uh, doubling into a broader base and then narrowing down into that shot sand blast that is typical of all atomic bombs. This bomb is not mushroomy, as did the former ones. The one on April the twenty second, however, from where we stand here, forty miles away it does look as though it is more intense. So there seems to be more fire, more power in this particular bomb . . . And now it is, um, beginning to go into a totem pole effect. Again, losing that mushroom effect, quicker than it has ever before. This is more like a spouting geyser, a giant jet of water shooting up into the sky. But still retaining those [long pause] beautiful colors of purple, white, and mostly gray now as I see them through my glasses, um I can't see it through the naked eye, it's almost lost. But, I go back to my glasses and I'm still able to appreciate the beautiful colors. We did not [long pause] and now let me take you down to the base of the, uh, of the explosion. Here we see a typical kind of the shock wave that has spewed out the sand and this is the fireball rising, uh, thick at the bottom, narrowing somewhat. Narrowing again and then blossoming out [inaudible] . . . and now here comes the full effect of the mushroom. And I wouldn't be surprised if in a few seconds we get the full effect of the shockwave [inaudible] and we have not felt it up here at the 9,000-foot altitude and that's part that this bomb might have been exploded at a lower altitude [inaudible] It is still a gorgeous sight—a frightening sight that one should never forget. ("Atomic/ Nuclear Bomb Nevada Test - 5/1/1952")

The sight was indeed awe-inspiring. In retrospect, "a frightening sight" is the most accurate way of describing the event. Yet Martyn quickly changed course and added, "We are happy to be bringing to you on your television screens in its full glory." As the sounds in the background continually echoed the roar of thunderous explosion, Martyn provided a summation as: "an awe inspiring sight and a fearsome sight" ("Atomic/Nuclear Bomb Nevada Test - 5/1/1952").

As the majestic mushroom cloud was slowly about to begin its dissipation, he added a hopeful statement. Martyn ended his broadcast by saying it was a "fearsome creature that we sincerely hope will be used in a peaceful effort and not in other ways." But the atomic bombs soon gave way to hydrogen-type thermonuclear bombs with the intent of supplying the American military with weapons for a possible war with the Soviet Union.

The KTLA news crew was only one segment of a large contingent of reporters given access to witness the detonation. Another eyewitness was newspaper journalist Hugh Baillie of the *Las Vegas Sun*. He described the event for his readers as:

> Hell burst from the skies over Yucca Flat this morning as America's latest model atom bomb exploded with enough force to devastate much of New York, Chicago, Los Angeles or any other big city. The spectacular detonation, televised to a nationwide audience for the first time in history, was believed to have been at least as powerful as any exploded on the Nevada test site since it was activated 18 months ago. (Baillie, "TV Audience Views Atomic Bomb Test for First Time," n.p.)

Unlike the awe and spectacle of the later television broadcast, Baillie recognized the military connection of the atomic testing.

In fact, the experiment did have military implications. The purpose was for the Army to gather information on how quickly a ground force could move into the blast zone to secure the objective. Prior to the test, U.S. Army infantrymen were stationed in foxholes just four miles away from the blast site. At the time, so-called "radiological safety units" estimated that the minimum amount of waiting period before entering the blast zone was 58 minutes. Baillie knew of the deployment part of the test as he reported, "The atomic flash was spotted 430 miles away in southern Idaho, yet cocky GIs and grinning generals popped out of their foxholes within the shadow of the fearsome bomb less than ten seconds after it exploded." Some generals later assessed that the bomb was too big and deployment time could be reduced to about 30 minutes. The military summation was "that troops could more easily capture an enemy object if a smaller bomb was used." A spokesperson for the Army also disclosed that as part of the test, a deployment of 120 paratroopers were dropped into the explosion zone about one hour and 40 minutes after the detonation. Brigadier General Frank Dorn claimed, "Not a single hair was singed, a single neck twisted or a single head injured. The only 'casualties' were the fellows who got a mouth full of dirt when the bomb went off."

At the time, the only medical concern was for the physical appearance of either personal injury such as a radiation burn or physical property damage. No concern, or full knowledge, of the aftereffects of radiation fallout was either known or cause for concern. Some seismic effects were felt in Las Vegas, but the U.S. Army claimed "without any apparent damage." Seismic conditions were felt more than 200 miles west of Yucca Flat in Cedar City, Utah. Baillie reported:

> The blast, however, hit the community of Cedar City with tremendous force . . . who reported two earth shocks, each about five seconds apart, which approached the fifth magnitude of earthquake density. The waves struck about 14 minutes and 48 seconds after the initial blast. ("TV Audience Views Atomic Bomb Test for First Time," n.p.)

All sorts of disclaimers and documentary films provided information on how to safely "survive" a nuclear attack. The concern, however, was not about being vaporized in the initial explosion or even suffering burns from the blinding

Members of U.S. Army 11th Airborne Division at Frenchman's Flat in Nevada watch a mushroom cloud of an atomic bomb blast prior to entering into the test site. (Library of Congress)

flash. At the time, the nuclear fallout was either not known, or information was deliberately withheld from the public. At the time, simple protection was usually enough to just "duck and cover."

BERT THE TURTLE SAYS: "DUCK AND COVER"

Throughout the 1950s, Americans were constantly aware of the "threat" of a nuclear attack by the Soviet Union. In retrospect, we know that no attack ever happened. However, that did not lessen the fact that the "threat" was actually going to happen. With the aid of declassified documents, it is apparent that the event was highly unlikely because no critical situation arose that might have caused a war between the United States and the Soviets. One real showdown that did bring the United States close to the brink of using nuclear weapons was in 1962 during the Cuban Missile Crisis. During the 1950s, however, no event came as close.

For those young individuals coming of age in the 1950s, news of atomic bombs became a routine part of the American culture. Schoolchildren were regularly provided with helpful information to deal with a nuclear attack, similar to how later generations learned to practice for a fire drill evacuation. Information was distributed, mostly in the grade schools, through pamphlets and educational videos. In 1951, a 10-minute short documentary *Atomic Alert* was prepared by the Encyclopedia Britannica Film Division for viewing in the elementary schools. A significant portion of the film sought to explain the process of fission as well as detecting radiation by the use of a Geiger counter. The film also explained the precautionary steps for elementary schoolchildren to take in case of an atomic bomb alert. That alert would come by way of an air-raid siren alert and the children had to be prepared to "duck and cover." The premise of "duck and cover" was to avoid the blinding flash and also as protection against any shattered glass or other flying debris. The instructional film did provide valuable information, yet it was another educational film with a lovable turtle who is best remembered for delivering the message of "duck and cover."

In 1952, elementary school age children were introduced to the animated cartoon figure aptly named "Bert the Turtle." The short film *Duck and Cover* provided children with information on what to do in the event of a nuclear attack. Ye, it differed than the others in that *Duck and Cover* was embraced by schoolchildren who warmed to the lovable Bert the Turtle. The film was eventually distributed all throughout the nation and viewed by millions of children. Movie posters provided along with the film distribution announced Bert as the "Star of the Official U.S. Civil Defense Film." The film began with a smiling Bert, wearing an Army helmet, walking upright down a park-like path while a catchy tune is played in the background. The song lyrics were as follows:

> [Chorus] Dum, dum, deedle dum dum,
>
> Dum, dum, deedle dum dum,
>
> There was a turtle by the name of Bert,
>
> and Bert the turtle was very alert;
>
> when danger threatened him he never got hurt
>
> he knew just what to do . . . [Firecracker explodes]
>
> He'd duck and cover! Duck and cover!
>
> [Male singer] He did what we all must learn to do
>
> You, and you, and you, and you. [Another firecracker explosion]
>
> Duck, and cover! do, do, do, do, do, dah, do, do, do. [Song ends]

As Bert is huddled within the safety of his shell, an announcer, who replaced the singing chorus, said:

> [Announcer] Be sure and remember what Bert the Turtle does, dear friends,
>
> Because every one of us must remember to do the same thing.
>
> That's what this film is all about. "Duck and Cover."

[In a deeper, serious voice], another announcer read the following words which appeared on the screen:

[Announcer] This is an official Civil Defense film
produced in co-operation with the
Federal Civil Defense Administration
and in consultation with the safety
commission of the National Education
Association.
Produced by Archer Productions Incorporated.

The announcer asks Bert to come out and "greet the nice people." An ever-cautious Bert reaches out for his helmet, puts in on his head and carefully looks around. He realizes it is safe and comes out of his shell. At that point, the animation cuts away to a real-life schoolroom about to practice "duck and cover." Throughout the film, various scenes of "all-American" family life is shown, such as a picnic or schoolroom. From time to time, the activity is disrupted by an emergency call to respond. The announcer provides able commentary instructions on what to do depending upon time and location. But the most memorable was Bert and his parting words of remembrance.

[Bert asks] "Tell me, what are you supposed to do when you see the flash?"
[Children shout] "Duck and Cover."
[Bert retreats into his turtle shell]

At the time, some critics claimed that telling schoolchildren the truth that "an atomic bomb is very dangerous" was scaring them. In deference to the children, the producers never did show an actual atomic explosion. But in reality, the entire Civil Defense program was predicated upon keeping an entire nation in a constant state of fear and readiness for an atomic attack. *Duck and Cover* did receive a "stamp of approval" from all the Civil Defense federal agencies including the National Education Association. With the release of *Duck and Cover*, Archer Productions also prepared an explanatory booklet with

In 1952, millions of American schoolchildren were introduced to the animated figure "Bert the Turtle" in the short film, *Duck and Cover*. In the educational film, Bert provided helpful information on what to do in the event of a nuclear attack. As explained by Bert the Turtle, to survive an atomic attack you must "duck and cover." (Photofest)

information provided by the Civil Defense Administration. The booklet *Duck and Cover: Introducing Bert the Turtle* was dated February 7, 1952. and authored by Milt Mohr. To alleviate any problem that might be associated with bringing the subject matter to children, Mohr wrote:

> What makes this motion picture singular from previous treatment on the atomic subject is the fact that the film warns, but does not frighten . . . [it] teaches, but does not alarm.

Yet the critics were in fact seeking the truth be told about the futility of any nuclear attack. In turn, any speaking of the "truth" during the 1950s was quickly quieted by claims of it being Communist inspired. One rebuttal came within a few months after the release of *Duck and Cover*. In May 1952, a Civil Defense public information officer for Nassau County, New York, named Forrest E. Corson, issued the following statement:

> It is unfortunate that the critics of *Duck and Cover*, in their misapprehension over the psychological effect of the film on schoolchildren, are unwittingly following the Communist party line laid down in their official publications. It is the Communist policy to deride Civil Defense wherever possible, to question and ridicule its necessity, and to "abhor" the effect of "air raid drills on tender impressionable young minds." (Quotes are from the *Daily Worker*.) I am sure that all thinking parents want their children to be prepared for catastrophe. It is exactly what Civil Defense is trying to do.

The debate subsided quickly, as did just about any that challenged the American patriotic mission of building nuclear weapons of such mass destruction capable of eliminating all humankind from the planet Earth. Those anti-war and anti-nuclear protests would be more prevalent in the subsequent decades.

After *Duck and Cover*, dozens of other educational films about atomic warfare and thermonuclear destruction were produced. Yet of all the other Civil Defense films, Bert the Turtle became the lasting and most endearing image. The impact of both Bert and *Duck and Cover* was significant enough for preservation. In 2004, *Duck and Cover* was one of 25 films added to the National Film Registry. (See Film chapter.) In naming the film for preservation for future American generations, the short synopsis reads:

> *Duck and Cover*—This landmark civil defense film was seen by millions of schoolchildren in the 1950s. As explained by Bert the Turtle, to survive an atomic attack you must "duck and cover."

The selection of *Duck and Cover* was in line with the National Film Registry's mission to choose "films that continue to have cultural, historical, or aesthetic significance."

THE UNITED STATES ATOMIC ENERGY COMMISSION

The nearby, growing gambling mecca of Las Vegas experienced two phenomena from the ongoing series of atomic tests at Yucca Flat. First off, many of the hotels found an economic benefit by advertising special package deals with roof-top access to witness an atomic explosion. In contrast, many of the residents and building owners of the city felt "seismic effects" after an atomic test. Some building owners reported broken glass and some other damages, prompting the U.S. Atomic Energy Commission to set up claim stations for reimbursement.

JOINT TEST ORGANIZATION
CAMP MERCURY, NEVADA

February, 1955

A MESSAGE TO PEOPLE WHO LIVE
NEAR NEVADA TEST SITE:

You are in a very real sense active participants in the Nation's atomic test program. You have been close observers of tests, which have contributed greatly to building the defenses of our own country and of the free world. Nevada tests have helped us come a long way in a few, short years and have been a vital factor in maintaining the peace of the world. They also provide important data for use in planning civil defense measures to protect our people in event of enemy attack.

Same of you have been inconvenienced by our test operations. At times some of you have been exposed to potential risk from flash, blast, or fall-out. You have accepted the inconvenience or the risk without fuss, without alarm, and without panic. Your cooperation has helped achieve an unusual record of safety.

In a world in which free people have no atomic monopoly, we must keep our atomic strength at peak level. Time is a key factor in this task and Nevada tests help us "buy" precious time.

That is why we must hold new tests in Nevada.

I want you to know that in the forthcoming series, as has been true in the past, each shot is justified by national and international security need and that none will be fired unless there is adequate assurance of public safety.

We are grateful for your continued cooperation and your understanding.

James E. Reeves
Test Manager

Chart 3.1

ATOMIC TEST EFFECTS
IN THE
NEVADA TEST SITE REGION

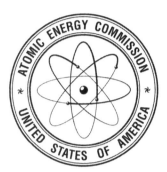

UNITED STATES
ATOMIC ENERGY COMMISSION
JANUARY 1955

TABLE OF CONTENTS

Chart 3.1 (*Continued*)

The Record of Past Tests

Thirty-one atomic fission weapons, weapon prototypes, or experimental devices were fired in Nevada from January 1951 to January 1955. All were relatively small in explosive power. . . . . compared to the tremendous forces released by the large fission and hydrogen weapons tested in the Pacific. So-called "H-bombs" are not tested in Nevada. . . .

Despite their relatively low yield, Nevada tests have clearly demonstrated their value to all national atomic weapons programs. . . . . Because of them our Armed Forces are stronger and our Civil Defense better prepared.

Each Nevada test has successfully added to scientific knowledge needed for development and for use of atomic weapons, and needed to strengthen our defense against enemy weapons.

Staging of some tests in Nevada, instead of carrying out all of them in the distant Pacific, also resulted in major savings in time, the most important factor, and in manpower, and money.

An unusual safety record has been set. No one inside Nevada test site has been injured as a result of the 31 test detonations. No one outside the test site in the nearby region of potential exposure has been hurt.

There were instances of property damage from blast, such as broken windows. Some cattle and horses grazing within a few miles of the detonations suffered skin deep radiation burns, but the damage had no effect on their breeding value nor the beef quality of the cattle.

THE SPRING 1955 TEST SERIES

The new series, scheduled to begin in mid-February, will conform generally with the pattern of the Spring 1953 series in Nevada. . . . Those who live near the test site know that experience . . . Any atomic detonation, even though small enough to be fired in Nevada, involves powerful forces. The low level of public exposure to the off-site effects of Nevada detonations has been made possible by very close attention to a variety of on-site and off-site procedures. . . . There will, however, always remain a possibility of off-site effects from flash, blast, and radioactive fall-out. The potential exposure of the public will be low and it can be reduced still further by continued public cooperation.

Chart 3.1 (*Continued*)

Exposure to Flash

If you look directly into the sun or at a photographer's flash bulb, you get black spots in front of your eyes and you can't see for a few seconds or a few minutes. If you were much closer to the sun or if you used binoculars, greater eye damage might result. Common sense precautions will protect your eyes from the bright flash of an atomic test.

On-site the thermal (heat) waves which accompany flash can injure eye tissues and cause permanent eye damage if the eye looks directly at the fireball. This is also true in the air immediately above the test site. At shot time all personnel on or above the test site wear extremely dark glasses or turn away; binoculars are prohibited; and road traffic is halted.

Off-site the flash can cause "black spots", so that momentarily you can't see . . . The greatest caution needs to be used by drivers of vehicles or the pilots or aircraft who might easily have an accident if momentarily unable to see, or if they were simply startled.

The brightness of the light striking your eyes depends, of course, on whether it is day or night, whether there is direct line of sight to the fireball, on distance, on atmospheric conditions, and to some extent on the power of a detonation. . . .

Off-Site Warnings and Procedures for Flash

Casual or commercial air flight above the test site is prohibited. The CAA will try to stop air traffic within the surrounding area up to 80 miles . . . . If a shot is postponed every effort will be made by radio and highway patrol to advise you so that you may proceed, or may know if it will be fired at a later time.

Chart 3.1 (*Continued*)

THE SOUND OR BLAST

The Phenomenon of Blast

Shock waves go out in all directions from the detonation. Some strike the earth and are dissipated. Some bounce back to earth from various atmospheric layers. If they reach earth at an inhabited point they may be felt or heard.

... Waves propagated through the troposphere (up to 6 miles high) cause sharp cracks and bangs in the nearby site region. Off-site damage to buildings or windows within 100 miles has resulted only from waves in the troposphere. ... Inasmuch as there is a possibility of jarring blast, which can break windows, on any Nevada shot, the effect should be anticipated for every shot and precautions taken throughout the nearby region.

Off-Site Warnings and Procedures for Blast

The Test Organization has a major safety program for anticipating where blast may strike. ... When a possibility of light damage to any community is indicated, the community is warned to open windows and doors to equalize pressure.

The warning procedure, coming as it usually must only a few minutes before shot time and usually in predawn hours when people are asleep, is not fully effective.

The most effective precaution is for you in the nearby region to anticipate blast from every shot and to take simple measures such as opening windows and doors. Persons driving or sitting in automobiles should open the car windows. Another simple precaution is not to stay near large glass windows at shot time.

The scheduled date of each shot, and usually its scheduled hour, will be announced.

Chart 3.1 (*Continued*)

FALL-OUT FROM THE ATOMIC CLOUD

We cannot see, feel, nor hear radiation and consequently it is more difficult for the public to understand than are light and sound waves from Nevada tests. In order to help you comprehend the phenomenon of radioactive fall-out, we have appended to this booklet a discussion of natural radiation, of how we measure radiation, of how it affects people . . . The appendix includes a discussion of the guide which will be used by the Test Organization in its efforts to hold any public exposure to a minimum.

The Atomic Cloud

At the instant of detonation, very powerful radiation is released in the firing area very close to the burst. . . .
As the fireball rises and forms the atomic cloud, dirt and debris are sucked up, become radioactive, and immediately start falling. . . .

The heaviest fall-out of radioactive particles is in the firing area. The area of quite heavy fall-out may extend several miles from ground zero . . .

As the cloud moves on, it becomes dispersed and usually within a few hours is no longer visible, having spread into an air mass. With each minute, its radioactivity loses strength.

Even though the cloud becomes invisible, it can be traced by the trail it leaves in the air and on the ground beneath it. . . . It does not constitute a serious hazard to any living thing outside the test site.

Chart 3.1 (*Continued***)**

Controls, Warnings and Procedures
Related to Radiation Fall-out

Every practical control and procedure is followed by the Test Organization to keep off-site fall-out at a minimum level.

. . . Additional limitations have been placed on the yield of shots to be fired under various circumstances. For instance, some shots will be fired from 500-foot towers solely to decrease the amount of radioactive fall-out off-site. . . . Your best action is not to be worried about fall-out.

TESTS AND THE WEATHER

You have lived next door to the test site long enough to know that weather is very important to us. We sometimes wait for days and days until the right weather comes along so that we can fire a shot. We don't create weather; we use it as it goes by.

. . . The U. S. Weather Bureau experts, and those in our Armed Forces, have reviewed all of the facts during the last year and a half and they have found no indication at all that Nevada tests change the weather anywhere in any respect.

APPENDIX
GUIDES TO UNDERSTANDING FALL-OUT

What Radiation Does to People

Uncontrolled radiation, like uncontrolled fire or carelessly used electricity, can be very dangerous. It does different things to people depending upon what kind it is and upon the amount to which a person is exposed. . . . But, overexposure to radiation can cause injury.

Similarly, the sun will give you a pleasant suntan, but if you are overexposed it can burn the skin and make you quite sick. . . .

The Range From Harmless to Serious Exposures

The body may safely receive considerably greater doses of radiation because the effects are repaired almost as rapidly as they are produced. . . .

Radiation exposure of the public is, however, different from that which atomic workers voluntarily accept. It is involuntary. The numbers of people involved may become large, and there is no discrimination as to age or occupational relationship. The population includes pregnant women, young children, and many persons in the active child bearing age. Exposure which the public should be asked to accept involuntarily should be--and is--lower than that atomic workers accept voluntarily.

For this reason, the Atomic Energy Commission has established a much lower guide for future Nevada test operations. It is essentially one-fourth the guide used for atomic test workers. The standard to be used will be 3.9 r. in 1 year, instead of a like total in 13 weeks.

Chart 3.1 (*Continued*)

To waylay any fears, "official" correspondence from the U.S. government provided informational pamphlets, booklets, and film documentaries on how to deal with atomic energy as part of everyday public life. One example was a booklet dated January 1955, carrying the official seal of the U.S. Atomic Energy Commission, that provided answers to many of the most commonly asked questions. The booklet accompanied by a letter from the "Joint Test Organization" located at Camp Mercury, Nevada, served as a public announcement aimed at the residents of Nevada and its surrounding region. An edited version of the booklet appears as follows:

THERMONUCLEAR AND HYDROGEN BOMBS

In 1952, the first tactical nuclear bomb placed in active U.S. military service was the Mark-7 atomic bomb. Nicknamed "Thor," the MK-7 was a nuclear fission "atomic" bomb carried on external under-wing mounts of fighter aircraft. From 1952 to 1963, over 1,700 were made with an increasing yield from different models that varied from 8 kilotons (kt), 19 kt, 22 kt, 30 kt, and finally an astounding 61 kt. The MK-7 series remained in active service until 1967, longer than any other tactical bomb in the entire U.S. nuclear arsenal. Fighter aircraft such as the F-84, F-100, and F-101 deployed by both U.S. Air Force and Navy jet fighters carried these weapons as easily as the smaller-type impact bombs of the Second World War. The MK-7 could also be carried inside the bomb bay compartments of larger bombers such as the B-57. (A defused casing of an MK-7 can be seen at the Wings over the Rockies Museum in Denver, Colorado.)

With a continuing fear of Communism and paranoia of a nuclear attack from the Soviets, the way to fight the new "Red Menace" was often answered with the need to build more powerful atomic weapons. (Scientists termed the pursuit of a more powerful nuclear weapon as "The Super.") Yet with the physical knowledge of the destructive powers as evidenced by the two bombs dropped on Hiroshima and Nagasaki, many scientists often spoke out against the dangers of larger weapons. Undeterred, the United States government proceeded forward and enlisted the aid of scientists willing to undertake the challenge. The result was a "Thermonuclear Bomb" (often called a "Hydrogen Bomb"). The misleading term applied throughout history as a "Hydrogen Bomb," or "H-bomb," was spread by media accounts unaware of the exact technicalities of the newer devices. Because the fusion in the thermonuclear bombs included hydrogen isotopes, the media sources called it a Hydrogen Bomb.

As a nuclear weapon similar to an atomic bomb the H-bomb also created energy, but from two different sources. The first source of energy was created from a similar nuclear fission reaction as in the atomic weapons. In the thermonuclear device, the primary fission reaction was used to "ignite a secondary nuclear fusion reaction." The simplest definition provided by *Merriam-Webster* dictionary describes *fission* as an action that causes the "dividing or splitting something into two or more parts." Similarly, yet slightly different, *fusion* is "the process or result of joining two or more things together to form a single entity." As for a description of a thermonuclear fusion bomb, an explanation as provided by the curators at the Wings over the Rockies Museum is as follows:

Thermonuclear weapons derive their explosive energy from the combined power of nuclear fission (a nuclear reaction in which an atomic nucleus splits into fragments) and fusion. An initial fission reaction generates the high temperatures needed to trigger a secondary—and much more powerful—fusion reaction. A fusion reaction is usually started with a fission reaction, but unlike the fission (atomic) bomb, the fusion (hydrogen) bomb derives its power from the fusing of nuclei of various hydrogen isotopes into helium nuclei.

The result of this combination of fission and fusion was an increased explosive power when compared to the single-stage fission atomic weapons of that had been made in the previous five to 10 years.

American experimentation for a "deliverable" thermonuclear/hydrogen bomb was proven a reality in March 1954 at the Bikini Islands in the Pacific Ocean. The South Pacific area, about halfway between the Philippines and the Hawaiian Islands, was not a new nuclear testing site. In early 1946, the United States sanctioned nuclear testing at the Bikini Islands, called "Operation Crossroads." Those atomic bombs were the fourth and fifth, respectively, that were ever detonated after the first at the Trinity Site in New Mexico and the two on Hiroshima and Nagasaki. Other nuclear testing continued at the Eniwetok Atoll as well as the New Mexico and Nevada deserts. All of these test sites were designated as U.S. military "Proving Grounds." As with all of the atomic or thermonuclear tests, each was given a code name. The tests conducted at the Bikini Atoll within the Marshall Islands in the South Pacific, as one example, was given the code name "Operation Castle." Each of the six tests was given an individual code name beginning with the word "castle." One of the tests, "Castle Bravo" (the first of the six) was the first successful test of a "dry fuel" thermonuclear bomb that could be delivered by an aircraft.

The Castle Bravo explosion was expected to yield somewhere in the magnitude of 6 megatons. (A megaton is equal to one million pounds of TNT.) Upon detonation, the actual explosion was much larger than anticipated, at a yield of 15 megatons. From one perspective, the high yield was a pleasant surprise. From the more practical concern for humanity, it was catastrophic. Declassified military reports rate it as "the most significant accidental radioactive contamination ever caused by the United States." The term "accidental" is debatable, as the U.S. military was aware of the radioactive "burns" from studying survivors of Hiroshima and Nagasaki. The radioactive fallout from Castle Bravo spread out over an area of 6,800 to 7,000 square miles. The fallout affected not only the inhabitants of neighboring islands, but also the American military personnel taking part in the tests and occupants of a nearby Japanese fishing boat. (A 1955 *New York Times* article provided a comparison of the destructive force of the Bikini Atoll test explosion. The story explained that the 7,000 square mile range of the blast "would have killed virtually every exposed person in an area about the size of New Jersey.") For many years after the test, all sorts of strange and horrible disfigurements were recorded due to the radioactive fallout of Castle Bravo. Of immediate concern, radioactive fallout from the event was also detected in many other parts of the world and led to international discord. Some of that discussion took place in the newly formed United Nations while others protested for nuclear disarmament ("Highway History: Civil Defense, 1955," n.p.).

THE CAMPAIGN FOR NUCLEAR DISARMAMENT
AND THE PEACE SYMBOL

Protests demanding nuclear disarmament began throughout America and other NATO countries including Great Britain. One result from the growing number of people protesting against the catastrophic implications of not just building but also using nuclear weapons was one of the world's best-known icons—the peace symbol. In 1958, a symbol of protest for nuclear disarmament became universally known as the "peace symbol." A professional designer and a conscientious objector during World War II named Gerald Holtom designed the symbol in England. Holtom, who opted to work on a farm rather than enter military service, had allied with a local peace group called the Campaign for Nuclear Disarmament (CND).

In preparing a logo for the group, Holtom combined the letters "N' and "D" from the position taken from semaphore flag symbols used by naval personnel to transmit information from ship to ship. Each position of the flags represented a single letter. He created a logo by using single line strokes within a circle, thus combining the downward "V" with a perpendicular straight line. When overlapped and placed within the circle he therefore created one of the best-known symbols throughout the world. In the United Kingdom it was recognized as the logo for the CND, whereas in America it was widely known as a universal peace symbol. Holtom later explained that his inspiration came from an 1814 painting by Francisco Goya titled *The Third of May 1808* that protested Napoleon's occupation of Spain. Holtom wrote to one journalist and explained.

> I was in despair. Deep despair. I drew myself: the representative of an individual in despair, with hands [and] palm outstretched outwards and downwards in the manner of Goya's peasant before the firing squad. I formalized the drawing into a line and put a circle round it. ("Origin of the Peace Symbol," n.p.)

Goya's famous painting is widely hailed as a continued source of Spanish national pride. The main focus is upon a Spanish guerilla fighter standing defiantly upright while facing a French army firing squad. The Spaniard has his arms outstretched and slightly angled upward. Therefore, Holtom's remembrance of the painting might have been a little confused. His statement of "outstretched outwards and downwards" is incorrect. Goya's figure does in fact have his hands "outstretched outwards," but they are upward not downward. Nevertheless, the inspiration was true to both instances. Whereas Goya's resistance stood up in the face of overwhelming odds, the anti-nuclear peace movement was willing to stand up and do the same. As Holtom's logo was widely accepted in Britain, it gained recognition in other countries. An aide to the Reverend Martin Luther King, who took part in the anti-nuclear protest marches in England, brought a copy of the symbol back to America. It was then adopted for the civil rights marches during the late 1950s and thereafter as an anti-war protest symbol against the Vietnam War during the 1960s and into the 1970s. The overall hope of the movement was to eradicate any and all devices that relied on nuclear energy ("Origin of the Peace Symbol," n.p.).

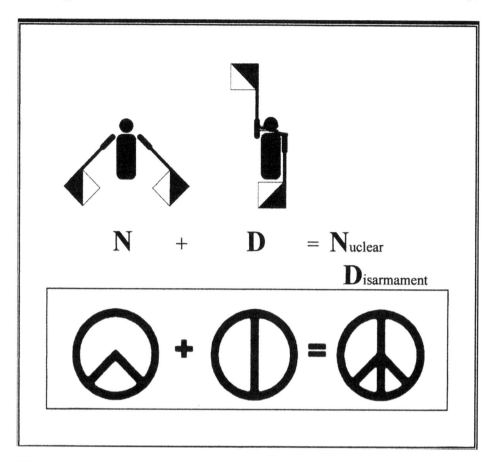

Chart 3.2

PRESIDENT EISENHOWER AND "ATOMS FOR PEACE"

President Eisenhower, the former supreme allied commander during World War II, was concerned over the possibility of "atomic warfare" teetering on the brink of human annihilation. Therefore, on December 8, 1953, Eisenhower spoke on the use of "Atoms for Peace" to an international meeting of the General Assembly of the United Nations in New York City:

> I feel impelled to speak today in a language that in a sense is new—one which I, who have spent so much of my life in the military profession, would have preferred never to use. That new language is the language of atomic warfare . . . My country wants to be constructive, not destructive. It wants agreement, not wars, among nations. It wants itself to live in freedom, and in the confidence that the people of every other nation enjoy equally the right of choosing their own way of life. . . . To the making of these fateful decisions, the United States pledges before you—and therefore before the world—its determination to help solve the fearful atomic dilemma—to devote its entire heart and mind to find the way by which the miraculous inventiveness of man shall not be dedicated to his death, but consecrated to his life. ("Atoms for Peace," n.p.)

As a result of the UN speech, a government-funded program was launched to supply public information on nuclear energy and atomic warfare.

On the surface it appeared that the message of peace was for the good of the American people, but rather it was an American Cold War propaganda campaign of "balancing fears of continuing nuclear armament with promises of peaceful use of uranium in future nuclear reactors." To the unsuspecting public and the UN, Eisenhower appeared to be making a call for worldwide peaceful co-existence in the use of atomic energy. For some countries, the United States supplied not only information, but also built the facilities in foreign countries. As part of that campaign, an American company built nuclear reactors in Pakistan, Israel, and Iran.

BUILDING A THERMONUCLEAR ARSENAL

The detonation at Castle Bravo produced an initial "fireball" explosion measuring more than four miles across followed by the familiar sight of a "mushroom cloud." The burst was visible more than 250 miles away on neighboring islands and the distinctive cloud rose to above 47,000 feet in about one minute. The magnitude of the blast in the first minute was certainly a formidable sight, but it was not over. Within the next 10 minutes, the blast cloud climbed to over 130,000 feet and expanded to a diameter of over 62 miles.

Despite the fact that the detonation of the thermonuclear bomb at the Bikini Islands Atoll was the single-largest explosion in the history of America, it was not the largest ever. The largest-known explosive nuclear device ever detonated belonged to the Soviet Union. In comparison, the American bomb detonated at the Bikini Atoll was about one-third the power of the Soviet bomb. On October 30, 1961, the Soviets detonated RDS-220, more commonly known as the "Tsar Bomba." Only one was known to be built and was exploded in the upper northern reaches of the Arctic Circle in the Novaya Zemlya archipelago of the USSR. The bomb was dropped from a Russian TU-95 bomber and slowed down in its descent by a large parachute allowing the piloted aircraft to fly away to a safe distance before the detonation. Film of the actual Tsar Bomba can be seen in the documentary *Trinity and Beyond: The Atomic Bomb Movie* (Visual Concept Entertainment, 1995). The film also contains actual film footage of the development of all nuclear bombs from the Trinity test site through 1992.

The explosion of the Soviet Tsar Bomba was rated at 50 megatons (equal to 50,000 kilotons) and spewed a unique circular cloud that reached upwards of 35 miles into the sky and was seen hundreds of miles away. U.S. Army reports placed the explosion power of the Tsar Bomba at the equivalent of 3,800 Hiroshima bombs. As astounding and unimaginable of the devastation that a bomb of that size could have created, it was even more powerful than the measured explosion. Apparently, the Soviet bomb was a three-stage explosive device of which only two of the stages were detonated, producing the 50-megaton yield. If the third stage of the bomb was released it would have produced a yield of an astounding 100 megatons (Scharf, "Dragon M65 Atomic Annie," 59).

The United States had a comparable two-stage weapon with a much lesser yield than the Soviet Tsar Bomba. One of the mainstays of the American nuclear

COMPARATIVE NUCLEAR BOMB CHART

TSAR BOMBA

CASTLE BRAVO

HIROSHIMA

Ground Level   Ground Level

The above chart indicates the comparative size between the 1945 Atomic Bomb dropped on Hiroshima with the 1954 U.S. Castle Bravo test and the 1961 Soviet test of the Tsar Bomba. Drawing by: Author.

Chart 3.3

arsenal was the 10-megaton MK-36 nuclear bomb. It was an upgraded version of the TX-21 "Shrimp" tested as part of Operation Castle. As a two-stage ther-monuclear weapon, the MK-36 created explosive power from a multi-stage fusion system. From 1956 to 1958, military contractors made a total of 940 MK-36 type bombs. During that production run another 275 of the MK-21 types were converted to meet the MK-36 specifications. At the time, the MK-36 was the main weapon for the U.S. Air Force representing about half of the entire U.S. nuclear weaponry. Similar to other thermonuclear bombs of the period it was designed to be dropped by a bomber such as the B-47 Stratojet, B-52 Stratofortress, B-58 Hustler, and B-36 Peacemaker. By the beginning of 1962, the MK-36 was replaced by the MK-41 with a yield of 25-, according to the Wings Over the Rockies Museum website.

The United States military also tested other options to deliver a nuclear device rather than by aircraft. Tests were also successful from a tractor-trailer driven mobile artillery unit. On May 25, 1953, an artillery shell with an atomic warhead was loaded into a 280mm long-range cannon and fired at the Nevada Proving Grounds. (Declassified film footage of the cannon is included in *Trinity and Beyond*.) Only 20 of the M65 mobile artillery type were built, but they remained a viable option for military ground forces until 1963 (Scharf, "Dragon M65 Atomic Annie").

"UNDERWAY ON NUCLEAR POWER"

The U.S. military desire to capitalize on delivering nuclear devices in as many ways possible extended to experimenting with launching a missile from a submarine. The diesel and battery powered submarines from the Second World War were not adaptable; therefore, they were replaced by new submarines powered by nuclear energy. In July 1951, the United States Congress approved appropriations for a submarine designed and built from the keel up, completely powered by nuclear energy. The "Atom Sub," as it was called at the time, relied on a nuclear power propulsion plant. The power plant was a Submarine Thermal Reactor (STR) later redesignated S2W (Submarine, Model 2,

USS *Nautilus* (SS-571), the Navy's first atomic-powered submarine on its initial sea trials enters New York City harbor in May 1956. (Library of Congress)

Westinghouse) designed by a joint group of scientists and engineers at the Naval Reactors Branch of the Atomic Energy Commission. On June 14, 1952, President Truman presided over a keel-laying ceremony at the Electric Boat Division of General Dynamics Corporation in Groton, Connecticut. The Groton shipyard had been building war-ready submarines since the very first purchased by the U.S. Navy in 1900. Footage at the time of commissioning provided by a Universal Studios newsreel called the submarine "a revolutionary chapter of the atomic age."

As the USS *Nautilus* left for its first mission on January 17, 1955, Commander Eugene P. Wilkinson radioed what would be a historical first: "Underway on nuclear power." Over the next few years, just about every mission set a new record for submarines including speed, distance, and submerged depth. Another historic first occurred during a top-secret mission with the code name "Operation Sunshine." The sub left from Pearl Harbor Naval Base in Hawaii on July 23, 1958, and the mission was accomplished on August 3, 1958, as the *Nautilus* became the first ship of any kind to cross the geographic North Pole. Commander William R. Anderson announced to his crew, "For the world, our Country, and the Navy—the North Pole." The implication from a military standpoint was that deployment of a military submarine could approach the Soviet Union from a much shorter distance than traveling the circumference of the globe.

By mid-1959, other nuclear-powered U.S. submarines had the ability to deliver and launch Polaris-type missiles with nuclear warheads. The first deployment of an operational Intercontinental Ballistic Missile (ICBM) was on October 31, 1959. As a result, by 1960, the United States had far-ranging nuclear capabilities well beyond anything imagined in 1950. The USS *Nautilus* remained in active service until 1980. On March 3, 1980, SSN-571 was officially decommissioned after traveling more than half a million miles. In May 1982, the *Nautilus* was designated as a national historic landmark and received a "historic ship" restoration at Mare Island Naval Shipyard in California. In 1985, the submarine, which had previously traveled by nuclear power, was towed to the Submarine Force Museum located where the ship was first built in Groton, Connecticut ("History of the *USS Nautilus*," n.p.).

POLIO: A "REAL THREAT" WITH A REAL CURE

Unlike the constant fictional fear of "subversive Communists" or an imminent Soviet attack, one of the most prevalent real threats to the American public during the 1950s was polio. For the most part, it was an acceptable part of American life with no known cure. The New York State Department of Health defines it this way:

> Polio is a viral disease, which may affect the spinal cord causing muscle weakness and paralysis. The poliovirus enters the body through the mouth, usually from hands contaminated with the stool of an infected person.

The medical term is "poliomyelitis," more commonly known as "infantile paralysis" because it was most prevalent in infants and younger children.

When adults were stricken, it was usually contracted when an infection was present. Many millions throughout history were affected, either mildly or severely, by the poliovirus. The most famous victim was former President Franklin D. Roosevelt. At the time, Roosevelt, like so many other polio victims, kept the affliction hidden from the public.

Two prominent entertainers of the 1950s who were polio victims were pop singer Dinah Shore (1916–1994) and teen idol Ray Peterson (1935–2005). Shore's popularity as a singer extended from the early 1940s into the 1950s. She was also in a few Hollywood movies and later became a prominent TV host. Peterson, called one of the "Golden Voices" of the Rock 'n' Roll era, signed a major contract with RCA Victor Records in 1957. He had a few charted hits such as "Goodnight My Love" and "Tell Laura, I Love Her," but his major success was the song "The Wonder of You." That song placed on the Billboard Top 30 chart in mid-1959. It became most famous as a signature song for Elvis Presley who recorded a similar arrangement and released it as single in 1970. The two pop icons of the 1950s later became close friends.

Of all the polio victims, it was President Franklin D. Roosevelt who first advanced the fight to find a cure for polio. In 1937, he said only a complete "conquest of the disease" was acceptable. To further the cause for a cure, he announced the formation of a National Foundation for Infantile Paralysis (NFIP) to "lead, direct, and unify the fight of every phase of this sickness." Soon thereafter, the NFIP acquired an easily recognizable nickname as the popular comedian and radio personality Eddie Cantor made a plea not for dollars but dimes. He asked his millions of listeners to "send their dimes directly to the President at the White House." He added, "We could call it the March of Dimes" (Rose, "A History of the March of Dimes," n.p.).

Although poliovirus was a common affliction, there was a steady, visible rise in the number of cases from 1945 to 1955. Those years coincided with the sudden rapid rise in the American birth rate known as the "Baby Boom." In simple terms, as the number of births increased so did a comparable percentage of those born with the poliovirus. It was not confined just to newborns; children and adults were also affected in larger quantities than ever before. In 1952, the worst ever recorded polio epidemic year, more than 3,000 Americans of all ages died from the virus. In addition, hundreds of thousands were either partially crippled or completely incapacitated. The poliovirus was not the only epidemic of the decade. Other devastating epidemics included a 1950 tuberculosis outbreak that resulted in 34,000 deaths. In 1957, an outbreak of influenza caused the death of more than 62,000 people. In comparison, the number of polio deaths was not as great. But millions of individuals who survived lived a life limited by various degrees of paralysis.

During a polio epidemic, public places were routinely closed. Those who were incapacitated were confined to a home or an institution in a device known as an "iron lung." Similar to an incubator, it was a large tank respirator in which the entire body was encased with only the patient's head exposed. The device was intended to aid in the patient's breathing with a hope of clearing the lungs of mucus. Many hospitals were reluctant to provide treatment using the tank respirators because it was usually considered short-term care. In essence, a patient

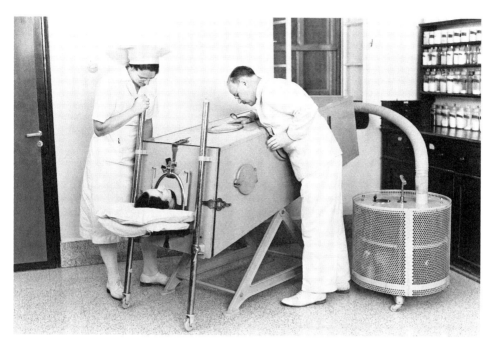

An "Iron Lung" breathing machine in a missionary hospital. Some incapacitated patients were homebound in a device known as an "iron lung." Similar to an incubator, it was a tank respirator to aid in the patient's breathing with a hope of clearing the lungs of mucus. (Library of Congress)

who needed a tank respirator was immobilized and was permanently confined indoors.

For those not totally incapacitated, aid was available through the use of crutches, metal leg braces, and wheelchairs. During the 1952 outbreak, those devices were in short supply and therefore even mild cases were confined to the home. In addition, very few if any public accommodations existed for individuals with any type of disability. (The United States-mandated Americans with Disabilities Act (ADA) did not become law until 1990.) At the time, all sorts of barriers such as steps, public bathrooms, swimming pools, movie theaters, and all other places of public accommodation existed that restricted access for a person on crutches, in braces, or in a wheelchair. American culture of the 1950s did not overtly promote compassion for any person who was deemed different or viewed as not capable of being useful to society. In fact, the defined "difference" also included Negroes, Hispanics, Italians, Jews, Atheists, workingwomen, unwed mothers, homosexuals, or basically any non-conformist, among many others. To add further insult, those persons labeled as different were routinely subjected to derogatory terms. Disabled individuals, for example, were often called "retarded," "crippled," or just "handicapped."

That opportunity to eradicate polio was provided on April 12, 1955, as Dr. Jonas Salk engaged in a long televised interview with host Edward R. Murrow on his CBS-TV *See It Now* program. Murrow's audience allowed millions of viewers to be aware of the available vaccine. As to the cost that any American might need to pay for this "miracle cure," Murrow asked the fateful question, "Who owns the patent on this vaccine?" Salk's simple response was, "Well, the people, I would say. There is no patent. Could you patent the sun?"

By the time of the news conference, Salk had performed years of painstaking research. Over the course of eight years, he was not alone, as he logged information from more than 200,000 volunteers, 20,000 physicians, and dozens of public health officers. Once a workable vaccine was developed, a test group was organized. On April 24, 1954, testing began on 650,000 children who received the vaccine, and another 1.18 million received a placebo. Salk's former teacher Thomas Francis oversaw administration of the program. Management of such a large-scale project included more than 150,000 volunteers in over 15,000 schools and coordination with Department of Health organizations in 44 states across the United States. The official historic date of "finding the cure" was listed as April 12, 1955, as Francis announced to a packed room of journalists, "The vaccine works. It is safe, effective, and potent" (Markel, "The Day Polio Began Losing Its Grip on America").

In 1956, Albert Sabin developed an oral polio vaccine and the disease was virtually eliminated from American society. (The last reported "natural case" in the United States was in 1979, and most of the worldwide cases were also eliminated.) Unknown to a large segment of the late 20th century and 21st century population was not necessarily the fact that the poliovirus was no longer a common part of American life, but rather that it still existed. The success of the vaccine by Jonas Salk and Albert Sabine was given to every newborn in America and in many nations throughout the world. Simply put, each newborn baby received the polio vaccine (IPV) as part of a child's series of immunizations during early development. Therefore, the poliovirus was not evident, but without a continuous vaccination and immunization program it could easily return. Salk's work was not complete as he secured funding by the late 1950s to build the Salk Institute for Biological Studies, which opened in 1963 in La Jolla, California. The research institute, designed by renowned American architect Louis Kahn, is considered one of the greatest works in architectural history—both aesthetically and ideologically.

SPUTNIK, EXPLORER, AND THE RACE FOR SPACE

By the mid-1950s, Americans began exploring the outer reaches of space. A major reason was to find an opportunity to deliver nuclear warheads by intercontinental ballistic missiles. At the beginning, the program could best be described as "infantile." The first step was to launch an artificial satellite into space orbit. In response, two different programs operated in separate joint ventures. One joint venture was between the U.S. Navy and the National Academy of Sciences known as *Vanguard*. The other was the Army Ballistic Missile Agency (ABMA) and the Jet Propulsion Laboratory (JPL) known as the "ABMA-JPL," which produced *Explorer*. The *Vanguard* design was selected in 1955 and mounted on a Viking-type rocket. The Navy design was chosen solely on the fact that the *Vanguard* did not interfere "with the high-priority military missile programs." By

1957, as the *Vanguard* was approaching a test launch, the Soviets surprised the world with a successful launch of their own (Bilstein, *"Orders of Magnitude,"* n.p.).

On October 4, 1957, the Soviet Union placed the first artificial satellite in outer space called *Sputnik I*. The orbital sphere emitted a "beep-beep" sound, which was picked up by tracking stations all around the world. With the growing tensions of a possible nuclear attack and the lingering "Red Scare," the *Sputnik* launch sent the American public into a panic. The mere thought of the Soviets controlling space with possible military capabilities was too much to fathom. In *Orders of Magnitude: A History of the NACA and NASA, 1915–1990*, Roger E. Bilstein wrote:

> The American public's response was swift and widespread. It seemed equally compounded of alarm and chagrin. American certainty that the nation was always number one in technology had been rudely shattered. Not only had the Russians been first, but *Sputnik* 1 weighed an impressive 183 pounds against *Vanguard's* intended start at 3 pounds and working up to 22 pounds in later satellites. In a cold war environment, the contrast suggested undefined but ominous military implications.

As the United States was re-grouping, the Soviets launched *Sputnik* 2 in November 1957. The second *Sputnik* was a much larger satellite weighing more than 1,000 pounds, but also added a live passenger. The live passenger was a dog named Laika, but just the thought of any living creature surviving proved that a human could eventually be launched into orbit. The surprise launch of not one, but two *Sputnik* satellites also revealed that the slow progress of the American program needed acceleration.

The United States was finally able to place the ABMA-JPL *Explorer* satellite in orbit on January 31, 1958. With the successful launch, a legislative bill was placed before Congress on April 2, 1958, for the authorization to establish "a national aeronautics and space agency." The new agency was named the National Aeronautics and Space Administration, which quickly became known as "NASA." In authorizing the new space agency, the Congress stated it was, "an Act to provide for research into the problems of flight within and outside the Earth's atmosphere, and for other purposes." In reality the program was in response to a pressing need by the military to meet the Soviets in space. The launching of the first satellite *Sputnik* by the Soviets had far-reaching military implications. With a growing paranoia that the Soviets might have an advantage, the argument for the new NASA agency therefore became a matter of "national defense." Soon, the "Space Race" became another phase of the Cold War.

CIVIL DEFENSE, NUCLEAR FALLOUT, AND FALLOUT SHELTERS

The uncertainties and previous failures such as the *Vanguard* launch explosion, as well as others, only heightened American fears that Soviet domination of space could easily launch a nuclear attack upon the United States. In no way can the paranoia created by *Sputnik* be understated. Americans were not only afraid of a nuclear war, but also of the Soviet "threat" from outer space. In response, Americans by the thousands built backyard fallout shelters for protection in the event of a nuclear attack. As the nation's schoolchildren continued to learn to "duck and cover" when and if the bomb would fall, they also learned to respond to an early warning system to take cover in an approved national Civil Defense shelter.

As part of the Civil Defense plan, the United States expanded the wartime "Ground Observer Corps" program. During World War II, the program was set up as a civilian volunteer organization to provide an early warning system in case of an impending German invasion on the East Coast or a Japanese invasion on the West Coast. The ground observers included over 8,000 volunteers who were able to access and sound air raid sirens in an emergency. By 1950, the federal government responded to heightened public anxiety by creating the Federal Civil Defense Administration (FCDA), later called the Office of Civil Defense (CD). The program known as "Operation Skywatch" grew to include more than 200,000 volunteers participating in various types of nationwide drills. The program continued to grow with at least 750,000 volunteers eventually serving in various capacities. By the end of the decade, the volunteers provided nationwide surveillance from a distribution of more than 16,000 CD posts. By 1959, new technological developments, such as a military expansion known as NORAD, provided radar tracking and satellite transmission that soon eliminated the need for civilian volunteers and the program ended.

A lasting effect of the program was the sounding of an air raid siren in the case of an attack. In order for the program to actively warn the nation of an impending attack and thereby take the necessary precautions was the sounding of an air raid siren. As a result, hundreds of thousands were installed all across the country. The system was tested each day at noon. The sound became very familiar to Americans as the tests continued every day until the end of the century. An additional warning test was conducted over the radio airwaves as well as television screens. The radio and TV warning varied slightly across the region, but most stated: "This has been a test of the emergency broadcasting system. If this had been an actual emergency, you would have been instructed where to tune in for official information." Printed instructions were also distributed all over the nation. The simple statement read, "If there is enough warning time, your local Civil Defense director may order a general evacuation of the area to get away from the bomb or its effects before its explosion."

In turn, many of the mass-market magazines routinely provided informational safety tips in "the event of a nuclear attack" that were issued directly from the federal government. One example was a 1955 pamphlet published by the Federal Civil Defense Administration titled "Facts About Fallout." This pamphlet illustrated 1950s conventional thinking about the threat of nuclear war, radioactive fallout, and their consequences. One statement read as follows:

> If there is enough warning time, your local Civil Defense director may order a general evacuation of the area to get away from the bomb or its effects . . . If you don't have time to evacuate, seek the best available shelter. An underground shelter with 3 feet of earth above it will give you almost complete protection if it is equipped with a door and an air filter.

The fallout shelter became a common part of everyday life. Throughout the country official signs were posted to indicate a safe shelter location for the public to enter in case of a nuclear attack. These signs contained distinctive yellow letters of "Fallout Shelter" on a black background underneath upside down yellow triangles against a black circular background. Many schools and church basements were designated as safe fallout shelters. The application of a bright yellow and black sign was affixed to all of the CD approved facilitiesAll sorts of posters, pamphlets, and booklets to aide in Civil Defense became part of the 1950s landscape.

21st-CENTURY NUCLEAR BLASTS AND FEMA

With instances such as the devastation caused by the 2005 Katrina Hurricane in New Orleans; Hurricane Sandy along the northeast coast of the United States in 2012; and of course the September 11, 2001, attacks, Americans became astutely aware of FEMA (Federal Emergency Management Bureau). The FEMA agency was responsible for emergency response in the aftermath of either a natural or manmade disaster. Yet often overlooked by Americans in the 21st century was the language contained in the FEMA publications, especially in the event of a nuclear attack. One example from a FEMA website Ready.com in 2016 defined a nuclear blast as follows:

> A nuclear blast is an explosion with intense light and heat, a damaging pressure wave, and widespread radioactive material that can contaminate the air, water, and ground surfaces for miles around. A nuclear device can range from a weapon carried by an intercontinental missile launched by a hostile nation or terrorist organization, to a small portable nuclear devise transported by an individual. All nuclear devices cause deadly effects when exploded, including blinding light, intense heat (thermal radiation), initial nuclear radiation, blast, fires started by the heat pulse and secondary fires caused by the destruction.

In a disclaimer attached to ease the fear, FEMA authorities felt the necessity to remind the public that the old Cold War threat was non-existent:

> The nuclear threat present during the Cold War has diminished; however, the possibility remains that a terrorist could obtain access to a nuclear weapon. Called improvised nuclear devices (IND), these are generally smaller, less powerful weapons than we traditionally envision. While experts may predict that a nuclear attack is less likely than other types, it is still important to know the simple steps that can save your life and the life of your family.

Information on "duck and cover" that was so common to every American schoolchild of the 1950s was resurrected in June 2010. A 130-page report issued by the U.S. National Security Council titled "Planning Guidance for Response to a Nuclear Detonation" provided the following definition and explanation if someone chose Bert the Turtle's preferred method of survival:

> Duck and Cover—A suggested method of personal protection against the effects of a nuclear weapon, which the United States government taught to generations

of school children from the early 1950s into the 1980s. The technique was supposed to protect them in the event of an unexpected nuclear attack, which, they were told, could come at any time without warning. Immediately after they saw a flash they had to stop what they were doing and get on the ground under some cover, such as a table or against a wall, and assume the fetal position, lying facedown and covering their heads with their hands.

FURTHER READING

Michael Barson and Steven Heller. *Red Scared: The Commie Menace in Propaganda and Popular Culture*. San Francisco: Chronicle Books, 2001.
Roger E. Bilstein. *Orders of Magnitude a History of the NACA and NASA, 1915–1990*, "Chapter 3: Going Supersonic." Washington, DC: NASA, 1989.
David Halberstam. *The Fifties*. New York: Metro Books, 2001.
Ken Hollings. *Welcome to Mars: Politics, Pop Culture, and Weird Science in 1950s America*. Berkeley, CA: North Atlantic Books, 2014.
Stuart A. Kallen, ed. *The 1950s. America's Decades*. San Diego, CA: Greenhaven Press, 2000.
Paul A. Offit. *Vaccinated: One Man's Quest to Defeat the World's Deadliest Diseases*. New York: Smithsonian Books/Collins, 2007.
Victoria Vantoch. *The Jet Sex: Airline Stewardesses and the Making of an American Icon*. Philadelphia: University of Pennsylvania Press, 2013.

CHAPTER 4

Music

Despite the massive worldwide carnage of World War II, the American home-front was far removed from physical warfare. In preparation for overseas deployment, it was heavily involved in training a military fighting force. As young men and women from all parts of America, both rural and urban, traveled to basic training camps in such places as Nebraska, Oklahoma, and Texas, they were exposed to different cultures, especially music. The drudgery of constant training was made bearable by looking forward to non-military recreational activities such as Saturday night dances. The United Servicemen's Organization (USO) organized many of the dances with music popular among the young 18-to-25-year-old enlisted men and USO hostesses. The music included the big band sounds such as Glenn Miller and Benny Goodman. Another music genre experienced by the fledging GIs was country and western, often accompanied by square dancing. Many of the country and western bands in the southwest United States were influenced by the popular big bands that played a format known as western swing. Both of those music formats continued into the 1950s as did popular song standards. By the middle part of the 1950s, a new genre called Rock 'n' Roll would shatter all the conformity standards of the previous popular music genres.

POPULAR SONGS, COUNTRY AND WESTERN, AND RHYTHM AND BLUES

In the 1950s, *The Billboard* (as it was then known) was the most influential trade magazine for recorded music. At the time, their rankings divided American music into three basic categories: Popular, Country and Western, and Rhythm and Blues. (The previous year the three charts were labeled: Popular, Hillbilly, and Race.) Basically, the popular, or pop, charts were marketed to white urban areas offering a song catalog from mostly white, smooth-singing crooners, big

Chart 4.1   Top Ten Best-Selling Records, 1950–1954

1950

1.   "Goodnight Irene"—The Weavers
2.   "Mona Lisa"—Nat "King" Cole
3.   "Third Man Theme"—Anton Karas
4.   "Sam's Song"—Gary and Bing Crosby
5.   "Simple Melody"—Gary and Bing Crosby
6.   "Music, Music, Music"—Teresa Brewer
7.   "Third Man Theme"—Guy Lombardo
8.   "Chattanoogie Shoe Shine Boy"—Red Foley
9.   "Harbor Lights"—Sammy Kaye
10.   "It Isn't Fair"—Sammy Kaye and Don Cornell

1951

1.   "Too Young"—Nat "King" Cole
2.   " Because of You"—Tony Bennett
3.   "How High the Moon"—Les Paul/Mary Ford
4.   "Come On-A My House"—Rosemary Clooney
5.   "Be My Love"—Mario Lanza
6.   "On Top of Old Smokey"—The Weavers
7.   "Cold, Cold Heart"—Tony Bennett
8.   "If"—Perry Como
9.   "Loveliest Night of the Year"—Mario Lanza
10.   "Tennessee Waltz"—Patti Page

1952

1.   "Blue Tango"—Leroy Anderson
2.   "Wheel of Fortune"—Kay Starr
3.   "Cry"—Johnnie Ray
4.   "You Belong to Me"—Jo Stafford
5.   "Auf Wiederseh'n Sweetheart"—Vera Lynn
6.   "Half as Much"—Rosemary Clooney
7.   "Wish You Were Here"—Eddie Fisher
8.   "I Went to Your Wedding"—Patti Page
9.   "Here in My Heart"—Al Martino
10.   "Delicado"—Percy Faith

1953

1.   "Song from Moulin Rouge"—Percy Faith
2.   "Vaya Con Dios"—Les Paul and Mary Ford
3.   "Doggie in the Window"—Patti Page

(continued)

Chart 4.1   Top Ten Best-Selling Records, 1950–1954 (*continued*)

4.	"I'm Walking Behind You"—Eddie Fisher
5.	"You, You, You"—The Ames Brothers
6.	"Till I Waltz Again with You"—Teresa Brewer
7.	"April in Portugal"—Lee Baxter
8.	"No Other Love"—Perry Como
9.	"Don't Let the Stars"—Perry Como
10.	"I Believe"—Frankie Laine

1954

1.	"Little Things Mean A Lot"—Kitty Kallen
2.	"Wanted"—Perry Como
3.	"Hey There"—Rosemary Clooney
4.	"Sh-Boom"—The Crew Cuts
5.	"Make Love to Me"—Jo Stafford
6.	"Oh My Pa-Pa"—Eddie Fisher
7.	"I Get So Lonely"—Four Knights
8.	"Three Coins in the Fountain"—Four Aces
9.	"Secret Love"—Doris Day
10.	"Hernando's Hideaway"—Archie Bleyer

Chart compiled by author.

bands, Broadway show tunes, and the like. Occasionally some Latin and African Americans such as Nat King Cole, Billy Eckstine, or Ella Fitzgerald were included within the pop category. Rhythm and blues were strictly African American recording artists with a strong lineage coming out of the Delta blues type of music. The music was characterized with a solid downbeat that would be the forerunner of Rock 'n' Roll music. Country and western (sometimes listed as "folk" and in previous years as "hillbilly") was marketed to mainly white rural areas of the United States. Not included as part of the popular mainstream was American roots music known as the "blues." At the time, some of the most influential of all blues artists such as Willie Dixon, John Lee Hooker, Muddy Waters, and Howlin' Wolf recorded some of their best work. However, due to segregation, very few of those artists received radio airplay. A few white artists such as country and western star Patsy Cline did record some blues-type music with considerable radio success. An offshoot of blues music was rhythm and blues.

BIG BANDS AND POPULAR SINGERS

In the immediate postwar years, many of the big bands and crooners from the late 1930s and early 1940s maintained some continued popularity. With the wartime rationing restrictions gone and growing prosperity, entertainment venues such as nightclubs experienced a resurgence. Some wartime bands such as the Glenn Miller Orchestra continued despite the loss of its namesake during

World War II. In 1947, under the direction of new bandleader and vocalist Tex Beneke, the remnants of the Glenn Miller Orchestra opened to a large crowd of over 6,500 eager dancers at the Hollywood Palladium. Sadly, many music historians cite that single show as the final "high point" of the big band era. As the 1950s progressed, the trend moved towards singular popular vocalists and eventually small combos playing either rhythm and blues, jazz, or the new sounds of Rock 'n' Roll. Historian Leo Walker, who wrote about the era of the big bands, said, "The ten-year period comprising the 1950s was one of steady decline of the dance band business from its once top position as a form of live entertainment to a situation where only a few of its former great names could prosper" (113, 211).

Between 1947 and 1955, music genres and dancing styles were changing. The big bands were no longer financially viable as the trend moved towards mellow pop standards and be-bop jazz. Former bandleader Paul Whiteman (one of America's all-time top entertainers) claimed that the transition from the band as a focal point to that of the lone vocalist caused the decline. Many other bandleaders said the decline was attributed to the newer jazz-style be-bop bands that did not play in "dance tempo." In small part, that was true as millions of Americans stopped going out for entertainment. Yet many were captivated by television and were firmly entrenched within their living rooms.

FRANK SINATRA

Unlike the misplaced nostalgia of later generations, Rock 'n' Roll was not accepted as an innocent attachment of the youth. The venomous attacks against the music can be summed up by famed American musical icon Frank Sinatra. During 1957, as Rock 'n' Roll was in fact "rolling" over all other types of popular American music, Sinatra was not impressed: He said:

> Rock and roll is the most brutal, ugly, degenerate, vicious form of expression— lewd, sly, in plain fact, dirty—a rancid-smelling aphrodisiac and the martial music of every side-burned delinquent on the face of the earth.

Sinatra's dislike of the music genre is certainly evident. Yet, unlike most critics who disliked Rock 'n' Roll due to its roots in African American culture, Sinatra was a long-time proponent of equality and integration.

In July 1958, *Ebony* magazine printed an article written by Sinatra regarding race relations in America. *Ebony*, in publication since its inception in 1945, focused on sports, entertainment, music, and other issues relating to African Americans. In an article titled "The Way I Look at Race," Sinatra, who at the time was America's top entertainer, spoke candidly on race relations, religion, and prejudice in American society. The editors added that Sinatra was against "racial epithets" and termed bigotry "a disease." Of his own close personal friends, he said, "they are of many colors and religious faiths, rich and poor, intellectual and illiterate." As for those of his friends that he "liked," he wrote:

> I don't like according to the color of a man's skin or his place of worship. And I have never picked a friend because of nationality. I simply like people, a lot of them, and my personal relationships are not determined by the boundaries of a

country or what society thinks of certain kinds of human beings. I'd personally like to see more friendships forged across color and religious lines, for I feel this is the surest way to erase all the lines that divide people everywhere. The world is suffering from a shortage of love, between nations and individuals, and something drastic and dramatic is needed to meet this hunger. (p. 34)

Frank Sinatra (1915–1998) was one of the biggest names of the entire 20th century. Many also attribute him as America's greatest entertainer of all time. Sinatra first gained fame as a singing sensation to a generation of "teenyboppers" during the early 1940s, however, as he grew older so did his fans along with him. To place him in the definition as solely a musical performer during the 1950s would be inaccurate. He did record some of his best songs during the time, but he also was among the early TV pioneers, as well as a major Hollywood movie star.

As the new decade began, Sinatra attempted to restart his singing career after a two-year break from live performances. On January 12, 1950, at the age of 35, he returned to the live stage for a concert in Hartford, Connecticut. Around the same time, he crossed over from the older Hollywood-styled musicals and embraced both dramatic and lighthearted movie roles. He auditioned for a dramatic role in the Hollywood movie *From Here to Eternity*. Soon thereafter, he was offered the role as an Italian-American U.S. soldier named Angelo Maggio. Released in 1953, the movie was a major hit and earned Academy Awards for Best Picture and also a Best Supporting Actor for Sinatra. He followed with key roles in hit movies including *Guys and Dolls* (1955), which he co-starred with Marlon Brando, and *The Man with the Golden Arm* (1955). As a result, his career was reinvigorated as Capitol Records signed him to a new record deal.

He also dabbled in radio and television. As for television, the musical variety *The Frank Sinatra Show* aired on CBS-TV from 1950 to 1952. From 1953 to 1954, he starred in an NBC radio drama as the self-titled *Rocky Fortune*. He returned to television in another self-titled musical variety show on ABC-TV from 1957 to 1958. His career was booming on all ends and he soon set the style for live stage performances in the newly opened Las Vegas gambling casinos. Sinatra's reinvigorated film and television career also propelled him back to singing with a new record deal.

In 1952, Sinatra signed a new recording contract with Capitol Records. By most accounts, he also recorded his best work at this time. During a 10-year period with Capitol, he worked with many of the finest musical arrangers of the era, most notably Nelson Riddle, Gordon Jenkins, and Billy May. His first record release in 1954 quickly brought him back to the top of the charts. By the end of the year, the title song of his 1954 movie with Doris Day "Young at Heart" (part of a two-sided 10-inch 78-rpm record) was named Song of the Year by *The Billboard*. That same year his eight-song ten-inch LP *Swing Easy* was named Album of the Year and Sinatra was named "Top Male Vocalist" by the major trade magazines *The Billboard*, *Down Beat*, and *Metronome*.

With a series of albums featuring darker emotional material, Sinatra reinvented himself and also explored new recording technology. A 1955 collaboration with Nelson Riddle produced *In the Wee Small Hours*, which was his first album on the new 33 1/3 LP 12-inch record format. His next Capitol project was his first

Chart 4.2   List of Capitol Albums by Frank Sinatra

Album Title	Year	Label	Arranger
Songs for Young Lovers	1954	Capitol	Nelson Riddle
Swing Easy!	1954	Capitol	Nelson Riddle
In the Wee Small Hours	1955	Capitol	Nelson Riddle
Frank Sinatra Conducts Tone Poems	1956	Capitol	Gordon Jenkins
Songs for Swingin' Lovers!	1956	Capitol	Nelson Riddle
Close to You	1957	Capitol	Nelson Riddle
A Swingin' Affair!	1957	Capitol	Nelson Riddle
The Man I Love	1957	Capitol	Nelson Riddle
Where Are You?	1957	Capitol	Gordon Jenkins
A Jolly Christmas from Frank Sinatra	1957	Capitol	Gordon Jenkins
Come Fly with Me	1958	Capitol	Billy May
Frank Sinatra Sings for Only the Lonely	1958	Capitol	Nelson Riddle
Come Dance with Me!	1959	Capitol	Billy May
No One Cares	1959	Capitol	Gordon Jenkins
Sleep Warm	1959	Capitol	Pete King

Chart compiled by author.

stereo LP *Where Are You?* (1957) also with Riddle as the arranger. In 1956, the release of *Songs for Swinging Lovers*, a third collaboration with Nelson Riddle as arranger, was both a critical and financial success. Each of the 15 tracks became mainstays of his future singing career, but none more so than one in particular. The album featured a recording of "I've Got You Under My Skin," which has often been called the single greatest arrangement of any American song during the entire 20th century.

THE CONFORMITY OF ROSELAND

For older adults desperately trying to resist any change in a post-World War II society, there were dance halls like Roseland in New York City. Roseland Ballroom was one of the few dance halls to maintain a "refined atmosphere" throughout the Rock 'n' Roll era. In October 1957, Stanley Frank, writing in the *Saturday Evening Post*, predicted, "Rock 'n' roll, guitars with, off-key tenors with forelocks overhanging beetling brows—this too, will pass away. Everything in pop music and dancing eventually passes except Roseland." The variety of dances and accompanying music included the waltz, fox trot, rumba, mambo, samba, cha-cha, or occasional swing. By 1957, it was under the same ownership since its inception in 1919 and over 20 million paid admissions had passed onto the Roseland dance floor.

Roseland held open dancing sessions every evening as well as a weekday matinee session. Located in midtown Manhattan, the large dance floor could accommodate at least 1,250 couples. At least 500 individuals were regulars who attended at least once or twice a week; almost all of them were over the age of 40. Owner Louis J. Brecker boasted, "You won't find a better-behaved crowd anywhere." In keeping with the social conformity of the time, Roseland maintained a strict house rule against any exuberant dance styles. Brecker's rules stated the acceptable sedate dance styles "excludes youngsters more effectively: rock 'n' roll, the jitterbug, and similar antics are prohibited." Another house rule explicitly stated any swing dancing must be "a restrained Lindy Hop, but the gentleman's feet never leave the floor and the lady never winds up in the chandelier" (Frank, "They'd Rather Dance Than Eat," 116).

BE-BOP JAZZ

The exuberance of the young dancers' antics was reminiscent of their own parents who went wild over the 1930s' swing and jazz bands. Yet, as the 1950s were a time of both of strict conformity and subtle sub-culture changes, jazz as an art form found new expression. The emergence of Be-bop was a musical derivative of pre-war jazz that was often played away from a continuous metronomic dance beat. For the most part the music was intended for the ear and not the dancing feet. The development of be-bop was in effect a rebellion in music by African American artists. According to musical composer Galt MacDermot (the creator of the 1960s Broadway musical *Hair*), "Black musicians were sick of the social system. So they created music that was not necessarily off the beat, but was too complicated for white people to understand. I don't know why they wanted to do that but they did." Be-bop historian Ira Gitler added, " 'It was said that black people didn't dance to bebop and, for the most part this was true, but black people figured out a way to make those fast tempos by cutting the time in half whether they were doing a new dance called "The Apple Jack" [sic] or the older Lindy Hop" (McQuirter, 83–85).

THE MAMBO AND LATIN MUSIC

Between 1947 and 1954, dance music and dancing was in a state of transition. During the late 1930s and World War II, the big bands' focus was dance music. Many of the venues were cavernous dance halls. Another significant venue for live music was nightclubs. In the post-war years, the nightclubs usually booked the popular singers of the day as well as Latin musicians. Often overlooked was the overwhelming popularity of the Latin-inspired music and dances from places such as Puerto Rico, the Dominican Republic, and Cuba. Throughout the decade, American relations with Cuba were quite good. The capital city of Havana was a major tourist attraction for well-to-do Americans as the vacation resorts had legal casino gambling and excellent native entertainment and dancing. Immigration from the island also moved freely into major U.S. cities such as New York, Chicago, Miami, San Francisco, and Los Angeles. Some of the dominant cultural influences combined the music with dances for the mambo, calypso, merengue, and the cha-cha.

The beginning of the mambo craze in the United States dates from 1947. At that time, both Tito Puente (1923–2000) and Tito Rodriguez (1923–1973) introduced a Latin *conjunto* style (the literal translation is "combo") into the American main-stream musical lexicon. Puente, born in New York City to Puerto Rican parents, was billed as the "King of the Mambo." He recorded more than 120 albums during his lifetime. Pablo "Tito" Rodriguez was a singer and percussionist who was born in Puerto Rico and later immigrated to the United States. He was known for singing with popular Latin orchestras including Xavier Cugat, Noro Morales, and José Curelo before forming his own band (Roberts [1999], 125–130). The success of mambo music and dance was overwhelming and a craze swept the nation as many adults learned to dance the mambo. Many dance studios found a lucrative endeavor in teaching adults how to mambo. The popularity extended into popular culture as one 1950s episode of *The Honeymooners* television show featured Ralph (Jackie Gleason) and Norton (Art Carney) attempting to learn the mambo.

FOLK MUSIC AND THE WEAVERS

In 1950, the folk music group The Weavers charted the overall #1 song of the year with "Goodnight, Irene." By 1955, *The Billboard* was considered the industry standard, but prior to that time many other trade magazines were in publication. Despite the different publications, all of them rated the song at or near the top of their charts. *The Billboard* placed it overall at #2; *Your Hit Parade* rated it #6; it landed at #1 with *Variety*, and *Cash Box* placed it at #2. For the recording of the nationwide smash hit "Goodnight Irene," the group partnered with singer Gordon Jenkins. The original group known as The Weavers that had formed in the late 1940s included Ronnie Gilbert, Pete Seeger, Lee Hays, and Fred Hellerman. (In 1958, Erik Darling replaced Pete Seeger.) In her obituary in 2015, Bruce Weber described Ronnie Gilbert's voice as "crystalline, bold contralto [that] provided distaff ballast for the Weavers, the seminal quartet that helped propel folk music to wide popularity and establish its power as an agent of social change" ("Ronnie Gilbert," p. A19).

The Weavers as a group were known for recording the genre known as folk music. It is defined by the *Free Dictionary* as:

> Music originating among the common people of a nation or region and spread about or passed down orally, often with considerable variation. Every nation has its own form of traditional folk music.

As American folk music, groups like The Weavers also reflected the realities of life in rural areas, farms, and factories. The music by The Weavers, and other folk artists of the time, usually promoted progressive political messages such as supporting labor unions and civil rights. The format included "work songs, union songs, and gospel songs." Some of the enduring songs that became American standards and very often part of the lexicon of grade-school children in later generations all across America included: "On Top of Old Smokey," "Goodnight, Irene," "This Land Is Your Land," and "The Hammer Song" (a.k.a. "If I Had a Hammer"), among many others. Of The Weavers, in particular, Bruce Weber added that the group is often credited with "a sing-along populism that

laid the groundwork for a folk-music boom in the 1950s and 1960s and its con-
comitant [to naturally accompany] earnest strain of 1960s counterculture."

Despite the reverence of folk music for the American heartland, it came under
scrutiny during the Red Scare. At the time of their #1 hit, The Weavers were in
the midst of a nationwide two-year tour. They appeared on numerous radio
and television shows and "were among the biggest musical stars in the country"
(Weber, Ronnie Gilbert, A19). In June 1950, their fast-rising career was usurped
by the Red Scare. A pamphlet titled *Red Channels* that proclaimed itself in support of the American patriotic mission to expose "Communist infiltration of the
entertainment industry" named The Weavers and other folk artists as Communist sympathizers. Despite the wide-ranging accusations, singer Ronnie Gilbert
(1926–2015) was singled out by the HUAC due to her parents' activism in labor
unions.

Despite the HUAC accusations, The Weavers influenced a new generation
of later folk groups and singers such as Bob Dylan, Joan Baez, Simon and Gar-
funkel, and the Kingston Trio, among dozens of others. In 1958, the Kingston
Trio charted the #1 nationwide hit "Tom Dooley," which also earned a Grammy
Award. (In a quirk of the awards show, the category was for "Best Country &
Western Performance," although the song was distinctly folk.) "Tom Dooley"
was a remake of a traditional folk song traced to the Kentucky Blue Ridge
Mountains. The original title was "Tom Dula," but the song lyrics were basically the same. The group was often credited with bringing American folk music
into the popular American consciousness, as well as spreading it beyond the
nation's borders to an international audience (Weber, "Ronnie Gilbert," A19).

COUNTRY AND WESTERN

In many rural areas of the nation and some southern and southwestern cities
the dominant music genre was country and western. This is not to say that the
music format was restricted to those areas. Country and western (C&W) held
various levels of prominence all throughout the nation. During the 1930s and
1940s, for example, the *WLS Barn Dance* radio program in Chicago was just as
influential as any other C&W radio station in America. One of the most notable C&W singers of the post-war period was Eddy Arnold. In his May 9, 2008,
New York Times obituary, Arnold was described as a singer who "personified the
evolution of country music in the years after World War II from a rural ver-
nacular to an idiom with broad mainstream appeal."

Arnold's career eventually spanned seven decades totaling record sales in
excess of 85 million copies. As for dominance on *The Billboard* C&W music
charts, it was Eddy Arnold who had more combined weeks at the #1 spot than
any other C&W artist. A few of his hits also crossed over to the traditional pop
chart. Overall he placed 37 of his C&W singles on the popular music charts.
His most successful #1 single on both charts was "Make the World Go Away"
that was released in 1965 in the midst of the Beatles' and the British musical
invasion (Friskics-Warren, "Eddy Arnold," p. C11).

At the time, a new sound emerged that was built upon many of the country
and western traditional artists. Western swing music historian Stephen Thomas

Erlewine probably said it best when he wrote, "In time, all of it became raw material for rock and roll" (Erlewine, n.p.). Regardless of the labeling, it was Rock 'n' Roll that ended the nationwide appeal of country and western music. The format did remain in high demand, but mainly in regional rural areas. Many of those influenced by western swing morphed into the honky tonk sounds of the likes of Ernest Tubb, Webb Pierce, Lefty Frizzell, and Hank Williams. But quite a few, such as Buddy Holly and Bill Haley, incorporated the western swing sound into what some called rockabilly, but others such as Cleveland radio disc jockey Alan Freed called it Rock 'n' Roll.

Chart 4.3   Top Ten Best-Selling Records of the Rock 'n' Roll Era, 1955–1959

1955
1. "Rock Around the Clock"—Bill Haley
2. "Cherry Pink & Apple Blossom White"—Perez Prado
3. "Yellow Rose of Texas"—Mitch Miller
4. "Autumn Leaves"—Roger Williams
5. "Unchained Melody"—Les Baxter
6. "Ballad of Davy Crockett"—Bill Hayes
7. "Love Is a Many Splendored Thing"—Four Aces
8. "Sincerely"—The McGuire Sisters
9. "Ain't That a Shame"—Pat Boone
10. "Dance With Me Henry"—Georgia Gibbs

1956
1. "Heartbreak Hotel"—Elvis Presley
2. "Don't Be Cruel"—Elvis Presley
3. "Lisbon Antigua"—Nelson Riddle
4. "My Prayer"—The Platters
5. "Wayward Wind"—Gogi Grant
6. "The Poor People of Paris"—Les Baxter
7. "Whatever Will Be (Que Sera Sera)"—Doris Day
8. "Hound Dog"—Elvis Presley
9. "Memories Are Made of This"—Dean Martin
10. "Rock and Roll Waltz"—Kay Starr

1957
1. "All Shook Up"—Elvis Presley
2. "Love Letters in the Sand"—Pat Boone
3. "Little Darlin' "—The Diamonds
4. "Young Love"—Tab Hunter
5. "So Rare"—Jimmy Dorsey

(continued)

Chart 4.3   Top Ten Best-Selling Records of the Rock 'n' Roll Era, 1955–1959 (*continued*)

6.	"Don't Forbid Me"—Pat Boone
7.	"Singin' the Blues"—Guy Mitchell
8.	"Young Love"—Sonny James
9.	"Too Much"—Elvis Presley
10.	"Round and Round"—Perry Como
1958	
1.	"Volare"—Domenico Modugno
2.	"All I Have to Do Is Dream"—Everly Bros.
3.	"Don't"—Elvis Presley
4.	"Witch Doctor"—David Seville
5.	"Patricia"—Perez Prado
6.	"Sail Along Silvery Moon"—Billy Vaughn
7.	"Catch a Falling Star"—Perry Como
8.	"Tequila"—The Champs
9.	"It's All in the Game"—Tommy Edwards
10.	"Return to Me"—Dean Martin
1959	
1.	"Mack the Knife"—Bobby Darin
2.	"Battle of New Orleans"—Johnny Horton
3.	"Personality"—Lloyd Price
4.	"Venus"—Frankie Avalon
5.	"Lonely Boy"—Paul Anka
6.	"Dream Lover"—Bobby Darin
7.	"Three Bells"—The Browns
8.	"Come Softly to Me"—The Fleetwoods
9.	"Kansas City"—Wilbert Harrison
10.	"Mr. Blue"—The Fleetwoods

Chart compiled by author.

ALAN FREED: "MR. ROCK 'N' ROLL"

In the midst of the late 20th-century nostalgia craze for the 1950s, a biopic movie titled *American Hot Wax* (1982) presented a brief period in the life of Cleveland radio disc jockey Alan Freed. The movie was highly fictionalized, but did provide a fairly accurate presentation of the societal problems associated with promoting a Rock 'n' Roll show at the Brooklyn Paramount Theater during the 1950s. The attempt at a serious portrayal of the chaotic events surrounding Rock 'n' Roll, however, was lost within the nostalgia-crazed upbeat portrayals of other significant 1950s-themed movies such as *American Graffiti* (1973), *Grease* (1978),

Alan Freed, the Cleveland radio disc jockey who coined the term "Rock 'n' Roll." (Photofest)

and top-rated TV show *Happy Days* (1974–1984). For the most part, the mainstream American public was totally unaware, or had just simply forgotten, the legacy of Alan Freed as the father of Rock 'n' Roll.

In many ways, his legacy was resurrected on September 2, 1995, when the Rock and Roll Hall of Fame and Museum was opened in downtown Cleveland. The choice to locate the museum in Cleveland was not by coincidence. The site selection had everything to do with the fact that Rock 'n' Roll was "born" in Cleveland. Designed by renowned American architect I.M. Pei, the signature pyramidal glass building located along the shore of Lake Erie quickly became an architectural icon. In reverence to Freed as the founder of the music genre, an "Ohio Historical Marker" was placed outside the museum entry in 2003. The information on the bronze plaque provides a brief summation of Freed's connection to the music. It reads as follows:

BIRTHPLACE OF ROCK 'N' ROLL

When radio station WJW disc jockey Alan Freed (1921–1965) used the term "rock and roll" to describe the uptempo black rhythm and blues records he played beginning in 1951, he named a new genre of popular music that appealed to audiences on both sides of 1950s American racial boundaries—and dominated American culture for the rest of the 20th century. The popularity of Freed's nightly "Moon Dog House Rock and Roll Party" radio show encouraged him to organize the Moondog Coronation Ball—the first rock concert. Held at the Cleveland Arena on March 21, 1952, the oversold show was beset by a riot during the first set. Freed, a charter inductee into the Rock and Roll Hall of Fame, moved to WINS in New York City in 1954 and continued to promote rock music through radio, television, movies, and live performances.

The Ohio Bicentennial Commission
The Rock and Roll Hall of Fame
The Ohio Historical Society

The basic information on the plaque is accurate, but it does not convey the tumultuous birth of the music genre, nor is does it fully recognize the turmoil placed upon Freed.

In 1951, radio disc jockey Alan Freed started "The Moon Dog House" that aired late at night from 11:15 PM to 1 AM on WJW-850 AM, a 50,000-watt Cleveland radio station. (Twenty-first-century digital technology, such as YouTube, provides access to the original broadcasts. One source is a WJW-AM air check for April 6, 1954.) Freed's music selections were intended for a new, growing demographic—the teenage listening audience. His music choice was mainly rhythm and blues (R&B) sung by black recording artists. The music and lyrics were sometimes risqué, but more often than not the lyrics were humorous, playful, and exciting. Most important, the music was defined by a heavy backbeat and it was danceable. The R&B music selected by Freed appealed to teenagers both black and white. He soon began calling it "Rock 'n' Roll." Ultimately, Rock 'n' Roll became not only a dominant and continuing mainstream American art form; it also became a cultural, social, economic, and political global force.

Freed's notoriety as a popular radio personality and promoter of Rock 'n' Roll stage shows had actually started five years earlier in Cleveland on March 21, 1952. His first show advertised as the Moondog Coronation Ball, in the Cleveland Arena sold out in advance for more than 10,000 enthusiastic teenagers. Thousands of others expecting to purchase tickets at the door were turned away, causing a near riot. At the time Freed billed himself as the "Moondog" and also began using the on-air term "Rock and Roll" to differentiate the music aimed at teenagers. In 1955, Freed's first New York area stage shows on January 14 and 15 were billed as a "Rock 'n' Roll Ball." Music historian James Miller reported that this might be the first use of the phrase with apostrophes bracketing a lower case "n." From 1951 to 1955, placards, posters, theater marquees, and albums promoting the Freed shows listed the term with misplaced apostrophes as either Rock 'n' Roll; Rock 'n Roll; or Rock n' Roll." After Freed's move to New York, many of the newspaper and magazine stories printed the phrase with the apostrophes placed as "Rock 'n' Roll" and also credited Freed with coining the phrase (Miller, *Flowers in the Dustbin*, 86).

Freed's live stage shows brought together many of the same acts he played on the radio and drew a faithful audience of teenagers, both black and white. During a time of strict segregation, the Rock 'n' Roll shows were the first time that music and dancing were presented to racially mixed audiences. The appeal was due in part to Freed's insistence on playing R&B songs as recorded by the original black artists and not the 1950s practice of re-recording the songs by white singers known as "white cover versions," in which a white singer or group re-records a proven hit radio song that had previously been recorded by a black artist.

WHITE COVER VERSIONS

The bottom line for radio airplay was money from advertising dollars based on the popularity of a particular show. In turn, the radio airplay garnered attention from a record-buying public. Most of the profits from sales went to the record producers with a small amount to the artist. At the time, the mainstream radio stations and record-buying public were mostly white and within a strictly segregated American society; profits were controlled by white businesses. Basically, white DJs played white recording artists and in a limited segregated market, black DJs played recordings by black artists. Despite the segregation, almost all the radio stations were owned by white men. As Rock 'n' Roll gained a larger audience, established record producers soon noticed the profit potential. Rather than succumb to integration, many producers hired a white artist or group to re-record a popular song as a "cover version." A significant amount of cover versions occurred during the years 1954 to 1956 when Rock 'n' Roll was gaining a wider audience and popularity. One early example was by the white group the Crew Cuts who in 1954 released two successful hits with cover versions of the songs "Earth Angel" and "Sh-Boom." As those songs rose to the top of the pop charts, very few were aware of the original version of "Earth Angel" by The Penguins and "Sh-Boom" by The Chords were each rhythm and blues hits before the Crew Cuts recordings (*Rock and Roll: The Early Days* video).

One white singer who had tremendous success was Pat Boone, who sold more than 20 million records during the time. His wholesome, clean-cut image of devoted husband and father was a perfect fit for the conformist-minded 1950s. His popularity extended to hosting a television show and publishing a best-selling book *Twixt Twelve and Twenty: Pat Talks to Teenagers* (1958). The book provided teen advice on activities such as "going steady" and the dangers of kissing. Boone advised strict abstinence especially when it came to allowing a date to get to "first base," slang for kissing. Boone noted, "Kissing for fun is like playing with a beautiful candle in a room full of dynamite" (Time-Life Books, "Rock & Roll Generation," 46–47). At a time when even kissing for teenagers was not tolerated, the thought of anything more was shocking. As reasoning for why white cover versions were necessary, Boone explained:

> It was at that time an absolute wall, an impenetrable wall, between pop and R&B [Rhythm & Blues]. There were R&B stations, R&B artists [and] there was R&B music. But, it was not gonna get played in its original form on pop stations. It was just too ragged. "Oh in some cases it was a little suggestive or more in some cases even explicit." (*"Rock 'n' Roll Explodes"* video)

However, Boone's "Rock and Roll" (he eliminated the apostrophes for the purpose of grammatical correctness) did not expend much stage energy beyond some foot tapping and finger snapping to an up-tempo cover of Little Richard's "Tutti Frutti." The absurdity of the cover versions included Boone's own attempt to cover Fats Domino's "Ain't That a Shame." Boone wanted to change the title to a grammatically correct "Isn't That a Shame." He was convinced otherwise and recorded the song as written by Domino. But in concert, Boone actually took to apologizing for the grammatical error of the song. In later years he took it as a joke and good-naturedly made fun of his own earlier confusions (Miller, *Flowers in the Dustbin*, 102). Boone might not have been a true Rock 'n' Roll singer, but he did appeal to mainstream America. In contrast, Alan Freed refused to play cover versions, insisting instead on playing the original R&B versions by the original recording artist or group.

ALAN FREED'S "ROCK 'N' ROLL DANCE PARTY"

With Freed's insistence on playing original music with sometimes suggestive lyrics leading to integrated dances, the controversies over the music intensified. It was not only the music and dancing, however, it was the association of the phrase itself that caused concern among white Americans. At the time, the phrase was actually slang for sexual fornication. A song title such as the 1949 single, "All She Wants to Do Is Rock" by Wynonie Harris, as one example, implied much more than dancing. Actually, among the slang terms for sexual activity, one could either "rock" or one could "roll," one could be done without the other, yet the terms were still considered overtly sexual.

As the words were applied by Freed, with the apostrophes linking the two words, the phrase became one singular word to denote the music. Regardless of the use of the wording, either singular or connected, many Americans still viewed it as a sexual reference. To put it in the context of the time period, sex, either marital or premarital, was not openly discussed, especially if it involved teenagers. During the time, an overt puritanical suppression was overwhelmingly prevalent when it came to any manner of sexual education, film portrayal, or television reference. In fact, any television show that had a scene in a bedroom did not include anything remotely resembling affection, touching, or romantic kissing. Scenes within the bedroom were limited. When in the bedroom, there were always twin beds, an obvious indication that a married couple did not actually sleep together in the same bed. This look back to the popular culture references of the time leaves later generations wondering how the couples ever managed to produce a pregnancy. But then again, the word "pregnant" was not allowed to be spoken on either television programs or even within the context of a mainstream Hollywood movie. It was within that nationwide prudence of sexual mores that Elvis Presley caused such a sensation with his suggestive hip movements. More on Presley later, but before and during Presley's rise to fame, Alan Freed was embroiled in a continuing controversy of Rock 'n' Roll music. In 1954, Freed left Cleveland for the much larger and lucrative radio market at WINS-AM in New York City.

In New York, he continued the same Cleveland tradition of promoting live stage shows. In 1955, on January 14 and 15, Freed's first New York show was advertised on the marquee as a "Rock 'n' Roll Ball." Regardless of its use in Cleveland, New York, or basically anywhere in the country, the phrase still was associated as slang for fornication and having a sexual good time. It was with the combined thought of teenagers engaging in both interracial dancing and premarital fornication that was the cause for a major backlash by the conformist media as well as municipal and religious leaders. Freed's troubles soon began in New York, and eventually spread nationwide (Miller, *Flowers in the Dustbin*, 86).

To place the importance and to also understand the complete role reversal of Rock 'n' Roll from its inception and acceptance into mainstream American culture is to fast forward 20 years. In June 1977, a NASA explorative space vehicle named *Voyager* was sent into the far reaches of the universe. Included was a gold record master disc containing a 90-minute sampling of world music. One representative song for the United States was Chuck Berry's rendition of

"Johnny B. Goode." In 1955, however, the song would never have been selected, as the cultural acceptance was very different. In retrospect, Berry remembered the differences that 20 years could make:

> I doubt that many Caucasian persons would come into a situation that would cause them to know the feeling a black person experiences after being reared under old-time southern traditions and then finally being welcomed by an entirely unbiased and friendly audience, applauding without apparent regard for racial difference. (quoted in Miller, *Flowers in the Dustbin*, 107)

Without the pioneering efforts of Alan Freed, Berry would never have been afforded the opportunity to have his music heard, or even have performed in front of a white audience. In a short time, Freed's stage shows quickly became legendary among the teenage faithful. For those who could not make it to the location of a live performance, the experience was recreated through Hollywood movies.

During the height of his career and over a two-year period, Freed starred as himself in five movies. All were based on the new musical style and featured dozens of the acts that he played over the radio airwaves and whom had also appeared at Freed's live stage shows. In 1956, his first movie capitalized on the sensation of the new hit record by Bill Haley and His Comets with the song as the movie title, *Rock Around the Clock* (1956). Two others followed that same year with similar titles: *Rock, Rock, Rock* (1956) and *Don't Knock the Rock* (1957). The movies were popular among the same teenage listeners and also profitable for the movie studio. The success prompted two more movies in the following year with *Go, Johnny, Go!* and the semi-autobiographical *Mister Rock and Roll*. The somewhat fictionalized storyline presented the "saga of how Alan Freed discovered rock and roll. The new musical sounds are traced back to their roots in jazz, blues and gospel." Regardless, the highlight of the movies was not just the music but also the scenes of teenagers dancing along to the music.

Prior to Alan Freed, *The Billboard* music charts clearly delineated between sedate pop, rollicking rhythm and blues (labeled "Race Records" during the late 1940s), and down-home country and western. Throughout the 20th century the newly renamed *Billboard Magazine* was the preeminent trade magazine and the "go-to" source for chart statistics. The rhythm and blues chart was definitely reserved for the segregated African American market. Freed's presentation of the so-called "Rock 'n' Roll" was merely a different name for rhythm and blues. However, during an interview with *Rolling Stone* magazine, singer Ruth Brown was asked to identify the time when rhythm and blues became Rock 'n' Roll. She simply replied, "When the white kids started to dance to it." The record that started them dancing was "(We're Gonna) Rock Around the Clock" (Johnson, "How Dancing in Rock Became Uncool," n.p.).

BILL HALEY AND HIS COMETS ROCK TO THE TOP

Bill Haley and His Comets played a mix of country and western, rhythm and blues and western swing. Although he was closely associated with the nationwide teenage Rock 'n' Roll craze of the 1950s, Haley was actually a late-1940s outgrowth of the prototypical western swing band of his time. In fact, prior to settling on the name of his band as Bill Haley and His Comets, the names of his two previous bands included Bill Haley and the Four Aces of Western Swing and Bill Haley and the Saddlemen. During the late 1940s and into the early 1950s, Haley added the influences of rhythm and blues, jive, and honky tonk, a sound emerged that was most often described as rockabilly. Some of his contemporaries called his music western bop. Haley himself once described his musical style as "western jive," that he described as "country & western together with rhythm & blues, and that was rock." Yet it was one single recorded by Bill Haley and His Comets that was best remembered for establishing the 1950s Rock 'n' Roll era: "(We're Gonna) Rock Around the Clock." It was one par-ticular version of the song that was recorded at Decca Recording studios in New York City in 1954 that is credited as starting a trend that had teenagers dancing as never before. One journalist remembered, "Before ['Rock Around the Clock'] became a hit in summer 1955 . . . rock 'n' roll was virtually an underground movement, [it was] something kids listened to on the sly" ("Bill Haley Biography," n.p.).

In contrast, the Rock and Roll Hall of Fame and Museum claim that Haley's 1951 recording of Jackie Brenston's R&B hit "Rocket 88" might have been "the first rock and roll record." Because Haley, who was white, had actually performed a "cover" version of Brenston's song, it would also make that recording "the first rock and roll recording by a white artist." Other similar titles that his band performed in 1952 and 1953 included "Rock This Joint" and "Crazy, Man, Crazy." The Rock Hall said of "Crazy, Man, Crazy" that it was an example of "an original amalgam of country and R&B that arguably became the first rock and roll record to register on Billboard's pop chart."

It was those songs that created interest in Haley among Decca Records. At the time, Decca was a major recording label located in New York City. The very first Decca session for Haley and His Comets in May 1954 produced a two-sided single with "Thirteen Women" intended as the "A-side" release for radio airplay. The "B-side" of a single was usually just an industry standard as a filler song not intended for promotion as a radio single. In the case of the Decca session for Haley, the choice was "(We're Gonna) Rock Around the Clock." Their ver-sion was recorded in an upbeat rockabilly style that was unlike the version that was recorded by a novelty group Sunny Dae and His Knights possibly only a few weeks before in Philadelphia. At the time, neither version of "Rock Around the Clock" created much interest. Haley's version did chart at #23 on *Billboard* but quickly faded away. As part of the same Decca sessions, the group did release another song in July 1954 that became a huge hit. Haley's cover ver-sion of Big Joe Turner's R&B "Shake, Rattle and Roll" achieved national radio airplay and sold more than one million copies.

The following year, the forgotten song was picked to accompany the opening credits for the Hollywood movie *The Blackboard Jungle* (1955). Internet Movie Data Base (IMDb.com) claims that lead actor Glenn Ford had heard his teenage son playing the record and suggested the song for the movie. Ford starred in the lead role as "Mr. Dadier," a former marine who through the use of the G.I. Bill had graduated college with a teaching degree. His first assignment was in an urban high school filled with rebellious teenagers. The movie became a hit and earned four Academy Award nominations. The title song also became a nationwide sensation as a symbol for the rebellious youth and for teenage dancing during the Rock 'n' Roll era. "(We're Gonna) Rock Around the Clock" quickly went to #1 and stayed at the top of the *Billboard* Pop charts for eight weeks. By the end of the year, sales totaled more than six million records. The song, which soon became known simply as "Rock Around the Clock," sold over 25 million records worldwide (Miller, *Flowers in the Dustbin*, 91–93).

"Rock Around the Clock" also kicked off a new trend in teenage dancing. Dance historian Ian Driver said that this one song "reaffirmed the role of dancing as part of the social ritual of boy-meets-girl, which had been the case in ballrooms and dancehalls since the turn of the century" (184). Music legend Dick Clark remembered, "Its initial impact was incredible. Kids hadn't been dancing since the end of the swing era. Suddenly, this spirited tune with a bouncy, rhythmic beat had the kids clapping and dancing" (Uslan, 17). It was also after the release of "Rock Around the Clock" that Alan Freed's term of "Rock 'n' Roll" was traditionally accepted as the proper designation of the music. Upon Bill Haley's 1987 induction into the Rock and Roll Hall of Fame, it was noted, "If only for the impact of 'Rock Around the Clock,' Haley would deserve a place in the Rock and Roll Hall of Fame. Yet his impact in the early days of rock and roll went well beyond that milestone." From 1952 through the end of the decade, Haley continued charting records. Overall, Haley and His Comets sold more than 60 million records ("Bill Haley Biography").

Teenagers and pre-teens loved the music, but the conformist adult society sought to suppress and condemn all things associated with Rock 'n' Roll. Newspapers nationwide blared headlines such as, "Rock-and-Roll Called Communicable Disease"; "Teenage Music Craze Has Parents Worried"; and "We're Losing Control of Our Own Children!" Other newspaper headlines asked, "Does Rock and Roll Cause Delinquency?," "Why They Rock 'n' Roll—And Should They?" and "Music or Madness? Rock and Roll Music Has Stirred Up a Whirlwind of Adult Protest" (*Rock and Roll: The Early Days*," video). Time-Life Books, in remembering the Rock & Roll generation, said FBI director J. Edgar Hoover called the music "a corrupting influence." One Baptist preacher called it a "new low in spiritual degeneracy." *Time* magazine likened the concerts to "Hitler mass meetings." The onslaught continued as the *New York Times* decried, "Rock 'n' roll exploits this same heavy beat [as Rhythm & Blues]—by making it heavier, lustier and transforming it into what has become known as The Big Beat. It is a tense, monotonous beat that often gives rock 'n' roll music a jungle-like persistence" (Samuels, 16).

In reality, much of the protest stemmed from the fact that many of the recording artists were African American. In similar fashion, the white Rock 'n' Roll musicians did not appear to harbor any ill will towards blacks. But in a time of legal segregation built on an American tradition of more than 300 years of slavery, legal subjugation, servitude, and unpunishable lynching of African Americans, white citizens would have nothing to do with the possible integration caused by Rock 'n' Roll. In one filmed television statement, the Executive Secretary of the Alabama White Citizens Council decried, "The obscenity and vulgarity of the Rock and Roll music is obviously a means by which the white man and his children can be driven to the level of the n*****." His cohort, the Chairman of the Alabama White Citizens Council, a local business owner of a used car lot, arrogantly displayed a sign that read, "We serve WHITE customers Only." He steadfastly added, "We set up a twenty-man committee to do away with this vulgar and cannibalistic n***** rock and roll bop" (*Rock and Roll: The Early Days*).

THE ROCK 'N' ROLL MENACE

Alan Freed braved the onslaught and continued promoting his Rock 'n' Roll shows. One extravaganza in early 1957 at the Manhattan Paramount Theater attracted the largest crowd to date in the 31-year history of theater. The double promotion over two days on February 23 and 24 was not only a live stage show but also the premier of the movie *Don't Knock the Rock*. The movie starred Freed as himself, and also many musical performers who were scheduled to appear in person. Similar to the past frenzy of Freed's shows, more than 5,000 teenagers were already in line ready for the 8:15 A.M. opening. As the theater quickly filled to a capacity of 3,650, a long line of teenagers waited outside. The box office eventually reached a total of 15,220, in a line that lasted for 18½ hours. Each of those waiting in line came with the singular purpose of having a good time watching the movie—listening to music—and dancing. A report of the day's event was carried the following day in *The New York Times*. One reporter described the innocent scene:

> Inside the theater, boys and girls danced in the aisles, the foyer, and the lobby, [they] stood in their seats and jumped up and down, screamed with delight as performers were announced, stamped their feet in time with the music and sang with the singers.

At one point, the balcony crowd caused concern as the vigorous feet stamping in time to the music worried the theater owners. A manager called in both the fire department and buildings department to determine the safety of the balcony. As a precautionary measure, more than 1,000 youngsters were ordered removed from the overhanging balcony sections (Asbury, "Rock 'n' Roll Teen-Agers Tie Up the Times Square Area," pp. 1, 12).

The second day provided a similar crowd occurrence as over 16,000 showed up for the extravaganza. In anticipation from the preceding day, the New York City Police Department (NYPD) dispatched 279 officers plus an additional 25 theater-police both outside and inside the theater. In an attempt to maintain crowd control, the scene outside the theater was accentuated by a police patrol both on foot and on horseback. During the course of the performances, *The New York Times* reported that "men and women police patrolled the aisles, chasing would-be dancers back to their seats and ordering those who stood up in their seats to sit down. . . . the police managed to thwart attempts to repeat Friday's dancing in the aisles. The youngsters kept trying, however" (Asbury, "Times Sq. 'Rocks' for Second Day," p. 37).

As Rock 'n' Roll was growing in popularity, dozens of regional television stations aired local teenage dance shows. Television was the ultimate commercial venture for entrepreneurs and product advertisers. As a result, commercial television provided product advertisers seeking larger and often a specific "target market" audience the ability to focus on a single point location of the American teenager. In simple economic sense, outlets such as radio and television provided that opportunity. With both Rock 'n' Roll and Alan Freed in its national ascendancy, the marriage with television seemed a perfect fit. In July 1957, ABC-TV signed Freed to host a nationwide Friday evening prime-time television dance show titled *Alan Freed's Big Beat* (sometimes listed as *The Big Beat*).

But the reality of the innocent power of Rock 'n' Roll's to actively change the status quo of a segregated America became all too apparent. Criticism of the inclusive nature of the music that bridged the races was becoming seen as a "danger" to the American way of life. In addition, the idea that Rock 'n' Roll promoted raw sexuality through the energetic response of its young male and especially female fans was beyond the allowance of mainstream America. The nature of the strict conformity of American segregation came within the second week of Freed's television debut. It should not come as a surprise that the outcry involved dancing. At the time, the fun of teenage dancing was not viewed as innocent, especially when it involved partnering between the races.

The severity of interracial dancing was brought to nationwide attention on one of Freed's television shows. One of the more popular and energetic artists of the genre, Frankie Lymon was a guest on *The Big Beat*. Lymon, who was the lead singer of The Teenagers, was known for hits that included "Goody, Goody," "I'm Not a Juvenile Delinquent," "Why Do Fools Fall in Love," and "Little Bitty Pretty One," among many others. During his customary energetic performance, Lymon was positioned on a raised platform in the middle of dancing teenagers. At one point, Lymon innocently reached down into the audience and brought up a young white girl to dance. The producers were appalled at the incident, especially ABC's southern affiliates, at the so-called "blatant" disregard for the rules of segregation. Without any hesitation, ABC cancelled Freed's TV dance show (Jackson, 55–56; Fong-Torres, "Alan Freed Biography," n.p.).

Sadly, most of the hatred was due to the fact that a black man was dancing with a white woman. (In a legally enforced segregated society, African Americans were lynched even upon an accusation of a relationship with a white woman.) Therefore, Lymon's actions were viewed as the ultimate violation of a woman's purity. In the eyes of not just the segregationists, but also all American adults, dancing led to fornication. For the segregationists, it led to a "mongrelization" of the races. Severe hostility towards the act of intercourse between a white woman and a black man existed, especially in the 11 former Confederate states. At the time, the situation even for a "mixed race" married couple (called "miscegenation") was against the law in almost all of the United States. Legal marriage status between a man and a woman was not granted until 1967, as the U.S. Supreme Court Decision *Loving v. Virginia* invalidated all laws prohibiting interracial marriage (U.S. Supreme Court 388 U.S. 1, 1967).

ELVIS PRESLEY, "THE KING OF ROCK 'N' ROLL"

Teenagers not only listened to Rock 'n' Roll on the radio, they also bought the music. After 1955, the sale of Rock 'n' Roll records accumulated at an astounding rate. In 1950, Americans of all ages purchased more than 190 million records. By mid-decade, the number doubled and by 1960, it had reached an astounding 600 million records sold. By that time, teenagers accounted for more than 70 percent of the record-buying public. The sales were driven at first by the success of songs such as "Rock Around the Clock" and soon overtaken by Elvis Presley. In 1956, Presley sold almost 4 million recordings alone. In that same year, more than 10 million portable record players were sold, attributed to the fact that people wanted to play Presley's records. By 1960, he had released dozens of hits that amounted to more than 28 million records (Halberstam, 474).

Elvis Presley became the definitive image of Rock 'n' Roll. As his first record producer Sam Phillips once said, "If I could find a white singer who sounded black, I could make a [fortune]." In Elvis, Phillips found that fortune maker—a young, white musical pioneer whose music sounded black. The dominant factor was that Elvis and his song styles crossed the cultural barrier between black and white, thereby transcending segregation. In an interview for the documentary video *Rock 'n' Roll Explodes*, singer Ruth Brown, herself an accomplished R&B singer, explained:

> So when Elvis Presley came on the scene, the only thing I can say is he did it right, he did it good, and again where Elvis was concerned there was no color line, because everybody liked his music. And Elvis Presley was what they were lookin' for to get that music, not necessarily accepted because it was already accepted, but permissible for the white kids to listen to openly.

His popularity soon surged as he signed with a manager by the name of Colonel Tom Parker. (The title of "colonel" remains a mystery.) When reporters asked Elvis who he sounded like, he often replied, "I don't sound like nobody." Beyond his singing, it was his live appearances that attracted not only media attention, but also adoring, screaming, female fans. First and foremost, Elvis was extremely good looking, courteous, and personable. His gyrations on stage, however, were completely unprecedented. Coming from an era and a preceding decade when singers such as Frank Sinatra hugged the microphone and simply swooned as they sang, Elvis broke all barriers of stage decorum. He reacted to the music and swiveled his hips, quivering and shaking his whole body, thereby causing all sorts of negative attacks against his singing style.

The difference was that Elvis moved and danced in a way that no other *white* entertainer had done before. His dancing was not new, but for the first time white audiences were seeing dancing and moves from the pelvic and hip area that in the past were strictly confined to the segregated jook joints and honky tonks of African Americans. The segregation extended so far and deep that mainstream America was totally unaware of African American culture. In an early moment of humility, Presley could not understand the objections to his performance style. He explained, "The colored folks been singing it and playing it just like

I'm doin' now, man, for more years than I know. They played it like that in the shanties and in their jook joints, and nobody paid it no mind 'til I goosed it up. I got it from them" (quoted in Miller, *Flowers in the Dustbin*, 136). In an interview for *Rock 'n' Roll Explodes*, musician and songwriter Hank Ballard said of Elvis:

> See in white society the movement of the butt—shakin' the leg, all that was considered obscene for white folk. And here is this white boy and that grind—rollin' his butt and shakin' that notorious leg [laughs] . . . I hadn't even seen a black dude doin it—Elvis he had some movements I had never witnessed.

Due to such risqué body movements, Presley was often told to tone down his stage act. At separate performances during 1955 in San Diego and Florida, authorities warned Presley that if he moved at all during his show "he would be arrested on obscenity charges" (Johnson, "How Dancing in Rock Became Uncool," n.p.).

Despite the attempt at suppression, Elvis continued singing and performing in his own way, which only added to his nationwide appeal. In late 1955, a new contract was negotiated with the prestigious RCA recording label for an unprecedented amount of money. By January 1956, his first RCA single "Heartbreak Hotel" was a nationwide hit as sales quickly jumped over one million copies and his career skyrocketed. As a result, his national television debut came on January 28, 1956, appearing on Tommy and Jimmy Dorsey's *Stage Show.* The Dorsey Brothers, although major musical stars of the 1930s and 1940s swing era, were well past their youthful prime and appealed to an older adult audience. Their sedate television show format usually had a guest performer who sang accompanied by the Dorsey studio orchestra. The booking of Elvis was due strictly to his popularity and as an attempt to boost ratings.

The nationwide controversy started on April 3, 1956, as Presley made another national television network appearance on *The Milton Berle Show.* Unlike Dorsey, Berle had welcomed the changes in the entertainment business. (See Television chapter for a discussion on Milton Berle.) Only one month prior to the Presley booking, Bill Haley and His Comets appeared on Berle's show, singing "Rock Around the Clock" while teens gleefully danced for the studio audience. A segue from the song included a contingent led by Berle, followed by his regulars and other guest celebrities, demonstrating all types of dance styles in a Broadway-style rendition of "Rock Around the Clock."

In announcing full acceptance of Elvis, Berle told a nationwide viewing audience, "It's no secret that Elvis Presley is the fastest rising young singer in the entertainment industry today." On the top-rated Berle show, Presley was allowed to perform as he wished as the cameras focused on his full gyrating body from head to toe. The host recognized the audience reaction and invited the singer for another appearance. For the follow-up performance on June 5, 1956, Presley sang an upbeat Rock 'n' Roll version of a rhythm and blues song titled "Hound Dog." Actually Elvis chose the song (a #1 R&B Hit for "Big Mama" Thornton) simply to have fun. He sang in front of a small combo composed of a standup bass, rhythm guitar, and drums. As he sang the cameras drew back to show his whole body, performing and dancing as only Elvis could with gyrating pelvis and hip movements. "Hound Dog" became an immediate hit with his fans, selling millions of copies. But the media fallout was not favorable and somewhat predictable.

Despite Berle's support and the good-natured approach to the song "Hound Dog," criticism mounted. Most of the criticism did not come from the ultra-conservative south, but rather from New York. One example was from noted television critic Jack Gould of *The New York Times*. Gould was both particularly harsh and possibly even tone deaf, as he decried, "Mr. Presley has no discernable singing ability," comparing it to a "whine." He added insult by saying, "He is a rock-and-roll variation of one of the most standard acts in show business: the virtuoso of the hootchy-kootchy, that heretofore has been primarily identified with the repertoire of the blonde bombshells of the burlesque runway." New York City-based congressman

A full-length picture of Elvis Presley performing live during the mid-1950s. He was often shown full-length in earlier performances and on the Milton Berle television show. However later images and television appearances often showed him only from the waist up. (Photofest)

Emanuel Celler spoke of "the bad taste that is exemplified by the Elvis Presley 'Hound Dog' music, with his animal gyrations which are certainly most distasteful to me, are violative of all that I know to be in good taste." Another New York journalist described it as "the weirdest and plainly planned, suggestive animation short of an aborigine's mating dance." The *New York Daily News*, with one of the largest circulations in America, described it as "suggestive and vulgar," adding that Presley's song represented a "kind of animalism" (quoted in Miller, *Flowers in the Dustbin*, 132–33).

On July 1, 1956, Presley made another national television appearance to sing "Hound Dog," this time on *The Steve Allen Show*, which was also filmed in New York. However, Allen said, "I will not allow him to do anything that will offend anyone" (Miller, *Flowers in the Dustbin*, 135). In doing so, to lessen any suggestive nature of the lyrics, they insisted that Presley appear wearing a tuxedo and sing his hit "Hound Dog" to a real live dog. It was also explicitly added that any suggestion of pelvic movement was eliminated and "against the rules." Elvis felt snubbed and vowed to never succumb again to restraint.

Later that same night, after the performance on *The Steve Allen Show*, Presley appeared in a split-screen telephone interview on the popular nationwide television show *Hy Gardner Calling*. During the almost 10-minute interview, Presley appeared a bit perturbed, yet was ever respectful and humble about his success and performance style. During the exchange with celebrity host Hy Gardner, the talk opened with discussion on Presley wearing a tuxedo for the first time and also about Cadillac cars. Gardner eventually asked about the controversy surrounding Presley's performance style. The exchange went as follows:

> **Gardner**: And do you think that you've learned anything from the criticism leveled at you?
>
> **Presley**: No, I haven't.
>
> **Gardner**: You haven't, eh?
>
> **Presley**: Because I don't feel that I've been doing anything wrong.
>
> **Gardner**: Do you think that your rocking and rolling has had an evil influence on teenagers or do you think that . . .
>
> **Presley**: I don't see that any type of music would have any bad influence on people, it's only music, I mean, I can't figure it out, I mean in a lot of the papers they say that rock 'n' roll is a bad influence on juvenile delinquency. I don't think it is, 'er juvenile delinquency is something that 'er, that's 'er, well, it's just, I don't know how to explain it, but I don't see how music can have anything to do with it at all.
>
> **Gardner**: I understand that Mitch Miller at Columbia Records defines rock 'n' roll as a safe form of rebellion against mother, father and teacher—do you go along with this analysis?
>
> **Presley**: I don't know exactly what he means by rebellion, I mean 'er, how would rock 'n' roll music make anybody rebel against their parents?

Despite the negativity, Presley's fame was skyrocketing. A few weeks later Elvis made the first of three appearances on *The Ed Sullivan Show* and became a sensation the likes of which had never been seen before (*"Rock 'n' Roll Explodes"* video).

The Ed Sullivan Show was the premiere showcase for the American TV viewing audience and also considered the arbiter of "good taste" in America. Therefore, as the hottest act in the country, it was a natural fit for an appearance by Elvis. As it turned out, Presley proved bigger than expected, as his appearance was the single-largest viewing audience for one television episode. On September 9, 1956, an estimated 42 million people (an astounding 82 percent of the entire nationwide viewing audience) watched his Sunday evening prime-time performance on *The Ed Sullivan Show*. After the show, Sullivan, as did others across the nation, thought Presley's gyrations and wiggling hips were too vulgar for the family-oriented audience. On January 7, 1957, during Presley's third and final appearance, Sullivan instructed the cameras to only show Elvis from the waist up ("Why They Rock 'n' Roll—And Should They?," 16).

Despite the camera censorship, Presley still captivated a nationwide audience who most of all wanted to not only *hear* him, but most important wanted to *see* him. Beginning with his hit song "Love Me Tender" in early 1956, his widespread appeal also proved profitable for Hollywood movies. His first movie was a Civil War drama of the same title of his recent hit, *Love Me Tender* (1956). The movie was a huge success and led to a profitable movie career. The following year, he starred in *Loving You* and *Jailhouse Rock*, followed by *King Creole* in 1958. Although movies starring Elvis were profitable and large legions of fans attended, it was still his tumultuous list of hit songs from 1956 through 1959 that made him the ultimate Rock 'n' Roll sensation. Despite all attempts to criticize or censor him, Elvis continued to sell records as no one else before him ever had. In 1957, Presley's single "All Shook Up" sold an astonishing 2.5 million copies. "Hound Dog" was even more popular, with another unheard-of 7 million copies added to his total. Before the decade was done Presley records amounted to more than 28 million records sold ("Why They Rock 'n' Roll— And Should They?," 16).

The popularity of Elvis Presley and Rock 'n' Roll can in no way be underestimated. Although reporters, critics, and the media relentlessly attacked him and his so-called "dirty body movements," Elvis represented a cultural phenomenon unlike any other. According to historian David Halberstam, beginning with Elvis Presley "the new music had entered the mainstream of American culture" (479). Presley was soon labeled as the "King of Rock 'n' Roll" as both he and the music were just too profitable to be ignored. To paraphrase an early Presley recording, "Mystery Train," the Elvis train appeared to be rolling along and gaining steam full speed ahead without stopping. But in 1958, one singular somewhat fictitious figure did what no critic or arbiter could succeed in doing, which was remove him from the stage. In 1958, "Uncle Sam" called and drafted Pvt. Elvis Presley into the United States Army. At the time, Selective Service was an active part of every young man's life. The random act of selecting individuals for military service remained virtually intact from 1940 through 1974. With few exceptions, American youth were required to serve in the active military, many overseas. For Pvt. Presley, it was active duty in Germany guarding against a possible Soviet Cold War invasion along its borders. As a result of his induction, both his music and movie careers were interrupted. Upon his release in 1960, he welcomed his fans with another musical titled *G.I. Blues*. Many other Elvis musicals added vacation themes such as *Blue Hawaii* (1961), *Fun in Acapulco* (1963), and *Viva Las Vegas* (1964). None of those films or his later music contained the same raw vitality of his pre-military career. Regardless, he was still a very profitable entertainer and entered into the realm of legend.

FURTHER READING

Victor Bondi, ed. *American Decades: 1950–1959*. Detroit: Gale Research, 1996.

Ralph G. Giordano. *Country & Western Dancing (American Dance Floor Series)*, Santa Barbara, CA: ABC-Clio, 2010.

Ralph G. Giordano. *Social Dancing in America Lindy Hop to Hip Hop 1901 to 2000, Volume Two*. Westport, CT: Greenwood Press, 2007.

Grace and Fred M. Hechinger. *Teen-Age Tyranny*. New York: Fawcett, 1963.

John A. Jackson. *American Bandstand: Dick Clark and the Making of a Rock 'n' Roll Empire*. New York: Oxford University Press, 1997.

James Miller. *Flowers in the Dustbin: The Rise of Rock and Roll*. New York: Simon & Schuster, 1999.

Phillip Norman. *Rave On: The Biography of Buddy Holly*. New York: Simon & Schuster, 1996.

Michael Uslan and Bruce Solomon. *Dick Clark's the First 25 Years of Rock and Roll*. New York: Dell, 1981.

CHAPTER 5

Literature

Despite the socially conservative nature of American society during the 1950s, a large selection of critically acclaimed, nonconformist literature was published. Some of those publications were novels that questioned the "status quo" as well as outright criticized American society and culture. Some of those critiques came in the form of dystopian settings as well as science fiction themes of time travel or of aliens from far away planets. This is not to say that an overwhelming number of best-selling books, especially in nonfiction, promoted the joys of conformity and consumerism.

PEYTON PLACE AND LIBRARY SERVICES

The novel that helped shed the fake veil of American society was *Peyton Place*. Written by Grace Metalious, *Peyton Place* (Julian Messner, Inc., 1956) was set in a fictional town of the same name in idyllic New Hampshire. In its first 10 days of release, it sold an astounding 60,000 copies. The novel brought out the vicious nature of class privileges as the story centered on three female characters. The main character, Constance Mackenzie was an unmarried mother with an illegitimate daughter named Allison. The third character was a young girl named Selena Cross who was stuck in poverty and was subjected to a sexually violent stepfather. The hypocrisy of American society was prevalent as Metalious wrote of adultery, incest, promiscuity, and other hidden small-town secrets. The editors at Barnes & Noble wrote, "In an era when keeping up appearances ruled, this book's exploration of the darkness lurking behind even the most brightly painted doors ignited readers' imaginations."

Within 18 months, *Peyton Place* was the best-selling novel of all time and was on *The New York Times* bestseller list for 59 weeks. In an article on February 2, 1958, *The New York Times* noted that less than two years after its release, *Peyton Place* had passed Margaret Mitchell's *Gone with the Wind* as the top-selling American novel of all time. Ten years later it still remained as the top-selling fiction title in America, with more than ten million copies sold. It still sold well into the 21st century with reported sales of more than 20 million copies to date. It was made into a 1957 Hollywood movie of the same title, and it also attained wide popularity as a TV primetime soap opera from 1964 to 1969. At first it aired two nights a week. As viewership topped 60 million, the show was aired three nights a week and eventually ran for a total of 514 episodes.

After an initial downturn in reading caused by the early television years of 1947 to 1953, reading took an upturn and grew steadily. Book sales of all kinds sold very well. In 1955, book sales totaled more than 400 million. By 1960, book purchasing doubled to over 813 million per year. Sales continued to rise, as within the next five years more than 1.3 billion books were sold, of which a significant amount were paperbacks. The best-selling book of the period was the Bible with more than 26.5 million copies. At the start of the 1950s, comic books offered over 650 titles as total sales exceeded over 300 million each year. Library circulation saw an increase of more than 40 percent. The increase in library book circulation was aided by federal sponsorship of the Library Services Act of 1956, which provided for new library services in 169 towns and cities. The act also added more than 200 bookmobiles servicing rural areas and provided additional access to over 4 million individuals. Improvement at existing library facilities throughout the nation served an additional 32 million people (Whitfield, 84; Kaplan, 14–15).

THE GREAT BOOKS PROJECT AND *READER'S DIGEST*

In 1952, the editors of the prestigious Encyclopedia Britannica announced the culmination of an ambitious literary release, *Great Books of the Western World*. Known as "The Great Books Project," the purpose was to allow any individual to be part of "the great conversation about the great ideas." In doing so the collection would provide the reader with a concise collection of valuable classic literature to make him or her a well-rounded, knowledgeable individual in the history of Western society. The vast array of topics was contained within 54 volumes that included the great works of drama, economics, ethics, fiction, history, philosophy, poetry, politics, and the sciences, among others. The set could easily compare to the famous *Encyclopedia* compiled by Denis Diderot and Jean le Rond d'Alembert from 1751 to 1772. That 18th-century publication had compiled similar subjects and is cited as a major publication leading to the Enlightenment period of world history. Many scholars point to that period of development towards the French Revolution as the beginning of the idea of liberty and the growth of Western democracy.

The idea of promoting Western democracy was transformed during the 1950s as the topics of *Great Books of the Western World* were grouped into four subjects: Imaginative Literature, Mathematics and the Natural Sciences, History and Social Science, and Philosophy and Theology. The first three volumes of the set provided an alphabetical listing of subject matter with a brief encyclopedic overview of the subject topic. The remaining volumes were arranged in chronological order providing classic works that were relevant to modern-day

American society. Volume Four began with Homer's classic story of *The Iliad* and *The Odyssey* followed by works from Ancient Greece such as *Agamemnon, Oedipus,* and more by writers and philosophers including Aristotle, Plato, and Sophocles. Others included Ancient Rome such Marcus Aurelius, Virgil, and Plutarch. Scientific discourse included *On the Revolutions of Heavenly Spheres* and works by Nicolaus Copernicus, Johannes Kepler, Isaac Newton, and Albert Einstein. Religious doctrine was represented by Thomas Aquinas' *Summa Theologica,* among others. The early works of literature included Dante's *Divine Comedy,* Chaucer's *Canterbury Tales,* Machiavelli's *The Prince,* Hobbes' *Leviathan,* and all of the works by William Shakespeare. A sampling of Enlightenment works included Montesquieu's *The Spirit of the Laws,* Rousseau's *The Social Contract,* and Adam Smith's *The Wealth of Nations.* Important documents from the founding of the United States included the Declaration of Independence, Articles of Confederation, and the Constitution of the United States of America. Other writings from the founders of America included those by Alexander Hamilton, John Jay, and James Madison. Political and scientific discourse was provided by Charles Darwin, Karl Marx, and multiple writings of Sigmund Freud. Some literary classics included Herman Melville's *Moby Dick,* Tolstoy's *War and Peace,* as well as multiple writings from Mark Twain, Henrik Ibsen, and William James. Some of the more contemporary literary works included Samuel Beckett's *Waiting for Godot,* as well as writings by James Joyce, F. Scott Fitzgerald, William Faulkner, Ernest Hemingway, Franz Kafka, Eugene O'Neill, George Orwell, and Virginia Woolf.

The successful sales of the Great Books Program encouraged other reading-relating consumer products. One such endeavor was *Reader's Digest,* which offered a "condensed" book program with a monthly mail order subscription over 500,000. From its inception in 1922, *Reader's Digest* was a conservative-minded magazine based in Chappaqua, New York, that promoted wholesome family values. No mention was ever made of the displeasure of suburbia, civil rights, native ancestries, or homosexuality, among other taboo subjects. During the 1950s and well into the 1960s, the editors of *Reader's Digest* took every opportunity to provide patriotic support of the American way and also published virulent anti-Communist articles. The publication did from time to time bring forward some of the inherent dangers promoted by American capitalism. One instance in 1952 was a series of articles called "Cancer by the Carton" that "linked smoking with lung cancer" (Kammen, 180).

During the 1950s, *Reader's Digest* was the top-selling consumer magazine in the United States with a monthly circulation of more than 13.3 million. Many of the subscriptions were delivered by postal mail directly to a family household. (By 2013, it still maintained a circulation of over 4.5 million.) At the time, the magazine maintained its long-standing format of providing 30 articles per issue. (The idea was one article of reading per day.) It also provided other items such as jokes and a vocabulary page. Two regular humor features in patriotic support of the nation were provided in "Life in these United States" and "Humor in Uniform." Each offered funny anecdotes on everyday life, mostly suburban, and the joy of military life. One longer article was usually reserved as a condensed and edited popular book (Kammen, 181).

FICTION AND NONFICTION BOOKS OF THE TIME

At the time, many notable fiction works were published that received wide literary acclaim. Quite a few of them also became required reading for many of the nation's high school and college students throughout the remainder of the century and into the 21st century.

Fiction Bestsellers

- *The Chronicles of Narnia* (1950–56) by C.S. Lewis
- *I, Robot* (1950) by Isaac Asimov
- *The Martian Chronicles* (1950) by Ray Bradbury
- *The Catcher in the Rye* (1951) by J.D. Salinger
- *Charlotte's Web* (1952) by E.B. White
- *East of Eden* (1952) by John Steinbeck
- *Invisible Man* (1952) by Ralph Ellison
- *The Old Man and the Sea* (1952) by Ernest Hemingway
- *The Crucible* (1953) by Arthur Miller
- *Fahrenheit 451* (1953) by Ray Bradbury
- *Waiting for Godot* (1953) by Samuel Beckett
- *Lord of the Flies* (1954) by William Golding
- *The Lord of the Rings Trilogy* (1954) by J.R.R. Tolkien
- *Lolita* (1955) by Vladimir Nabokov
- *Howl* (1956) by Allen Ginsberg
- *Night* (1956) by Elie Wiesel
- *Peyton Place* (1956) by Grace Metalious
- *The Cat in the Hat* (1957) by Dr. Seuss
- *Doctor Zhivago* (1957) by Boris Pasternak
- *On the Road* (1957) by Jack Kerouac
- *Profiles in Courage* (1957) by John F. Kennedy
- *Breakfast at Tiffany's* (1958) by Truman Capote
- *The Witch of Blackbird Pond* (1958) by Elizabeth George Speare
- *The Haunting of Hill House* (1959) by Shirley Jackson
- *A Separate Peace* (1959) by John Knowles

Nonfiction Bestsellers

Some of the nonfiction literary bestsellers included: *Betty Crocker's Picture Cook Book* (1950); Thor Heyerdahl, *Kon-Tiki* (1950); *Better Homes and Gardens Garden Book* (1951); *Better Homes and Gardens Handyman's Book* (1951); Rachel L. Carson, *The Sea Around Us* (1951); *Thorndike-Barnhart Comprehensive Desk Dictionary* (1951); *How to Play Your Best Golf* (1953) by Tommy Armour; *Better Homes and Gardens Diet Book* (1954); *Webster's New World Dictionary of the American Language* (1956); *Betty Crocker's Picture Cook Book*, 2nd ed. (1956); *Better Homes and*

Chart 5.1   Best-Selling Books of the Decade, 1950–59

Year	Fiction Bestsellers	Nonfiction Bestsellers
1950	Henry Morton Robinson, *The Cardinal*	*Betty Crocker's Picture Cook Book*
1951	James Jones, *From Here to Eternity*	Gayelord Hauser, *Look Younger, Live Longer*
1952	Thomas B. Costain, *The Silver Chalice*	*The Holy Bible: Revised Standard Version*
1953	Lloyd C. Douglas, *The Robe*	*The Holy Bible: Revised Standard Version*
1954	Morton Thompson, *Not as a Stranger*	*The Holy Bible: Revised Standard Version*
1955	Herman Wouk, *Marjorie Morningstar*	Anne Morrow Lindbergh, *Gift from the Sea*
1956	William Brinkley, *Don't Go Near the Water*	Dan Dale Alexander, *Arthritis and Common Sense*
1957	James Gould Cozzens, *By Love Possessed*	Art Linkletter, *Kids Say the Darndest Things!*
1958	Boris Pasternak, *Doctor Zhivago*	Art Linkletter, *Kids Say the Darndest Things!*
1959	Leon Uris, *Exodus*	Pat Boone, *Twixt Twelve and Twenty*

Source: Publisher's Weekly. Chart compiled by author.

Gardens Barbecue Book (1956); *Better Homes and Gardens Decorating Book* (1956); Art Linkletter's *Kids Say the Darndest Things!* (1957); *Better Homes and Gardens Flower Arranging* (1957); *Better Homes and Gardens Salad Book* (1958); Abigail Van Buren, *Dear Abby* (1958); Thor Heyerdahl, *Aku-Aku: The Story of Easter Island* (1958); William Strunk Jr. and E. B. White's *The Elements of Style* (1959); and *The General Foods Kitchens Cookbook* (1959), among dozens of other similar titles.

DWIGHT MACDONALD AS "MAC THE KNIFE"

Included among the literary works of the 1950s were a significant amount of titles that criticized American society. According to Eric Foner writing in *The Story of American Freedom*, books such as William Whyte's *The Organization Man* (1956) and Vance Packard's *The Hidden Persuaders* (1957) were "a critique of the monotony of modern work, the role of bureaucracies, and the emptiness of suburban life, created the vocabulary for an assault on the nation's political institutions and social values that lay just over the horizon." At the time Russell Kirk, writing *The Conservative Mind* (1953), defined many of the values of American society. Yet at the same time he criticized the consumer culture created for mass society. Despite the criticism, the overall majority of the affluent middle class and suburban households seemed unfazed by the "widespread complacency about the American way of life." Some of those other critiques came

from "intellectuals" such as Ralph Ellison, Betty Friedan, and Dwight Macdonald (Kirk, 270–71).

At the time, books of all kinds were a valued part of American culture as was
the literary critic. One of the best known was Dwight Macdonald (1906–1982), an
individual who during the 1950s was well known as both a literary critic and
also as a cultural critic. At the time, writers such as Macdonald held sway over a
large segment of the American population. In a biographical essay, "Mac the
Knife: On Dwight Macdonald" in *The Nation*, Jennifer Szalai described his
influence as:

> If one were to point out that the wider authority of literary criticism is barely dis-
> cernible today, one could hardly be accused of courting a controversy or kicking up
> a fuss. There certainly is a coterie [small group] of Americans for whom literature
> and its criticism is a matter of urgency or livelihood or both, but the notion of
> the literary critic as a cultural gatekeeper, whose judgments shape tastes and move
> units, sounds either fanciful or anachronistic, depending on whether you believe
> that such a creature ever really existed. Our culture is now so big and so varied, the
> population so diverse and so fragmented, that the very idea of anything or anyone
> having "wider authority" sounds silly, if not absurd. (Szalai, "Mac the Knife: On
> Dwight Macdonald," n.p.)

As an influential writer living during the height of the Red Scare and the
wild accusations posed by the likes of Senator Joe McCarthy, Macdonald was
well-aware of the possible consequences of any attachment to Marxism. In
1952, he wrote a series of essays in a public debate with Norman Mailer. Within
those public debates, Macdonald denounced Communism and its leader
Joseph Stalin. The next year, he issued a revised version of an earlier 1940s
essay, "The Root is Man," in which he praised the virtues of Western democracy. (Examples of Macdonald's work from the 1950s were compiled and edited
by John Summers in *Masscult and Midcult: Essays Against the American Grain*,
New York Review Books Classics, 2011.) In keeping with the climate of the day,
Szalai summed up, "Macdonald specialized in the ruthless takedown." One of
his targets was the Great Books Project, which he sarcastically labeled "The
Book-of-the-Millennium Club." His criticism was published in 1952 in *The New
Yorker* simultaneously with the release of the multi-volume compilation. Macdonald wrote, "The problem is not placing these already available books in
people's hands . . . but getting people to read them, and the hundred pounds
of densely printed, poorly edited reading matter assembled by Drs. Adler and
Hutchins is scarcely likely to do that" (Szalai, "Mac the Knife," n.p.).

In his introduction of Macdonald's essays in *Masscult and Midcult*, Louis
Menand said, "Macdonald understood how this culture was contrived and which
buttons of vanity and insecurity it pushed so successfully." Macdonald's criticism was mainly leveled at what he called the "Lords of Kitsch." It was they
whom Macdonald accused of manufacturing the wide variety of consumer
products based on an advertiser's created want of a product rather than as an
essential need. He often claimed that the products were not built of a sustained
quality to be savored by an individual, but rather "for a herd of mass men,
ripe for manipulation." Macdonald was firmly focused on the constant and

overwhelming burden of consumer culture that was placed upon the American middle class. Much of that burden was placed upon the white, suburban, middle-class housewife.

MIKE HAMMER AND THE BACHELOR PAD

An attitude of the approval of the sexual prowess and masculinity of the American male was reflected in the popular novels by author Mickey Spillane. In 1947, Spillane's first hardcover of *I, the Jury* introduced the fictional private detective Mike Hammer to the American public. As an expensive and cumbersome hardcover, the book sold only about 15,000 copies. With the availability of inexpensive paperback publishing, the book sold more than 2.5 million copies. Spillane's *I, the Jury* caused concern over the free use of coarse language, violence, and sexual innuendos. The covers also sparked some criticism, especially from conservative religious groups due to the provocative images of seductive women. Despite the early controversies, the success of *I, the Jury* spurred Spillane to churn out more novels with the same fictional character. By the mid-1950s, all of his books had the theme of the "hard-boiled" tough guy. The fictional Mike Hammer viewed women with disdain as nothing more than sexual playthings. Yet with the growing paranoia of the Red Scare of Communism, Hammer was soon promoting American patriotism and fighting Communists. Spillane continued his next six novels on the same theme, as each sold more than three million in paperback sales. By 1956, seven of Spillane's books were among the top-ten best-selling fiction titles in the history of American publishing (Halberstam, 60–61).

One of the most prevalent symbols of masculine virility was the idea of owning a "bachelor pad," a living space, usually an apartment in an urban setting, where an unmarried (termed "single") adult male lived. In some cases, the apartment was kept as an extra living space where a businessman could have an extramarital affair. The life of the male bachelor was portrayed in all sorts of media such as Hollywood movies as enjoying a freewheeling, sexual lifestyle. Oftentimes, they bedded (implied but not shown visually) "easy females" and "dumb blondes" such as stewardesses and cocktail waitresses. All throughout every aspect of society, the virulent male was viewed with respect and envy. The morality aspect was usually satisfactorily applied as the freewheeling bachelor was eventually looking to "settle down" and get married. Of course there was no social equivalent for the single woman. Any woman who might not be a virgin was viewed with disdain and often criticized with harsh language. The ultimate irony was that the bachelor would actually be having sex with a willing woman. Yet society, on the surface, only acknowledged "good girls" as living the wholesome lifestyles as wives, mothers, grandmothers, sisters, and daughters.

A CRITIQUE AGAINST CONFORMITY

The critique that basically shredded the myth of an idyllic, affluent American lifestyle was evident in two best-selling novels. Both Sloan Wilson's *The Man in the Gray Flannel Suit* (Da Capo Press, 1955) and William Whyte's *The Organization*

Man (Simon & Schuster, 1956) brought forward the monotony of the 9-to-5 office worker. Others such as C. Wright Mills criticized the post-war defense industry in *The Power Elite* (Oxford University Press, 1956). A similar critique, although mainly upon white corporate America, was provided in 1950 by sociologist David Riesman's *The Lonely Crowd.* Riesman, who wrote with Nathan Glazer and Reuel Denney, said that the corporate man was "defining himself in terms of the opinions and goals of others, or in terms of the bureaucratically established goals of the organization." Yale University Press claimed "*The Lonely Crowd* is considered by many to be the most influential book of the twentieth century." Todd Gitlin, writing for *The New York Times Bookend*, added, "As accessible as it is acute, *The Lonely Crowd* is indispensable reading for anyone who wishes to understand American society. After half a century, this book has lost none of its capacity to make sense of how we live."

Vance Packard (1914–1996) introduced the concept of motivational research within advertising agencies in his best-selling book *The Hidden Persuaders* (D. McKay Co., 1957). Packard's book sold more than one million copies under the pretext of exposing the advertising world. The novel did not actually reveal very much of the real inner workings of Madison Avenue. Packard, however, did manage to add more fuel to the existing paranoia of Americans who were now fearful of having their minds manipulated. Sidra Stitch, writing in *Made in U.S.A.,* said *The Hidden Persuaders* "focused on depicting the value conflict between old Protestant ethic of self-reliance thrift, and hard work, and the new organizational ethic that fostered belongingness, consumption, and leisure" (10).

THE UNIQUE CRITIQUE OF VONNEGUT AND JACKSON

Two other notable writers that offered a unique critique of American society were Kurt Vonnegut and Shirley Jackson. Kurt Vonnegut (1922–2007) had an active writing career that lasted 50 years. He eventually published 14 novels, five books of nonfiction, a few plays, and numerous short stories that were released in compilation book form. Some of his works were also made into Hollywood movies and television shows. All of his work contained a satirical view of American society, yet he was often classified as a writer of science fiction. His work was summarized by Biography.com: "He is known for his satirical literary style, as well as the science-fiction elements in much of his work." In many ways the title is appropriate as he shaped his ideas based on the "science" he saw as he worked as a publicist for General Electric (GE) from 1947 to 1950 in Schenectady, New York. His work was also "fiction," as his characters and situations were fictional. Yet he combined the fictional with some of the real themes of "science" that he saw firsthand while working at GE. At the time, GE was a leader in advancing all types of science and technology ranging from military items to consumer needs. The GE labs were also staffed by the prototypical 1950s conservative conformist corporate lifestyle. The workers became the company and none of them either dressed flamboyantly or displayed lifestyles other than the married male with a stay-at-home wife with children and a suburban home. During the years after his discharge from the U.S. Army (Vonnegut served in World War II and was captured at the Battle of the Bulge), he worked as a writer in GE's company newspaper, also writing press releases for distribution to the wider public.

Vonnegut never saw himself as living the life of the "Company Man" and began writing short stories. At the time, numerous magazines existed for writers to make a decent living by writing short stories for publication. Throughout the decade there was a large increase in specialty magazines aimed at the growing interest in literature, fantasy, sports, recreation, and leisure. (Almost 7,000 magazines of all types were published. At least 45 magazine titles had a circulation of at least one million per year.) The most popular of the mass-market magazines included *Collier's, Cosmopolitan, Life, Look, Saturday Evening Post,* and *Time,* among dozens of others. Specialty science-fiction magazines were also common such as *Amazing Stories, Argosy, Astounding Stories, Galaxy Science Fiction,* and *Infinity.* During the early part of the 1950s, Vonnegut had a few short stories published, which encouraged him to leave GE and embark on a full-time career as an author. His short stories soon appeared in many of the prestigious magazines during the decade.

Vonnegut's first novel, *Player Piano* (Charles Scribner's Sons, 1952), was derived from his experiences at GE. The story set at the "Ilium Works" in upstate New York was a pseudonym for Schenectady and General Electric. (It was published again in 1954 as *Utopia 14* and re-issued as *Player Piano* in 1966.) The story set in the "near future" is centered on a scientist named Dr. Paul Proteus who contemplates the fact that his skills are not being used to benefit society. Vonnegut's second novel, *The Sirens of Titan* (George T. Delacorte, 1959), is set among the planets of Earth, Mars, and Mercury. He also provides locations on some of the moons of Saturn. A major character is a robot named "Salo" from the fictitious planet Tralfamadore. Vonnegut returned to Tralfamadore in his most famous novel *Slaughterhouse-Five* (1969). The main character, the time-tripping Billy Pilgrim, is heavily based upon Vonnegut's own wartime experiences. As an Army private, Vonnegut was captured during the Battle of the Bulge. He was a POW who survived the incendiary bombings of Dresden in Germany.

A website devoted to the legacy of Shirley Jackson (1916–1965) describes her as "one of the preeminent authors of classic American mystery and suspense fiction." She is often credited as the creator of the modern suspense fiction. Authors could write a few pieces a year and secure a steady paycheck while waiting for either an advance from a publisher or a royalty check. For Jackson, a significant amount of her work also included real-life "household stories." Biographer Ruth Franklin said, "[S]he also had a genuine gift for this mode of writing. Her household stories take advantage of the same techniques she developed as a fiction writer: the gradual buildup of carefully chosen detail, the ironic understatement, the repetition of key phrases and the unerring instinct for just where to begin and end a story" (Franklin, BR31).

For a short time, the family lived in Westport, Connecticut, with their four children while husband Stanley Edgar Hyman traveled to Manhattan while working for *The New Yorker*. (Hyman later secured a teaching position at Bennington College and the family moved to Vermont.) Each professed a love of reading and literature and kept a personal library of more than 100,000 books in their home. Jackson and Hyman were known as being generous hosts to literary talents, including Ralph Ellison. During that time, Ellison was a guest in residence as he wrote his soon to be famous novel *Invisible Man*. On the surface it appeared that Jackson was living the life of a suburban housewife, raising children and taking care of household duties. Yet she continued to write and publish.

Jackson's first novel *The Road Through the Wall* was published in 1948. About the same time, her short story of "a classic horror tale," titled "The Lottery" appeared in *The New Yorker*. Jackson set the tale in a fictional small town that held a random lottery each year that selected one person who was stoned to death by the local townspeople. "The Lottery" was only the beginning of a notable career. During the 1950s, Jackson wrote a series of four soon-to-be classic dark Gothic suspense novels that told of abnormal psychology, ghosts, and witchcraft. They included *Hangsaman* (1951); *The Bird's Nest* (1954); *The Sundial* (1958); and *The Haunting of Hill House* (1959). Many literary critics have rated *The Haunting of Hill House* as the "quintessential haunted house tale." Many of the great authors of the genre, including the famed Stephen King, cite Jackson as the measure for all great horror tales. One reviewer, with a bit of humor, said Jackson wrote "not with a pen but a broomstick" (Franklin, BR31).

Jackson was not limited to horror tales. She also published two well-received humorous novels of family life. The first was *Life Among the Savages* (1953); the other was *Raising Demons* (1957). She continued writing short stories as well as other novels until her untimely death in 1965 at the age of 48. In her obituary "Shirley Jackson, Author of Horror Classic, Dies," of August 10, 1965 (she had died the day before), the editors of *The New York Times* described her versatility: "She could describe the delights and turmoils of ordinary domestic life with detached hilarity; and she could, with cryptic symbolism, write a tenebrous horror story in the Gothic mold in which abnormal behavior seemed perilously ordinary." Jackson did not live the life of an "ordinary" 1950s suburban housewife. Yet many women were regulated to a hidden life lost among the sameness of suburban developments. One individual who brought forward the hidden life of such conformity was Betty Friedan.

THE HOUSEWIFE, *THE FEMININE MYSTIQUE*, AND DR. SPOCK

During the 1950s and early 1960s, magazines, television, and Hollywood movies continually portrayed the glory and happiness of middle-class motherhood and marriage. Commercial advertisers such as Betty Furness, among others, supported the image. Furness, as one example, promoted the joys of domesticity through the purchase of home products such as refrigerators and washing machines. (See more in Media and Advertising.) The constant image of a happy marriage devoid of any hints of divorce was considered the norm. Another example was by the married celebrity dance couple Marge and Gower Champion of Hollywood movies and television fame. In their book, *Let's Dance with Marge and Gower Champion* (Grosset & Dunlap, 1954), the Champions suggested, "Many a happy marriage can be made happier if the husband and wife will re-live the romance of their earlier years on the dance floor" (Thomas, 7).

The continuous media image of the "new American woman" devoted herself to raising a family, being a homemaker, and supporting her husband's decisions. A career for a married woman was simply out of the question. Once married, a woman was supposed to stop working and change her last name to that of her husband. (In fact, a married woman completely lost her own identity. Upon marriage, a wife was referred to with both her husband's first and last name preceded by a married prefix such as "Mrs. Robert J. Smith.") Social historian Gloria Steinem summed up the real-life situation saying, "A woman became the man she married."

At the time, gender roles were clearly defined, but not within certain designations of responsibility such as "Chairman" or "Congressman." Those positions were reserved almost exclusively for men. During the decade, the total number of female elected representation never exceeded three percent of the total number in Congress. The U.S. Senate only had three elected female members. They included Margaret Chase Smith of Maine serving from 1949 to 1973; Eva Kelly Bowring of Nebraska who served briefly from April to November in 1954; and Hazel Hampel Abel, also from Nebraska, who replaced Bowing in November 1954 and served only 53 days. In the House of Representatives, only 23 women were elected during the entire decade.

The gender problem was not confined to the secrecy of any type of sexual activity or lifestyle, but also a new problem among young women in the fledgling suburban developments. Throughout the late 1950s, author Betty Friedan (1921–2006) documented a social "problem with no name" among the young suburban housewives. Friedan never intended to become what her *New York Times* obituary labeled as a "feminist crusader and author." After graduating *summa cum laude* from Smith College in 1942, she, as did so many other women of her time, put aside her career for marriage. Friedan forgoed continuing her PhD in psychology. Instead of a professional career, she married and became a "suburban housewife" as the mother of three children. At the time, all the media and medical professionals claimed that women like her were the embodiment of the "American Dream." Friedan realized, however, that something was drastically missing from in her life.

Friedan came to realize that she was missing her own identity. She began to interview other suburban housewives, almost exclusively young, white, newly married mothers. She soon discovered an almost universal malaise among the middle-class housewives. More often than not, the common complaint claimed they were not content to be isolated in suburbia performing the daily housekeeping, child rearing, and keeping up with the barrage of consumer products. In general, some wanted to go out and work or pursue a meaningful career. In reality, women wanted an opportunity to express their talents and shape the world more profoundly than just shuffling the children off to school, performing housework, going to the supermarket, or attending community meetings.

Friedan compiled her findings in a major best-selling book, *The Feminine Mystique* (W.W. Norton, 1963). The work might have been published in the 1960s, but it served as an excellent example of middle-class culture of the 1950s. The most profound revelation was how many of the real-life situations and problems were either simply ignored, hidden, or not discussed openly. Friedan's interview subjects were mainly her former Smith College classmates who also put aside their professional lives for marriage and the seclusion of suburbia. When asked to describe accomplishments, the talk was all about what their husbands had achieved and of their home, furnishings, appliances, and children. When Friedan explored further questions, she came to a startling revelation. In all, it revealed a reality to other women who thought they alone suffered from the malaise. The isolation of suburbia and the struggles felt by the young housewife was aptly summed up by Friedan:

> Each suburban wife struggles with it alone. As she made the beds, shopped for groceries, matched slipcover material, ate peanut butter sandwiches with her children, chauffeured Cub Scouts and Brownies, lay beside her husband at night—she was afraid to ask even of herself the silent question—"Is this all?" (1)

In a short time, the universal malaise became known by a term labeled by Friedan as "the problem with no name." Her first interview subjects were from a select group of suburban housewives, but after publication thousands of other women spoke out about the same problems and frustrations of suburban life.

The Feminine Mystique also came to reveal that the reluctance to actually name the problem came from the male-dominated medical and psychological associations. In fact, the problem was not totally unknown, nor was it kept in total secret. Many media outlets often hinted at some "female problems" such as depression. The solution to end any depression was often advertised as buying new consumer products like a washing machine or vacuum cleaner. Some magazines and publications offered simple marital advice such as to cook an exciting dinner. On a more troublesome note many doctors and psychiatrists suggested highly addictive prescription drugs such as barbiturates and Valium. Some medical professionals would prescribe the pills and simply dismiss the problem with instructions such as "take one pill a day and go out and buy a new dress." Some others prescribed having another child. In contrast, Friedan wrote, although these women were well educated, talented, and intelligent, no outlet for personal satisfaction was ever prescribed. She wrote, "The feminine mystique has succeeded in burying millions of women alive." In her 2006 obituary, *The New York Times* noted that Friedan and *The Feminine Mystique* "permanently transformed the social fabric of the United States."

Almost all of the mainstream media promoted the ideal of a dutiful wife who enjoyed motherhood. Bringing up a child within the confines of suburbia could provide its own unique problems. For the most part, the young mothers (the average marriage age was 19) were usually often alone and removed from any other family structure that could offer advice. Many of the new mothers found helpful advice on raising children from Dr. Benjamin Spock's *The Common Sense Book of Baby and Child Care* (1946). The book remained controversial throughout its history. Unlike the previous decades that promoted alienation of affections and strict upbringing of children, Dr. Spock's book stressed nurturing, caring, and affection in child rearing. The inexpensive paperback book was literally a godsend for the young mothers. In a short time from 1946 to 1952, it

became a nationwide bestseller with more than four million copies sold. By 1960, over 30 million copies were in print and continued to sell at a steady rate of more than one million per year until 1970 (West, 234).

RALPH ELLISON AND INVISIBLE ETHNIC GROUPS

The factual situation among African Americans was depicted quite accurately in a 1952 classic *Invisible Man* by Ralph Ellison (1914–1994). The often repeated line from Ellison was: "I am an invisible man, I am invisible, understand, simply because people refuse to see me." In later years, the book, which earned the National Book Award in 1953, was often required reading in high schools and colleges. Yet well into the 21st century the novel was often banished from high school reading lists.

During the time of Ellison's *Invisible Man*, any instances of promoting any type of social integration were also either legally forbidden or shunned by society. One thought to lessen the stigma placed upon racial relations by an adult society was to teach children different attitudes. Some of the books of the time did attempt to provide children with a nonracist attitude of understanding the benefits of social integration, but were met by resistance. In 2015, Linton Weeks, writing for the NPR History Department, called them "Hot-Button Kids' Books." They included:

- *Swimming Hole* (Morrow Junior Books, 1950) by Jerrold Beim (1910–1957) with illustrations by Louis Darling told the story of a young boy who finds out "it doesn't matter what color people are." The book provided situations in which children both black and white went swimming together and shared similar play experiences. In 1956, the Associated Press (AP) reported that a South Carolina state senator said that type of behavior was "a monstrosity and an affront."

- *The First Book of Fishing* (Watts, 1952) written by Steven Schneider was an attempt to educate young readers on the simple basics of fishing. An AP report of July 1959 claimed that the head librarian at the Shreve Memorial Library in Louisiana issued an order to remove it from circulation. The reason was cited as "it contained illustrations of white and black children fishing and picnicking together." The Shreve Library had a long history of removing books from public circulation. The same AP report noted that an order was also issued to remove *Black and White* (Harper & Brothers, 1944) by Margaret Wise Brown, a story of an old "grumpy black man" and a caring "white lady." The reason was cited as it was "insidious racial propaganda."

- *The Rabbits' Wedding* (Harper Collins, 1958) written and illustrated by Garth Williams (1912–1996) told a simple story of marriage between a white rabbit and a black rabbit. Many southern states rejected the book. Alabama, which had a state director to oversee all the public libraries, issued a directive to remove the book from the library shelves. The AP reported the decision was "because critics complain it is pro-integration."

The idea of racial integration was strictly recognized as a societal taboo. Laws remained on the books throughout the nation prohibiting integration in public facilities including restaurants, bathrooms, schools, swimming pools, sporting activities, among every other aspect of American society. So it should come as no surprise that even comic books were found offensive to public morals.

COMIC BOOKS AND THE COMICS CODE AUTHORITY

In July 1955, novelist Ralph Ellison took part in a roundtable discussion with other writers and editors discussing the topic "What's Wrong with the American Novel?" Ellison spoke of the "individual man" missing from the reality of the world around him. Granted, the reference to "individual man" could certainly be reflective of his own novel *Invisible Man* (Random House, 1952) as an African American who was very much "invisible" in 1950s American culture. Yet Ellison's discussion provided a more viable reference. Rather than speaking of finding the reality in a contemporary novel, he made note of another literary genre. Ellison said the individual man "is more apt to get a sense of self-awareness and a sharper reflection of his world from a comic book than most novels" (Stitch, 220). Comic book self-awareness often came as a result of individual superheroes who had special powers to protect themselves and others from all sorts of troubles.

Comic books could often be confused with the four-frame comic strips in the daily newspapers. Those features were often humorous, sometimes confined to a one-day parable or a continuation of a storyline. During this time, one of the most endearing of all the newspaper comic strips, *Peanuts,* first appeared. Drawn and conceived by Charles M. Schulz (1922–2000), the *Peanuts* strip gave America the lovable Charlie Brown and his dog Snoopy. Distributed through United Features Syndicate, "Good 'ol Charlie Brown" made his first appearance on the printed newspaper pages on October 2, 1950. Two days later, America was introduced to Charlie Brown's lovable dog Snoopy. By 1959, Charlie Brown, Snoopy, and the Peanuts gang were syndicated in more than 100 newspapers nationwide. Megan Friedman, writing in "A Brief History of Peanuts" for *Time* magazine on October 1, 2010, noted that Schulz would eventually become "the highest-paid and most widely read cartoonist of all time." The strip was eventually syndicated in more than 2,000 newspapers and read by over 355 million people.

Unlike the newspaper comic strips, comic books were small, magazine-like animated stories printed and sold as separate entities. In 1938, Detective Comics (a subsidiary of National Comics) introduced the fictional superhero Superman in *Action Comics* No. 1. Superman was widely popular and many cite this instance for launching the modern age of comic books. In the next few years, the company introduced other fictional superheroes including Batman, Robin the Boy Wonder, Flash, Green Lantern, and Wonder Woman, among others. One competitor, Marvel Comics, had Captain America. In February 1940, Fawcett Publications issued a version of their own superhero named "Captain Marvel" who appeared in *Whiz Comics* No. 2. Almost immediately Captain Marvel became the best-selling comic book in America, outdistancing Superman. The superhero character was the most prevalent, but many other popular subjects included crime tales, horror tales, humor, jungle stories, and westerns, among others.

At the time, comic books were the most popular form of entertainment, selling between 80 and 100 million copies per week. (Television would later become the most popular form of entertainment.) During the late 1940s and extending into the 1950s, comic books were attacked by church organizations, civic groups, community leaders, literary critics, and teachers, among others. Some school agencies claimed that the reading level of comic books diminished the ability to read school textbooks. Church groups objected to content based on morality. Some literary critics did not rate the comic books on the same level as novels. Those accusations piggybacked off of a self-regulatory agreement made in 1948 by the Association of Comics Magazine Publishers (ACMP). The ACMP agreed on a set of guidelines for all content as follows:

1. Sexy, wanton comics should not be published. No drawing should show a female indecently or unduly exposed, and in no event more nude than in a bathing suit commonly worn in the United States of America.

2. Crime should not be presented in such a way as to throw sympathy against the law and justice or to inspire others with the desire for imitation. No comics shall show the details and methods of a crime committed by a youth. Policemen, judges, government officials, and respected institutions should not be portrayed as stupid, ineffective, or represented in such a way to weaken respect for established authority.

3. No scenes of sadistic torture should be shown.

4. Vulgar and obscene language should never be used. Slang should be kept to a minimum and used only when essential to the story.

5. Divorce should not be treated humorously or represented as glamorous or alluring.

6. Ridicule or attack on any religious or racial group is never permissible.

Later in 1948, the widely read *Collier's Magazine* published an anti-comic book essay "Horror in the Nursery" written by New York psychiatrist Fredric Wertham (1895–1981). Professor Frank Nickell of Southeast Missouri State University recalled quite a few incidents that occurred as a result of Wertham's article. In "The Burning of the Comic Books," Nickell said, "By the end of 1948 large comic book burnings occurred in such places as Spencer, West Virginia, and Binghamton, New York, and the movement spread to Cape Girardeau [Missouri]." The national paranoia and fear were an easy sell to the American public. In 2008, David Hajdu, writing in *The Ten-Cent Plague: The Great Comic Book Scare and How It Changed America* (Picador, 2009), explained, "That was the peak of the HUAC. If you get a copy of any newspaper from 1948, it is full of stories of paranoia. It was all of a piece, the deep fear that our values [were] under threat, that our young people [were] changing, that something is happening that is out of our control" (2). The paranoia did not end, but continued in intensity during the 1950s.

On November 1, 1953, the *Los Angeles Times* warned its readers of, "Sex and Sadism Rampant: It's Time Parents Awakened to Danger in Comic Books." Other newspaper stories followed the same pattern of sensationalizing the supposed dangers faced by children reading of comic books. Headlines warned not only of the "Horror in the Nursery," but also "The Curse of the Comic Book," among dozens of similar headlines (Hajdu, 7).

The media assault continued with a scathing editorial in *The Hartford Courant*, an influential Connecticut newspaper. On January 28, 1954, columnist Thomas E. Murphy chose comic books as his topic for an editorial piece, "Design for Murder." In regards to the comic books in the hands of innocent children, Murphy decried:

> Many of the comic books seem to be the products of diseased minds. It is not the violence that is objectionable, but the sadism, the torturing, the decay and the perversity that are daily served the little ones in the guise of entertainment. (Hajdu, 223)

The article was read throughout the nation when it was reprinted concurrently in the *Reader's Digest*, the *Catholic Digest*, and *Editor and Publisher.* At the time *Reader's Digest* was the largest circulating monthly magazine in America. Both the *Catholic Digest* and *Editor and Publisher* also held prominent sway. All three maintained strict adherences to conservative, wholesome, American family values. The attention placed upon Murphy's editorial prompted *The Hartford Courant* to assign reporter Irving Kravsow to write an in-depth story. The result was a four-part series published over consecutive days in February 1954, carrying the headline "Depravity for Children—10 Cents a Copy." As suburban parents looked at the page-one story on the morning of February 14, 1954, they were awakened with previously unknown fear about what was lurking within their own homes. Kravsow wrote:

> This morning I want to talk about murder and how the how the children of Connecticut are being served a poison diet. I don't think anybody has the right to poison the minds of my children with depraved, degenerate bits of scatology, I wished strongly that I had my hands on the human scum that conceived them and published them to make money. (Hajdu, 224)

At one point, Kravsow said that the reading of comic books placed children upon the path to not only juvenile delinquency, but also put them firmly on a "short course in murder, mayhem, robbery, rape, cannibalism, carnage, sex, sadism and worse." Kravsow's attack was relentless and he sensationalized his story with all sorts of scare tactics. For added emphasis, he also told parents that the children were being exposed to "lust, sadism, necrophilia, depravity, and just plain filth" (Hajdu, 225).

In a society that was fearful of any nonconformity, the power of a scare-tactic article, such as written by Kravsow, provided the direct path to censorship. Yet he was typical of so many others who knew full well their power of persuasion by using the innocence of children to put false scares into the minds of parents (Hadju, 6–7).

In 1953, a U.S. Senate subcommittee was already in place to investigating the causes of juvenile delinquency. With the growing media sensation of comic books, the Senate made what they thought was an obvious link between the fictional stories and the real-life cause of teenage crime. The accusations were aided by a new book, *Seduction of the Innocent* by Dr. Fredric Wertham, that was released when the Red Scare and concern over juvenile delinquency was in full swing. Wertham published the results of a long research study on comic books. The "seduction" implied the harmful messages comic books placed upon the "innocent" children of America. Wertham claimed his study proved the comics provided all sorts of depictions that led children into juvenile delinquency. As a psychiatrist, he claimed that the images affected the "mental health" of the young readers. The only solution, according to Wertham, was a nationwide ban on comic books. According to the legendary Stan Lee of Marvel comics, Wertham was taken seriously because "he was a psychiatrist, so people listened." In the eyes of the Senate investigative committee and of the American public, *Seduction of the Innocent* only confirmed the ongoing accusations in the series of newspaper articles and national magazines. Wertham's book and his professional "credibility" as a psychiatrist just added to the reasons for Congress to launch an investigation (Hajdu, 6).

By the spring of 1954, the U.S. Senate Subcommittee on Juvenile Delinquency expanded its role to launch an investigation into the fictional world of comic books. Their first concern was the graphic cover images of "crime and horror" that was put before the eyes of millions of American children each month. The hearings were held in New York City for maximum media coverage on April 21 and 22. They reconvened on June 4, 1954. During the hearings, specific issues of comic books were put into evidence and some experts were called to testify. One noted exchange took place between Senator Estes Kefauver and publisher William Gaines of Entertainment Comics. At the time, Entertainment Comics (known mainly as "EC") was the leading comic book publisher. EC publishing, headed by William Gaines, focused primarily on horror and crime with both cover artwork and story art often providing images of killers, blood, and sometimes a severed head. Sometimes the images were accused of being too sexy, with "the occasional cleavage or bare foot showing."

In June 1954, a U.S. Congressional hearing focused on this particular 1954 comic book cover of "The Vault of Horror" published by EC Comics. The hearing led to the formation of the Comics Code Authority. (Photofest)

Kefauver was looking to make a name for himself for a possible U.S. presidential run. He had also recently received major media attention for leading a Senate inquiry against organized crime in America. For the comic book hearings, Kefauver squared off against Gaines as the investigation focused on a single 1954 EC issue. The comic in question was "The Vault of Horror" in which a woman was about to have her head "dismembered." The exchange led to a front page story the following day in *The New York Times* that carried the sarcastic title, "No Harm in Horror." Yet the hearings were no laughing matter as the industry was facing extinction by the court of public opinion. In an attempt to save the industry, the comic book publishers formed a self-regulatory agency (Nyberg, "Comics Code History," n.p.).

As a result of the negative media publicity combined with the so-called credibility of the U.S. Senate subcommittee, the comics book industry was at a

In order to publish a comic book issue for sale to the public, the seal (shown above) stating: "Approved by the Comics Code Authority" was necessary.

Chart 5.2

Chart 5.3   1959 Monthly Circulation of Comic Books

Rank	Publisher	Monthly Sales
1.	Dell	9,686,424
2.	National (DC)	6,653,485
3.	Harvey	2,514,879
4.	Charlton	2,500,000
5.	Marvel	2,253,112
6.	Archie	1,608,489
7.	ACG	975,000
	Total	26,191,389

Source: The information was derived from John Jackson Miller of *The Comics Chronicle* from the archival N.W. Ayer & Sons Directory, which was an annual publication that gathered information for use by advertising agencies. Chart compiled by author.

crossroads. In an attempt to save their industry, the publishers announced the formation of a self-regulatory agency: the Comics Magazine Association of America (CMAA). In October 1954, the CMAA, soon known as the "Comics Code Authority" or just "CCA," was voluntarily placed in charge of monitoring the content of comics while promising to promote "wholesomeness and virtue." The CCA soon took on a censorship initiative to preserve contemporary American values. In doing so, the CCA instituted a list of 41 taboo items. The "problem areas" defined provisions that banned sexual innuendos, scantily clad images of women, crime, horror, intimacy, violence, and any other content not in keeping with the Comics Code standards. The code continually stressed respect for government and parental authority. Language was monitored, often eliminating contemporary slang. In order to publish an issue for sale, the comic book required a seal that resembled a stamp, stating: "Approved by the Comics Code Authority" (Hajdu, 319).

In order to receive approval, publishers submitted each comic issue to the CCA. The entire issue including cover art, story art, subject matter, and language was reviewed for adherence to the code. If in compliance, and the content was suitable for young readers, the publisher's title would receive authorization to use the Seal of Approval. The seal was displayed on the cover of the comic book and therefore eligible for sale to the American public. The official approval from the CCA became an absolutely necessity, as wholesalers and retailers would only sell comics that carried the seal of approval.

The situation drastically affected the overall sales. At the start of the 1950s, about 20 publishers offered more than 650 comic book titles as total sales exceeded 80 to 100 million copies each month (Hajdu, 5). By mid-decade, only about 250 titles remained; and by the end of the decade, sales showed a sharp decline from the pre-Congressional hearings. The overall number dropped to a little more than 26 million per month, with a yearly total of over 314 million copies (Tilley, 383–84).

JAMES BALDWIN IN *GIOVANNI'S ROOM*

The great fear over protecting children extended to all facets of American life. In doing so, all sorts of subjects were broached as to what might be harmful and what was acceptable means of behavior. On the other hand, 1950s society did not even want to admit that homosexuality existed. One novel that broached the subject was *Giovanni's Room* (Dial Press, 1956) written by James Baldwin (1924–1987). Granville Hicks writing for *The New York Times Book Review* on October 14, 1956, described Baldwin "to be one of our gifted young writers. His most conspicuous gift is his ability to find words that astonish the reader with their boldness even as they overwhelm him with their rightness." Baldwin wrote the novel at a time when most of the conservative Christian-minded American society viewed homosexuality as deviant and abnormal. One way that the novel could pass the scrutiny was to realize that the gay affair had lasted only one night and therefore could easily be passed off as experimentation. The righteous view of the time period would certainly agree that the "deviant" murderer was executed and could also relate to Giovanni's supposed "sin" of homosexuality. David's misstep is certainly corrected as he chooses marriage to his female interest Hella. Some cultural critics have placed Baldwin's publication as a companion to the 1936 novel *Nightwood*, written by the American writer Djuna Barnes (1892–1982), that is considered "a cult classic of lesbian fiction." Barnes tells the story of two women who fall in love while in Paris.

Giovanni's Room was placed within the context of Baldwin's acceptance of his own sexuality as "being poor, black, and gay." History Display, a website from the University of Illinois, places the real-life situation of Baldwin within the context of the novel. In 1948, the then 24-year-old Baldwin had left America and moved to Paris. In Paris, living as a gay man, he was not subject to the discrimination he had faced in his home country. While there, he found comfort in a friend and a lover named Lucien Happersberger. *Giovanni's Room* brought Baldwin "critical acclaim as a powerful American writer." He continued as a prolific writer of poems and novels. His other literary works included *Notes of a Native Son* (1955), *Nobody Knows My Name* (1960), and *The Fire Next Time* (1963). Baldwin also became a social activist and early advocate of gay and lesbian rights. During the 1960s, he was actively involved in the American Civil Rights movement and spoke out against the Vietnam War.

HOMOSEXUALITY, THE BIBLE, AND THE KINSEY REPORT

The late 1960s stood in stark contrast to the 1950s for the social acceptance of gays and lesbians. Milt Ford, a professor of liberal studies at Grand Valley State University in Michigan, provides a good summation in an essay, "A Brief History of Homosexuality in America." He traces the "definition" of homosexual as a relatively recent phenomenon from about 120 years or so in the past. Ford writes that the term was first applied in the late 19th century as American society sought a way "for distinguishing homosexual and heterosexual selves." The cause was due to a restructuring of society as millions of Europeans and

Americans were moving from rural areas into cities in search of work created by the Industrial Revolution. During the late 1860s and 1870s in Europe and 1890s in America, city officials noticed a trend that many people had developed lifestyles "not around family, household, and reproduction but around various forms of sexual pleasure." Various studies looked at the non-nuclear family groups that deviated from the rural family structure and labeled them "deviants." Deviation is not a harmful word as the most common definition is "the action of departing from an established course or accepted standard." Yet the term "deviant," which described someone who departed from "social or sexual behavior," has since come to describe an unwanted predator (usually sexual). It was also about this time that the term "homosexual" was applied as one distinctive "deviant class."

One of the first to describe a difference in sexual preference came from noted psychologist Sigmund Freud (1856–1939). Freud, who revolutionized the study of psychology both in Europe and America, described homosexuality as an "object choice." His ideas later became the basis for many aspects of American society that became immersed within 1950s American culture. Even the average American during the 1950s was aware of Freud and either knowingly or unknowingly blindly accepted any part of his thesis. It can easily be said that in the post-war years, Freud's ideas had not just permeated the culture, but rather saturated it. In 2009, Daniel Akst writing for *The Wall Street Journal* provided a historical perspective: "Freud's ideas would grow into a kind of orthodoxy in America, becoming a staple of medical training in psychiatry and permeating the larger culture. By the 1950s Freudian therapy was almost commonplace for those who could afford it, and its basic doctrines were familiar even to those who had never reclined on an analyst's couch" (Akst, n.p.).

The acceptance of Freud's notion of sexuality had everything to do with promoting the sanctity of the nuclear family—mainly for financial profit. During the 1950s, the prevalent consumer culture was heavily dependent upon marketing products for purchase by the nuclear suburban family. The pervasive image of a supposedly happily married couple with children was necessary to continue the desire to buy more and more consumer products. Attached to that need was portraying the American male as not only the "breadwinner" but also as a strong, undeterred force capable of defeating Communism. Therefore, any weakness or deviation, such as homosexuality, was not viewed as a masculine response necessary to fight Communism.

At the height of the Red Scare, a 1950 U.S. Senate report titled *Employment of Homosexuals and Other Sex Perverts in Government* said "those who engage in overt acts of perversion lack the emotional stability of normal persons." This led to a situation where any public disclosure of homosexuality was enough to get most people fired from their jobs. The loss of employment was coupled with being ostracized in the community and also within their own family. By 1953, it was legal to fire a person who was gay or lesbian. President Eisenhower issued Executive Order 10450, making homosexuality a sufficient reason to fire an employee from a government job. (The executive order remained from 1953 until 1993.) By extension, any employer could in turn fire an employee simply for either being gay or even suspected of being gay. The fear generated by

Senator McCarthy also linked homosexuality with Communism. Oftentimes homosexuality was compared to perversion and in turn labeled subversive. Senator Kenneth Wherry (R-Neb) said, "I don't say every homosexual is a subversive, and I don't say every subversive is a homosexual. But a man of low morality is a menace in the government, whatever he is, and they are tied up together" (Whitfield, 43). Throughout the decade, all sorts of homophobic attacks came from the media, newspapers, religious organizations, and even school hygiene films.

In 1997, W. N. Eskridge writing for the *Yale Law Journal* also noted that the use of the term "homosexual" was barely a "century old." The use of the word was traced to an 1880s campaign begun by the Church of Jesus Christ of Latter Day Saints (commonly known as Mormons). The group revived their campaign against gays and lesbians during the 1950s in the midst of Cold War rhetoric. The Reverend Billy Graham associated gays, lesbians, and Communists all in the same group. He said it is "the pinks, the lavenders, and the reds who have sought refuge beneath the wings of the American Eagle." Other religious groups joined in claiming the declining role of the American family was due to Communist infiltration that had also weakened religion (Whitfield, 44–45).

To waylay the fear, many Americans, especially Christian Fundamentalists, embraced religion as a weapon to fight Communism. As a result, the best-selling book of the decade was the Bible; actually, it was titled the *Revised Standard Version of the Bible* (1952). Within the first year of publication, the Bible sold over 26.5 million copies. Prior to the Cold War paranoia, many bookstores had placed the Bible in a separate section devoted to either "Religion" or in its own section labeled as "The Bible." Yet, by the 1950s, no bookstore would ever lay claim that the biblical stories were in any way a work of fiction. Mounting pressure from religious groups claimed the literary truths were contained in the "factual" accounts, especially the Old Testament. As a result, the Bible was listed on the "nonfiction" list where it remained #1 for most of the decade. Overall it was the largest seller by far of any other book published during that time (Whitfield, 84).

The overwhelming success of the Bible led to the publication of many other religious books. One of the most popular was *The Power of Positive Thinking* (1952) by the Reverend Norman Vincent Peale. It quickly became a best seller and remained as the second best-selling book behind the Bible for three years running. In another publication, *Stay Alive All Your Life* (1957), Peale advised "a Higher Power . . . can do everything for you. . . . This power is constantly available. . . . This tremendous inflow of power is of such force that it drives everything before it, casting out fear, hate, sickness, weakness, moral defeat . . . restrengthening your life with health, happiness, and goodness" (Whitfield, 84). Other popular novels containing Christian themes included:

- *The Greatest Story Ever Told* (1949), Fulton Oursler
- *The Cardinal* (1950), Henry Morton Robinson
- *The Silver Chalice* (1952), Thomas B. Costain

- *The Seven Storey Mountain* (1948), Thomas Merton
- *A Man Called Peter* (1952), Catherine Marshall
- *The Day Christ Died* (1957), Jim Bishop

Other concerns of declining "masculinity" were dominant throughout America. Noted historian Arthur Schlesinger voiced his displeasure in a 1958 *Esquire* magazine article "The Crisis of American Masculinity." K. A. Cuordileone, writing in *The Journal of American History,* claimed, "American males had become the victims of a smothering, overpowering, suspiciously collectivist mass society—a society that had smashed the once autonomous male." All sorts of religious organizations and groups also joined in about the declining role and also weakening of the American male. Some of the publications of the time that promoted American masculinity included:

- Norman Mailer's *The Naked and the Dead* (1948) told of World War II soldiers fighting in the South Pacific. Its shocking revelations included frank and raw language of warfare.
- *The Caine Mutiny* (1952) by Herman Wouk promoted the virility of the American military. It sold more than three million copies and was translated into 17 languages.
- *The F.B.I.* (1954) written by Quentin Reynolds was the story of the Federal Bureau of Investigation telling tall tales of the agency that had tracked down notorious criminals of the past as well as its present-day fights against Communism, thereby keeping America safe from internal threats.

Within the pages of *The F.B.I.*, Reynolds quoted director J. Edgar Hoover's summation of what was required of an agent. Hoover said, "[W]hen a young man files an application with the F.B.I., we do not ask if he was the smartest boy in class. We want to know if he was truthful, dependable, and if he played the game fair. We want to know if he respects his parents, reveres God, honors his flag and loves his country" (65). That statement by Hoover can only be described with the utmost of irony. It was later revealed that Hoover, who was a "confirmed bachelor," spent most of his private adult life as a cross-dressing female. He also spent many years living in "intimate company" with Clyde Tolson (1900–1975). Tolson was Hoover's protégé who served as Associate Director of the FBI from 1930 until 1972 in charge of "personnel and discipline." Despite Hoover's veil of deceit, he maintained a vicious campaign as he ruined other people's lives by vigorously prosecuting alleged homosexuals and Communists. He added to his legacy as he also used the agency to hinder the progression of the Civil Rights movement during the mid-1950s and into the 1960s.

Throughout the decade, any and all means were employed to counteract the decline of masculinity. Images in newspapers, magazines, and television, among many others, abounded with strong virile men portrayed as the ultimate catch for a lucky female. Of ironic note, one of the more common images promoting the ideal American male as rugged, strong, and handsome was the Hollywood actor Rock Hudson (1925–1985). He was often paired in romantic

comedies with attractive
actresses, such as with Doris
Day in *Pillow Talk* (1959) and in
All That Heaven Allows (1955)
with Jane Wyman; and in dramas such as *Giant* (1956) with
Elizabeth Taylor. An October 3,
1955, issue of the nationwide
Life magazine featured a cover
story proclaiming Hudson
as "Hollywood's Most Handsome Bachelor." He was often
pictured in romantic poses with
some of the most attractive
Hollywood starlets of the day
including Marilyn Monroe,
among many others. Yet
unknown to the mainstream
American public was that Hudson was gay.

In fact, no American stated
publicly that homosexuality
existed. A study that explored
American sexuality was by
Alfred Kinsey. During the late
1940s and early 1950s, he led a
research group on American
sexual attitudes and lifestyles.
He released his findings in two
separate publications, *Sexual
Behavior in the Human Male*
(1948) and *Sexual Behavior in
the Human Female* (1953). Both
of the titles attracted a lot of

Images in newspapers, magazines, and television
abounded with strong virile men portrayed as the
ultimate catch for a lucky female. One of the more
common images promoting the ideal American
male as rugged, strong, and handsome was Hollywood actor Rock Hudson. Yet, unknown to the
mainstream American public was that Hudson was
gay. This October 3, 1955, issue of the nationwide
Life magazine featured a cover story proclaiming
Hudson as "Hollywood's Most Handsome Bachelor." (Photofest)

media attention, as they became known simply as "The Kinsey Report." The
first of Kinsey's research findings on the American male was not viewed with
as much open criticism and denial as his subsequent release of the sexual attitudes of the American female.

Sexual Behavior in the Human Male was viewed with interest but not too much
surprise. The study released information on the sexual habits of the American
male such as premarital sex and extramarital affairs. At the time, that kind of
information was often taken for granted as acceptable male behavior that was
often dismissed as "boys will be boys." Yet when Kinsey revealed that sometimes boys played with themselves through masturbation, the criticism
increased. The ultimate criticism was reserved for Kinsey when he wrote that
men sometimes had sexual relationships with other men. In doing so, Kinsey
revealed publicly the existence of homosexuality. His report brought forward

the information that this pattern of behavior was not part of some small minority of deviant individuals, but rather part of mainstream America.

The furor over the male behavior in Kinsey's report eventually subsided, yet the publication of *Sexual Behavior in the Human Female* unleashed an intense fury of attacks. In simple terms, Kinsey revealed that the sexual attitudes of the males were common to those of females. It almost becomes laughable to think that sexual prowess among men was acceptable and bragged about. Yet, when it was revealed that women also enjoyed sexual intercourse, masturbation, and experimentation as much as men did, the idea was beyond the bounds of acceptability. Kinsey also revealed that some women also loved other women. The mainstream American media and religious groups seemed not just surprised, but also appalled by the Kinsey revelations as they applied to females.

In fact, both books followed the same pattern of questions and answers compiled as statistical data, one specifically on male behavior patterns and the other focusing on female behavior patterns. Within the books Kinsey provided the results of statistical research findings on both heterosexual and homosexual lifestyles. The research revealed information on such taboo subjects as premarital sex, extramarital affairs, sex within marriage, and masturbation, among other topics. Yet each study was met with much criticism and also denial.

* * * * *

ON BEING GAY IN AMERICA DURING THE 1950s

Omar Swartz

Major catalysts in the 1950s for the emergence of a gay consciousness as a positive identity were crucial for the community building and civil rights activism of the following decades. Mobilization of soldiers, nurses, and workers for the Second World War (and for war-time industries) gathered millions from long-isolated socially repressive communities, providing an opportunity for same-sex sociability. The Cold War followed with severe anti-gay repression, causing Harry Hay (1912–2002) and others to spearhead the homophile movement, thereby reinventing the way homosexuals viewed themselves. (In 2002, Eric Slade directed a PBS documentary film *Hope Along with the Wind: The Life of Harry Hay.*) Subsequent legal battles extended First Amendment protection to the homosexual media to convey a positive new identity. Meanwhile, scientist Alfred Kinsey helped the public rethink traditional notions of sexuality.

Wartime experiences encouraged permissiveness among people who experienced same-sex attractions and such relationships flourished. Previously, such people were isolated, confused, and scared; homosexuals hid, accentuating their political/social marginalization. Challenging the hatred and degrading language that described and limited gay people was almost unthinkable. The echo chamber of society reinforced the belief that to be gay was to be in some way broken or dysfunctional, an appraisal accepted by many gay people. Homosexuals returned from the Second World War to a society in which they were targeted as criminals, subversives, and security threats. Thousands of gay (or suspected gay) civil servants were fired or forced to resign. State laws equating homosexuality with public order threats were common and law enforcement shared investigations with the private sector to further terrorize homosexuals. To be homosexual was to be an *enemy* of the people.

The twenty-first century idea of "gay consciousness" did not exist in the 1950s, such vocabulary had to be forged. Few people "knew" they were gay in the way that we think currently, as a normal and natural condition. They had no positive vocabulary to describe how they felt. Gay people lived in a world of shame, lacking language to articulate their struggles. Harry Hay, who was widely recognized as the "founder" of the Gay Liberation movement in the United States, filled this void. He argued that gay people constituted a distinct cultural minority from which a gay identity, so central to gay power and liberation, could be cultivated. Hay's insights evolved out of his years as a community organizer against racism and poverty. His work with the Mattachine Society of Los Angeles fueled the Homophile movement, precursor to the Gay Rights movement. The Daughters of Bilitis, the first lesbian rights organization, was formed in 1955 by Del Martin and Phyllis Lyon. The work of these groups was important for bringing the concerns of gay people out into the open in terms set by the gays themselves, to establish a sense of community.

Print media was essential to the homophile movement and the creation of *One Magazine: The Homosexual Viewpoint* (1953–1967) marked the first national magazine dedicated to discussing homosexuality written by, and for, homosexuals. Featuring political and literary articles, and circulated the ideas of the Mattachine Society, *One Magazine* was challenged by the U.S. government as obscene because it portrayed gays sympathetically. In 1958, *One Magazine* prevailed in a legal battle as the U.S. Supreme Court held that magazines featuring homosexual content could not be prohibited. A year earlier the Court had rewritten obscenity rules by overruling the common-law "bad tendency" test. That law banned materials that might "deprave and corrupt those whose minds are open to such immoral influences." Prosecutors were held to a more exacting challenge to prove that a work was "utterly without redeeming social importance," a nearly impossible standard for political or erotic writings about same-sex desire. Gay-themed literature could no longer be considered obscene and suppressed. The ruling opened the possibility for the gay media to proliferate openly and proudly, contributing instrumentally to the founding and sustaining of gay communities nationally.

Media resources to communicate, however, were not enough. A message that resonated beyond a small insular group and a messenger with the respectability to be taken seriously by society was necessary. The myth of the homosexual as deviant, perverted, or sick had to be proven as the falsehood and lie that it was. This task fell to scientist Alfred Kinsey. After collecting evidence on human sexuality, a successful argument was provided by Kinsey that homosexuality, far from being a rare abnormality or something deviant among human beings warranting repression, was an experience shared by a large percentage of people without harm. Kinsey thus undercut the argument that homosexuals, as "sexual deviates," constituted a social threat. Sexual attraction, he documented, is a biological phenomenon without moral implications. Moreover, Kinsey established that sexual identity exists as a *continuum* (not a binary in which people could be exclusively homosexual or heterosexual); most people experienced some degree of same-sex attraction. To fear homosexuality, he argued, is to fear that part of ourselves that recognizes the existence, naturalness, and desirability of same-sex sexuality. The only thing "unnatural" about our sexuality is the socially constructed confines in which we live and the discrimination we are made to suffer.

Kinsey's work changed the thinking about homosexuality in two ways. First, he successfully brought knowledge to bear on understanding homosexuality—its prevalence and normalcy, its important dimension in human affairs. Being homosexual was as normal as being heterosexual. Second, he provided an impetus for homosexuals to use this knowledge to construct positive self-images in order to cease being "homosexuals" by happenstance, and, instead to actively learn to be "gay" and "lesbian" or, more recently, "queer." This shift in language mattered; with each identification came a new political/social reality—such as the association of the word "homosexual" with pathology. Subsequently, gays and lesbians began forming vibrant communities in places such as Los Angeles, New York, and San Francisco where they worked for self-help and, ultimately, social change. What was once experienced as a *personal* defect and reason for shame became an identity to be *shared* and a community to be affirmed.

Source: Omar Swartz is an associate professor of humanities and social science at the University of Colorado Denver.

Many aspects of American society were being addressed in the literary works of the day. Yet, the mainstream publication on subjects such as homosexuality, feminism, African Americans, ethnicity, and Native Americans, among others in literature did not begin to flourish until the later part of the 1960s.

FURTHER READING

John D'Emilio. *Sexual Politics, Sexual Communities: The Making of a Homosexual Minority in the United States, 1940–1970.* Chicago: University of Chicago Press, 1983.
Eric Foner. *The Story of American Freedom.* New York: W. W. Norton & Company, 1998.
Betty Friedan. *The Feminine Mystique.* New York: W.W. Norton & Company, 1963.
James Kepner. *Rough News, Daring Views: 1950's Pioneer Gay Press Journalism.* Binghamton, NY: Harrington Park Press, 1998.
David Hajdu. *The Ten-Cent Plague: The Great Comic Book Scare and How It Changed America.* New York: Farrar, Straus and Giroux, 2008.
Amy Nyberg. *Seal of Approval: The History of the Comics Code.* Jackson, MS: University Press of Mississippi, 1998.
David Riesman. *The Lonely Crowd.* New Haven, CT: Yale University Press, 2001.

CHAPTER 6

Sports

Not all Americans embraced sports as the national ideal. One American-born daughter of a Hungarian refugee family noted, "Americans place great emphasis on sports, football, and baseball (to watch) and golf and fishing. My parents were never raised with this kind of sports enthusiasm and have never learned to like them." Many immigrants of the pre-war years, as well as many refugees entering America, often held that same sentiment during the post-war era. As immigrants assimilated with native-born Americans, spectator and participation sports also became a major part of leisure time enjoyment. Many of those activities included fishing, boating, hunting, and swimming. A 1959 survey claimed that more than 33 million Americans actively participated in swimming. That information also placed swimming as the most popular recreational activity in the country. Swimming was also a major competitive sport in colleges and also part of the international Summer Olympic Games. Recreational fishing and social dancing were also high on the list, with each activity having 32 million participants. Other popular activities included hunting at more than 16 million, and 11 million men and women participated in amateur baseball and softball (Kaplan, 72).

Bowling was another popular sport as a fun family recreational activity or as an opportunity for a date night. A significant number of individuals also bowled in friendly competitive leagues that numbered more than 33,000 nationwide for both men and women. At least 18 million people engaged in one form or another of bowling. In 1952, a technological device for mechanized pinsetters was introduced (prior to that time, the pins were set by hand). The new device increased participation and also resulted in the demand for the construction of many new bowling facilities. Unlike the older bowling facilities of the past, the newer alleys during the decade provided improved lighting and food service, and some even offered babysitting services among other amenities that further enhanced bowling's appeal to women and married couples. As a result, by the end of the decade, at least 30 million Americans of all ages bowled on a regular basis (Braden, 273).

THE PRESIDENT'S COUNCIL ON PHYSICAL FITNESS AND NATIONAL PARKS

On many occasions throughout the 1950s, President Eisenhower was criticized by his opponents for portraying a life of relaxation and leisure. That aspect of his legacy actually began while he was campaigning for the presidency. One July 1952 *New York Mirror* newspaper cartoon titled "The Escapist" parodied the then-candidate relaxing with a friend around a campfire. An image held in the Library of Congress Prints and Photographs Division showed the former General Eisenhower as being nonchalant about an upcoming political nominating convention. The caption read, "That reminds me, Ike—there's something going on in Chicago this week." The comment was in direct reference to the fact that although Eisenhower had by that time secured the Republican presidential nomination, his forthcoming opponent was about to be selected at the Democratic presidential nominating convention taking place in Chicago. Rather than focusing on who his opponent would be, Eisenhower instead took a fishing vacation in Colorado following his own selection (Albrecht, 238).

A unique aspect of Eisenhower's presidency was a focus on promoting recreation and leisure pursuits for Americans. One notable point was a program that began in 1956 as the President's Council on Physical Fitness. The idea was to challenge all Americans in attaining a certain level of physical fitness. A major focus was aimed at young children in grade school and high school teenagers with the basis to maintain an ongoing activity program. A series of events was setup including sit-ups, rope climbing, and running, among others. Upon completion, the student was awarded a certificate with the signature of the President of the United States. Other aspects of the program sought to encourage adults to also develop fitness programs. Part of the promotion to maintain total physical fitness included numerous exercise activities such as bicycling, jogging, swimming, and walking, to name a few.

The end of the Eisenhower era did not end the President's Council on Physical Fitness. The program continued for many years thereafter. The transition during the early 1960s to President John F. Kennedy (1917–1963) offered the same devotion to outdoor recreation. The public display of recreational activities by both Eisenhower and Kennedy prompted the federal government to increase public access to outdoor recreation.

During the 1950s, almost every state gained more land for recreational use. Over one million acres were added nationwide to the existing 4.6 million acres. Another 1,100 state parks were added, bringing the nationwide total to 2,664. More than 60 percent of the new parkland was devoted to camping, fishing, and boating activities. Funding to maintain these programs was mainly from the federal government. Supplemental funding was secured by individual states placing fees for entry, hunting and fishing licenses, and taxes on ammunition, guns, and fishing tackle, among other sources of revenue. Some states differed in their approach to use of state parks depending upon their unique culture. The summer-like climate of southern California, for example, led the state to acquire and develop oceanfront areas for both surfing and beachgoers. Nationwide attendance figures maintained a steady increase from 92.5 million per year in 1946 to over 259 million by 1959, a rate five times faster than the population growth (Madow, 95–96).

WINTER SPORTS AND THE 1952 OLYMPIC GAMES

Most of the sporting-type activities were dependent upon calm and warm weather conditions. Yet winter sports participation and spectators were also quite common. A major boost for both participation and fan interest was provided by the success of the American team at the 1952 Winter Olympics held in February in Oslo, Norway. In previous Winter Olympics, the United States was not known for achieving much success. In contrast, the U.S. Olympic team earned its first-ever gold medals in skiing and figure skating. In all, the United States team earned an unprecedented total of 11 medals (4 gold, 6 silver, and 1 bronze), finishing a surprising second in total medals to Norway, which earned 16 total medals (7 gold, 3 silver, and 6 bronze). The surprise success of the American team created a surge of participation in winter sports in America. A March 1953 story in *Time* magazine reported on an international competition held at Iron Mountain, Michigan. The surprise factor was that more than 30,000 spectators witnessed the exhilarating competition. The event attracted more than 100 international athletes to compete in ski jumping, in which skiers launch off a long slide and fly into the air before landing (some in excess of 550 feet). The launch brought them to altitudes near 300 feet while attaining speeds in excess of 60 mph. A later 1959 poll showed a large increase in winter sports of all kinds. Over three million were active participants in downhill skiing and over six million regularly ice-skated as a recreational pursuit.

American participation in winter games continued. It reached a political high point in 1980 as the sports world was mesmerized by the "Miracle on Ice" as an amateur American hockey team defeated the overwhelming favorite Soviet Red Army team in the Winter Olympics in Lake Placid, New York. The event played out the long post-war political posturing in the Cold War between the Soviet Union and the United States since the 1950s. But the 1980 Olympic hockey match was not the first time the Cold War was played out on the sports arena. One of the first occurred during the 1952 Summer Olympic games between American Horace Ashenfelter and the Soviet athlete Vladimir Kazantsev.

THE "COLD WAR" OF THE 1952 SUMMER OLYMPIC GAMES

Horace Ashenfelter (1923–) was a premier American distance runner during the 1950s. He served in World War II and attended college at Penn State under the G.I. Bill during the late 1940s. During his college career at Penn State, he held numerous NCAA records in both the indoor and outdoor two-mile run. During the 1950s, he was an AAU national champion in cross-country (1951, 1955, 1956), the steeplechase (1951, 1953, 1956), the three-mile outdoor run (1954, 1955), the indoor three-mile run (1952 through 1956), and the six-mile

(1950). His crowning achievement was representing the United States as an Olympic athlete.

In the 1952 Olympics, Ashenfelter became the only American to win the gold medal in the Steeplechase event. His preliminary heats set the Olympic record for the event, yet his winning time of 8 minutes and 45 seconds broke the current world record by an astonishing six seconds. That same year he earned the prestigious Sullivan Award as the outstanding amateur athlete in America. As an amateur athlete, Ashenfelter supported his own training while he maintained a day job as well as a growing family. His training occurred after work for about an hour each night often jumping over local obstacles such as park benches. What separated Ashenfelter from the other athletes was not his unique training regime, or even his military service, but rather that he was an agent for the Federal Bureau of Investigation ("Horace Ashenfelter," n.p.).

* * * * *

HORACE ASHENFELTER AND THE COLD WAR ON THE TRACK AT THE 1952 OLYMPICS

By Jeff Benjamin

In the year 2012, Horace and Lillian Ashenfelter arrived at Fitzgerald's Restaurant in Glen Ridge, New Jersey, to be inducted into the National Distance Running Hall of Fame on the 60th anniversary of his gold medal and world record performance at the 1952 Helsinki Olympics. He reminisced not only about his 1952 Olympic performance and other athletic exploits, but also his fears of the Cold War time. "When our team arrived in Finland, we had to take a train to Helsinki," the then 89-year-old legend remembered. "Our windows were painted black because we were traveling through a Soviet-occupied area and we feared we'd be hit!" This was no hollow statement. [The year] 1952 was one of the "hottest" years of the U.S.-Soviet Cold War. Fear of a nuclear holocaust, McCarthyism, and the Korean War were on the minds of millions of people, including the Olympic athletes. "Everyone knew what was going on, that there were conflicts going on between the two countries," said Ashenfelter. Then he pointedly stated, "But NOT between the athletes!"

Horace Ashenfelter, competing in the 3000-meter steeplechase, was a true underdog. The greatest "steeper" of the time, Soviet athlete Vladimir Kazantsev was the overwhelming favorite. However, in a previous interview, Ashenfelter stated, "I didn't even consider that I was the underdog. I was there to represent the United States, do my best and that was it." When he surprised many by setting the Olympic record in his semi-final time of 8:51.00, the Soviets, who were competing in their first Olympic Games, instructed Kazantsev to run on Ashenfelter's right side, forcing the Soviet to run extra steps, which suited Ashenfelter just fine. "I knew I was going to win," Ashenfelter said modestly, as if it was just a fact. In the perceptions of the time, it was also noted that Ashenfelter worked for the FBI, while Kazantsev had some sort of KGB connections, a fact that fit nicely right into the Cold War category.

Neck and neck entering the final lap, Lillian Ashenfelter, sitting in the stands, decided to close her eyes until she heard the loud cries from the crowd, which would indicate the race was over. At the final water barrier, Kazantsev jumped straight down into the water, while Ashenfelter leaped angularly, pretty much clearing most of the water and launching a furious sprint and finishing in a new world record of 8 minutes, 45.4 seconds, nearly 6 seconds in front of Kazantsev and a delirious crowd, along with an open-eyed, happy Lillian. The Olympic champion returned home to Glen Ridge, New Jersey, as a national hero. He would continue to break world records for the indoor two-mile. From 1952 to 1956, he was the indoor three-mile champion. He also won a silver medal in the 1955 Pan-American games along with many AAU titles. In 1957, at age 35, he announced his retirement from competitive running. In 2015, at the age of 93, he still got out to jog in a local Thanksgiving traditional event named after him, the "Ashenfelter 8K Race" run by thousands in Glen Ridge every year.

Source: Jeff Benjamin is an American history teacher at New Dorp High School in Staten Island and a regular contributor to American Track and Field Magazine *and* RunBlogRun.com.

"Marvelous" Mal Whitfield

Another Sullivan Award winner and gold medal winner at the 1952 Helsinki Summer Olympics was the American track athlete Mal Whitfield (1924–2015). Like many athletes of his generation, his career was interrupted due to wartime service. During the Second World War, he served as a tail gunner on bombing missions with the famed Tuskegee Airmen. (The 1944 Olympics were suspended due to the war and resumed at the 1948 London Games.) While participating in the 1948 London Olympics, Whitfield earned two gold medals, one in the 800 meters and a second as part of the 4×400-meter relay team. In between Olympics he served on active military duty in Korea as part of the Army Air Forces. In 1952 at Helsinki, he won the gold once again in the 800 meters. Overall, in two Olympic appearances, he earned a total of five Olympic medals, adding one silver and one bronze. After release from military duty, he returned to Ohio State University and competed on the track team. During his amateur athletic career, he won eight U.S. track titles (six outdoor and two indoor). He set six world records including the outdoor 880 and the indoor 600. Sportswriters called him "Marvelous Mal." In 1954, Whitfield became the first African American to receive the Sullivan Award as the nation's top amateur athlete. He competed for a third Olympic appearance in 1956 but did not qualify (Litsky, "Mal Whitfield," B14).

Whitfield retired from competitive track shortly thereafter and spent the next 47 years as a coach in more than 20 foreign nations serving as a goodwill ambassador representing the United States Information Service as an athletic mentor in Europe, Africa, and the Middle East. In all of his years of service, he said he visited more than 130 countries. Whitfield recognized the high caliber of desire demonstrated by the foreign athletes. At one point during the late 1950s, he was quoted in *Time* magazine as saying, "If I could get all the athletes who want to train in America to come over, I could fill every university from New York to San Francisco." In 1974, Whitfield was elected into the U.S. National Track and Field Hall of Fame followed in 1988 with entry into the U.S. Olympic Hall of Fame (Litsky, "Mal Whitfield," B14).

RACIAL INTEGRATION, WOMEN IN SPORTS, AND TITLE IX

The post-war years were often praised as a time when major league baseball ended its segregation policy with Jackie Robinson playing with the Brooklyn Dodgers. Despite his achievements, the post-war era did not overwhelmingly accept racial integration or even female professionals. The legal segregation of the time was prevalent as was the overt sexist view of women. According to various sources in the "African American Celebrity and the Civil Rights Movement" compiled by The Authentic History Center, some notable changes in professional sports did happen. They included:

- COLLEGE BASKETBALL: In 1956, the Harvard basketball team had accepted an invitation to play in a winter tournament in New Orleans for a series of games scheduled for December 21, 1956, to January 8, 1957. The event never materialized, as the schedule was wiped clean. Unknown to the team was that the previous July, the Louisiana Legislature defied desegregation laws and voted to ban "interracial athletic activities like dancing and pastimes like cards, dice, and checkers." Not only was any integrated play banned, spectator seating was also segregated. Other southern states enacted similar legislation. At the time, Harvard was an "all-white team," but the preceding three years their center was Bob Bowman, an African American who had recently graduated. One player Philip Haughey recalled, "And our reaction was, 'So Bob wouldn't have been able to come?' There was no debate after that. We weren't going. Yes, we were now an all-white team, but if that was their attitude, then no one was going" (Pennington, B15).

- COLLEGE FOOTBALL: At Syracuse University, Ernie Davis became the first black athlete to win the Heisman Trophy. At the end of the 1959 season, the Syracuse football team was invited to play in the Cotton Bowl in Texas on January 1, 1960. The game was filled with all sorts of racial slurs, taunts, and illegal hits upon Davis. Despite the situation, Syracuse defeated the University of Texas 23-14. Davis was named the game's MVP. In presenting the award at a post-game banquet, Davis was told the facility was segregated and therefore he could accept the award, but could not eat with the other dinner guests.

- PROFESSIONAL BASEBALL: In 1947, both Jackie Robinson in the National League and Larry Doby in the American League became the first African Americans to break the so-called "color barrier." Each faced severe opposition and racial taunts from both players and fans.

- PROFESSIONAL GOLF: In 1948, Ted Rhodes was the first African American since the First World War to compete in a sanctioned PGA tour event. Yet, throughout the 1950s, no black player received PGA tour playing privileges until Charlie Sifford in 1961.

- PROFESSIONAL GOLF LPGA: In 1950, the Ladies Professional Golf Association (LPGA) was founded with 14 sanctioned tournaments, with total prize money barely totaling $50,000. Among its 13 founding members was Louise Suggs (1923–2015). (Other notable founders included Babe Didrikson Zaharias and Patty Berg.) Suggs was the dominant player of the era, winning 61 tournaments, including 11 major championships, including the LPGA's Grand Slam in 1957. Legendary pro golfer Ben Hogan offered praise as he once said, "Her swing combines all the desirable elements of efficiency, timing and coordination. It appears to be completely effortless." From its founding until her retirement in 1962, Suggs won at least one LPGA tournament for 13 consecutive years. In 1953, she won nine tournaments, including the LPGA Championship. Yet, at a time when the men's PGA tour was glamorous and filled with stars such as Hogan and Sam Snead, the women had to contend with less than ideal conditions. Suggs recalled, "Some courses had so little grass, and it was in clumps that we took farm machines, tractors with discs, to outline fairway and rough. Between rounds, we set the pins for the next day, called newspapers with the day's scores and tried to charm potential sponsors" (LPGA.com)

- PROFESSIONAL BASKETBALL: In 1950, the National Basketball Association (NBA) Boston Celtics became the first team to draft an African American player named Chuck Cooper. In later rounds of that same year, other blacks picked were Earl Lloyd by Washington and Nat Clifton by the New York Knicks. Lloyd became the first to play in the NBA on October 31, 1950.

- PROFESSIONAL TENNIS: In 1950, Althea Gibson was the first black American (male or female) to compete at any of the major U.S. tennis matches. She competed at the famed Wimbledon Championship in England the following year. She also became the first African American, man or woman, to win a major championship when she won the 1956 French Open. By 1958, she had won twice at Wimbledon and added two U.S. championships. She also earned six major doubles titles.

- PROFESSIONAL HOCKEY: In 1958, Willie O'Ree became the first black professional hockey player with the Boston Bruins. He was not an "African American" because he was a Canadian citizen. He did note "racist remarks were much worse in the U.S. cities than in Toronto and Montreal," two Canadian cities that are part of the National Hockey League (NHL). He remembered, "Fans would yell, 'Go back to the South' and 'How come you're not picking cotton?' Things like that. It didn't bother me. I just wanted to be a hockey player, and if they couldn't accept that fact, that was their problem, not mine." During his 15-year career he was the only black professional hockey player.

For females, the full acceptance into sports of all kinds did not begin until 1972, when federal legislation known as "Title IX" was enacted. The act granted females equal access to higher education. As a result, equal opportunity was afforded to females not only in the classroom, but also on the playing field.

ORANGE AND WHITE, BUT NO BLACK

At the end of the 1951 college football season, only eight post-season bowl games were sanctioned for NCAA play. Playing in a bowl game was financially lucrative to the school as well as possibly voted on by sportswriters as the national champion. One forgotten incident was the Orange Bowl game played on January 1, 1952, in Miami, Florida, between Baylor and Georgia Tech. The selection of Baylor University as an opponent came after a committee snubbed the undefeated University of San Francisco Dons. Unlike the Rose Bowl played each year in Pasadena, California, between the winner of the Midwest Big Ten Conference and winner of the West Coast Pac-8 Conference, the Orange Bowl did not have a set format. An invitation was reserved for the best available opponent for the Southeast Conference (SEC) winner. At the end of the 1951 season, the SEC champion was Florida University.

The top NCAA college football team of 1951, however, was the undefeated University of San Francisco Dons (USF). The reason for not inviting the USF team is attributed to the fact that the team had two African American players, running back Ollie Matson and linebacker Burl Toler. Historian Kristine Clark, who described the events of that season in *Undefeated, Untied, and Uninvited* (Griffin Publishing, 2002), said USF was invited to play in the Orange Bowl with the stipulation, "The white players were invited to go, as long as they left Ollie [Matson] and Burl [Toler] behind." (Matson would play in the NFL for 14 seasons, earning Pro Bowl honors six times, and was later elected into the Hall of Fame. Toler later became the first black NFL official.) The players had a vote and unanimously decided that they would only go together as a team or not at all. USF player Dick Columbini remembered, "It was no question in our mind we were teammates, and we lived together in the dormitories. We ate together. We played together. We went to school together. They were our teammates." Running back Bob Springer recalled, "So we told them, screw those guys . . . Hey, we're just going to end the season right here.' And we did."(Littlefield, "The 1951 USF Dons," n.p.).

The predicament of hateful legal segregation in the south precluded the team from not only playing in Miami, but had also caused previous problems. At one point, during the 1951 season, as the USF team traveled to play in Tulsa, Oklahoma, Matson and Toler were denied sharing the same hotel with their white teammates. In turn, the white players were not allowed to share space with their teammates in a "Colored Only" hotel. Clark said of the team, "All they were looking at was the talent. So they were fairly naïve as to what was going on, as were a lot of the other people in the United States." As it turned out, the 1951 football season was the last played at the University of San Francisco. In 1952, citing financial restraints, the school disbanded the football program. In retrospect, it could only be determined that the funds received from an Orange Bowl appearance might have kept the program going. The situation was not an isolated one as it persisted in many areas of collegiate football throughout the decade and well into the 1960s (Littlefield, "The 1951 USF Dons," n.p.).

FOOTBALL MERGER OF THE AAFC AND THE NFL

The AAFC All-American Football Conference was formed immediately after the war in 1946. One of the teams, the Cleveland Browns, was an extension of a wartime service team from the Great Lakes Naval Training Station coached by Paul Brown. The first three years, the league had eight teams in two divisions of four teams each. The final year was comprised of a single division of six teams that included the Cleveland Browns, San Francisco 49ers, the Brooklyn-NY Yankees (a merged team), Buffalo Bills, Chicago Hornets, Los Angeles Dons, and the Baltimore Colts. During the short time of the AAFC, the Cleveland Browns dominated as they compiled an overall record of 45 wins against only four loses and three ties. During the 1948 season, they completed an undefeated season with a perfect record of 14–0. Their dominance of the league also extended to winning the championship title all four years.

As the rival National Football League (NFL) completed its 30th regular season in 1949, a merger was announced with the AAFC for the upcoming 1950 season. Three AAFC teams—the Cleveland Browns, Baltimore Colts, and San Francisco—joined the established NFL in a 13-team realignment as follows:

American Conference (East): Cleveland Browns (AAFC), Chicago Cardinals, New York Giants, Philadelphia Eagles, Washington Redskins, and Pittsburgh Steelers.

National Conference (West): Baltimore Colts, Chicago Bears, Detroit Lions, Green Bay Packers, Los Angeles Rams, New York Yanks (AAFC), and San Francisco 49ers (AAFC).

The Baltimore Colts left the league after the 1950 season and rejoined in 1953. The New York Yanks played two seasons, transferred as the Dallas Texans and were disbanded after the 1952 season. From 1953 through 1959, the NFL was a solid 12-team league in two geographically named divisions as follows:

East Division: Cleveland Browns, Chicago Cardinals, New York Giants, Philadelphia Eagles, Pittsburgh Steelers, and Washington Redskins.

West Division: Baltimore Colts, Chicago Bears, Detroit Lions, Green Bay Packers, Los Angeles Rams, and San Francisco 49ers.

NFL FOOTBALL AND "THE GREATEST GAME EVER PLAYED"

Television would mark the transition of professional football into a major spectator sport. The turning point was the result of the 1958 NFL championship game between the Baltimore Colts and New York Giants. The season-ending game was also the first NFL championship to be seen live on national television. It also provided a surprise ending, as the game was tied at 17–17 at the end of regulation play and, as the rules dictated, the first team to score in overtime, known as "Sudden Death," would win immediately. The anticipation of a sudden score that would end the game was also added with the fact that play would continue as long as necessary until one team scored. In overtime, the Colts scored on a long drive engineered by legendary quarterback Johnny Unitas, culminating in a short touchdown run by fullback Alan Ameche. The final score of 23–17 captivated the national television audience and set the stage for an increased interest in the sport. By 1960, attendance at profession football games increased to more than three million per year. But the real impact was the television audience that numbered over 30 million.

The NFL has since hailed the game as "The Greatest Game Ever Played." The Professional Football Hall of Fame described its distinction this way:

> Professional football was on the rise in the 1950s and reached a crescendo during the latter part of the decade. Much of the popularity can be traced to a single game—the 1958 NFL Championship Game between the Baltimore Colts and New York Giants.

The 1958 championship game is cited as being the catalyst for bringing the NFL into a leader among professional sports leagues. By the 21st century, it blossomed into a multi-billion-dollar industry in an eight division, 32-team league.

BASEBALL AND TELEVISION

Throughout the 1950s, baseball was the most popular American spectator sport. At the beginning of the decade, more than 17 million fans attended games at 14 stadiums of Major League Baseball (MLB) teams. In 1952 and 1953, a slight drop in overall attendance was at 14 million each year. The reduction is often attributed to the popularity of television, which was responsible for a large decline in all kinds of going-out types of entertainment such as restaurants and movie theaters. Unlike some other entertainment venues that did not recover due to the switch to TV, baseball was just the opposite.

The widespread popularity of television soon added to the growing popularity of American sports including baseball. Many found that they could enjoy watching the games within the comforts of their own homes. But the excitement of being among a crowd was an exhilarating feeling often unmatched sitting alone at home. However, a person did not have to go into a baseball stadium to be part of the excitement. Legendary TV personality Steve Allen said, "The same thing happened in the typical tavern, where a [television] set behind the bar virtually guaranteed a full house. Sports events that might attract a [stadium] crowd of 30,000 or 40,000 suddenly, with the addition of TV cameras, had audiences numbering in the millions" ("Television in the United States").

By the end of the decade, live attendance was at a high of more than 19 million. Television, however, drastically affected attendance at minor league games. Small cities and towns that were usually located too far from the larger baseball cities had relied on a local minor league affiliate for their baseball entertainment. With the increase in the number of MLB games broadcast on live nationwide television, a large number of fans stopped going to minor league games. In 1949, prior to the ascent of television, attendance at minor league stadiums numbered more than 42 million among 58 minor league teams. By 1957, after a steady yearly decline, the number was only at 15 million (Olson, 286).

By 1958, major league baseball maintained a steady stream of nationwide broadcasting of regular season games and also set the stage for a major breakthrough in society. The networks found that televising a sporting event proved economical. The stadiums were already in place; therefore, no expensive sets were needed. In addition, the production costs were lower because salaries were not required for writers or actors. This made sports inexpensive to produce, a primary concern when the audience was small and not yet generating large advertising revenues. The first televised sporting event was a college baseball game between Columbia and Princeton in 1939. The game was covered by one camera focused along the third base line. Sports soon became a fixture on prime-time network programming, such as the first network sports broadcast of NBC's *Gillette Cavalcade of Sports*, often accounting for one-third of the networks' total evening fare.

BASEBALL, THE COLOR BARRIER, AND THE NEW YORK YANKEES

In 1947, Jackie Robinson (1919–1972) is credited as breaking the color barrier as the first African-American player in the modern era, joining the Brooklyn Dodgers in the National League. Often overlooked is Larry Doby (1923–2003), who became the first African American in the American League, joining the Cleveland Indians a few months later that same year. The color line might have been broken, but the league was slow to embrace the change. By 1949, only the New York Giants added another African-American player to their roster as they signed Monte Irvin (1919–2016). At the start of the 1950s, Major League Baseball (MLB) was more than 95 percent white. By the end of the decade, many of the teams had signed African Americans, yet the percentage of white players remained high at 85 percent. Overall the number was quite low, but some of the African-American players signed during the 1950s turned out to be some of the best and most exciting in all of baseball history. They included future Hall of Fame members such as Hank Aaron (Braves), Ernie Banks (Cubs), Willie Mays (Giants), and Frank Robinson (Reds), to name just a few. Hank Aaron, as one example, entered the league in 1954 and would go on to break Babe Ruth's all-time major league home run record. The number of African-American players reached an all-time high of about 18 percent of the league in 1980. Yet each year thereafter, the total number dropped consistently to only 7 seven percent by the year 2012. (Many attribute the drop to the growing lucrative contracts offered by the NFL and NBA, as blacks dominated those leagues in large numbers.) In contrast by 2012, the number of Hispanic players topped 28 percent of the league. That statistic can be traced to Roberto Clemente's entry into the league.

In 1955, Roberto Clemente (1934–1972) earned the distinction as the first Puerto Rican baseball player in the major leagues. (The previous year Pittsburgh had signed its first African-American ballplayer Curt Roberts, becoming only the ninth MLB team to do so.) Clemente went on to an MVP career as a four time National League batting leader (1961, 1964, 1965, 1967), played in 15 All-Star games, had two World Series wins (1960 and 1971), and earned 12 consecutive Gold Glove Awards (1961–1972). Of tragic irony, Clemente joined the prestigious 3,000 MLB hit club on his final at bat of the 1972 season. A few months later, on December 31, 1972, he died as a result of a plane crash while on a humanitarian mission. He was posthumously elected into the Baseball Hall of Fame in 1973.

Integration was slow in baseball, yet those that did sign during the 1950s turned out to be some of the best and most exciting in all of baseball history. Three pictured here left to right were future members of the Baseball Hall of Fame, Roberto Clemente (Pirates), Willie Mays (Giants), and Hank Aaron (Braves). (Photofest)

The racial changes were an important step to a better quality level of play. Some important changes in MLB during the 1950s included:

- Lights for playing night baseball (and prime-time television) were installed at all the major league parks except Wrigley Field in Chicago.
- Teams were enticed to move to new stadiums, often located outside the urban areas. As a result, going to a game by car was becoming a regular occurrence.
- Air travel made the relocation of teams to the West Coast more easily accessible than train travel for teams playing away games.

The changes were numerous, but some constants remained the same. One event was the World Series to determine the champions of baseball. The series was a contest that put the winner of the American League (AL) and the National League (NL) in a best-of-seven-games contest. The most dominant team was the New York Yankees. Over a period of 18 years, the Yankees appeared in 15 World Series, winning the title 10 times. Their most dominant period was throughout the 1950s as they won the American League Pennant eight times and the World Series six times.

The total number of wins by the New York Yankees is even more impressive, when the World Series wins in 1947 and 1949 made it six titles in seven years. In addition, after the 1950s ended, the Yankees appeared in consecutive World Series from 1960 to 1964. In 1960, the team lost to the Pittsburgh Pirates (NL) in a dramatic last-at-bat seventh game home run. The Yankees returned as champs the next two seasons, winning in 1961 over the Cincinnati Reds (NL) in seven games, and again in 1962, winning in seven games over the San Francisco Giants (NL). The following year they lost to the Los Angeles Dodgers (NL) in four straight games. In 1964, the series went to seven games as the Yankees lost to the St. Louis Cardinals (NL).

BASEBALL MOVES EAST TO WEST WITH
A MIDPOINT IN BETWEEN

During the early 1950s, the New York Yankees led the league in total stadium attendance with 2.1 million in 1950, 1.95 million in 1951, and 1.6 million in 1952. The following year, the attendance leader was the Milwaukee Braves as the relocation of the Braves from Boston, Massachusetts, to the Midwest in Wisconsin is often overshadowed by the advent of West Coast baseball. Prior to leaving Boston, the Braves could not compete with the neighboring Red Sox for fan attendance. In three successive years, the Braves went from a fairly respectable yearly attendance of 944,000 in 1951 to a sharp decline the following year of only 488,000. That season was followed by an embarrassing total attendance of barely 281,000 for the entire 1952 season. In 1953, when the Braves relocated to Milwaukee, it was the first MLB franchise move in more than 50 years. (In 1966, the Braves relocated to Atlanta.) The move to Milwaukee County Stadium proved to be a bonanza as they jumped from last to first (supplanting the Yankees) in total attendance for 1953, attracting over 1.8 million fans. The Braves continued as the league leader in attendance figures each year from 1953 through 1958, averaging between 1.8 and 2.2 million fans. Other MLB teams relocated for similar attendance reasons. In 1954, the St. Louis Browns relocated to Baltimore and changed their name to the Orioles. In 1955, the Athletics left Philadelphia moving to Kansas City. (In 1968, they moved once again to Oakland, California.)

In 1959, the top-attendance figure shifted to the Los Angeles Dodgers (NL), who had recently relocated from Brooklyn to the West Coast. While in Brooklyn, the numbers were quite good as they consistently averaged between 1 million and 1.2 million die-hard fans each year. Once in Los Angles, however, their attendance consistently topped two million each year. The Dodgers' move coincided with another move from the East Coast to the West Coast, when the New York Giants (NL) relocated to San Francisco. Unlike the Dodgers, the Giants were not doing well in attendance. During the early part of the decade, from 1950 to 1954, the team averaged about one million per year. After that, a steady decline in yearly attendance went from 824,000 in 1955 to 629,000 in 1956 and 654,000 in 1957. The move to San Francisco provided immediate results, as attendance was at 1.3 million in 1958 and 1.4 million in 1959.

Chart 6.1 Comparative Attendance Figures for Relocated Major League Baseball Teams

Year	Braves (NL)	Total	Dodgers (NL)	Total	Giants (NL)	Total
1905	Boston	944,391	Brooklyn	1,185,896	New York	1,008,878
1951	Boston	487,475	Brooklyn	1,282,628	New York	1,059,539
1952	Boston	281,278	Brooklyn	1,088,704	New York	984,940
1953	Milwaukee	1,826,397	Brooklyn	1,163,419	New York	811,518
1954	Milwaukee	2,131,388	Brooklyn	1,020,531	New York	1,155,067
1955	Milwaukee	2,005,836	Brooklyn	1,033,589	New York	824,112
1956	Milwaukee	2,046,331	Brooklyn	1,213,562	New York	629,179
1957	Milwaukee	2,215,404	Brooklyn	1,028,258	New York	653,923
1958	Milwaukee	1,971,101	Los Angeles	1,845,556	San Francisco	1,272,625
1959	Milwaukee	1,749,112	Los Angeles	2,071,045	San Francisco	1,422,130

Source: ballparksofbaseball.com. Chart compiled by author.

BOXING AND ROCKY MARCIANO

Professional boxing was a major sport in the 1950s comparable with Major League Baseball as the most popular spectator sport of the time period. A major factor that contributed to the popularity of both of these sports was television. At the time, especially during the early part of the decade, TV cameras were in their early stages of development. They were a single fixed-lens camera not capable of offering multiple angles or zooming. Therefore, sports such as boxing and even wrestling were a perfect match for a fixed-lens camera, as the action was located within a defined area and could be easily followed by the viewer. TV programs such as the *Gillette Cavalcade of Sports* provided a weekly lineup of top-notch boxing matches. Sports historian Scott Levinson of ProBoxing-Fans.com said, "Many people consider the '50s the golden era of boxing." Unlike the 21st century, with many different boxing organizations and dozens of champions, the 1950s had a total of only eight weight classes, each with one champion. Many of those fighters who became household names included:

- *Sugar Ray Robinson* (1921–1989) won titles at both the welterweight (140–147 lbs.) and middleweight divisions (154–160 lbs.). Often considered the greatest fighter of all time.

- *Jake LaMotta* (1921–2013), middleweight champion in 1949. He fought six classic fights against Sugar Ray Robinson; the last match was on February 14, 1951. He continued fighting, eventually retiring in 1954. In later years, he was the main subject of the Hollywood movie *Raging Bull* (1980).

- *Rocky Graziano* (1919–1990) was immortalized in a popular 1950s Hollywood movie *Somebody Up There Likes Me* (1956) with legendary actor Paul Newman in the title role. As one of the most popular fighters of any time period,

Graziano fought as both a welterweight and middleweight. Most of his fights were during the 1940s, yet 19 of his 83 career bouts occurred during the early 1950s, his last fight coming on September 17, 1952.

- *Archie Moore* (1913–1998) won the light heavyweight division (165–178 lbs.) in 1952 at the age of 39 and held the title until 1962. He moved up in weight and fought for the heavyweight title, losing two notable decisions to Rocky Marciano and Floyd Patterson.

- *Floyd Patterson* (1935–2006) was a 1952 Olympic Gold Medalist who fought for the vacant world heavyweight title after Rocky Marciano retired. He won the title on November 30, 1956, knocking out Archie Moore in the fifth round, becoming the youngest heavyweight champ at 21 years old. He lost the title to Ingemar Johansson on June 26, 1959. Patterson became the first ever to regain the title by beating Johansson in a rematch on June 20, 1960 (KO5).

- *Willie Pep* (1922–2006) entered the decade as the reigning featherweight champion (119–126 lbs.). He lost two notable bouts to Sandy Saddler (1926–2001) and was forced to retire after a car accident in 1956.

Other notables included Carmen Basilio (1927–2012), Ezzard Charles (1921–1975), Gene Fullmer (1931–2015), Kid Gavilan (1926–2003), Joey Maxim (1922–2001), and Jersey Joe Walcott (1914–1994), among many others. One of the greatest fighters of all time, Joe Louis (1914–1981), fought his final fight on October 26, 1951, which he lost against an up-and-coming Rocky Marciano (1923–1969).

In an era filled with great fighters, none stood out more than "The Brockton Blockbuster" Rocky Marciano. The "Brockton" part of the nickname referenced his hometown in Massachusetts where he was born as Rocco Francis Marchegiano on September 1, 1923. The "Blockbuster" part was derived from his devastating punching power. Marciano was not known for his crafty coordination, but rather for his pure power, stamina, and an undeterred willpower. In many of his fights, he was often on the brink of losing and was known for making incredible comebacks, which very often ended with him winning with a spectacular knockout. Debate about the greatest boxing heavyweights of all time is often discussed among boxing fans and historians. During the post-war time, the three names mentioned most often were Muhammad Ali, Joe Louis, and Rocky Marciano. Sometimes they are ranked in that order; other times Marciano is rated as the top heavyweight of all time. That top rating is often based on the fact that Marciano was the only heavyweight boxing champion to ever retire undefeated.

Marciano certainly did not have the boxing skills of an Ali or a Louis, nor did he have the ideal physical size of a classic boxing heavyweight. Whereas both Louis and Ali were each lean, tall, and over 200 lbs., Marciano was short, stout, and often fought at a weight under 190 lbs. As a result, for Marciano to be effective he had to get in close to an opponent while usually suffering tremendous punishment. But his tenacity and ability to keep on "coming at" an opponent drove his growing legion of boxing fans into an appreciative frenzy.

Marciano took up boxing after he was drafted into the U.S. Army in 1943. After the war, he boxed as an amateur and turned to a professional career in

Chart 6.2   Comparative Physical Features of Muhammad Ali, Joe Louis, and Rocky Marciano

Boxer	Height	Weight	Reach	Record	Title Held
Muhammad Ali	6'3"	236 lbs.	78 in.	56–5 (37 KOs)	1964 to 1969
					1974 to 1978
Joe Louis	6'2"	200 lbs.	76 in.	50–4 (43 KOs)	1937 to 1949
Rocky Marciano	5'11"	188 lbs.	67 in.	49–0 (43 KOs)	1952 to, 1956

Source: Chart compiled by author.

1947 after a failed tryout as a baseball catcher with the Chicago Cubs. He gained attention and built a loyal legion of local fans in and around the Boston area, as he often fought close to home. Twenty-eight of his 49 professional bouts took place at the nearby Rhode Island Auditorium in Providence. Twice he fought in Boston, once in Holyoke, Massachusetts, and once in Hartford, Connecticut. As his fame grew, his bouts were held in larger stadiums and arenas. Four of his fights were shown on live television. His other big fights were available to the public on closed-circuit TV shown in movie theaters.

On October 26, 1951, he defeated Joe Louis with a knockout in the eighth round at New York's famed Madison Square Garden. (He would fight a total of five times at Madison Square Garden, considered the mecca for boxers and fans alike.) After the Louis fight, Marciano was rated as a top contender for the heavyweight title. He was placed among contenders to take part in a World Heavyweight Title Eliminator fight held at Yankee Stadium. On July 28, 1952, after knocking out Harry Matthews in the second round, he was in line to fight for the title. On September 23, 1952, Marciano won the Heavyweight Championship title in Philadelphia by knocking out defending champion Jersey Joe Walcott in the 13th round. Prior to the knockout, Marciano was suffering severe punishment and was way behind in points and losing the fight. He rallied with a brutal knockout punch that was captured in a photograph by Herb Scharfman of International News Photos and is considered one of the most famous photos in boxing history. The following day on September 24, 1952, the *Boston Globe* described the knockout:

> MARCIANO REBOUNDS AFTER KNOCK OUT
> Jersey Joe Walcott never saw the right glove of the hard-bitten Marciano
> as it came whirling out of the night. It hit him on the side of the jaw and a
> splatter of blood shot from an old eye wound.
> The champion's face went blank. His mouth hung open and his
> mouthpiece dribbled slowly from between his lips. Then he sagged
> forward and collapsed gently on the ring floor, his forehead on the canvas,
> supported by his knees and elbows.
> The Bull from Brockton stood over him on his shaggy pillars of legs,
> drenched in his own hot blood on this cool damp night.
> The referee Charlie Daggert tolled the count, which you couldn't hear in
> the tumult that filled the auditorium. Right in the middle of his count, at

precisely five, Walcott's knees and elbows refused to prop him up any
longer, and he sort of went down on his face like a flat tire.
And the new champion of the world was Rocco Francis Marchegiano of
Brockton, Massachusetts.

The new champion only defended his title six times, winning all of them
with five by a knockout. His first title defense came on May 15, 1953, in a
rematch against Walcott, whom he knocked out in the first round. During his
reign as heavyweight champion, Marciano was named "Fighter of the Year"
by *The Ring Magazine* in 1952, 1954, and 1955. On three separate occasions his
bouts were also voted as "Fight of the Year" by that same magazine.

Marciano was more than just a boxer; he was a national celebrity. He made
three appearances on the widely popular Sunday night variety program *The
Ed Sullivan Show*. His first was in 1951, a second occurred in 1954, and his last
appearance was on September 25, 1955, a few days after his successful title
defense. His last fight on September 21, 1955, at Yankee Stadium drew over
60,000 fans as he won with a ninth round knockout over reigning Light-
Heavyweight Champion Archie Moore. (The closed-circuit TV audience was
estimated at half million.)

Rocky Marciano officially retired from boxing at the age of 32 on April 27,
1956. He explained the reason for his retirement in *The New York Times*, saying,

Jersey Joe Walcott (right) lands a blow to the body of champion Rocky Marciano during the
first round of their championship bout at Chicago stadium on May 15, 1953. Marciano and
his legendary punching power knocked out Jersey Joe in the first round. (AP Photo)

Chart 6.3   Boxing Matches by Rocky Marciano during the 1950s

Date	Opponent	Decision
March 24, 1950	Roland La Starza	W MD 10
June 5, 1950	Eldridge Eatman	W KO 3
July 10, 1950	Gino Buonvino	W KO 10
September 9, 1950	Johnny Shkor	W KO 6
November 13, 1950	Ted Lowry	W UD 10
December 18, 1950	Bill Wilson	W KO 1
January 29, 1951	Keene Simmons	W KO 8
March 20, 1951	Harold Mitchell	W KO 2
March 26, 1951	Art Henri	W KO 9
April 30, 1951	Willis Applegate	W UD 10
July 12, 1951	Rex Layne	W KO 6
August 27, 1951	Freddie Beshore	W KO 4
October 26, 1951	Joe Louis	W KO 8
February 13, 1952	Lee Savold	W KO 6
April 21, 1952	Gino Buonvino	W KO 2
May 12, 1952	Bernie Reynolds	W KO 3
July 28, 1952	Harry Matthews	W KO 2
September 23, 1952*	Jersey Joe Walcott	W KO 13
May 15, 1953*	Jersey Joe Walcott	W KO 1
September 24, 1953*	Roland La Starza	W TKO 11
June 17, 1954*	Ezzard Charles	W UD 15
September 17, 1954*	Ezzard Charles	W KO 8
May 16, 1955*	Don Cockell	W KO 9
September 21, 1955*	Archie Moore	W KO 9

* Indicates heavyweight title fight.
MD=Majority Decision KO=Knockout
UD=Unanimous Decision TKO=Technical Knockout
Source: Chart compiled by author.

"I thought it was a mistake when Joe Louis tried a comeback. No man can say what he will do in the future, but barring poverty, the ring has seen the last of me. I am comfortably fixed, and I am not afraid of the future." In the succeeding years he made some personal appearances, most connected with boxing. He also did a few acting stints on some television series. On August 31, 1969, his life was cut short as he was killed in a private plane crash near Des Moines, Iowa. By the time of his tragic death, Rocky Marciano was an American celebrity known by millions outside the boxing world.

FURTHER READING

Scott Levinson. "Boxing," ProBoxing-Fans.com. Accessed March 22, 2016. www
.proboxing-fans.com/boxing-101/history/1950s-boxing/

"Rocky Marciano, The Brockton Blockbuster." Estate of Rocky Marciano. Accessed
March 22, 2016. www.rockymarciano.net/about/bio.htm

John F. Steadman. *The Greatest Football Game Ever Played: When the Baltimore Colts and
the New York Giants Faced Sudden Death.* El Paso, TX: Press Box, Inc., 1988.

Mal Whitfield. *Beyond the Finish Line.* Washington, D.C.: The Whitfield Foundation,
2002.

CHAPTER 7

Art and Architecture

In the early 20th century, *The New York Times* cultural critic Michael Kimmelman noted, "Perhaps no decade in the history of American art continues to generate quite so much debate as the 1950s, when the United States, and in particular New York City, supplanted Europe as the primary focus of international attention" ("Art of the 50's"). Art historian Sidra Stitch, writing in *Made in USA: An Americanization in Modern Art*, described the art style as a "mid-century focus on a visibly American subject matter" (6). The most prevalent example of the new art was known as "abstract expressionism," created by artists such as Willem de Kooning, Franz Kline, Barnett Newman, Robert Motherwell, Jackson Pollock, and Mark Rothko, to name a few of the most prominent. In 1951, Motherwell organized an exhibition titled *School of New York* that might represent the beginning when New York replaced Europe. Sidra Stitch, explained the shifts:

> The dominant trend in western painting throughout the 1950s began with a handful of American artists later termed Abstract Expressionists. Their paintings were often made of shapes, lines, and forms not meant to depict a "reality" from the visible world. They believed that non-representational painting could express spiritual and emotional truths in the most direct way. These artists often used a spontaneous and physical process in order to present an immediate response to emotion. (6–7)

A significant amount of the artists' inspiration came from Europe. Many were inspired by the pre-war artists such as Piet Mondrian and Max Ernst, who had recognized the growing tensions on the European continent and left for a safer haven in America.

   The new style shifted the center of the western art world to New York City, more specifically the borough of Manhattan. (Both Pollock and de Kooning had studios on the less than affluent Lower East Side.) It should serve to note that one of the very few areas in the entire world to escape the unimaginable physical destruction and human genocide of the war was the United States. In deference to Europe, the severe loss of human life and the shameless destruction of the cities and countryside alike prevented any quick return to any kind of normalcy, therefore art did lag behind. Because the continental United States was unaffected, art was able to flourish.

THE DECADE OF AMERICAN ART

During the early 1950s, the Neo-Dada art style was introduced by artists such as Robert Rauschenberg (1925–2008) and Jasper Johns (b. 1930). Neo-Dada was often described simply as "anti-aesthetic" (Stitch, 9). A PBS documentary on the *American Masters* series noted that Rauschenberg and Johns often concerned themselves with the everyday life of post-war America. Their work is often cited as a forerunner to pop art as Neo-Dada often applied popular images and easily recognizable items from everyday American life. Other notable artists such as Andy Warhol and Roy Lichtenstein often rejected abstract expressionism. Warhol and Lichtenstein were part of a movement termed "pop art" that connected popular culture imagery with fine art. They included diverse images from television, film, print media, and everyday life that were presented in sculpture, collages, posters, line drawings, and paintings, among other media. Warhol explained, "Pop artists did images that anyone walking down the street would recognize in a split second" (Warhol, 3).

Many of the artists who set up studios in New York were not actually born in the city. Motherwell, for example, had moved to New York just prior to the war in 1940. At the time, other artists such as Pollock, de Kooning, Rothko, and Kline had previously set up studios. As noted in a film biography on Motherwell for the PBS *American Masters* film series:

> These painters renounced the prevalent American style, believing its realism depicted only the surface of American life. Their interest was in exploring the deeper sense of reality beyond the recognizable image. Influenced by the Surrealists, many of who had emigrated from Europe to New York, the Abstract Expressionists sought to create essential images that revealed emotional truth and authenticity of feeling.

Motherwell, as did the others of his time, explored psychological and philosophical themes within his work. Art, however, was not Motherwell's first pursuit as he had studied philosophy at both Stanford and Harvard. His philosophical path led him to the American philosopher Alfred North. It was North who encouraged Motherwell to pursue abstract art as "the process of peeling away the inessential and presenting the necessary." In later years, Motherwell often described his approach to his work as, "To end up with a canvas that is no less beautiful than the empty canvas is to begin with" (*American Masters*).

At a time of growing conformity, the total break into the abstract world of art was often met with harsh criticism. The tensions created by the overt suppression of free speech throughout the decade were also applied against the new art styles. Serge Guilbaut, writing in *How New York Stole the Idea of Modern Art*, explained:

> It is ironic but not contradictory that in a society . . . in which political repression weighed as heavily as it did in the United States, abstract expressionism was for many the expression of freedom: the freedom to creative controversial works of art, the freedom symbolized by action painting, by the unbridled expressionism of artists. (201)

Former President Harry Truman, for example, was not a fan of modern art, or any type of leisure pursuit, for that matter. In 1955, as Truman appeared for a *Person to Person* TV interview with host Edward R. Murrow and was asked, "What do you do to relax?" Truman replied, "My only relaxation is to work, and I never have known anybody to be injured by too much hard work. It is the lack of it that kills people." Truman also criticized the famous artist Pablo Picasso (1881–1973). At the time, Picasso was well established with more than a half-century of work to his credit. (In the early 21st century, a 1955 Picasso painting titled *Les Femmes d'Alger (Version 'O')* became the single highest-priced painting sold at a Christie's auction for a price of $179.4 million.) Yet in 1955, Picasso's work was often criticized as Communist subversion. Actually, any modern art, abstract expressionism, and the like was often decried as Communist subversion. Truman added, "I dislike Picasso, and all the moderns—they are lousy. Any kid can take an egg and a piece of ham and make more understandable pictures" (Geselbracht, "Harry Truman Speaks," n.p.).

As a Missouri native, Truman epitomized the American mid-western ideals of Protestantism, hard work, and conformity. He was also wary of the supposed lost ideals of an American way of life. Therefore, when political figures such as Truman spoke, his voice was often reflective of a large segment of the American population. In turn, the media attention attached to his name also served as credibility to current public opinion. His description of museum work was often filled with the melodramatic, as Truman viewed art from a nostalgic point of view. He said,

> It is too bad that our age has forgotten those things that make real art appealing—or they are too lazy to take the pains to do real work. I saw a bronze monstrosity in one of the art galleries and asked the director if it was meant to be a bronze picture of a devil's darning needle, [or] a vicious-looking bug that's scary to look at. The director turned pale and told me it was a modernist conception of love at first sight! Then I fainted. (Geselbracht, "Harry Truman Speaks," n.p.)

Unknown to the likes of Truman was that the artistic response was to reject the conformity of the time. Lisa Phillips, writing in *The American Century: Art & Culture, 1950–2000,* described it as "a group of American artists moved away from representation and realism toward a completely nonrepresentational style, which became known as abstract expressionism." The term "abstract expressionism" often defies definition, yet is often considered the first truly American art form in painting. As an art form, it was actually characterized by the use of abstract forms. Sources such as the Museum of Modern Art (MoMA) cites examples that "convey strong emotional or expressive content." Some also define it as "spontaneous" painting as evident by the works of artists such as Willem de Kooning (1904–1997) and Jackson Pollock (1912–1956). Another facet was provided by many of the artists, such as de Kooning, who had left a war-torn Europe and in turn rejected all previous European styles of painting.

Unlike the previous European masters of the early 20th century, the abstract expressionists working in America, such as Pollock, created large works on canvas. As the canvas was much too large for an easel, he was known to place the canvas on the floor of his studio and hover over it while he applied the paint. His improvisational art style was aided by listening to jazz music. (Jazz at the time was moving towards expressive abstractionism and improvisational staccato, breaking from traditions of the past.) Willem de Kooning was another abstract expressionist who listened to jazz. One of his personal favorites was Miles Davis, of whom he wrote, "He doesn't play [the notes], he bends them. I bend the paint" ("Abstract Expressionism," n.p.).

Many other artists, such as Pollock, also rejected the traditional artist easel to express a break from past traditions. As described by MoMA curators:

> Pollock began laying canvas on the floor and pouring, dribbling, and flicking enamel paint onto the surface, sometimes straight from the can, or with sticks and stiffened brushes. The density of interlacing liquid threads of paint is balanced and offset by puddles of muted colors and by allover spattering. The pictorial result of this tension is a landmark in the history of abstract expressionism. (Stitch, 6–7)

A similar painting, *Number 1, 1950 (Lavender Mist)*, also painted in 1950 was an oil on canvas measuring 7'3" high and 9'10" wide, held by the National Gallery of Art in Washington, D.C. Of interesting note, writer Clement Greenberg, whose 1955 article "American Type Painting" promoted the new style, suggested the title even though there was no actual "lavender" color within the painting. Curators at the National Gallery of Art noted that the assemblage of colors did form a "mauve glow that inspired Greenberg . . . to suggest the descriptive title" (Stitch, 7).

In 1951, the first training center for the study of American art and culture was established at the Henry Francis Dupont Winterthur Museum in Delaware. A few years later in 1954, the Metropolitan Museum of Modern Art (MoMA) sponsored its first exhibit of solely American art. The art style gained national attention on December 24, 1956, as *Time* magazine provided a cover story on American art. The story featured American realist painter Edward Hopper (1882–1967) advertising "A Christmas Treasury of American Painting." By 1958, American art was being championed throughout the nation. During that year, a massive exhibit at New York's renowned Madison Square Garden titled *Art: USA: 58* featured more than 1,540 paintings and 300 sculptures (Stitch, 8).

One noted artist, Ray Johnson provided a contrast to abstract expressionism in his *Elvis Presley No. 1* (c. 1955). (In 1955, Presley was still in the early stages of his career and would not become a national star until 1956.) For his project, Johnson "embellished" a Presley publicity photo with a red tint and some red geometric highlights. A noticeable addition was an application of red drips that resembled teardrops coming from the singer's eyes. Johnson claimed the red teardrops were a satirical statement to abstract expressionism. He was quoted as saying, "I'm the only painter in New York whose drips mean anything" (Stitch, 128).

ABSTRACT EXPRESSIONISM AS A WEAPON IN THE COLD WAR

During the Cold War, American ideology was pitted against Soviet ideology. Each promoted a "way of life" that was better than the other. The Soviets even promoted an "official" style of art, socialist realism, as the official Soviet government sanctioned doctrine from 1932 until the 1980s. The editors at *Encyclopedia Britannica* wrote, "The primary theme of socialist realism is the building of socialism and a classless society. Socialist realist paintings and sculptures used naturalistic idealization to portray workers and farmers as dauntless, purposeful, well-muscled, and youthful." Unlike modern American art, which provided a look toward the future, socialist realism looked back to the style of romanticism. The old style was prevalent during the 18th century by a growing conservative movement in Europe looking to suppress the enlightened will of the individual to the absolute will of the monarchial state.

Despite harsh public and political criticism from Truman, Senator Joe McCarthy, and mainstream America, abstract expressionism did receive a fair share of European exhibitions. They included:

- *Masterpieces of the Twentieth Century* (1952) in Paris;
- *Modern Art in the United States* (1955), which toured major museums throughout the United States;
- *The New American Painting* (1958–1959), which toured major European cities.

The touring exhibition of *The New American Painting* shown in Paris and London included works by Pollock, de Kooning, and Motherwell, among others. These exhibitions were funded by a group known as the Congress for Cultural Freedom (a U.S.-funded global group with offices in 35 countries). The group started in 1950, claimed backing from wealthy American financiers such as the Rockefeller family.

Despite the public perception fueled by the criticism of Truman and McCarthy, late 20th-century reports from declassified documents and retired government personnel claimed the actual source of funding for the Congress for Cultural Freedom was provided by the U.S. Central Intelligence Agency (CIA). In 1995, Tom Braden, who was the first head of the CIA's International Organizations Division, confirmed the full involvement by the spy agency. From the standpoint of the CIA, Braden thought American art could be used in a "psychological war against the Soviets":

We wanted to unite all the people who were writers, who were musicians, who were artists, to demonstrate that the West and the United States was devoted to freedom of expression and to intellectual achievement, without any rigid barriers as to what you must write, and what you must say, and what you must do, and what you must paint, which was what was going on in the Soviet Union. I think it was the most important division that the agency had, and I think that it played an enormous role in the Cold War.

Braden added that the reason to operate in secret was due in part to a Congress that was in the midst of overt suppression to any non-conformity as Communist subversion. The former CIA director also said there was significant "public hostility to the avant-garde" (Stonor Saunders, "Modern Art was CIA 'Weapon'").

Journalist Sam Biddle also wrote about the uncovered CIA involvement in a 2010 article. He explained the need for the CIA secrecy and the American public opinion against abstract expressionism:

> The reason it [the art] disgusted so many Americans then (and now) was that it was the exact antithesis of the older stuff. Norman Rockwell stuff. It didn't just break the rules of painting; it was entirely rule less—ditto the work of Pollock's peers. Abstract Expressionism was meant to be the unmitigated will of a human being, blasted onto a canvas in the form of paint. And, thought the CIA, it was American as hell.

Unknown to the American public was that the full extent of the ideological war against Communism had deep implications, especially in the field of architecture.

AMERICAN ARCHITECTURE VERSUS SOVIET COMMUNISM

An attempt at a peaceful post-war world was proposed by a collaborative effort of promoting an alliance among the nations of the world. In doing so, the formation of the United Nations (a 1942 term applied by President Franklin D. Roosevelt) on October 24, 1945, drew representatives of 50 countries to meet in San Francisco. The idea was to propose a charter agreement on how to resolve future problems and/or conflicts between nations. According to the official United Nations website:

> The United Nations officially came into existence on 24 October 1945, when the Charter had been ratified by China, France, the Soviet Union, the United Kingdom, the United States and by a majority of other signatories. United Nations Day is celebrated on 24 October each year.

Yet the formation of a group such as this could not be just on paper alone; a permanent home and a building were necessary.

In 1950, the United Nations (UN) building opened on the east side of Manhattan in New York City. It not only signified a new era of the international political world in post-war society, but also a new phase in American architecture. From an architectural standpoint, the United Nations headquarters is a mastery of post-war modernism and design expression. Architectural historian Jackie Craven, writing for the *Picture Dictionary of Modern Architecture*, cited the United Nations Secretariat building as a "famous example of the International Style." (The name was derived from the title of a book co-authored by architectural critic Henry-Russell Hitchcock and architect Philip Johnson in 1932 titled *The International Style*.)

In keeping with the spirit of international cooperation, a design team of architects from various UN member nations was formed. The Archives of the United Nations credits architect Oscar Niemeyer (1907–2012) as head of the team to provide a conceptual design for the new building. At first, Niemeyer's role on the design committee was solely as Brazil's international representative. In 1947, it was Niemeyer's ideological concept that provided the basis for the eventual completed project:

> When we make a building for the UN, we must have in mind what is the UN? It is an organization [that] set the nations of the world in a common direction and gives to the world security. I think it is difficult to get this into steel and stone. But if we make something representing the true spirit of our age, of comprehension and solidarity, it will by its own strength give the idea that that is the big political effort, too. (www.UN.org)

According to UN Archives, the completed project was "based primarily on Niemeyer's design." Despite Niemeyer's critical influence, the final design was officially credited to the team of Wallace K. Harrison (1895–1981) and Max Abramovitz (1908–2004). Yet, it was Oscar Niemeyer who made the decision to eliminate the idea of one large building, thereby favoring an Assembly Hall as a distinctive element separate from the rest of the complex. The idea was to provide visual architectural identity to a meeting hall that brought all the world's representatives together on common ground.

In proposing an architectural ideology to reflect the "true spirit" of the post-war time, Niemeyer was one of a group of architects of international statue who provided a new dynamic to the profession. (The iconic Charles-Édouard Jeanneret-Gris (1887–1965), known universally as "Le Corbusier," was another proponent of the style. He also contributed some significant ideas for the eventual final design.) At the time, the Brazilian Niemeyer was best known for his Ministry of Education and Health building in Rio de Janeiro, designed in conjunction with fellow Brazilian architect Lúcio Costa (1902–1998). Prior to his work on the UN building, Niemeyer was a well-known international architect. His previous work in America was not overabundant, but his influence was. While working with the offices of Lúcio Costa, Niemeyer designed the Brazil pavilion for the 1939 New York World's Fair. The design so impressed then New York City Mayor Fiorello La Guardia that Niemeyer was declared "an honorary citizen of New York."

Yet it was the completion of the United Nations building that brought him widespread professional acknowledgement in the United States. As a result, Niemeyer was offered the prestigious architectural position of Dean of the Harvard Graduate School of Design. That position never came to be as his application for a work visa was denied by the U.S. government. The rejection was due to his past membership in the Brazilian Communist Party. Niemeyer became another victim of the time when just the mere accusation of being a Communist in the United States was met with all sorts of ramifications, including job forfeiture and sometimes jail sentences ("Oscar Niemeyer Biography," n.p.).

For Niemeyer, who had joined the party in 1945, Communist ideology was also an expression of his architecture. In 1956, one example was his masterful work for the public buildings in the new capital of Brazil known as Brasilia. Niemeyer applied his Communist party ideology as a "utopian vision of government." With that vision, Brasilia was a city built entirely from the ground up in a former uninhabited interior area of Brazil. As many of the architects of the time who subscribed to the International Style, the preferred exterior building material was concrete. Niemeyer said, "I tried to push the potential of concrete to its limits, especially at the load-bearing points, which I wanted to be as delicate as possible so that it would seem as if the palaces barely touched the ground." The new capital city was completed in 1960, but his statue fell out of favor in 1964 as a military coup labeled him as a threat due to his Communist ideology.

Due to his political conflicts in the United States and Brazil, Niemeyer relocated to Europe where he continued working well past his 100th birthday. In 1988, he was awarded the profession's highest international honor: the Pritzker Prize. In retrospect, his ideology was not as overtly political as some might think. When properly analyzed, it was not at all dangerous when placed within the "Red Scare" tactics by the likes of Senator McCarthy. The real "danger" was due to the architectural style breaking with conformity. Niemeyer placed his ideology within his architecture for "a better world through better design." In his outspoken manner, he noted, "It is important that the architect think not only of architecture but of how architecture can solve the problems of the world. The architect's role is to fight for a better world, where he can produce an architecture that serves everyone and not just a group of privileged people" ("Oscar Niemeyer Biography," n.p.).

Yet the 1950s presented a contrast in building types and design excellence. The dominant building of the time was the one-family single-story house of Levittown fame. Although hailed as a "revolution" in American building design, many would be hard-pressed to call the simple wood-frame houses "architecture." Those suburban areas represented a development sprawl in direct contrast to the pattern of planning and design associated with the architectural profession. For the most part, the single-family homes and large-scale suburban developments were in contrast to Niemeyer's ideology, as the single-family home design that swept the nation was in fact for "a group of privileged people." The privileged included white, non-ethnic, middle-class Americans living in areas far removed from the inner cities of mixed ethnicity.

The post-war period was notable for the almost universal overhaul and demolition of the urban center of America's major cities. With a mass migration to the suburbs, which became known as "white flight," the inner cities faced a double dilemma. One was a burgeoning "baby boom" and housing shortage for people of all races. Many of the inner cities oversaw the building of large-scale housing developments that were built over razed pre-war neighborhoods. The addition of the massive interstate highway system was a boon to the American traveler and suburban dweller, but it often dissected established city neighborhoods and added to the urban blight. For other American architects, the post-war buildings of significance searched to present a dialogue quite different than the "cookie cutter" conformity of suburban development and American society in general.

FRANK LLOYD WRIGHT AND DEMOCRATIZING GREAT ARCHITECTURE

During the 20th century, and especially within the decade of the 1950s, many notable architects created dozens of structures worthy of architectural historical significance. No one was more well known than Frank Lloyd Wright (1867–1959). His legacy of designing iconic architectural structures extended well over a period of 60 years. During his long career, he is credited with completing 1,141 projects and also wrote an abundance of essays and a few books on architecture. Wright's designs of his early "prairie-style" residential houses (mostly in and around the Chicago suburb of Oak Park and the Midwest from 1890 to the 1930s) and other work such as the Imperial Hotel in Tokyo have all been well-documented. Some of the more famous iconic projects have included the Kaufmann House known as "Fallingwater" (1935) in Pennsylvania, and the Johnson Wax Building (1939) in Wisconsin. By the start of the 1950s, he was firmly established as America's greatest architect, who had provided a vast body of work with very few equals throughout architectural history. As hard as it might be to imagine, his most memorable public work occurred during the last years of his life.

During the 1950s, Wright produced some of his most important buildings. Yet the decade started with one of his best works actually torn down. In 1950, the growing reliance by Americans upon the automobile led to the destruction of many older pre-war buildings. One example was Wright's 1904 Larkin Company that was demolished to create room for a parking lot. Within the original office building, Wright had paid careful consideration to the comfort of the worker. The main office area rose six stories above the central work area with a cathedral-like atmosphere created by the abundance of natural sunlight directed in by clerestory windows. Architectural historian Spiro Kostof called it "the first classic example of the open plan office block" (117). (The open plan concept was routinely applied to office space throughout the 1950s and became widely popular in the 21st century for tech businesses.) Kostof likened the destruction of the Larkin Building as "one of the biggest losses in American architectural history."

Wright did lose one of his most impressive works, but during the decade he produced a long list of impressive designs. By that time, he was based fulltime at his studio and home in Arizona known as "Taliesin West" that he designed and built in 1936. A brief list follows:

- Zimmerman House, Manchester, New Hampshire, 1950
- Unitarian Meeting House, Madison, Wisconsin, 1951
- Boomer Residence, Phoenix, Arizona, 1953
- Harold Price Jr. Residence (Hillside), Bartlesville, Oklahoma, 1954
- Price Tower, Bartlesville, Oklahoma, 1956
- Marin Civic Center, San Rafael, California, 1957
- Florida Southern College, Lakeland, Florida, 1936–1958

At Florida Southern College, located in the central part of the state, Wright designed 10 campus buildings and two auxiliary structures. Design began in 1936, and a groundbreaking ceremony for the first building was held in 1938. Construction slowed a bit due to the war, but continued after the end of the war with the completion of the first seven buildings. Wright visited the campus for a Memorial Day celebration in 1950 and many other times throughout the decade as the final three buildings were constructed. They included the Lucius Pond Ordway Building, a student center and cafeteria, completed in 1952; the William H. Danforth Chapel, completed in 1955; and the last of the original 10, the Polk County Science Building, completed in 1958. The structures were still an active part of the college during the 21st century as they underwent renovation.

During a time when thousands of suburban residential single-family houses were being built in places such as Levittown in Long Island, Frank Lloyd Wright's residential contribution is often dismissed from the standard history books of the 1950s. In fact, Wright did not necessarily favor tall buildings. Throughout his career his buildings often emphasized horizontal lines that embraced nature, rather than the tall, vertical, and narrow structures that came to dominate the post-war period. Nor did he favor cities or the new urban renewal policies. One post-war criticism by Wright was leveled at an urban renewal project in Pittsburgh, Pennsylvania. By the end of war, the city of Pittsburgh, as did others, explored the process of urban redevelopment. At the time, officials sought the advice of many experts, including America's best-known architect. Wright, who was never known for a long explanation, especially if he rejected a proposal, simply suggested, "It'd be cheaper to abandon it." When asked a similar question on how to improve the quality of the city of Detroit, Wright delivered a similar message to its City Council. He said, "I suggest you tear it all down and start over." Those responses were typical of Wright's unique personality, which was often described as smug (Teaford, 120; and Jackman, n.p.).

In contrast to the popularity of Levittown (see later this chapter), some architects such as Frank Lloyd Wright would not conform to the sameness of style. One architecture critic said, "The fact that what the people really wanted was a little brick Georgian house or a little Cape Cod cottage or something that drove [Wright] crazy. He hated it. His own work appealed to much more sophisticated people" (Lubow, n.p.).

In reality, Wright favored the single-family home as the ideal American democratic expression. Yet during the 1950s, he differed from the assembly-line fashion of the houses with the sameness of bland style that were being built in the American suburbs such as Levittown in Long Island. Often overlooked by the uninitiated, but not by the architectural profession, is Wright's long history of preference for the single-family residential house. Throughout his 60-year career his unique prairie and Usonian styles offered some of the same qualities for individual home ownership as Levittown, but were vastly different in quality and design aesthetics. It was Wright's work within this period, which was often described as "quintessentially American," that provided some notable additions to the residential landscape (Lubow, n.p.).

One of the standard features of the mass-produced suburban houses, such as those at Levittown, was the distinctive high-pitched roof, attic dormers, and double-hung windows. In contrast, Wright opposed the use of those building features. In regard to the double-hung windows, he called them "the guillotine window" (Wright, 91). He often wrote of the ideal American home:

> First, get rid of the attic, therefore the dormer. Next, get rid of the basement. Use one chimney only. The human being is the scale . . . bring the scale down. . . . Walls are not to have holes punched in them for windows. (90)

His attention to a complete building design package also involved designing each piece of interior furniture, much of it built-in. He did not see the need for the "client" to bring in any other furniture other than what Wright determined was needed. He often claimed the client's furniture did not belong within a Wright design. Despite the fact that the client would be living within the home and also claim ownership, Wright felt that once the building was designed, the client would simply occupy, but not own, the space. This personality trait of Wright placed the building as his own.

During the 1950s, a prime example of Wright's Usonian design was the "Turkel House" located in the Palmer Park suburb of Detroit, Michigan. Palmer Park was not a run-of-the-mill neighborhood; rather, it was a pricey suburb removed from the inner city, but still within the city limits. The request for his design services came from future homeowner Dorothy Turkel, who wanted to have a home built for her and her four children. In 1955, she had contacted the architect after reading Wright's recent book *The Natural House* (Horizon Press, 1954). Within the book, Wright provided a complete description of all the elements of his Usonian house style that was supplemented by numerous illustrations. He wrote of his vision for each part of the building process from site location, foundation, building materials, furnishings, and also the mechanical elements of adequate heating and cooling. Within the dust jacket cover for the book, the editors promoted its contents as follows:

> The world's greatest architect here meets the urgent problem of suitable shelter for the family in a democracy, in a magnificent and—as was to be expected—challenging book. Here, presented at last in full detail, is the natural house. The moderate cost houses described in this book and profusely illustrated with 116 photographs, plans and drawings, are houses—of infinite variety for people of limited means—in which living has become for their owners a purposeful new adventure in freedom and dignity. Mr. Wright tells the story of the world famous "Usonian" houses, so that we now see, in text and illustrations, how they have

evolved from original conception to final execution. He has also written a step-by-step description of the "Usonian Automatic," explaining just how that remarkable house is built—a simplified method of construction so devised that the owners themselves can build it with great economy and beauty. For this purpose, there are, in addition to Mr. Wright's text, special photographs and drawings of the method and materials, showing clearly how the Usonian Automatic is built.

The idea of the Usonian house was also to dispel the idea that Wright only designed and oversaw the construction of homes "for the rich." The editors added, "This book is convincing evidence of the error of that notion."

The basic Usonian house were considered small at around 4,000 square feet. The single-story design, with either a low-sloping or flat roof, was often an "L-shaped" floor plan. Dorothy Turkel lived in the home with her family from 1957 to 1997. By the 21st century her home, as well as many other Wright designs, was preserved and often opened up to public tours. In 2015, writing for the *Detroit Metro Times*, journalist Michael Jackman said, "To walk through the Turkel house is to have a tour of Wright's artistic temperament." Unlike the prairie-style homes, the Usonians were ideally suited for a flat piece of land situated on a small lot. A significant idea of this style home was the use of a construction material known as "Usonia blocks." These were cast-on-site concrete blocks, which in theory, could be cast by a homeowner who wished to build his or her own home. One Wright protégé who worked at Taliesin West during the 1950s was architect Lawrence Brink. Of the Usonian style, Brink said, "The Usonian automatics were almost prefab, but not totally, because it wasn't cheap. The intent was to be inexpensive, because the owners could put it together, but with contractors building it, it was expensive" (quoted in Lubow, n.p.).

The idea of an owner-built home was a long-standing ideal within the American tradition. At the time, it was also an attempt to provide a home within the affordable financial reach of the average American family. As John Gallagher of the *Detroit Free Press* wrote, "Although the Turkel and Affleck homes were done for wealthier clients, Wright designed the Smith House for a pair of schoolteachers with modest incomes, and indeed Wright's whole line of so-called Usonian houses was designed to get good architecture within reach." The ability to provide "good architecture" within reach was also demonstrated by a prefabricated home or to purchase one from a mail-order catalog. Little known is that towards the end of his career, Wright provided a series of well-designed prefabricated houses manufactured in Madison, Wisconsin, by Marshall Erdman Prefab Houses. The houses were shipped to various locations throughout the United States. One such unit was Prefab #1 that was shipped and assembled on site in Staten Island, New York. That unit known as "The Crimson Beech" was completed in 1959. In summation, as Gallagher added, these homes attributed "Wright's commitment to democratizing great architecture."

THE GUGGENHEIM MUSEUM AND THE PRICE TOWER

One of the most distinctive and well-known non-residential American building is Frank Lloyd Wright's Guggenheim Museum in New York City. The

Architect Frank Lloyd Wright standing in front of a model for the Solomon R. Guggenheim Museum, c. 1953. (Photofest)

building, located in the borough of Manhattan on the Upper East Side, is situated along Fifth Avenue directly across the street from Central Park. Construction began in 1956 and was completed to all sorts of praise and criticism by 1959. But Wright did not live to preside over the official opening on October 21, 1959. He had died just six months previously on April 9, 1959, at the age of 92 at his Arizona studio.

During the early 1940s, Solomon Guggenheim in consultation with his art advisor Hilla Rebay proposed a museum to display abstract and modern art. Rebay said to Guggenheim that the museum should promote "a temple of spirit, a monument." The selection of Wright as the architect was a natural. Temples were certainly part of Wright's body of work, yet as described by Arthur Lubow for *Smithsonian Magazine*, "To Wright's way of thinking, any building, if properly designed, could be a temple." The project developed over a 16-year period. As the design progressed, Wright's proposal of an inverted reinforced concrete spiral structure, that he described as an "inverted ziggurat," was met by resistance from artists, building code requirements, and the excessive cost of the design. In response to many of the critics, but most importantly to quell the concerns of his client and benefactor Solomon Guggenheim, Wright explained to his patron:

It is not to subjugate the paintings to the building that I conceived this plan. On the contrary, it was to make the building and the painting a beautiful symphony such as never existed in the world of Art before. ("Guggenheim," n.p.)

For those who described the curved walls within the distinctive spiral as "an awkward place to hang paintings"—well, they simply missed the point. For an architect who continually pushed the boundaries of structural limitations, space, and conformity, similar to the abstract expressionists, Wright also challenged the artists to accept new parameters. The spiral inversion was an ideological proposal to create a special form that, in Wright's words, would be one of "pure optimism." Within the museum the idea was not to provide a flat wall to hang a picture, but rather to challenge the artist to create within the nonconforming environment—in essence, not to provide paint on canvas, but rather create art to conjoin within the curvilinear interior (Lubow, n.p.).

Unlike many other influential architects throughout the 20th century, Wright designed only one building that could be termed a tall building or a "skyscraper." That was the 19-story H.C. Price Company Office Tower in Bartlesville, Oklahoma (1952–1956). The project, 25 years in the making, traced its roots to an earlier Wright design in a 1929 proposal for an apartment tower to be built in New York City. The proposed location was on a lot adjacent to St. Mark's Church in the East Village of Manhattan and was therefore given the name "St. Mark's Tower." For the tall building concept, he proposed a "treelike structure" with a central core reflecting an ideological connection to nature. Wright called it "dignified as a tree in the midst of nature, but a child of the spirit of man." Within the central core, Wright designed a unique structural stability and safety system. He explained, "This building, earthquake, fire and soundproof from within, by economics inherent in its structure weighs less than half the usual tall building and increases the area available for living by more than twenty percent." For many reasons, St. Marks Tower never began actual construction (Kostof, 47–48).

The New York project might have been scrapped, but Wright was able to apply a similar concept in Oklahoma. For the Price Tower, he designed a cantilevered shaft at the vertical central core to house the utilities. Each floor, with an alternate mix of office space and apartments, spread out from the center like the limbs of a tree. During the grand opening of the H.C. Price Company Office Tower, a question and answer session ensued. The session served as a good example of Wright's bravado in a brief exchange with his client Harold Price. One journalist asked Wright, "What's your first prerequisite?" The reply went as follows:

Wright said: "Well, to fulfill a client's wishes."
Price added: "I wanted a three-story building."
Wright said: "You didn't know what you wanted." (quoted in Jackman, n.p.)

In another, but far less than complementary description, famed architectural critic Ada Louise Huxtable of *The New York Times* once described Wright thusly:

An irascible mix of genius and charlatan, both a visionary who created works that evoked a rich, honeyed light and a tyrant who demanded total control of his projects—and whose disastrous cost overruns drained his clients' bank accounts. (quoted in Jackman, n.p.)

Frank Lloyd Wright might have had quite a few critics, especially as it applied to his often brash personality, but very few could match the bravado he delivered through his architecture. Very few people have entered the legacy of popular culture to the degree of Wright. Granted, it may be unlikely that the average American might be able to name or even recognize any of his architectural achievements, but so many recognize his name as an architect.

HOME OWNERSHIP, SUBURBIA, LEVITTOWN, AND THE AMERICAN DREAM

A professional architect, such as Frank Lloyd Wright, serving society as both an artist and with the ability to alter the built human environment is often misunderstood. It is the least likely understood of all the professions and often taken for granted. One reason might be the fact that architecture so shapes the daily lives of Americans that they simply do not notice. Famed architectural historian Spiro Kostof spent an entire career, which in his own words, he tried to "help people *see* America, and not take anything they saw for granted" (ix). Yet, when it came to owning an individual home, the average American seemed to take everything that "they saw for granted."

Over the course of the 20th century, individual homeownership maintained a steady rise. According to the U.S. Census Bureau, in 1900, less than half of the American population claimed individual home ownership. A large majority either rented in the city or in the rural landscape. The most dramatic increase occurred after the war. Throughout the 1950s, the percentage of individual home ownership increased from 55 percent to more than 62 percent of all American households. By the year 2000, home ownership was firmly entrenched in the idea of the "American Dream" with two out of every three households living within their own home. But as Spiro Kostof reminds us "this proportion is much lower for some ethnic minorities" (55).

The large increase in home ownership during the 1950s actually began just a few years earlier. In 1947, many large-scale suburban developments arose in many parts of the country. The most well known was Levittown in Long Island, New York. The fast-growing residential developments did not offer much from an architectural standpoint. Architectural historian Spiro Kostof probably said it best: "they spread like crabgrass" (60). The "crabgrass" reference was in response to the uniformity of the same style 4-½ room house on standard, flat 60×100 foot lots with the house only covering 12 percent of the land. Other development tracts that included thousands of lookalike houses were built in places such as Bucks County, Pennsylvania. In California, they included Los Angeles, Palo Alto, and Sacramento. The large development tracts sprung up around most American cities and rural enclaves.

Throughout the United States during the 20th and 21st centuries, the most easily recognizable architectural structure was a single-family house. For many in the post-war era, it was the purchase of a single-family suburban home that represented the fulfillment of the "American Dream." The home purchase also represented the single largest investment a person usually made in his or her lifetime. Those houses were all too often replicated in vast quantities of the

Chart 7.1   U.S. Census Bureau Homeownership Rates

Year	Pct.
1900	47%
1910	46%
1920	46%
1930	48%
1940	44%
1950	55%
1960	62%
1970	63%
1980	64%
1990	64%
2000	66%

Source: Chart compiled by author.

same style and size in side-by-side, uniform rows. The sameness of only one or two different type of houses within a large newly built neighborhood led to the use of the term "cookie cutter." Architecture critic Witold Rybczynski writing for Slate.com justified the conformity of suburban type houses: "While architectural critics frequently disparage the uniformity of housing, that is precisely what buyers demand; they don't want to be stuck with an odd or dated house at the time of resale. Contrarians [non-conformist] don't do well in the housing market." The ranch house was a product design of 1930s California and in some ways reflected the Prairie Style and Usonian houses of Frank Lloyd Wright. Initially, those homes were a "radical departure from tradition" (Rybczynski, n.p.).

A "ranch-house" style is not to be confused with a home built on a working ranch or farm. Rather, it is a one-story building composed of modest spaces including a kitchen, one living room, two or three bedrooms, a bathroom, and a utility room. Most did not include a basement, but sometimes added a built-in garage. A low sloping roof offset a simple exterior of either brick or wood. By 1950, almost nine out of every 10 new homes were built in the basic ranch style. A variation on the ranch style was another California innovation known as the "split level." The entry door was usually centered along the horizontal façade. Upon entry, the occupant faced a staircase leading half up and half down, thus split in two levels. Sometimes this occurred side to side within the building. A significant feature of all these new suburban style homes was a sunken living room that prominently placed a sofa facing a television. Later on, additional space was often added on or built into new designs known as a "play room" or "rec room" ("rec" for recreation).

What might be the most impressive statistic of the entire decade of the 1950s was the drastic increase in paved highways. Prior to the war, urban freeways or simply "highways" in the top 25 American cities amounted to a combined total of less than 400 miles. By mid-decade the federal government responded with the Federal Aid Highway Act of 1956, which upped the total within those cities to over 5,000 miles of urban freeways. Within that same authorization was the construction of a staggering 41,000 miles of interstate highways connecting the entire nation. Many of the new roads also provided easy access to the newly developing suburban building boom. Urban historian Jon C. Teaford, writing in *The Twentieth-Century American City*, said,

> Without the freeways, then, suburbia would have been more remote and less accessible to places of employment, shopping, and amusement in the central city. Freeway driving may not have been a pleasure, but the mammoth ribbons of concrete and asphalt did cut travel times between the increasingly dispersed fragments of the metropolis. (98)

Prior to the new highway construction, new housing starts were quite small at slightly over 142,000. As a result of the highway accessibility, within a year the number of new housing starts topped one million new units. By 1950, the number was placed at nearly two million and in each succeeding year until 1964, at least 1.2 million new housing starts were recorded (Teaford, 97–99).

AUTO-CENTRIC DESIGN, THE SUBURBAN SHOPPING MALL, AND THE LAWN

A major influence upon the overall architectural designs of the 1950s was the automobile. The most appropriately applied term is "auto-centric design."

With the massive population shift to the suburbs also came the need for shopping centers such as this one in Levittown in Long Island, New York. This 1957 photo shows the businesses centered on automobile accommodation. (Library of Congress)

Planned communities such as Levittown were designed based on a road pattern only accessible by automobile. With the movement to the suburbs aided by highway access, all sorts of ancillary businesses prompted designs centered on automobile accommodation. They included drive-in movie theaters, parking garages, drive-through fast food restaurants, drive-up teller windows at banks, and roadside motor lodges, among many others. The most notable of the auto-centric design features was the suburban shopping mall.

The construction of the shopping malls moved retailing away from the dense, commercial downtowns of the city into the largely residential suburbs. The formula of an enclosed space with many retail stores far away from downtown and accessible only by automobile became a standard way to build a mall across the nation. By 1955, more than 1,000 of the new suburban shopping malls were built. The following year, the total was more than 1,600 nationwide. One of the largest of the suburban shopping malls was in Long Island at the Roosevelt Field shopping plaza, containing 110 stores with paved parking for 11,000 cars. The location was close to one of the new highways being built by the Federal Interstate Highway Act and offered close proximity to the most famous of all the suburban housing developments at Levittown (Teaford, 105).

For many Americans, the post-war dream of owning a suburban home and being able to buy items that were in either short supply or non-existent during the war became a new craze of "consumerism." As the term implies, the idea was to consume as many new products as possible. Consumer values and the pressure of advertising to buy and keep up with their neighbors led many to buy on credit. In 1950, Diners Club introduced the first credit card, initially with the idea to pay for a dinner. In a short time, other business ventures applied the idea of buying on credit with the use of a plastic card. (A credit card allowed the consumer to pay back a third-party creditor in monthly payments with interest added.) In 1958, the American Express Company issued more than 250,000 cards. By the end of the decade, just about every major retailer provided a credit card service. One example was Sears & Roebuck with more than 10 million charge account customers (Giordano [2003], 148–149).

For the newborn in suburbia, a new way of life developed. It was far removed from the horrors of war and also completely ignorant of the growing social problems that occurred within American cities. As a result, those who grew up in the secluded suburban developments fostered a unique, innocent nostalgia. One good example is provided by Don and Susan Sanders who described their suburban upbringing:

> Each morning our fathers left in the family car to go to work. We went to school and our mothers stayed home in order to plan and cook that night's dinner, to attend PTA meetings and Tupperware parties. . . . Our lives had a predictable rhythm to them. . . . Every afternoon after school we would play outside with the other neighborhood children, [sometimes] throwing the football, riding bikes, playing Red Rover, and Hide and Seek. (6)

The Sanders' experience was no different than any other child living in the new suburban developments which some called the "American Dream." Yet no other proponent of the "American Dream" can be discussed without a further understanding of William Levitt.

WILLIAM LEVITT: "A SELLER OF THE AMERICAN DREAM"

Time magazine described William Levitt (1907–1994) as "a brash, rambunctious hustler." In contrast, *The New York Times* called him "a seller of the American Dream." As a typical American Dream, Levitt's own story could certainly relate through his rise as an entrepreneur. He was born in Williamsburg, Brooklyn, in a neighborhood inhabited by Jewish immigrants. His father Abraham was a real estate developer who had the foresight to purchase large tracts of land in Long Island during the Depression years of the 1930s. During the war, the company of Levitt & Sons procured an additional 200 acres of Long Island farmland. At that time, the younger Levitt served as a Seabee in the war, building various types of military projects including housing. In 1941, Abraham Levitt procured a significant government contract to build 2,350 homes in Norfolk, Virginia. The need was in response to the large influx of individuals who moved to Norfolk looking for work in the shipyards. In order to expedite the construction process, the company divided the building process into 27 distinctive steps (or trades). The division of labor created a system similar to an assembly line, thereby completing the houses quickly. The wartime experience of building in assembly line fashion was duplicated in their post-war development of suburban Levittown on Long Island in New York (Ruff, 46–48).

The Levitt building concept was quick, efficient, and used the least amount of materials. The first cost-saving feature was to build each house on a concrete slab (without a basement). Eliminating a basement not only saved time, but also eliminated a significant cost outlay for the developers in both time and material. The first Levittown homes were built with the same one-story floorplan of four and one-half rooms: a living room, kitchen, and two bedrooms. The "half room" was a bathroom. The exterior façades provided a choice from five slightly different exteriors. Each house had a high-sloping roof that provided the homeowner what Levitt called "an expansion attic." In a short time from 1947 and 1951, Levitt built 17,447 homes. The first advertisements offered the sale of each house for "$52 a month, For Veterans Only." (The "$52 a month" was part of a 30-year mortgage.) The Levitt homes also came stocked with all sorts of new convenience appliances such as refrigerators and washing machines. A multitude of advertisements in newspapers and magazines promoted the Levitt houses as the fulfillment of the new American Dream (Ruff, 47).

That American Dream in Levittown also included segregation and a complete break from the American city. The homeowner contract provided by William Levitt strictly eliminated any integration. One clause stated, "No dwelling shall be used or occupied by members of other than the Caucasian race." As Joshua Ruff noted in *American History* magazine, "Even after the 1948 U.S. Supreme Court decision in *Shelley v. Kraemer* [334 U.S. 1 (1948)] made racial covenants unconstitutional, the FHA continued to underwrite loans only to white neighborhoods." As was often noted, Levitt did in fact remove any restrictive racial language from his contracts. Nevertheless, the legal language might have been dropped, but Levitt steadfastly refused to sell his homes to any African American family. In fact, the following year he was quoted in the local *Levittown Tribune* as saying, "The elimination of the clause has changed absolutely nothing." Historian Crystal Galyean, in her article for *U.S. History Scene*, "Levittown: The Imperfect Rise of the American Suburbs," revealed a surprising statistic: "By 1953, the 70,000 people who lived in Levittown constituted the largest community in the United States with no black residents" (Teaford, 103; Ruff, 48).

Levittown remained exclusively white until 1957, when one African American family bought a re-sale. The house was sold despite the fact that angry neighborhood residents offered to pay the previous owner more than the initial asking price. The home was purchased by a Dr. William Meyers, who upon moving his family into the home was met by an angry mob of more than 200 Levittown residents. Rocks were thrown at the house, shattering a picture window. Harassment continued with taunts from Ku Klux Klan members, and angry town hall meetings calling for the Meyers' removal. The situation eventually caused the Meyers family to move to a more affluent neighborhood (Teaford, 103–104).

The racial segregation was not confined to Levittown in New York. Of the more than 60,000 residents of Levittown, Pennsylvania, in 1957, not one single family was African American. Throughout America, the situation was the same. Historian Eric Foner, writing in *The Story of American Freedom*, said, "If the suburbs offered a new locale for the enjoyment of American freedom, they retained at least one familiar characteristic: rigid racial segregation. Suburban homeownership long remained a white entitlement." Foner also recalled that federally funded mortgages "continued to insure mortgages with racially restrictive provisions, thereby financing housing segregation. In reality, all of America was complacent with segregation since it was the law of the land and also federally supported. Therefore, segregating suburbia was legal and ingrained in the American psyche as being normal to the American way of life" (Foner, 266–267).

MAIN STREET

With a massive population shift of Americans leaving the big cities for the outer-lying suburbs came a drastic reduction in the urban economic base both in tax revenue and business income. Prior to the 1950s, all of the major cities, as well as the smallest of towns, had a central shopping district. In the big cities it was known as "downtown"; in the small cities and towns it known as "Main Street." (Very often the name of the street was in fact Main Street.) Architectural historian Spiro Kostof said, "[Main Street] is much more than a place name to Americans. It is a state of mind, a set of values" (165). Often only a few blocks long, the small-town concept of Main Street, was the "main" commercial center of the town containing stores for necessary items such as hardware, toiletries, barbershops, grocery stores, banks, and professional services such as realtors, attorneys, doctors, and insurance agencies among others. In addition, it usually contained entertainment venues such as a movie theater and conveniences such as an ice cream parlor, a record store, and a newsstand. The indelible image was a central theme in Walt Disney's concept of a suburban theme park in Anaheim, California (see chapter on Game Changers). Many critics understood that the ideal of "Main Street" was more often than not just a mythical connotation of a false ideal.

A classic interpretation of the false ideal and conformity of small towns and so suburbia was often brought to the forefront as a science fiction theme. One example was the classic television series *The Twilight Zone* (1959–1964). In a first season episode, "The Monsters Are Due on Maple Street," writer and series creator Rod Serling portrayed an underlying paranoia in a typical 1950s white suburban neighborhood. The critique offered by Serling was that any deviation from conformity was viewed with suspicion. As the once-peaceful neighbors detect "strange occurrences," they lash out against each other, leading to a violent conflict. Another critique by Serling in this episode was aimed at the fear of any subversive element fueled by the 1950s fear of Communist infiltration that might exist in American society (Season 1, Episode 22, March 4, 1960).

PUBLIC HOUSING: STUYVESANT TOWN AND PRUITT-IGOE

Each of the top-20 American cities experienced a significant rise in the total overall population of African Americans during the decade. The three most populated American cities of New York, Chicago, and Philadelphia also showed a sharp increase in the population of African-American residents. There was also a sizable increase as to the total percentage of the entire population, but that anomaly was a result of a significant portion of white residents leaving the city for the suburbs. Urban historian Jon Teaford noted, "Overall, the black population in central cities having over 50,000 inhabitants rose 50 percent, climbing from 6,456,00 in 1950 to 9,705,000 in 1960." Some cities, such as St. Louis, Missouri, experienced a 29 percent rise in the African-American population (115–116).

All of the American cities had some sort of segregation policy, either legally or tacitly. Yet the shift in population and also the rising birthrate due to the post-war baby boom created a housing need for African Americans and white urban residents. In response, some cities funded central city housing projects. Two of the most notorious were Stuyvesant Town in New York City and the Pruitt-Igoe Housing Complex in St. Louis, Missouri.

Chart 7.2   Population Shift: Top 3 Most Populated American Cities

City	1950 Population	1960 Population	White	Black
New York	7,891,957	7,781,984	–7%	+46%
Chicago	3,620,962	3,550,404	–13%	+65%
Philadelphia	2,071,605	2,002,512	–13%	+41%

Source: Compiled from Jon C. Teaford, *The Twentieth-Century American City,* 2nd ed. Baltimore: Johns Hopkins University Press, 1993, pp. 110–115. Chart compiled by author.

A public housing project was not a new concept to the 1950s. One of the most successful of the type was Stuyvesant Town in New York City. (Throughout that century and well into the 21st century, it remained a successful venture.) The initial planning was to fill a wartime housing shortage that existed in New York. (All wartime production cities such as San Diego, Los Angeles, and New York, to name a few, experienced severe housing shortages.) During the war, significant New York City housing complexes were completed in the borough of the Bronx in Parkchester and Riverton. It soon became apparent that in the post-war, a significant amount of additional public housing was also a necessity. With Stuyvesant Town as one example, a portion of the completed apartment units would be allocated for returning war veterans ("Hearing Advances Big Housing Plan," 36).

The housing boom certainly filled a need, but that availability applied only to white Americans. Segregation was still the law of the land; all non-white customers were denied federally funded home mortgage loans. As Teaford noted:

> During the 1950s suburbia was booming, but this boom was deepening the fissures in metropolitan America, dividing central-city blacks from suburban whites, plebian [common] Levittowners from the country club set of Rolling Hills Estates, and farmers in Dairy Valley from manufacturers in Industry. (109)

For those returning white war veterans and wartime workers who sought to live in New York City, Stuyvesant Town was an affordable option. The $50 million apartment town plan was approved by the New York City Planning Commission in May 1943. The following day, more than 7,000 people applied for a rental unit. When the first tenants began occupying the building on August 1, 1947, rental units ranged from $50 to $91 per month. By that time, more than 100,000 applicants had applied for housing ("Hearing Advances Big Housing Plan," 36).

The project was one of the first to promote a public-private partnership. The "public" was the City of New York, which provided the land through eminent domain and a 25-year property tax exemption. The "private" funding for construction was the Metropolitan Life Insurance Company. During rental negotiations Metropolitan Life instituted a segregation policy by refusing to issue any rental agreements to African Americans. A public debate followed over the right of a private company that received public assistance from taxpayer subsidies to maintain the right to legally discriminate. *The New York Times* reported on May 6, 1943, that city planner Robert Moses voiced his strong support of segregated housing. Moses defended the right to discriminate, claiming the profits earned by Metropolitan "would be harmed." He also claimed that opponents to segregation were "obviously looking for a political issue and not for results in the form of actual slum clearance." The president of Metropolitan Life, Frederick H. Ecker, simply explained, "[N]egroes and whites do not mix." Lawsuits were filed, but by the time of occupancy in 1947, a New York Supreme Court ruling upheld the right of a private company to discriminate. The ruling stated in part:

It is well settled that the landlord of a private apartment or dwelling house may, without violating any provision of the Federal and State Constitutions, select tenants of its own choice even though it may result in the exclusion of prospective tenants because of race, color, creed or religion. [Supreme Court, Special Term, New York County, 190 Misc. 187 (N.Y. Misc. 1947)]

The ruling was of no major surprise as segregated housing was prevalent throughout the entire country. A unique situation to placate equal housing opportunities was proposed in St. Louis, Missouri.

Just prior to the war, St. Louis was faced with a dwindling population. In the preceding decade, the population dropped from 822,000 people in 1930 to just about 816,000. A significant cause was lack of employment. After the war, the city was faced with the same situation as most of the other major American cities with large numbers of white residents moving to suburbs. In an effort to slow the population loss, city commissioners undertook a restructuring of many of the St. Louis neighborhoods. (Similar efforts also took place throughout other major U.S. cities.) Mayor Joseph Darst proposed a solution based on the housing built at Stuyvesant Town in New York City. The plan was also to move forward with an optimistic projection that at least one million residents would be living within the city limits by 1970.

In 1947, St. Louis passed a bond issue to allocate $110 million for the construction of an apartment housing complex to satisfy the needs of both black

The segregated Pruitt-Igoe housing complex in St. Louis, Missouri, was praised as a shining example for the future or urbanization. The northern side, named after African-American World War II fighter pilot Wendell Pruitt, was for black residents. The southern half, named for former white Missouri Congressman William Igoe, was designated for white residents. (Collections of Ralph G. Giordano)

and white residents. (Additional funding was secured through a federal loan.) Pruitt-Igoe was slated as one of four St. Louis housing projects for immediate construction. The others included Cochran Gardens, Darst-Webbe, and Vaughn, for a combined total of 5,800 units. The complex was named for two prominent St. Louis natives, Wendell O. Pruitt (1920–1945) and William L. Igoe (1879–1953). Igoe was a white former Missouri U.S. Congressman. Pruitt was a World War II fighter pilot with the famed Tuskegee Airman of the 332nd Fighter Group in Europe. He flew 70 combat missions and was awarded the Distinguished Flying Cross. He was rotated back to the United States to serve as an instructor at Tuskegee where he was killed in a flying accident with a student pilot trainee (Wartts, n.p.).

In 1950, the design for the Pruitt-Igoe project was awarded to the architectural firm of Leinweber, Yamasaki & Hellmuth. Partner Minouro Yamasaki (1912–1986), who would later gain fame as the principle architect of the World Trade Center Twin Towers in New York City, was the principle design architect. At a time when architectural critics were exploring new ways of redesigning urban areas, Pruitt-Igoe was often praised as a shining example for the future of urbanization. One example was from *Architectural Forum*, which described Pruitt-Igoe as "vertical neighborhoods for poor people" and praised Yamasaki's design as "the best high apartment" of the year (Cendón, n.p.).

Pruitt-Igoe contained a total 2,870 units dispersed in 33 buildings, each of them 11 stories high spread over 57 acres on the north side of the city. From the beginning, the design was designated as segregated housing. The northern side of the site, designated for black residents, was named after Wendell Pruitt. The southern half of the 57 acres was designated for white residents and named for William Igoe. The Pruitt side was completed in late 1955 and the Igoe side completed four months later in early 1956. The racial split of the complex provides a historical reflection on the Missouri Compromise of 1819. That situation attempted to maintain an even balance between a country evenly divided between slave states and free states. Earmarking the buildings housing black residents on the north side of the site and the buildings for white residents on the south side should not dismissed as mere happenstance, but rather an ironic attachment to the American Civil War.

Occupancy began in 1954, with the first residents praising the housing units as "perfect." One female resident said it was "the nicest place [she]'d ever had." Yet almost as soon as racial segregation was declared illegal by the U.S. Supreme Court in 1955, white residents began moving out even before all the buildings were completed. Almost as soon as the paint dried, municipal fiscal problems arose. Within the following years, whites' reluctance to live in desegregated housing, combined with lack of additional funding, caused all sorts of complications. The elevator service was erratic, forcing residents to often use the stairs. Garbage disposal was insufficient as well as overall fresh-air ventilation. Without the problems resolved, other complications arose, such as vandalism and crime. As a result, the units never achieved 100 percent occupancy. By 1957, only 91 percent of the units were occupied. In the following years, occupancy rates continued to decline. Within a decade, more than half of the complex was vacant. By 1970, the population dropped by an additional 30 percent. The city of St. Louis also fell far short of the earlier projections of one million residents, as the total population was only 618,000. As a result, the tax base was severely crippled, leaving little option to provide a financial solution to Pruitt-Igoe. By 1971, 16 of the 33 buildings were unoccupied and boarded up. The remaining 17 buildings had barely 600 total residents. With very few options left the city of St. Louis authorized demolition of the entire complex.

In stark contrast, but with a focus on reality, Sara Fernández Cendón, writing for *The American Institute of Architects*, provided a post-mortem assessment:

> [Pruitt-Igoe] was perhaps the nation's most infamous public housing complex, [but] there's no longer much point in arguing that Pruitt-Igoe was not a failure. At the end of its brief 20-year existence, the Pruitt-Igoe projects in St. Louis crashed down with enough force to (allegedly) take down Modernism and, with it, the nation's faith in large-scale public housing.

Demolition of the first buildings began on March 16, 1972, and continued through July. The remaining buildings were demolished by implosion over the next three years with the last coming down in 1976. Of ultimate irony was that in the midst of the implosions, the only other significant design by Minouro Yamasaki, the World Trade Center Twin Towers, was opened in April of 1973. In a gruesome twist of architectural irony, those buildings were also destroyed by acts of terrorism on September 11, 2001.

INTERNATIONAL STYLE: "ORDER, SPACE, AND PROPORTION"

Of major significance was the presence of the international style of architecture that had begun in America during the 1930s and continued as a major architectural influence during the 1950s. The style is recognizable by using structural materials such as concrete, steel, and glass that are devoid of unnecessary ornamentation. The exterior of the building, either glass or concrete, often exposed the structural system viewable to the naked eye. An example is One Chase Manhattan Plaza in New York City designed by Skidmore, Owings, and Merrill. The 813-foot high tower was described by the Historical Preservation Commission of New York City as "faced with shimmering panels of natural color and black-enameled aluminum, H-shaped mullions and glass."

Possibly, the crown jewel of the prototypical modern glass office was Lever House in New York City, completed in 1952. The design was credited to the firm of Skidmore, Owings, and Merrill (SOM) and lead architect Gordon Bunshaft. For dozens of years, the Lever House design was credited only to Bunshaft, but by the 21st century, SOM architect Natalie de Blois was officially given equal credit for the design. (The oversight of De Blois was due to the "second class" status of professional women during the 1950s.) Lever House received the designation as an "official landmark" in 1982 from the New York City Landmarks Preservation Commission:

> Manhattan's Lever House . . . with its façade made of blue-green glass and stainless steel mullions, was one of the first glass-walled International Style office

buildings in the country. The structure consists of two intersecting masses, balanced in their proportions but contrasting in shape. A two-story horizontal block containing an open court occupies the entire site with a 21-story tower located on the north. The columns and the ground floor court create a large open plaza allowing entrances to the lobby to be located away from pedestrian traffic. . . . Within a decade of its construction, the initial enthusiasm for Lever House gave way to a universal recognition of its pivotal importance to American architecture.

When the SOM building was completed, it was the first steel-frame, glass-curtain wall structure in New York City. It also stood in stark contrast as a corporate office building along the prestigious Park Avenue masonry residential apartments. (The United Nations building was built at about the same time, but its use was not as a corporate office building.) The ground level of Lever House only rises a few stories before it terminates in a rooftop garden. Sitting upon that low element is a tall rectangular slender vertical mass placed in juxtaposition to the ground level horizontal structure. In *Shaping a Nation*, architectural historian Carter Wiseman complained that the horizontal street block "is actually a rather bleak area for pedestrians . . . the geometry compromised the impact on the street." He added that Lever House "owes a considerable debt to Mies's [van der Rohe] own earlier imagery of high rise design, but is fundamentally different in its composition" (178–180).

MIES AND "LESS IS MORE"

Ludwig Mies van der Rohe (1886–1969) is often considered the innovator of the international or modern style of architecture in the United States. He was a German-born immigrant known for his involvement with the Bauhaus school of art and architecture. The growing influence of the Nazi Party affected his profession, as the Bauhaus School of Design in Dessau was ordered closed in 1933 by Adolph Hitler. With mounting pressure from the Nazi Party, van der Rohe left Germany. In 1937, he immigrated to the United States and obtained American citizenship in 1944. As his fame and influence spread in America, he became affectionately known within the architecture community simply as "Mies." His most famous adage was the adaptation of and architectural style that "less is more." *The Illustrated Encyclopedia of Architects and Architecture* provided a description of Mies's adage:

> To create contemplative, neutral spaces through an architecture based on material honesty and structural integrity. Over the last twenty years of his life, Mies achieved his vision of a monumental "skin and bone" architecture. His later works provide a fitting denouement to a life dedicated to the idea of a universal, simplified architecture. (Sharp, 109)

Some of his most distinctive and influential works of the time were the Farnsworth House in Plano, Illinois (1950); the Lake Shore Drive Apartments (1951) in Chicago; Crown Hall (1956) at the Illinois Institute of Technology in Chicago; and the Seagram Building in New York City (1958). Of the Lake Shore Drive design, located along Lake Michigan, Christopher Beanland writing for the Chicago-based *Independent* said:

> The apartments—built in 1951—are the embodiment of Ludwig Mies Van der Rohe's guiding philosophy of "less is more." Just a steel frame wrapped around some windows, they are simple, elegant, powerful. At the same time, they are also the embodiment of America's guiding philosophy of "more is more." They are huge, their shapes and materials are unnatural—this is man's victory over nature; a place that cost a pile of money to build and costs a pile of money to live in. (Beanland, n.p.)

The design of Crown Hall at the Illinois Institute of Technology began as the Lake Shore Apartments were nearing completion. At Crown Hall, which opened in 1956, Mies applied a similar design philosophy. The low horizontal building structure was expressed by its exterior appearance of a flat roof suspended by I-beams, interspersed with floor-to-ceiling windows. It was at Crown Hall that Mies attached his own expression of the essence of architecture. He said:

> [Crown Hall] uses technological means, but it is not only concerned with a purpose but also with a meaning, as it is not only concerned with a function but also with an expression. . . . It is based on the eternal laws of architecture: Order, Space, and Proportion. (quoted in Zukowsky, 23)

Mies partnered with Philip Johnson in the design of the Seagram building located on the prestigious Park Avenue in New York City. The building was noteworthy for providing a new form of exterior glass walls instead of masonry. GreatBuildings.com called it, "Eloquent structural expression in façade which is ornamental rather than literal." As Mies described his own building, he said, "We can see the new structural principles most clearly when we use glass in place of the outer walls, which is feasible today since in a skeleton building these outer walls do not carry weight. The use of glass imposes new solutions" (Mies van der Rohe, 12).

Unlike many other office towers in Manhattan, the Seagram building made use of an open pedestrian plaza at street level. The tower was offset from the street and in doing so makes a break from the congested rows of office buildings lining the avenues. Mies did not intend to simply fill up all the space on a single lot with a building form. Similar to Frank Lloyd Wright, Mies always intended to create architectural space with dignity respectful of nature itself. He said,

> The essence of space is not determined by the mere presence of limiting surfaces but by the spiritual principle of this limitation. The true task of architecture is to let the structure articulate the space; it is not the building that is the work of art but space. (Mies van der Rohe, 86)

Mies was but one of the significant architects who provided great works of architecture during the 1950s. Some other important architectural works of the time included:

- Harvard Graduate Center, by Walter Gropius, Cambridge, MA, 1950
- Joe Esherick House, by Joseph Esherick, at Kentfield, CA, 1950
- California College of Arts, by SOM, San Francisco, CA, 1951
- Central Lutheran Church, by Pietro Belluschi, Portland, OR, 1951
- Ralph Johnson House, by Harwell H. Harris, Los Angeles, CA, 1951
- Walker Guest House, by Paul Rudolph, at Sanibel Island, FL, 1952
- Manufacturer's Trust Co., by Gordon Bunshaft/SOM, New York City, 1954
- University Art Center, by Louis I. Kahn, New Haven, CT, 1954
- Bavinger House, by Bruce Goff, at Norman, OK, 1955
- General Motors Technical Center, by Eero Saarinen, Warren, MI, 1955
- Kresge Auditorium, by Eero Saarinen, Cambridge, MA, 1955
- Kresge Chapel, by Eero Saarinen, Cambridge, MA, 1955
- Starkey House, by Marcel Breuer, Duluth, MN, 1955
- House at Kentwoodlands, by Joseph Esherick, Kentwoodlands, CA, 1957
- Bailey House, Case Study No. 21, by Pierre Koenig, Los Angeles, CA, 1958
- Yale Hockey Rink, by Eero Saarinen, New Haven, CT, 1958
- Trenton Bath House, by Louis I. Kahn, Trenton, NJ, 1959

(*Source*: Dennis Sharp. *The Illustrated Encyclopedia of Architects and Architecture*. London: Quarto Publishing, 1991.)

WELTON BECKET, DISNEYLAND, AND CAPITOL RECORDS

Los Angeles is a city that has produced many facets of American culture that include Hollywood artistry and West Coast baseball, among others. An iconic structure located very close to the famous intersection of Hollywood and Vine is the landmark Capitol Records Building. The unique circular tower designed by architect Welton Becket (1902–1969) is certainly not as well-known as the dozens of others throughout American history. Nevertheless, his design is one of the best-known structures in Los Angeles. As echoed by journalist Chuck Schmidt, "To the casual observer, the name Welton Becket doesn't mean all that much. To students of architecture, however, the name is legend" (Schmidt, n.p.). The so-called "legend" achieved early fame in partnership with architects Walt Wurdeman and Charles F. Plummer. The group became well known in and around Los Angeles. Together, they achieved wide critical acclaim with a stylistic modern design (sometimes "moderne") for Pan-Pacific Auditorium in 1935. Yet, in 1949, Wurdeman died and Becket left the partnership to start his own firm under the name of Welton Becket & Associates. Within 10 years or so, his firm was "one of the prominent architectural firms in Los Angeles" (Schmidt, n.p.).

Some notable projects produced by Becket's firm included: The Pauley Pavilion, an indoor arena on the UCLA campus; the Santa Monica Civic Auditorium; the Beverly Hilton Hotel in Beverly Hills; and the Nassau Veterans Memorial Coliseum, in Uniondale, Long Island, among many others. Those buildings were well known regionally but none could match the iconic status of the Capitol Records Building or, for that matter, his designs for the Walt Disney Company for the Contemporary and Polynesian resorts in Walt Disney World Florida. Also in conjunction with Disney, he designed the General Motors Pavilion and the Ford Pavilion at the 1964–1965 New York World's Fair in Queens, New York. Those Disney commissions did not come by accident, as Becket was in fact a friend of Walt Disney. The close friendship was beyond a business relationship as they often vacationed together with their respective spouses (Schmidt, n.p.).

The conceptual design for Disneyland in Anaheim, California, was designed by the architectural firm of Periera and Luckman, but Becket served as Disney's personal architectural consultant. Becket eventually advised Disney to fire Periera and Luckman and

This 1958 photo of the Capitol Records Building designed by architect Welton Becket opened in 1956. The unique 13-story building, which critics claimed looked "like a stack of record albums," was the first circular office building anywhere in the world. (Photofest)

recommended that Disney should provide his own concept. Becket said, "No one can design Disneyland for you. You have to do it yourself" (Schmidt, n.p.).

Disneyland and Disney World are two of America's most indelible contributions to pop culture. Yet the design that stands out among all Becket's works was for the Capitol Records Building that opened in 1956. The unique 13-story building, which critics claimed looked "like a stack of record albums," was the first circular office building anywhere in the world. The architectural significance is equally matched by the historic musical recordings that occurred within the building, including those by the Beach Boys, Nat "King" Cole, Paul McCartney, Les Paul, and Frank Sinatra, among hundreds of others. An interesting addition to the building was a 90-foot rooftop antenna. Atop was a blinking red light, which continuously blinked the word "H-O-L-L-Y-W-O-O-D" in Morse code. Another city tradition is the rooftop Christmas tree that has been placed atop the building every year since 1958.

FURTHER READING

Donald Albrecht, ed. *World War II and the American Dream: How Wartime Building Changed a Nation.* Boston: The MIT Press, 1995.

Diane Boucher. "The 1950s American Home." London: Shire Publications, 2013.

Serge Guilbaut. *How New York Stole the Idea of Modern Art: Abstract Expressionism, Freedom, and the Cold War.* Chicago: University of Chicago Press, 1983.

David P. Handlin. *American Architecture.* New York: Thames and Hudson, Inc., 1985.

Spiro Kostof. *America by Design.* New York: Oxford University Press, 1987.

Lisa Phillips. *The American Century: Art & Culture, 1950–2000* New York: Whitney Museum of Art. First Edition, June 1999.

Don and Susan Sanders. *Drive-in Movie Memories.* Union, NH: Carriage House, 2000.

Dennis Sharp. *The Illustrated Encyclopedia of Architects and Architecture.* New York: Quarto Publishing, 1991.

Sidra Stitch. *Made in USA: An Americanization in Modern Art, The '50s & '60s.* Berkeley, CA: University of California Press, 1987.

Jon C. Teaford. *The Twentieth-Century American City,* 2nd edition. Baltimore: Johns Hopkins University Press, 1993.

Mies van der Rohe. *Less Is More.* New York: Waser Verlag Zurich, 1986.

Carter Wiseman. *Shaping a Nation: Twentieth-Century American Architecture and Its Makers.* New York: W. W. Norton & Company, 1998.

Frank Lloyd Wright. *The Natural House.* New York: Horizon Press, 1954.

CHAPTER 8

Fashion

Nostalgia puts a fashion focus on the era when every high school girl wore a "poodle skirt" with saddle shoes and a high school sweater. The boys were remembered as wearing denim jeans, a white T-shirt and black leather motorcycle jacket, with slicked-back hair. But that is an image often portrayed in a promotional photo, a Hollywood movie image that has become firmly embedded in our collective memory of the past. Some female fashion styles that were prevalent during the time included swing dresses and swimsuits. A brief fashion trend among young female viewers of the nationally televised dance show *American Bandstand* (see Television chapter) was known as the "Philadelphia Collar," a style that came about as young teens often came straight from high school to appear on the afternoon TV show. Since the start of the television show coincided with the end of the school day, the girls who came from the local Catholic high schools did not have time to go home and change. Yet they were forbidden by administrators of the Catholic high schools to wear their school uniforms on air. So they would either change in the bathrooms of just simply pull a sweater over their uniforms displaying only a wide frilly collar. The high school boys were required to wear a sports jacket and a tie, which often gave the image that all teenagers were "clean-cut" (Jackson, 70–72).

Denim jeans were only worn by a select group of teenagers who were often viewed as rebels or just plain poor. Very few schools, if any, allowed denim jeans to be worn during the schoolday. The common fashion for many teenage girls soon included rolled-up jeans, bobbysocks, and saddle shoes. For a dress-up dance, girls wore a below-the-knee dress or skirt with a high-neck collar. Bouffant-styled hair was held in place with lots of hairspray. Boys sported collared button-down shirts, slacks, and crew cuts. For a dress-up dance, boys wore a sport jacket, shirt and tie, and either matching slacks or suit. Some young teenage boys wore "ducktail" haircuts, jeans, and white t-shirts. Tight black jeans and a leather jacket were the signs of a true "teenage rebel." In order to groom a ducktail, the hair was grown a little longer. Styling and shaping the hair into shape was achieved by the use of hair wax, Vaseline, or Brylcreem, leading to the term "greasers." Greasers were known to continually whip out a pocket comb and keep the hair in place. Both groups often wore white socks that were easily viewable with a rolled-up hem. More often than not the styles were copied from the movies.

AMERICAN FASHION STYLES

The images from the Hollywood movies continued to influence fashion styles, especially among teenagers. Yet more often than not, the stories of both the on-stage and off-screen lives of the movie stars were just as fictitious as in the movies. Nevertheless, the American public sought to emulate the movie stars for their types of parties, cars, and fashion. The powerful images of the movies were often responsible for the way all Americans, young and old, dressed, talked, and lived. That same notion continued in the 1950s. Examples included trendsetters Marilyn Monroe, James Dean, and Marlon Brando. In Brando's obituary for *The Washington Post*, Adam Bernstein described the influence:

> Brando also had a huge impact on public behavior. He was, at first, a strikingly muscular and vital figure who defined 1950s leather-jacketed masculinity. He wore jeans to swank parties, insulted star-making gossip columnists and flaunted his preference for dark-skinned women. ("Actor Marlon Brando, 80, Dies," n.p.)

It was Brando who provided teenagers with one of the best-known images of teenage rebellion against social conformity. One example is the movie *The Wild One* (1953), in which his character "Johnny" impacted a large segment of American youth with a fashion style of a plain white t-shirt, denim jeans, and a black motorcycle jacket. James Dean wore similar clothing in his iconic movie *Rebel Without a Cause* (1955).

The fashion style of jeans and t-shirts was gaining acceptance among the youth, but not among adults. Many school districts around the country, both public and private, enforced dress codes prohibiting denim jeans, t-shirts, and non-conformist hairstyles. One example was in Long Island at Hicksville Junior High School. An instructional video of the time showed unacceptable fashion attire. Fashion prohibition for girls included dungarees, ankle bracelets, and dropped earrings. An official decried an objection, saying, "This student is wearing an extremely tight skirt and tight sweater." For boys, the school official said, "Open shirts, black jacket, and dungarees are mentioned in the code and not proper student attire." The school board's ban on certain clothing was supported by parents, local municipalities, and religious leaders who linked fashion to juvenile delinquency, teenage gangs, and Rock 'n' Roll as cause for all the blame. In reality, adults were scared of change, scared of non-conformity, scared of heightened sexuality, scared of rebellion, mostly scared of the weakening of segregation. Therefore, most adults continued to promote conformity, especially in male fashion.

The acceptable fashion style for men did not change much during the decade. The dominant choice was a white shirt and dark tie when out in public. In just about all instances, an adult male wore a hat when in public. Male work clothing could include denim jeans and overalls, but was also topped with some type of hat or cap. For the most part, an adult male who worked in an office, usually in a city setting, did not go out in public, or on his way to and from work, without wearing a subdued color suit (such as gray or blue), white shirt, and skinny solid-color tie, topped by a fedora hat. For males within small-town America, a similar decorum included a white shirt and tie for workplace environments such as a grocery store clerk or a sales position. Even gas station attendants were usually clad in full-length sleeved shirts emblazoned with a station logo such as "Texaco," complimented with a bowtie and attendant hat. Away from work, casual wear included a white collared shirt, often short-sleeve (depending on weather). A more stylish version was an "Italian knit" polo shirt, or semi-dress shirt, over flannel pants.

Women's styles were changing, but it was still common to see traditional styles like dainty hats and formal gloves worn in public. More often than not, the prevalent images of the day were set by the "party-type" dresses worn by television celebrities such as Betty Furness and Lucille Ball. Full-length nylon stockings were also a necessity. An adult woman would not even consider going out in public without a full complement of hosiery. Etiquette from past generations on how a young girl should sit at a dinner table, talk, stand, walk, and subtly laugh, among other public manners, was still taught in public schools and private "finishing schools."

THE SCANDALOUS BIKINI

The idea of all the 1950s fashion was simple conformity and subdued colors. Yet during the same time, one of the most scandalous fashion items arose in the form of a two-piece bathing suit known as the "bikini." Some earlier styles of two-piece bathing suits had appeared in movies during the 1930s of a wide bra top, bare midriff complemented with a long bottom skirt. Adult women who frequented private upscale resorts sometimes displayed a similarly styled bathing suit. For a large majority of the American public, the two-piece swimsuits of that time were not necessarily acceptable at public beaches. Yet they were quite modest when compared to the 1950s-style bikini. Beth Duncuff Charleston, writing in the *Heilbrunn Timeline of Art History* for The Metropolitan Museum of Art, described it:

> The difference between the bikini and its two-piece predecessor is brevity. Simply defined, the bikini is an abbreviated two-piece swimsuit with a bra top and panties cut below the navel. Broadly defined, the bikini represents a social leap involving body consciousness, moral concerns, and sexual attitudes. Named after an A-bomb testing site on a remote Pacific atoll, the bikini has had a history and reputation deserving of its name. (Charleston, n.p.)

The origin of the post-war bikini is disputed between two separate fashion designers named Jacques Heim and Louis Reard. Each claimed to have produced the two-piece design that was first worn by European women at Cannes

One of the most scandalous fashion items was a two-piece bathing suit known as the "Bikini." In this photo, actress Vera Day wears the latest model. (Photofest)

in the summer of 1946. Nevertheless, the official birthdate of the bikini is listed as July 5, 1946, when it was part of a poolside fashion show in Paris. The French bikini design was quite different than two-piece bathing suits of the past. It was a combination of "triangles" with the breasts covered by two separate triangular bra cups connected in the middle with a fabric string around the neck and a strap around the back. The bottom was also two fabric triangles, one smaller in the front and another larger one covering the buttocks.

In reality, the advent of the bikini was not totally unacceptable as long as it was worn by women who the dominant male society viewed as sex objects. At the time, the bikini was considered too risqué and scandalous for the typical American housewife or daughter. The bikini was often worn by Hollywood starlets such as Ava Gardner, Rita Hayworth, Jayne Mansfield, and Marilyn Monroe, among other celebrities. They were often photographed in a bikini in publicity photo magazine advertisements. The bikini, as were other less scandalous bathing suits, was made from new synthetic stretch fabrics such as nylon and latex (each manufactured by DuPont during the 1930s). The fabrics were quick drying and also enhanced a woman's figure, features not often found in swimsuits of the past. The bathing suits were defined by bright colors and patterns such as polka dots. The bikini was immortalized in a summer song hit of 1960, "Itsy Bitsy Teenie Weenie, Yellow Polka Dot Bikini" performed by the teen idol Bryan Hyland. Later developments in the 1960s and 1970s led to even skimpier bikini styles such as halter-style tops and small triangular bottoms each exposing more shoulder skin and hips (Charleston, n.p.).

SEVENTH AVENUE AND DESIGNING WOMEN

As the advertising industry was collectively known as "Madison Avenue," the American fashion industry was collectively known as "Seventh Avenue." That name came from the New York City location along Seventh Avenue from

West 26th Street to 41st Street. The area had a large concentration of garment designers and shops that produced American fashion dating to the pre-war years and continuing into the 1980s. Some designers and fashion houses remained into the 21st century, but nowhere near the almost complete saturation of clothing-related businesses in that area during the 1950s. (In 1973, it was officially renamed "7th Avenue-Fashion Avenue" by the passage of NYC Local Law 35.)

Fashion was not new to New York or, for that matter, to the United States. What was new was the creation of a field of a non-formal fashion style known as "sportswear." Fashion historian Richard Martin, writing in the *Heilbrunn Timeline of Art History* for The Metropolitan Museum of Art, said,

> That phenomenon of an American sportswear was chiefly defined on Seventh Avenue, with some support from Connecticut and surrounding hillsides and from the sports- and car-oriented burgeoning West Coast, and was committed to making ready-to-wear and affordable fashion realistic and attractive to women of the epoch of the Great Depression through the American world of hegemony. A changeover in fashion styles was due in large part to a significant increase in prosperity for many Americans. With the war and the depression behind them, new consumer advertising also brought changes in fashion especially in de-emphasizing formal clothing for everyday life. (Martin, n.p.)

The changeover style was a step backwards from the traditional fashion styles that so often had been dictated by the European houses, especially those in Paris.

Many of the designers sought to emulate the new post-war lifestyle among middle-class America. In doing so, a significant change occurred to complement the newly structured lives of American women. The American fashion designers did not copy the European styles as much as their fashion was a new development in the fashion industry. The distinct styling was noted by the creation of "sportswear" to meet the needs of real-life situations. The "sportswear" style also coincided with the growth of department stores such as Lord & Taylor, Macy's, and Abraham & Strauss. The department stores were located both in the urban downtowns as well as in suburban shopping malls. Aided by advertising and television, the fashion styles were heavily promoted and soon led to an abundance of designs and manufacturing of new styled clothing, especially for women.

Unlike previous generations, and for that matter even during the 1950s, the leading impetus for the fashion industry occurred mainly among female designers who became associated with the acceptable new "sportswear" fashion style. Some of the noted American designers of the time included Bonnie Cashin, Elizabeth Hawes, Tina Leser, Vera Maxwell, Claire McCardell, and Emily Wilkins. Fashion historian Whitney Blausen confirmed this in the early 21st century: "We live today indebted to McCardell, Cashin, Hawes, Wilkins, Leser, and Maxwell, and other women who liberated American fashion from the thralldom of Parisian design. Independence came in tying, wrapping, stowing, eschewing ornament, harmonizing, and rationalizing that wardrobe."

Bonnie Cashin (1908–2000) based her design notion upon "fashion evolved from need." Some of her work of the early 1950s was inspired by a trip to Japan where she saw first-hand the "practical aspects" of a woman's kimono. She learned that the kimono served as a versatile garment especially as temperatures and climate changed. Upon returning to the United States, this concept led her to a design idea for layered clothing. The *Encyclopedia of Fashion* said her design was "long before the concept became a universal option." Fashion historian Whitney Blausen added, "Of course, people around the world had been dressing in layers to accommodate the climate for centuries, but . . . [f]ashion writers are ever grateful for something that looks new, and for a while layering was praised as the big new idea." Cashin is also credited with introducing fashion items such as canvas boots and raincoats into popular use in 1952. She also designed a jump suit that was acceptable to wear in public by 1956. Some of her other "signature pieces" included funnel-necked sweaters that doubled as a hood, and a bicycle sweater with large back pockets, toggle closures, and leather piping. She also had the distinction of pairing various types of fabrics in one ensemble. By the early 1960s, she designed some Coach bags.

Blausen described Elizabeth Hawes (1903–1971) as "a visionary and an iconoclast. She was a designer of inventive clothing and a fashion writer whose analytic prose still illuminates the world of Seventh Avenue." Hawes' contribution was mainly through her journalistic endeavors as a fashion critic and author. Her writing often suggested that both women and men "rebel against the status quo." In doing so she often recommended to let manufacturers know that they wanted clothes to accommodate their specific individual lifestyles and not what advertisers dictated. By the 1950s, her design influence was spread through popular publications such as *Why Is a Dress?* She was forthright in rejecting the lead of the Paris designers and also explained how the American garment manufacturers worked against the average consumer (Blausen, n.p.).

Tina Leser (1910–1986) was known for designing relaxed clothing that was affordable for many post-war women. In 1953, she designed industrial uniforms for the Ramsey Sportswear Company, which fashion historian Blausen described as displaying "sensitivity to the realities of life for working women." At a time when pants were not openly accepted for a woman to wear in public, Leser came up with a unique idea. For the working woman who was required to wear pants during work time, Hawes designed a playful skirt that could be worn over the pants while the woman traveled to and from work. She also employed different types of prints and fabrics such as Indian silks, denim, and chenille, among others. Derivations included a cashmere sweater dress, a sleeveless jacket, a strapless bodice, and wide-cuffed pants.

Vera Maxwell (1903–1995) derived her design style from many influences such as Viennese military officers. She is credited with designing the first jumpsuit for women with a mid-1940s coverall for women performing war work at the Sperry Gyroscope Corporation. Another design influence came from a meeting with famed scientist Albert Einstein. It was his tweed jacket that inspired Maxwell to design a series of gray flannel skirts and pants as fashion separates that she called suitable as a "weekend wardrobe." Fashion historian Jean Druesedow described Maxwell's clothes as "handsome, interesting, and eminently wearable" (Druesedow, n.p.). Maxwell was also influenced by both the design and business sense of the famed French fashion designer Coco Chanel (1883–1971). Chanel was known for providing early 20th-century women with a new "liberating" style of clothing that was free of the pre-1920s, restrictive, centuries-old corsets. She promoted more casual and sporty styles that were keeping in time with a progressive change for women occurring both in Europe and the United States in the years between the world wars. Chanel was involved in all sorts of fashion accessories; her most famous design product was the legendary perfume Chanel No. 5.

Unlike the other female designers who designed adult clothing, Emily Wilkens (1917–2000) was an American fashion designer who specialized in children's wear. In *The New York Times* of December 6, 2000, journalist Ginia Bellafante titled Wilkens' obituary "Designer Who Dressed Girls Like Girls." Prior to the 1950s, young girls and teenagers often wore dresses and clothing "as if they were their mothers in miniature." In contrast, her work ventured into new untapped areas of the teenage market. Wilkens changed that age-old notion by drawing on influences as diverse as Russian peasant dresses and paintings by the 19th-century artist Thomas Gainsborough. She was aware that young girls grew at a rate that often made their clothing too small within a year or less. Therefore, Wilkens provided washable cotton type dresses with adjustable waistlines allowing for growing hips while "maintaining an age-appropriate appearance." Fashion historian Richard Martin wrote, "Long before rock 'n' roll and James Dean movies, Emily Wilkens invented the American teenager, pegging her sensibility to young, playful, energetic women."

Claire McCardell and "The American Look"

Claire McCardell (1905–1958) is credited with pioneering "a style of clothing that was both casual and chic." She had studied in Paris during the mid-1920s and was also influenced by Coco Chanel. Yet it was her introduction of simple functional clothing designs that made her work uniquely American. According to the *Fashion History Encyclopedia*, "Claire McCardell's greatest contribution to fashion history was in creating and defining the American Look" (Martin, "American Ingenuity," n.p.). In previous years the European fashion designer placed the wearer at the will of the designer. Fashion historian Richard Martin called it "authoritarian and imposed on women, willing or not." In contrast, McCardell made it fashionable for women to make their own choices as they could buy a blouse, dress, or a skirt that did not necessarily match, but complimented each piece in coordinating colors. The economical idea was to mix and match combinations without any preconceived restrictions, thereby providing versatility with only a limited number of garments. As a result, Martin said, "American fashion addressed a democracy" ("American Ingenuity," n.p.).

McCardell's contribution was recognized both during her lifetime and continued after her death. In 1990, *Life* magazine listed her among the "100 Most Important Americans of the 20th Century." During her lifetime, she was one of the first American designers to attain an instant "name recognition." That came as a result of a cover story on *Time* magazine on May 2, 1955, which began:

> It was the end of April, and as the soft air turned the land green, American women were suddenly aware of a truth that bursts upon them every spring: Summer was at hand, and they did not have a thing to wear. Therefore, they were out in force in stores last week in search of the cool—and new—clothes to make the hot weather bearable. Tall girls looked for dresses that would make them seem shorter; short girls wanted to look taller. The plump wanted eye-foolers that would seem to take off weight. ("Claire McCardell," 4)

As any of those woman shopped for clothing, all of them would have been drawn to a McCardell design. Her clothes were not designed for just one body type. They often had adjustable components, such as drawstring necklines and waists, to accommodate many different body types. Therefore, short, tall, over-weight, or skinny, all women could be fashionably attired in a McCardell design.

In formulating the designs, McCardell often claimed that she designed clothing with herself in mind. In the same May 1955 *Time* article, she said, "I've always designed things I needed myself. It just turns out that other people need them too." Yet it was a special distinction that placed her in a different category from the other fashion designers of the time. Fashion historian Margo Seaman explained,

> The beauty of McCardell's clothes lay in the cut, which then produced a clean, functional garment. Her clothes accentuated the female form without artificial understructures and padding. Rather than use shoulder pads, McCardell used the cut of the sleeve to enhance the shoulder. Relying on the bias cut, she created fitted bodices and swimsuits, which flattered the wearer. Full circle skirts, neatly belted or sashed at the waist without crinolines underneath, a mandatory accessory for the New Look, created the illusion of the [thin] waist. (Seaman, n.p.)

A popular non-formal style was a simple dress style, often termed a "sundress," that was considered acceptable to wear either inside or outside the home. McCardell's sundresses made use of fabrics such as rayon, calico, seersucker, gingham, and also cotton voiles for evening wear. She also placed fasteners such as zippers, cording, and toggles in easy accessible locations. She came up with the idea of a playsuit, often advertised as adult "play clothes." Some stylish changes to the standard house dress came in the form of a "popover" dress. Her "kitchen-dinner" dress was made of silk with a matching apron. All of her designs were intended as stylish enough for those suburban women who entertained at home, but could not afford to employ a maid. In that same sense for those who could not fully afford to buy a dress in a department store, specially designed home patterns of McCardell dresses could be purchased from companies such as McCall's and Spadea. These companies sold a basic clothing pattern which a person could then purchase and cut her own material of the dress pattern and therefore, sew her own McCardell dress. Other influences came from fashion writing such as her popular publication of

What Shall I Wear (1956, reprinted Duckworth Limited, 2013). McCardell, as did the other designers, provided functional clothing with simple lines and decorative elements that provided the average woman as "subtly sexy." As a result, fashion historian Richard Martin said, "These designers established the modern dress code." Part of that dress code was casual attire that also made it acceptable for a woman to wear pants as part of her everyday wardrobe.

Most women who wore slacks during the 1940s did so as a practical means as war-workers in a factory-type setting. That image was immortalized by the image of "Rosie the Riveter" who wore denim jeans as a practical measure in the factories. Outside the factory, dresses were the acceptable mode of fashion and continued into the 1950s. Pants were not viewed as acceptable in public and were very rarely seen on television. Two popular, and somewhat acceptable, styles of pants for women were known as capris and skinny pants (sometimes known as "cigarette pants"). The popular color for both styles was black, with capris offering some other vibrant colors. The skinny pants were high-waisted with a single side zipper or back zipper that were slim fitted along the legs extending to just above the ankle. The capris were often considered as three-quarter-length pants since they were below the knee but still a bit higher above the ankle.

In the early 1950s, a fashionable casual female fashion style was black capri pants and a white ruffled blouse. Some of those styles were made popular by Hollywood stars such as the iconic actress Audrey Hepburn (1929–1993). Her "European" fashion presence as displayed in such popular movies as *Roman Holiday* (1953), *Sabrina* (1954), *Breakfast at Tiffany's* (1961), and *My Fair Lady* (1964) was emulated by Americans. For a brief time, the capri style was also marketed as "calypso pants" as Calypso-type music was popular on the radio and featured on TV shows. Some other fashion styles of the same design were also known as clam diggers, toreador pants, and pirate pants, among others. The only denim-type jeans that were considered fashionable for women included a version in the capri style, which came just below the knee with a rolled-up hem revealing a colorful plaid flannel lining.

In a similar, yet more semi-casual style, women for the first time were wearing a version of short pants in public known as "sport shorts." (In previous years some versions of short pants were acceptable for the beach.) During the time, the sport shorts came in different lengths and styles, but stayed within the realm of acceptable decorum of about six inches above the knee. The acceptable adult and teenage shorts were called "culottes," a version that sometimes had the hem looser and flair out a bit more on the thigh. (The term "culottes" is French, often attributed to an early 20th-century style of short pants. Yet the term is often traced to the "Sans-culottes," a French phrase for a societal class of people in Paris from the 18th century. That term was derived from their distinctive pantaloons, which later became a version of modern-day pants.)

The most common acceptable style was a version known as Bermuda shorts. (The term came from the fashionable male style on the British territorial island of Bermuda.) Some American men began wearing a similar version, but it was not a common male feature until the late 1960s. At the time, it was becoming more acceptable for women to wear the Bermuda shorts at a respectable length that came to about three inches above the knee with a high waist often and side-waist zippers. Another type of fashionable casual pants were called "pedal pushers." The term came from bicycle-styled pants that held the cuff tight and up from the ankle to avoid tangling on the bicycle chain or the pedals. A version was adopted mainly by teens that rolled up the cuff of their jeans.

One of the least accepted for adult women, but more readily accepted by younger unmarried teens, were "short shorts." These were pulled up very high with the short portion of the leg either rolled up or held in place with a safety pin, thereby showing as much of the thigh as possible. The short itself was often tight to the hips and buttocks. The musical group The Royal Teens provided a parody of the teen mania in a top-rated 1957 song titled, "Who Wears Short Shorts." The 1950s style of "short" would not be comparable to later generations of "short," since the hem was only about six inches above the knee and usually tight to the leg. A high waist offset the leg hem, unlike later generations that displayed a low-cut waist. Nevertheless, the teenage version was not openly accepted by regular societal standards of the day, and definitely not for any self-respecting adult women. The short shorts were most often reserved for the beach or poolside. Some were often seen in risqué magazine advertisements worn by the likes of Hollywood starlets such as Marilyn Monroe, or on pin-up models like Bettie Page.

THE FASHION PIN-UP: BETTIE PAGE AND CAMERA CLUBS

The quintessential "pin-up" whose sexuality rivaled, but was quite different from either Jayne Mansfield or Marilyn Monroe, was Bettie Page (1923–2008). Born Betty Mae Page in Nashville, Tennessee, she was described by TCM.com as "one of the first sex icons in America . . . a super successful 1950s pin-up model." Hannah Betts, writing Page's obituary in London for *The Telegraph*, called her "The Miss Pin-up Girl of the World." Yet her life was littered with myth, mystery, and sadness; eventually her fashion style led to a 21st-century cult following. Similar to other icons of the 1950s, like Marilyn Monroe and James Dean, Bettie Page memorabilia and clothing items continue to sell and garner cult-like status well into the twenty-first century. From 2005 thru 2010, her website, www.BettiePage.com, a commercial merchandising outlet offering the sale of 1950s-inspired apparel of dresses, swimwear, and shoes similar to those which Page wore in her modeling poses, received more than 600 million views.

Of all the iconic figures of the 1950s, Page seemed the least likely to be a fashion influence. As the oldest of six children, Page suffered through a childhood of an abusive father culminating in her parents' divorce. (Some sources say her age was 7, others 10, at the time of the divorce.) Page's single mom, often unable to make ends meet, once sent the young Betty to an orphanage for one year. In her teens, she acted in high school plays and was engrossed in drama. She was a straight "A" student—nearly missing earning the title of "valedictorian" of her graduating class. With her academic accomplishments, she was awarded a scholarship to the Nashville Peabody College for Teachers, graduating with a batchelor's degree. In all likelihood, she was about to settle into a typical 1950s life. She first worked as a secretary and married at the age of 20, which was the average age of females who married during the decade. Her husband was a sailor who left for service during the war. However, upon his return, things did not work out according to the 1950s idealized plan. She divorced from whom biographers say was a "violent husband," in either 1947 or 1948. (Sources vary, although Page did later marry on two other occasions; each of those also ended in divorce.) Soon thereafter, she moved to New York to study acting and supported herself working as a secretary (Sahagun, n.p.).

Page's "notorious" career (she disliked that description) began one day in October 1950, while walking along the famous Coney Island beachfront in Brooklyn, New York. During her stroll, an amateur photographer and full-time police officer, Jerry Tibbs, asked her to pose. At what many would consider an old age to begin modeling, Bettie was 27 when she appeared in her first photo shoot. Tibbs, however, was not looking for a fashion model, but rather someone to pose in risqué clothing.

At the time, risqué imagery, of both film and still photographs, was subject to strict censorship and possible criminal action. However, Tibbs told her of the "Camera Clubs" that technically made the work legal (Sahagun, n.p.).

In late-1940s America, "Camera Clubs" was a loosely defined term as a way to circumvent the morality codes of the time, especially regarding nude, erotic, or obscene images. Yet, most Camera Clubs were formed under the guise of an artistic endeavor promoting photography. They began in the 1940s, mostly in New York City. The "clubs" were loosely organized and sometimes served only as a way to label a photographer as an amateur working with a home-installed darkroom. The "amateur" status was only a front as professional nude photography was strictly taboo and often subject to criminal charges. Therefore, the clubs, with an amateur status, often presented erotic and sometimes nude photography, under the pretense as either "art" or "glamour"

Of her thousands of photographs, Bettie Page is often remembered for only a few as a "dominatrix" or in risqué clothing. As a "glamour model," Page developed a signature "look" shown here. Her blue eyes and shoulder-length black hair were accentuated by her trademark bangs draping a bit longer and wavier than the typical bangs of the 1920s flappers. (Photofest)

photography. The ruse was a safe way to sell the photographs to the growing
number of men's magazines of the time (the most famous was Hugh Hefner's
Playboy). Some of the images accompanied fictional crime stories in magazines
labeled as "True Detective Stories." The most well-known model at the time
was Bettie Page.

One such result to bypass prosecution was also applying the terminology
of "glamour photography." As a "glamour model," Page developed, with
the help of different photographers, a signature "look." Her blue eyes and
shoulder-length black hair (described as "raven") were accentuated by her
trademark bangs draping a bit longer and wavier than the typical bangs of the
1920s flappers. She herself said that the bangs offset her high forehead and
eliminated any photographic glare off the top of her head. Eventually she
posed for many different photographers, accumulating a total of more than
20,000 photographs. Almost all of the images were of Page as a solo model in
risqué poses of her wearing either bikini-type bathing suits or skimpy underwear. A few of her photographs were in bondage-type apparel, and thereafter
she was often associated with dominatrix. In an interview conducted in
June 1998, she responded to her title as the "Queen of Bondage":

> The only bondage posing I ever did was for Irving Klaw and his sister Paula.
> Usually every other Saturday he had a session for four or five hours with four or
> five models and a couple of extra photographers, and in order to get paid you
> had to do an hour of bondage. And that was the only reason I did it. I never had
> any inkling along that line. I don't really disapprove of it; I think you can do your
> own thing as long as you're not hurting anybody else—that's been my philoso-
> phy ever since I was a little girl. I never looked down my nose at it. In fact, we
> used to laugh at some of the requests that came through the mail, even from
> judges and lawyers and doctors and people in high positions. Even back in the
> '50s they went in for the whips and the ties and everything else. (Sharkey, n.p.)

Looking back from the 21st century, all of her photographs and films appear
quite innocent. Yet, at the time the non-nude, black-and-white images were
tantamount to graphic pornography. Well before the adult film industry and
the breakthrough of pornographic films into the mainstream during the 1980s,
it was "stag films" that were considered pornographic during the 1950s. The
stag films, most were just suggestive and risqué, yet some did include pornography, were shot on 8mm and 16mm film of eight to 10 minutes in length.
They were usually sold and offered for discreet sale in unsavory men's magazines. Page did appear in a few of these types of films, sometimes as a dominatrix, sometimes as a "bound victim." None of Page's film work, however,
displayed any nudity or sexual intercourse.

It was mainly her notoriety in still photographs that led to a different type of
film career. It later years it was often mistaken that she made more movies
than she actually did. Most of her film performances were burlesque-type,
black-and-white films of about 10 minutes in length. Page only appeared in four
film-like features that were barely one hour long. Her first was a 1950s short
film *Teaser Girl in High Heels* (1950). She later made *Striporama* (1953) and *Varie-
tease* (1954). Her 1955 film titled *Teaserama* was listed as a "documentary," but
actually was a titillating color film of a typical burlesque stage show. That film

listed Tempest Storm as the star with Page listed as a feature player under the name "Betty Page." *Teaserama*, as did her other work, was accompanied with suggestive burlesque-type music with dancers in lingerie and underwear; some settings were on a stage, others in bedrooms, but none included any nude scenes.

Most of her legacy was as a result of non-nude, 4×5–inch, black-and-white photographs. Some of those images appeared in the so-called "girlie" magazines of the time, with such titles as *Eyeful*, *Wink*, and *Glamour Parade*, among dozens of others. Those same magazines, catering strictly to men, also offered for sale photographs of Page, stag films, and others by mail order. In 1955, a professional fashion photographer by the name of Bunny Yeager provided better quality images of Bettie Page than many of the others working in the field. Some of those later images of her were nudes. One of those was a semi-nude image of a topless Bettie wearing a Santa hat kneeling before a Christmas tree with an ornament in hand. That image was sold to the fledging *Playboy* magazine and appeared in the January 1955 issue. The widespread circulation of the growing popularity of *Playboy* added to her own fame. In parallel with the same philosophy of *Playboy*, Page's own image captured the imagination of a generation with her free spirit and unabashed sensuality, during an era of strong sexual repression. While some of the societal taboos regarding nudity were slowly disappearing during the 1950s, Bettie Page was not widely accepted by mainstream society.

Suddenly, without fanfare, Page ended her career in 1959 as she became an evangelist and followed the teachings of Billy Graham. For the most part, throughout the 1960s, she remained in quiet seclusion, often working to spread the word of the Reverend Graham. A surprise resurgence in her image was later hailed by a 1970s generation of feminists as a pioneer. Some of that can be attributed to what Page heard from other young women. In a 2006 interview, she said, "Young women say I helped them come out of their shells, and 13 rock groups have written songs about me." But she still was unsure why, all of a sudden, she was embraced by younger generations of mostly female fans. Page added:

> I was not trying to be shocking, or to be a pioneer. I wasn't trying to change society, or to be ahead of my time. I didn't think of myself as liberated, and I don't believe that I did anything important. I was just myself. I didn't know any other way to be, or any other way to live. (Sharkey, n.p.)

Yet it was in the asking of her own question that provided the reason, because later generations of liberated women just wanted to express themselves without having to conform to either a male perception or societal conformity. In 2008, British journalist Hannah Betts explained, "In fact, as every schoolgirl ought, yet all-too frequently fails to know, such self-expression was one of the [feminists'] movement's most fundamental gifts" (Betts, n.p.).

From the 1980s onward, her image achieved cultlike status. Without prompting, all types of merchandising including t-shirts, photos, figurines, and books, among others, were avidly sought after by a new generation of fans, almost exclusively female. Yet so much of the sale of her merchandise was out of her control. She was often involved with trying to obtain royalties from the many unauthorized uses of her image. Although her popularity was growing in a society without the restrictions of the 1950s, she did not capitalize on it with public appearances. Her later life was plagued by mental illness, mood swings, and severe depression. In the late 1980s, she was declared insane by a judge after a long period of violent mood swings. One instance involved a knife attack upon her landlady in a rent dispute. Page was given a 10-year sentence to a mental institution, but was released after a few years in 1992. In an interview for *The Los Angeles Times* of March 11, 2006, she also reconciled the contradiction that some perceived between her risqué modeling career and religious conviction. Page reasoned, "Being in the nude isn't a disgrace unless you're being promiscuous about it. After all, when God created Adam and Eve, they were stark naked. And in the Garden of Eden, God was probably naked as a jaybird too!"

Her legend lived on enough to have a 2005 film produced about her life titled *The Notorious Bettie Page*. Although flattered by the attention, she was displeased with the inclusion of the word "notorious" in the title. Louis Sahagun, writing in her *Los Angeles Times* obituary, quoted her as saying, "Notorious? That's not flattering at all. They should have used another word." After the movie release, Page seemed surprised about her 1950s influence upon the 21st century. In a 2006 *Los Angeles Times* interview, she said, "I have no idea why I'm the only model who has had so much fame so long after quitting work." As a model who, in a short time span of the 1950s, was photographed professionally more than 20,000 times, she requested not to have herself photographed in her old age, adding, "I want to be remembered as I was when I was young and in my golden times . . . I want to be remembered as the woman who changed people's perspectives concerning nudity in its natural form" (Sahagun, n.p.). Despite the overwhelming interest in her fashion website, she never returned to the public realm and lived quietly in a one-bedroom Los Angeles apartment. Her consolation involved reading the Bible, listening to Christian and country music, watching television, or sometimes venturing outside to a vintage clothing store. Unlike the early tragic deaths of Marilyn Monroe and Jayne Mansfield, Bettie Page died in December of 2008 at the age of 85.

FURTHER READING

Beth Duncuff Charleston. "Christian Dior (1905–1957)." In *Heilbrunn Timeline of Art History*. New York: The Metropolitan Museum of Art, 2000.
The Bettie Page Biography. Biography.com. A&E Television Networks.
Jennifer Le Zotte. "How the Summer of Atomic Bomb Testing Turned the Bikini into a Phenomenon." *Smithsonian Magazine*. May 21, 2015.
Richard Martin. "American Ingenuity: Sportswear, 1930s–1970s." In *Heilbrunn Timeline of Art History*. New York: The Metropolitan Museum of Art, 2000.

CHAPTER 9

Media and Advertising

Throughout the decade, advertising dollars for all types of consumer products increased dramatically. Unlike the pre-war years, a change in the approach to creating ad campaigns incorporated all sorts of demographics and research studies. Another change was having the new visual medium of television to provide advertisers with a vast new way to reach consumers and tap into the "hidden desires" of the recently affluent American society. A considerable amount of advertising space was still purchased in newspapers and magazines, as well as promotional spots on radio. Yet the most notable increase in spending by advertisers was in the entertainment outlet of television. Within a few short years, the most dramatic and desired ad spot was a television commercial offering a visual enhancement, which radio could not match. In the first half of the decade, the newness of television and its limited distribution audience provided advertisers with the ability to sponsor an entire program. (In 1950, the number of TV sets totaled almost four million households or just 9 percent of the total population.) Some examples included the popular *Texaco Star Theater* hosted by Milton Berle, sponsored by the gasoline company; the toothpaste manufacturer *Colgate Comedy Hour*; the greeting card company *Hallmark Hall of Fame*; tire company *Goodyear TV Playhouse*; and food manufacturer *Kraft Television Theater*. As the popularity of television and the number of TV sets increased, sole sponsorship of a single show became too expensive. As a result, programs sought out multiple sponsors. By 1960, more than 45.8 million households had at least one television set, or in the words of ad lingo, TV had "reached 90 percent penetration." As the number of television sets increased, home viewership skyrocketed. Reports showed that Americans were staying home and watching more and more TV. As a result, advertisers bought more and more television commercial airtime. All sorts of advertising dollars were spent to promote consumer products. As a result, top-level advertising agencies secured large increases in ad revenues to levels never achieved in the past.

THE NEW AGE OF ADVERTISING AGENCIES

At the time, the best-known marketing ad agency in the world was the J. Walter Thompson Company. It was not new to the decade; in fact, the company had been in existence for more than 150 years. Thompson's main office was located in New York City, but the company also maintained an international advertising and communications network of about 10,000 employees in over 200 offices located in 90 countries. From 1945 to 1955, the company increased billings from $78 million to over $172 million. By 1960, the ad revenue for the year was over $250 million. Although companies such as J. Walter Thompson were spread out in many cities and countries, all of the advertising was referred to as "Madison Avenue." The reference was applied as almost all of the top advertising agencies listed office addresses along Madison Avenue in the midtown area of New York City. Other top names of the time included Batten, Barton, Durstine & Osborn; McCann-Erickson; and Young & Rubicam. The combined total billings for all the ad agencies in the decade grew substantially from $1.3 billion in 1950 to well over $6 billion by 1960. By mid-decade, a significant amount of that revenue came from creating television commercials, which became the number one form of advertising medium in America (Halberstam, 497–499).

Many of the Madison Avenue advertising agencies formed research departments to study consumer buying habits. All sorts of studies included

Chart 9.1 **Advertising Revenues Radio vs. Television (In Millions of Dollars)**

Year	Radio	Television
1949	145.2	34.3
1950	444.5	105.9
1951	450.4	235.7
1952	469.7	323.6
1953	475.3	431.8
1954	449.5	593.0
1955	453.4	744.7
1956	480.6	896.9
1957	518.3	943.2
1958	523.1	1,030.0
1959	569.0	1,163.9
1960	597.7	1,268.6

Source: www.tvhistory.tv/Radio_vs_TV_Revenues.jpg. Chart compiled by author.

psychology, color, packaging, and other motivational aspects that might be associated with a particular brand. One result was the creation of new fictional characters that became associated with a particular brand. Those included the Marlboro Man (from Leo Burnett Co.), the Maidenform Woman (Norman, Craig & Kummel), and the Hathaway shirt man (Ogilvy & Mather), among others (*Advertising Age*, "History: 1950s").

At the time, all aspects of commercial advertising provided patriotic support of American Capitalism over Soviet Communism. As explained by the trade publication *Advertising Age*:

> Capitalism claimed the technical innovations of wartime and transformed them into labor-saving convenience products. The aerosol spray can was a by-product of the war's South Pacific "bug bomb." Adding a spray top transformed the "bug bomb" into a dispenser for everything from processed cheese, whipped cream, shaving cream, hairspray and deodorant to furniture polish. Nylon, initially developed for parachutes, replaced expensive silk in stockings. Plastics and Styrofoam found new applications in everything from furniture to insulation. ("History: 1950s," n.p.)

Throughout, the mass-market magazines continually warned of the Soviet threat by printing all sorts of speculation and paranoia. In 1947, at about the same time that the House Un-American Activities Committee (HUAC) was gaining nationwide notoriety, the national *LOOK* magazine offered Americans suggestions on "How to Spot a Communist" (March 4, 1947). Another example from *LOOK* provided detailed information on a "real" impending Soviet threat. During the height of nuclear testing the editors told the American public, "We Are in a Life and Death Atomic Race" (July 14, 1953). As the decade ended, and entered into the 1960s, the false fear of Communism did not subside. Another example was the widely circulated *LIFE* magazine that suggested "What We Must do to Stop Communism" (November 10, 1961). All of these articles ran side-by-side with ads for new consumer products such as washing machines and automobiles.

Apparently the only way to "Stop Communism" was to continue to buy American consumer products. At least that is what the advertisers promoted. The new craze, termed "consumerism," continually stressed the message to own a suburban home and buy items that were in either short supply or nonexistent during the war. Consumer values and the pressure of advertising to buy and keep up with their neighbors, led many to buy on credit. In 1950, Diners Club introduced the first credit card as a way to ease the situation of paying for a dinner by eliminating the awkward situation of counting out cash in a restaurant. The idea of "paying with plastic" was soon the convenient way for buying on credit. (With a credit card, the consumer paid a third-party creditor in monthly payments with interest added.) In 1958, the American Express Company also went into the credit card business. Within the first year, over 250,000 applications were processed and subsequent credit cards were issued to select consumers. Within a few years, many banks and just about every major retailer provided a credit card service. One example was the department store Sears & Roebuck that had more than 10 million charge account customers.

A strong outlet to promote consumerism was television. Across the spectrum, the programs had commercial sponsorship of just about every type of consumer product available in America. In many cases, the content of the television programs coincided with the same idealized commercial images. Most television shows, and also the magazine images, glorified the happiness of middle-class motherhood and marriage. Those included suburban homeownership, marital fidelity, respectful children, and a loving housewife who understood that the idea that a "woman's place was in the home." Unlike the strong feminine woman such as the wartime "Rosie the Riveter," advertisers changed the definition of "feminine" to a dainty housewife who always deferred to her husband. The new image was constantly promoted through television commercials, sitcoms, variety shows, Hollywood movies, and all sorts of print media.

The new devoted woman was portrayed as content to stay home to raise a family in complete marital bliss. The "double standard" of gender roles was also provided in high school education courses that enrolled young males in vocational and professional courses such as auto mechanics, woodworking, and business. On the other hand, women were encouraged to take "home economics" courses such as cooking and sewing. Other women-geared courses included secretarial skills such as shorthand and typing. Women were also encouraged in such home leisure pursuits as interior decorating, quilting, and embroidery, among others. Historian David Halberstam wrote, "Gender, not talent, was the most important qualification. The boys in the family were to learn the skills critical to supporting a family, while daughters were to be educated [on how] to get married" (589).

BETTY FURNESS, DINAH SHORE, AND "SEE THE USA IN YOUR CHEVROLET"

All sorts of familiar slogans, musical jingles, and fictionalized characters such as Speedy Alka Seltzer and the Jolly Green Giant became embedded in the American consciousness. Timex watches, as just one of many examples, employed TV newscaster John Cameron Swayze to put the watch under all sorts of unusual weather conditions. The watch was shown to the viewers as unharmed, as Swayze proclaimed, "It takes a licking and keeps on ticking." Anacin pain relief tablets (picked by *Advertising Age* as one of the top ads of the entire 20th century) promoted relief from the "tension headache." The ad created by Ted Bates & Co promised that a dose of Anacin provided "fast, fast, fast relief." The idea of all the commercials was repetition and earning consumer trust for the product (*Advertising Age*, "History: 1950s").

The Madison Avenue advertising agencies came up with the idea of providing one single spokesperson for a particular product or an entire company. The idea was to find a celebrity or notable person whom the viewing public would like and eventually come to "trust." Two of the most famous of the time included Betty Furness (1916–1994) and Dinah Shore (1916–1994). (Of ironic coincidence, they were born less than two months apart in 1916, and each died within three months of each other in 1994.)

Betty Furness was a constant presence as a celebrity television spokesperson selling Westinghouse home appliance products throughout the entire decade. She became one of America's most recognized and trusted celebrities. In this photo she displayed a new Westinghouse refrigerator during a 1950s television commercial. (Photofest)

Furness, who had limited success as a Hollywood actress during the late 1930s and 1940s, was hired by Westinghouse. She first appeared in TV ads for the appliance company in 1949 during commercial breaks in the drama series *Studio One*. The American public quickly developed a comfort and trust in Furness. She appeared to stroll effortlessly through a studio kitchen attired in a party-type dress. She demonstrated to the viewers the ease of operating the appliances while also telling them of the prestige of purchasing a Westinghouse appliance for the kitchen or home. Furness enthusiastically promoted home products that included refrigerators, stoves, and washing machines, among other new household conveniences. She was a constant presence throughout the entire decade and became one of America's most recognized and trusted celebrities.

Of similar viewer trust was actress, singer, and entertainer Dinah Shore. Unlike Furness, Shore was a well-known popular singer before she began a career in television commercials. She had a knack for promoting a wholesome image of "the girl next door" look. Writing for PopHistoryDig.com, Jack Doyle described it as "a likeable mixture of Southern charm, good looks, and friendly hospitality." During the 1950s, Shore served as host of her own prime-time entertainment variety show. In 1956, her show garnered sponsorship from Chevrolet, a division of General Motors (known to car buyers as "Chevy"). At first the once-a-month NBC-TV show was billed as *The Chevy Show*. Her association with both the automaker and the song "See the USA in Your Chevrolet" became synonymous to the American public, so that the name of the show was changed to *The Dinah Shore Chevy Show*. The short song contained jingoistic reference to the greatness of the United States. The show remained as both a popular product sponsorship platform and also a viewer favorite until 1961.

Another popular entertainer who earned sponsorship from Chevrolet was singer Pat Boone. He was a consistent portrait of the clean-cut all-American male that was especially appealing to non-rebellious teenagers. In 1958, both Shore and Boone were paired in a single commercial promoting the new Chevy Impala model. It soon became the best-selling automobile in America. The trade publication *Advertising Age* looked back upon the 1950s as a time when Dinah Shore "helped make Chevy the unchallenged leader in America and the Chevy jingle one of the most famous in TV history."

IGNORANCE AND DEATH CAUSED BY SMOKING

During the 1950s, smoking was allowed just about everywhere in American society. It was common in all public places such as on an airplane, in a doctor's office, in movie theaters, on public transportation, in restaurants, and retail stores, just to name a few. The places where smoking was prohibited were almost non-existent. At one point, surveys revealed 70 percent of Americans over the age of 16 smoked at one point or another. The placement of a cigarette in a person's hand was evident in all portions of American society as a conformist prop. Many promotional photographs and images of the day were accentuated by the noticeable placement of a lit cigarette. Celebrities, athletes, newscasters, doctors, and notables from all walks of life promoted and advertised the "pleasures" of smoking. One example was TV host Rod Serling, who in real life did not smoke. During his introduction to his popular television series *The Twilight Zone*, he was seen holding a lit cigarette. Women, who smoked at a rate almost as high as men, were completely unaware of the dangers. Smoking (and drinking alcohol, for that matter) were acceptable during pregnancy.

Ads for cigarettes were everywhere in popular culture, including newspapers, magazines, radio, and television. They were in movies, on television programs, on billboards, given as birthday and Christmas gifts, part of prize giveaways, and radio promotions, just to name a few. A brief sampling of some of the more common clever "tagline" examples included:

- *Chesterfield*: "No Unpleasant After-taste to the world's most famous A, B, C's of Always Milder, Better Tasting, Cooler Smoking."
- *Lucky Strike* or "Luckies" were: "Cleaner, Fresher, Smoother and Nothing Tastes Better."

- *Camels*: "These smokers gave CAMELS 30-<u>Year</u> Mildness Tests," and "I'd Walk a Mile for a Camel."
- *Encore*: "Filters the Smoke but <u>not</u> the taste."
- *Pall Mall* "Reward yourself with the pleasures of smoking.—Outstanding and they are Mild!
- *Pall Mall* advertised: "Guard Against Throat-Scratch. Enjoy the <u>smooth smoking</u> of fine tobaccos—the *<u>finest quality</u> money can buy!*"

(*Note*: Capitalization and underlines are as they appeared in the ads.)

The advertisers hired pop- culture figures such as NFL football player Frank Gifford for Lucky Strikes; TV icon Lucille Ball for Philip Morris; Hollywood starlet Joan Crawford for Chesterfield; and rugged actor John Wayne for Camels. Celebrities such as actor James Dean and entertainer Frank Sinatra were rarely pictured without a cigarette either in hand or dangling from their mouths. Much of the advertising hinted at sexual pleasure. One such example was a Chesterfield ad promoted by Sinatra. The ad asked, "Like Your Pleasure Big?" The response adjacent to Sinatra was, "Man-size Satisfaction, Clean, smooth, fresh!" Notable actor and future U.S. president Ronald Reagan promoted, "My cigarette is the <u>MILD</u> cigarette, that's why Chesterfield is my favorite." The truth is none of the products were mild, pleasurable, smooth, or any other advertising jingo the ads promised. In truth they were all a fabrication; quite simply, the spokespersons were either ignorant or lying (Halberstam, 197–200).

Yet it was the false advertising that got Americans smoking and it was the addictive nicotine that kept them hooked on the habit. Smoking was certainly one of the most noticeable aspects of 1950s conformity. On the other hand, it was, and still is, one of the worst health hazards ever produced for human consumption. A misnomer existed that Americans smoked because they did not know of any associated danger. On the contrary, evidence of the destructive dangers of smoking did in fact exist and were widely publicized. According to a Stanford University report prepared by Dr. Robert N. Proctor: "Scholars started noting the parallel rise in cigarette consumption and lung cancer and by the 1930s had begun to investigate this relationship." In fact, research and evidence did exist and became more prevalent during the 1950s. The first test cases involved the connection with lung cancer and those who smoked (Proctor, n.p.).

A *CNN* article titled "Tobacco History" claimed that the first to bring public attention to the dangers of smoking was the widely circulated monthly magazine *Reader's Digest*. The magazine had a national following in small towns as well as the big cities. Beginning in December 1952, the magazine published a series of articles in the following months titled "Cancer by the Carton." The article positively linked "linked smoking with lung cancer." In 1953, the widely circulated national publications of both *Life* and *Time* magazines also devoted multiple pages to a research study that the hazards of smoking were proven "beyond any doubt." Similar language, as well as the severe dangers, was echoed the following year.

In 1954 researchers employed by the tobacco manufacturers concluded that the "odds of dying from lung cancer" increased dramatically for those who smoked. The incidence was also high among those who lived or worked in areas where they were subjected to "second-hand smoke." The conclusions were stated as "proven beyond a reasonable doubt." That same year, the American Cancer Society announced to the public "available evidence indicates an association between smoking, particularly cigarette smoking, and lung cancer." Despite credible evidence on the severity of the dangers of smoking, the tobacco manufacturers did not release their own research information to the public (Proctor, n.p.).

The initial reactions to the dangers of smoking did cause concern among both the public and tobacco manufacturers. So much to the point that some Americans stopped smoking and the overall stock prices of the big companies declined. In response, the most prominent of the large tobacco manufacturers gathered at the swank Plaza Hotel in Manhattan. The meeting resulted in a concerted agreement, which in effect was to simply deny the validity of the studies. A counter-campaign employing many of the same "trusted" celebrities and health professionals continued to promote not only the "pleasures" of smoking, but also the "safety." The counter campaign worked as smoking among the American public continually rose from the declining period of 1953 to a steady rise until 1982.

Many "confidential surveys" performed by tobacco manufacturers such as Philip Morris and RJ Reynolds concluded that their product was indeed dangerous and a cancer-causing commodity. Throughout it all, a complete sense of ignorance was displayed by the smoking public. More than half of all doctors and health professionals smoked, many while conducting an examination. Through it all, the advertisers continued with a barrage of healthy and happy individuals who "enjoyed the pleasures" attained by smoking.

The effects of the studies from the 1950s was the impetus for a 1964 U.S. Surgeon General report that warned of the health hazards. Although the manufacturers were aware of benzo[a]pyrene and "several dozen carcinogens" in their product such as "arsenic, chromium, nickel and polycyclic aromatic hydrocarbons" the results were kept from the consumers. An additional known fact was the overwhelming substance addiction caused by nicotine in the product, as well as the hundreds of thousands of excruciating deaths caused by emphysema. Smoking is the overwhelming cause of emphysema, which is a chronic condition that severely damages the lungs and drastically shortens life expectancy. Smokers with emphysema require continuous oxygen support to avoid suffocation. Death is often slow and painful.

Nearer the end of the 20th century, the rates of smoking declined, but it was still prevalent and cigarettes were a profitable consumer product within American society. A 2013 survey by the Center for Disease Control (CDC) and the U.S. Department of Health and Human Services (updated in October 2015) listed the following:

Tobacco use remains the single largest preventable cause of death and disease in the United States. Cigarette smoking kills more than 480,000 Americans each year, with more than 41,000 of these deaths from exposure to secondhand smoke. In addition, smoking-related illness in the United States costs more than $300 billion a year, including nearly $170 billion in direct medical care for adults and $156 billion in lost productivity. (Center for Disease Control, October 2015)

Selective memory often eliminates any remembrance of bad times. In all cases, it also forgets the filthy and dangerous aspect of either the highly addictive smoking habit or the awful smell. A good example was provided by famed American author Stephen King in his novel *11/22/63* (Gallery Books, 2012). King provided a "time travel" trip back to the late 1950s. In providing a historical setting to his story, he replicated some often forgotten common everyday occurrences, as he placed his main character back to the year 1958. It was soon discovered "they had forgotten how the past smelled" (36).

HOWDY DOODY, WALT DISNEY, AND THE TV CHILDREN'S MARKET

Advertising agencies also targeted children and teenagers as a separate demographic for the purchase of all sorts of toys, phonographs, record albums, transistor radios, magazines, clothing, and soft drinks, among dozens of other products. One of the most popular children's television shows to take advantage of the post-war advertising boom was *The Howdy Doody Show*. As children were entertained by the likable array of characters, the show was responsible for demonstrating the power of the new TV media format to sell consumer products. In an article for the Museum of Broadcast Communications, Suzanne Rautiolla-Williams wrote, "While Howdy and his friends entertained American children, they also sold television sets to American parents and demonstrated the potential of the new medium to advertisers" ("Howdy Doody," n.p.).

As television was in its developmental stage and tracking systems such as the Nielsen ratings were just beginning, *The Howdy Doody Show* inadvertently discovered a unique TV advertising phenomenon. As an educational program, the show once offered a lesson in the American presidential election policy. Prior to the final election results in 1948, Howdy Doody proclaimed that he was running for "President of all the kids." The idea was to provide the young viewers with the basic concept of how to elect a president of the United States. To replicate the national campaigns of Truman, Dewey, and Thurmond, the producers offered free campaign buttons for the viewing audience. No one foresaw the potential of a simple request sent out over the TV airwaves. In a short time, children mailed in more than 60,000 requests, delivered by the U.S. Postal Service directly to the production studios. The overwhelming numbers of mail requests added up to about one-third of all the TV sets in American homes up to that time. That was most likely the first time that anyone was able to know the actual number of people watching a particular program. As a result, the mail-in event provided the producers with solid evidence to sell commercial advertising time to sponsors interested in selling only children's products. The astute producers also encouraged the writers to incorporate consumer product messages and also display the products within the scheduled programs. In combination with selling commercial airtime, the producers also sold merchandising specific to *The Howdy Doody Show* cast and characters.

Products such as a Howdy Doody comic book published by Dell in 1949 sold well into the 1950s. Soon all sorts of merchandising such as hats, t-shirts, and various toys were licensed and sold to a wanting children's audience ("Howdy Doody," n.p.).

When it came to marketing children's merchandising on television, however, none could have foreseen the power of Walt Disney. In 1954, Walt Disney sought to bring a dream to life with the opening of a theme park in California (see Legacy chapter). In seeking financial backing for his construction project, Disney partnered with ABC-TV. In return, he agreed to produce a weekly children's variety type show. At first, the TV show was titled *Disneyland* (1954–1958), later *Walt Disney Presents* (1958–1961), and throughout its run from the fall of 1961 to 2008 as *The Wonderful World of Disney*. One of the proposed limited features was *The Adventures of Davy Crockett* with actor Fess Parker hired to play the lead role. For unexplained reasons, the program created an unexpected large popularity among its young audience. The young audience also looked to copy some of Davy Crockett's TV props, creating a large merchandising fad for coonskin caps. The potential for a continuing stream of both in-store merchandising and advertising dollars led to an extension of the Crockett features for two additional seasons. The success of the program also added to the growing interest in the new Disneyland theme park. Soon thereafter, all sorts of merchandise associated with Disney were produced, marketed, and sold to its young viewing audience.

TV ADVERTISING FOR THE ELECTION OF A U.S. PRESIDENT

In 1952, the American presidential election process was forever changed by corporate advertising. As Truman's term neared an end, the race was between Republican candidate Dwight D. Eisenhower (1890–1969) and the Democratic candidate Adlai E. Stevenson (1900–1965). During the course of the election, one of Eisenhower's top strategists was Rosser Reeves of the Ted Bates Advertising Agency. During his advertising career, Reeves came up with the idea of "Unique Selling Proposition" or "USP." (A USP, sometimes known as a Unique Selling Point, concentrated on what differentiated one product from another.) With the Eisenhower campaign, Reeves decided to break from the so-called "clutter" of the print media with a series of televised promotional ads. The idea was to provide the American public with a unique, private moment with General Dwight D. Eisenhower. Reeves arranged for a prerecorded spot by Eisenhower, who appeared to be speaking directly to individuals within the comforts of their own living rooms. Some of the television spots did not mention the military rank, but stressed his Midwestern roots as "The Man from Abilene." Some other commercial spots proclaimed the former wartime general as a "Man of Peace." Eisenhower did win the election handily, earning 442 electoral votes and 39 states carried as compared to Stevenson's 89 electoral votes and 9 states carried. The new age of television and the dominant news and advertising medium was also evident as the inauguration in 1953 of newly elected President Eisenhower was the first ever aired on nationwide live television.

Some critics, although few in number, thought Reeves had denigrated the political office by selling it just like any other consumer product of the time. Regardless, in the television age, the presidential election process was definitely a time when appearances such as marriage and family were very important to an overtly conservative American population. Eisenhower was often pictured with his wife Mamie (1896–1969). On the other side of the political candidacy, Adlai Stevenson was trying to downplay his own marital status. Stevenson, the former governor of Illinois, was divorced. At the time, candidates needed to promote the ideas of being happily married and American family values. At the time, future journalist Gloria Steinem was a young college student working on the Stevenson for President campaign. In later years, she wrote of the discorded nature of American public perception: Steinem recalled:

> Altogether, this Stevenson for President office was the most open and welcoming place I'd ever been. But one Saturday when I and the other young women arrived, we found ourselves stashed away on an upper floor. We were devastated. A staffer explained that Stevenson himself might drop in and must not be seen with any female unless she was old enough to be his mother. After all, he was that terrible thing—divorced—something no president had ever been. Though everyone seemed to know that Eisenhower had imported the beautiful young English woman [his mistress Kay Summersby] who was his driver during the war—and even arranged for her U.S. citizenship—he would have his wife, Mamie, as a proper First Lady. Appearances were all that mattered. (Steinem [2015], 131)

The irony of the contrast between the marital situations of Stevenson and Eisenhower was very much reflective of the societal values of the 1950s. At the time, simply put, a man's infidelity was not considered a scandal as long as he did not divorce.

NON-COMMERCIAL TELEVISION NEWS AND EDWARD R. MURROW

Throughout the 1950s, most Americans still received their news from daily newspapers. The idea of receiving daily news in print form slowly shifted towards a televised format. One the foundations for television news was *See It Now* with on-air host Edward R. Murrow (1908–1965). Throughout its history, *See It Now,* co-produced by Murrow and Fred W. Friendly (1915–1998), was a model of the news programs that maintained the utmost of journalistic integrity. Prior to the television era, Murrow was well known to the American people as a radio newscaster. Before the United States was involved in the war, he had provided live radio eyewitness reports to the American public during the German bombings of London in 1939–1940. He continued similar reporting throughout war-torn Europe and the Pacific. He transitioned into broadcast television with a legacy of having earned the trust of the American public. The Museum of Broadcast Communications stated that *See It Now* "remains the standard by which broadcast journalism is judged for its courage and commitment" (Simon, n.p.).

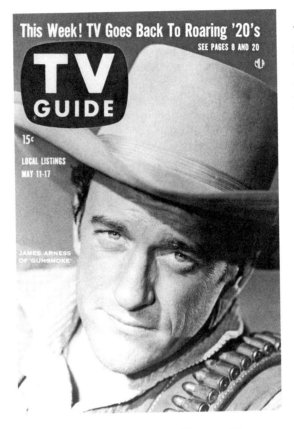

By 1959, *TV Guide* was the #1-selling weekly magazine in America with a combination of newsstand and home subscriptions totaling over 25 million per week. This issue from May 1957 featured actor James Arness from the TV western *Gunsmoke*, which replaced *I Love Lucy* as the top-rated TV show from 1957 through 1960. (Photofest)

The Archive of American Television added, "CBS News in particular established a protocol for television reporting—airing stories about topical, political and worldwide events that impacted its viewers. Plus, each night, viewers could see the newsmen they had trusted for years." Both Friendly and Murrow collaborated on the editorial content and are credited as "inventing the magazine news format" on network television. Without interference from a commercial sponsor, Murrow and Friendly could concentrate solely of journalistic content. The format was allowed to happen as the federal government mandated specific time slots for non-commercial editorial programming. The idea of non-commercial news programs held through most of the 1950s, but slowly gave way to the networks including commercials to make each program profitable venture. By the late 1950s, and well into the 21st century, journalistic integrity gave way to securing commercial advertising dollars to stay viable ("TV History," n.p.).

TV GUIDE: THE MAGAZINE FOR TELEVISION

One of the most popular television shows of the time, *I Love Lucy*, coincided with the rise in a major magazine heralding television. The stars of the show, Lucille Ball ("Lucy") and Desi Arnaz ("Ricky"), were married in real life and during the filming she became pregnant with their first child. (Their actual child did not appear on the series; the role was played by various child actors.) The real-life birth was written into the fictional script and was soon responsible for launching the most popular weekly magazine throughout America—*TV Guide Magazine*. Prior to April 1953, *TV Guide* was only a regional magazine that provided local listings of scheduled television programing. At the time, as they did throughout the late 20th and early 21st century, television listings were also carried in local newspapers. As the need arose for individuals to locate the numerous TV programs airing at all hours of the day, a new magazine format was launched. Unlike the newspapers, *TV Guide* was devoted solely to television. It offered all sorts of tidbits and stories "of their favorite stars, programs, and listings of the network schedule" (Logan, n.p.).

At the onset, *TV Guide* was only available in 10 of the largest American cities. It did attain a respectable first week circulation of 1.56 million copies. Later that year, circulation was extended to a total of 15 cities. The sales of the magazine soon equated to about the same number of TV households throughout the nation. During its first year the weekly circulation slowly moved up and down. By the end of the decade it was the number-one selling weekly magazine all over America, with a combination of newsstand and home subscriptions totaling over 25 million per week (Kammen, 182).

TV Guide went national with its first issue dated April 3, 1953, featuring a cover with the real-life baby of Lucille Ball and Desi Arnaz, claiming Desi Jr. was "Lucy's $50,000,000 Baby." (Their child was named "Desiderio Alberto Arnaz IV" but was known to all as "Desi Jr.") In a released statement to coincide with the 60th anniversary of the magazine, credit was given to that particular issue that "helped make *TV Guide Magazine* a hit right out of the box." The *I Love Lucy* show was already a major success at the time, but the birth episode did provide a boost in the ratings and soon turned in higher profits. The public mania with Lucy became even more widespread as the birth of her child amounted to an advertising merchandising bonanza. All sorts of dolls, games, books, and nursery items, including maternity wear patterned after those Lucy wore on TV were gobbled up by the American public. Desi even sang a song he wrote titled "There's a Brand New Baby in Our House," which also sold well as an individual record (Logan, n.p.).

THE TV DINNER'S IMPACT ON EVERYDAY LIFE

Although the term "Golden Age of Television" was sometimes applied in the early 21st century as the "Second Golden Age," the 1950s were a golden age for vastly different reasons. It was television as a vehicle for commercial advertising that changed Americans' leisure pursuits in the same manner that the automobile had in previous decades. Unlike the automobile, which allowed the freedom to roam far away from the home, with television, people stayed home. Many accounts indicate that the entire family, and sometimes neighbors, would all gather together to watch television. Studies showed when the television was turned on family conversations stopped and that television also interfered with the traditional family dinner hour. In connection with the new fascination was the promotion by advertising agencies of the frozen "TV Dinner."

The first prepackaged dinners appeared shortly after the end of the war. In 1945, Maxson Food Systems is known to have manufactured the earliest complete frozen meal for airline passengers, but called them "Strato-Plates." Others, such as Frozen Dinners, Inc., provided similar products by 1949. Although the true origin is unclear, the Science Reference Services at the

Library of Congress attribute C.A. Swanson & Son in 1953 (commonly known as "Swanson's") as the first company to coin the phrase and market it as a "TV Dinner." The following year, Swanson's launched a large advertising campaign with the trademark name of TV Dinner. Regardless, the advent of the frozen dinner was purely a byproduct of television itself ("Who Invented the T.V. Dinner," n.p.).

As a pre-prepared frozen meal, the TV dinner could be served much quicker and without the arduous preparation of a conventional dinner. Simply put, it was a pre-packaged frozen entrée, usually accompanied by a potato, vegetable, and a small dessert. The food was compartmentalized in an aluminum tray that was kept frozen in one of the new consumer products of the time known as a refrigerator/freezer. When needed, the frozen dinner was thawed and heated in a conventional oven. The heated dinner was usually placed on a snack tray and eaten while watching television. Eric Foner, in *The Story of American Freedom*, cited a contemporary food writer named Poppy Cannon, who in 1953 claimed the frozen dinner offered the post-war American housewife "freedom from tedium, space, work, and [her] own inexperience" (266).

SAUL BASS: *THE MAN WITH THE GOLDEN ARM*

A prominent, often overlooked, aspect of the art of filmmaking was the opening title sequence and the posters advertising the movie itself. During the 1950s, Saul Bass (1920–1996) provided a major change in the advertising and design of both the opening movie credits and advertising posters of the film industry. Born in New York City, Bass was a graphic designer with notable accomplishments in not only the film world, but also in the world of advertising. His most visual and long-lasting advertising work was for the design of corporate logos that included Alcoa Aluminum, AT&T, Continental Airlines, Quaker Oats, United Airlines, the United Way, and Warner Communications, among dozens of others. Bass used his innovative ideas and unique perspective of the world to influence his art. He engaged his audience with his work and in turn reshaped the graphic design industry. Biographer Alex Bigman, writing for *99designs,* said, "Saul Bass might be the single most accomplished graphic designer in history." As for the transition from an advertising logo to the realm of movie posters and title sequences, Bigman added, "Bass stepped up the sophistication of movie posters with his distinctive minimal style and he completely revolutionized the role of title credits in films" ("Saul Bass," n.p.).

Some of his most famous "advertising" work with the movie industry occurred during the 1950s. They included Otto Preminger's *The Man with the Golden Arm* (1955) and two Alfred Hitchcock classics, *Vertigo* (1958) and *North by Northwest* (1959). Although technically not within the 1950s, Bass also worked on Hitchcock's *Psycho* (1960). In 1968, Bass was featured on the premiere episode of the long-running prime-time television series *60 Minutes* in a segment called "Why Man Creates." As he ventured into other areas of graphic design, he continued working on film projects. During the early 1990s, his final work was for a series of iconic Martin Scorsese films: *Goodfellas* (1990), *Cape Fear* (1991), *The Age of Innocence* (1993), and *Casino* (1995). In addition to revamping title sequences and poster design, Bass's early work also included the developmental process of creating "storyboards." The storyboard was similar to a comic book in that the sequence of scenes for the movie story was illustrated in a sequential set of drawings. The drawings served as a tool for planning scene blocking, locations, and details in the production process. Often, the storyboard artist provided their own interpretation of the visual representation of the written script. For Saul Bass, his creative techniques were often incorporated with the movies themselves (Bigman, n.p.).

Prior to Bass, movie credits were often displayed on static screens. Those same titles did not have any type of flair or provide any attachment to the story. For the most part, the title sequence was not considered an important part of the creative movie process. More often than not, the opening credits were projected upon a set of closed curtains. When the credits finished, the curtains opened for the movie shown upon a projection screen. In contrast to the minimal approach to originality, Bass incorporated his graphic design knowledge to make the title sequence an actual part of the movie. In essence, his credits literally "set the stage" or more succinctly, "set the tone" for the upcoming story. To eliminate the problem of projection upon curtains, Bass provided special instructions for the "projectionist [to] pull curtain before titles." He developed what has often been described as his own "kinetic type" to enhance the movie going experience. (Kinetic refers to "movement" and that is exactly what Bass provided—movement of the text.) He also added other imagery and a soundtrack.

Bass's work in film came at the request of an independent producer/director named Otto Preminger (1905–1986). As Preminger was set for his 1953 release of *The Moon Is Blue*, he objected to the movie poster designed by United Artists who would distribute the film. Preminger felt the images and style portrayed the movie as "pornographic." Prior to the initial screenings of the movie, Preminger knew full well that imagery of that kind combined with a taboo subject could be extremely detrimental to a wide release. Therefore, Preminger hired Saul Bass to provide an alternative movie poster.

It was the 1956 release of Otto Preminger's *The Man with the Golden Arm* that was the ultimate artistic and advertising controversy for many reasons. The new artistic style of the opening credits of Saul Bass alone would be enough for an analysis of its use in the opening title sequence and graphics. The poster design for *The Man with the Golden Arm* provided Bass with certain challenges that placed him in direct contrast to the widely-held social decorum of the day. The situation was described by biographer Pat Kirkham:

> The challenge facing Saul was how to create a symbol that captured the drama and intensity of the film without resorting to sensationalism. He created an arresting image of a distorted, disjointed arm. The semi-abstract form helped distance the image from the harsh realities of shooting up, although they are implicit in the (dis) figuration. As well as being disconnected from a body, the black arm has the appearance of being petrified and transformed into something else, just as the Sinatra character in the film is transformed by his addiction. (Bass and Kirkham, 12)

But other items of controversy beyond the advertising poster included the subject matter, soundtrack, the director, and its star.

Saul Bass was a graphic designer with a long history of designing corporate logos for advertising. During the 1950s, he changed the way movie advertisement posters were designed. Shown here is one of his works during the time for Otto Preminger's *The Man with the Golden Arm* (1955). (Photofest)

New York Times critic Bosley Crowther added that despite opposition from the Catholic League of Decency (which Crowther called "that parochial disapproval"), he suggested that there should not "be any question about showing [the movie]." He described the basic plot as reflecting a real-life premise of "one man's battle to beat a craving for dope." At the time, real-life issues such as drug addiction were simply not talked about. For the most part, all forms of American news outlets and popular culture simply made believe the problem did not exist. Therefore, Crowther felt obliged to educate the public as to certain words used within the film. He told his readers of the word "fix" and described for the supposedly uninitiated to the world of drug addicts. Crowther explained, "A 'fix' in the lingo of the 'junkies' or addicts—is a shot of dope." The denial of real-life drug use was not as bad as the pressures by the distribution companies that requested some of the images for heroin preparation be cut from the film. Once again as explained by Crowther, "This was cut, we understand, to avoid trouble over instructing in the methods of taking dope." Yet the critic felt that the rawness of the sequence was enough to provide a non-drug user with enough "revulsion toward the habit of drugs." And it was that same erratic, uncertain destruction and the unsettling nature of addictive drug use that Saul Bass sought to emote in his poster design (Crowther, "The Man with the Golden Arm," n.p.).

Bass provided a continuum for all other advertising aspects of movies extending well into the 21st century. One of the highest praises was noted in the publication of *George Lucas's Blockbusting*. Editors Block and Wilson wrote:

> [Bass] would go on to reinvent key art—the central image of a movie used for promotional purposes—and develop the first holistic approach to presenting a motion picture. Before Bass's arrival, posters and opening credits had been very functional. They often featured a panorama of characters, a clever gag, or a visual bit. Bass also created imaginative title sequences that were more like little experimental films with great psychological and emotional impact. He saw that the graphic arts could be as artistically important as the fine arts. (335)

TELEVISION AND SEGREGATION

Instances of a backlash against integration are numerous. Television was a prime example, for it simply did not portray any positive images of blacks. The extent of segregation was often enforced by corporate sponsors. One example involved the Texaco Oil Company, which insisted on preventing black performers from appearing on its *Texaco Star Theater* with host Milton Berle. At the time, Berle was the most popular individual on television and his show was the most viewed TV program in the United States. (For more on Berle, see the Television chapter.) In defiance to his sponsors, Berle risked his stardom and defied the sponsor's request. At the time, it was not just sponsors that maintained rigid ideas of segregation, but southern television affiliates did not air programs that featured any black performers. In 1974, in his autobiography co-written with author Haskel Frankel, Berle recalled:

> I remember clashing with the advertising agency and the sponsor over my signing the Four Step Brothers [a famed dance team] for an appearance on the show. The only thing I could figure out was that there was an objection to black performers on the show, but I couldn't even find out who was objecting. "We just don't like them," I was told, but who the hell was "we"? Because I was riding high in 1950, I sent out the word: "If they don't go on, I don't go on." At ten minutes of eight—ten minutes before showtime—I got permission for the Step Brothers to appear. If I broke the color-line policy or not, I don't know, but later on I had no trouble booking [dancer] Bill Robinson or [singer] Lena Horne. (285)

Another notable example involved the very popular Alan Freed (see Music chapter). By the late 1950s, Freed had a growing nationwide following, mainly among teens and young adults who embraced Rock 'n' Roll. In July 1957, Freed was offered a television dance show titled *Alan Freed's Big Beat*. The weekly half hour intended to bring the flavor of his theater stage shows to a nationwide audience. However, an innocent incident involving dancing led to furor and subsequent cancellation after the third show. One segment featured the affable and energetic Frankie Lymon (1942–1968), an established Rock 'n' Roll singing star who had many hits with his group The Teenagers including

"Why Do Fools Fall I Love," "I'm Not a Juvenile Delinquent," and "Goody Goody." The energetic Lymon was positioned on a raised platform in the middle of some dancing teenagers. At one point, Lymon innocently reached down into the audience and brought up a young white girl to dance a jitterbug. The producers were appalled, especially ABC's southern affiliates, at the so-called "blatant" disregard for the rules of segregation. The show was cancelled immediately (Jackson, 55–56).

"PAYOLA"

In 1959, both Alan Freed and Dick Clark were national celebrities, each hosted a major network TV show, and also hosted a radio program. Yet the innocence of Rock 'n' Roll music and the coming together of the teenagers regardless of race was not lost upon the larger political world. In 1959, the U.S. Congressional House Oversight Committee began to look into deejays who took gifts from record companies in return for playing their records on their shows. The practice, known as "Payola," was quite common in the music business. In its simplest terms, a record promoter provided cash payment for a radio disc jockey to play a new record on the air. Some called it a "bribe," others said it was a simple "gratuity." In either case, it was apparently common and no actual laws prevented the custom. Within one year, the Oversight Committee questioned more than 300 disc jockeys. Many of the radio disc jockeys admitted accepting money; most said it was as a "consulting fee." Despite the fact that many were accused of Payola, the Oversight Committee only subpoenaed Freed to testify. He was offered immunity, but refused to testify. Freed, who at the time commanded major media attention, said, "What they call payola in the disc jockey business, they call lobbying in Washington" (Miller, *Flowers in the Dustbin*, 83).

As the investigations received more and more media attention, both Clark and Freed came under closer scrutiny. ABC-TV was concerned that advertising sponsorship would suffer. At the time, both were under contract to ABC and were asked to sign a statement confirming they had never accepted payola. Clark signed and also divested his financial interests in various record production holdings. Clark escaped without harming his career, as did almost all of the others. In contrast, Freed refused to sign "on principle" and was fired. A front-page banner headline in the *New York Daily News* of September 1960 announced:

WABC FIRES
ALAN FREED IN
'PAYOLA' PROBE

Freed lost his radio show on September 21, 1959, and also his *Big Beat* television show on November 23, 1959. Without a job, Freed was forced to leave New York. He worked briefly in 1960 at a few radio stations such as KDAY in Los Angeles, California. For a time, he also worked on-air at WQAM in Miami, Florida.

On February 8, 1960, his complications mounted as he was informed that a New York grand jury also would investigate Freed's involvement in the recording industry. On May 19, 1960, he was among eight men charged with receiving "illegal gratuities." This probe would lead to Freed being charged with income tax evasion by the IRS. A criminal trial began in December 1962. He eventually pleaded guilty to numerous counts of commercial bribery. His sentencing was light as he received a six-month suspended sentence and required to pay a $300 fine. But by that time, the media attention was overwhelming and his professional career was effectively over. His career might have been finished, but not his troubles. The accusations against Freed mounted, including the IRS claiming income tax evasion due to the unreported income for the years 1957–59. A federal grand jury indicted him on March 15, 1964, for tax evasion. His trial never materialized as his health failed. In January 1965, Freed died in Palm Springs, California, at the age of 43 (Fong-Torres, n.p.).

FURTHER READING

David Halberstam. *The Fifties.* New York: Metro Books, 2001.

Michael Kammen. *American Culture American Tastes: Social Change and the 20th Century.* New York: Basic Books, 1999.

Charles Panati. *Panati's Parade of Fads, Follies, and Manias.* New York: Harper Collins, 1991.

Bernard Rosenberg and David Manning White, eds. *Mass Culture: The Popular Arts in America.* Wilmington, IL: The Free Press, 1957.

This Fabulous Century: 1950–1960. Vol. 6. New York: Time-Life Books, 1970.

Stephen J. Whitfield. *The Culture of the Cold War.* 2nd edition. Baltimore, MD: Johns Hopkins University Press, 1996.

William H. Young and Nancy K. Young. *The 1950s.* American Popular Culture Through History series. Westport, CT: Greenwood Press, 2004.

CHAPTER 10

Controversies

When analyzing a controversy from the time period such as the 1950s, a reasonably intelligent person might find it a bit perplexing as to many major issues in society that were not exactly controversial, but rather widely accepted in American society. The first step is to actually define the word "controversy." The definitive American source for word definitions since 1828 is the *Merriam-Webster Dictionary*. An online search from Merriam-Webster.com defines it as:

> "An argument that involves many people who strongly disagree about something: strong disagreement about something among a large group of people."

A comparative scholarly source is the *Oxford Dictionary*, compiled by Oxford University Press that defines "controversy" as:

> "Disagreement, typically when prolonged, public, and heated."

Yet when providing information on so-called controversial issues such as anti-semitism, civil rights, female equality, gay rights, nuclear disarmament, public access for the disabled, religious toleration, and segregation, among many others, it can come as quite a surprise that the issues were more widely accepted as part of an American way of life than not. In fact, most of these human rights issues were kept out of mainstream American society by laws enacted at the local, state, and even federal levels.

During the 1950s, the issues were not necessarily "controversial" because a public debate either "for" and "against" an issue was not always adequately provided to the American public. A major reason was the prevalent atmosphere of the Red Scare perpetuated by Senator Joseph McCarthy. In just about all ways possible, McCarthyism completely suppressed any ideas of free speech or counter argument. As described by cultural historian David Hajdu,

"McCarthyism, a movement out of the heartland to purge the country of modes of thinking associated with Northeastern intelligentsia and the New Deal, was a form of anti-elitism as well as anti-Communism" (210). Some cases such as the *Brown v. The Board of Education of Topeka Kansas* Supreme Court decision did garner major media attention such as a banner headline in *The New York Times.* Yet, for the most part, resistance to segregation was widely accepted and did not begin to make headway into the mainstream until federal legislation occurred during the 1960s, 1970s, and beyond. At the same time, many of the aforementioned issues did exist, and the American response is often quite surprising.

LENNY BRUCE AND THE FIRST AMENDMENT

As the 1950s presented experimentation in all sorts of the arts such as abstract expressionism, Rock 'n' Roll, and be-bop jazz, to name a few, so did stand-up comedy by way of Lenny Bruce (1925–1966). He worked mainly in small venues such as jazz and burlesque clubs and attracted a faithful following as a "hip" and "rebellious" individual speaking against the social conformity of the time. In his autobiography, Bruce described the mid-1950s as a time for experimentation. He wrote: "Four years working in clubs—that's what really made it for me. Every night: doing it, doing it, doing it, getting bored and doing different ways, no pressure . . . so I could try anything" (Kifner, n.p.). The comedy routines performed by Bruce often pushed the boundaries of free speech, as he often incorporated what the court briefs later labeled as "obscene." By 1957, Bruce had developed a reputation as an edgy, innovative comedian. One of his most noteworthy sketches was "Religions, Inc." Within the routine he was critical of real-life religious leaders such as the Pope and the Reverend Billy Graham, whom Bruce said existed to fleece money from the faithful. The denouncement of religion was not as objectionable, at least in the courts, as was Bruce's use of the words considered "obscene" by the courts (Kifner, n.p.).

Bruce's reputation slowly gained national attention. In response, he was offered an appearance on the popular Steve Allen television show on April 9, 1959. Allen introduced Bruce "as the most shocking comedian of our time, a young man who is skyrocketing to fame—Lenny Bruce!" In February 1961, as his career was skyrocketing, Bruce appeared at the famous Carnegie Hall. The following year he was arrested on criminal obscenity charges and put on trial. In the trial defense, his attorney continually cited the First Amendment right to free speech. The irony of the arrests is that Bruce performed inside private clubs among adults who had paid for and knew full well the language content. In 1964, Bruce was put through a series of heavily publicized "obscenity" trials in New York and California. He was found guilty, but was free on bond as he formulated an appeal. Bruce spent most of the time filing countersuits. Within a few years, however, he died of a morphine overdose on August 3, 1966, in California.

In December 2003 in a *New York Times* story, "No Joke! 37 Years After Death Lenny Bruce Receives Pardon," journalist John Kifner described Bruce as "the potty-mouthed wit who turned stand-up comedy into social commentary."

Even into the 21st century, Bruce's legacy remained. In addition, the words of contention that called him "potty-mouthed" were still deemed objectionable for journalists. The focus in the story did concern a posthumous pardon that was declared by New York governor George Pataki—37 years after the fact. It is a wonder that the governor could even declare with all honesty that he believed the pardon was "a declaration of New York's commitment to upholding the 1st Amendment." In summation, at least Kifner injected a bit of satire, as he noted, "Being dead [since August 1966], Mr. Bruce is not expected to reap any immediate benefit from the pardon" (n.p.).

   Lenny Bruce was just one of many non-conformists, and therefore controversial figures of the time. Some other people and items that were also noteworthy included the following:

- **Dorothy Day** (1897–1980): Pacifist, journalist, and social activist; founder of the Catholic Worker Movement. On September 24, 2015, Pope Francis lauded praise upon Day as a positive representation "of the American people . . . using their dreams of justice, equal rights, liberty and peace to make America a better place." The Pontiff added, "Her social activism, her passion for justice and for the cause of the oppressed, were inspired by the Gospel, her faith, and the example of the saints." Day was instrumental in the publication of the *Catholic Worker* and in support of workers' rights and human dignity. In June 1955, she made headlines as she was arrested for failing to "take cover" during a nationwide civil defense drill. She was part of a group that handed out pamphlets stating: "We will not obey this order to pretend, to evacuate, to hide. In view of the certain knowledge the administration of this country has that there is no defense in atomic warfare, we know this drill to be a military act in a cold war to instill fear."

- **Christine Jorgensen** (1926–1989): The December 1, 1952, front page headline of the *New York Daily News* described it: "EX-GI BECOMES BLONDE BEAUTY. Operations Transform Bronx Youth." At that time, George Jorgensen, a former serviceman and professional photographer, "underwent gender reassignment surgery in Copenhagen, Denmark, to change from a male to a female." The *Daily News* claimed that this was the first operation of its kind in history. In preparation for the gender change, Jorgensen had begun hormone treatments in early 1950 and continued until 1952. In 1955, as Christine, she returned to the United States as a minor celebrity touring nightclubs.

- **Health and Hygiene Films:** Short educational films that were 10 to 15 minutes in length were shown to millions of American high school students during the 1940s and 1950s. Ken Smith, writing in *The New York Times*, said, "[T]hese films preached the joys of domesticity and uniformity." At the time, social theorists and educators believed that teenagers were "social mimics who would imitate whatever behavior they saw acted out onscreen." Therefore, films such as *What Makes a Good Party?* (1950) and *Mind Your Manners!* (1953) demonstrated to high school students life "not as it was," but rather as adults wanted life to be like. Other diverse subjects included reckless driving in *Last Date* (1950); social manners in *Right or Wrong or Wrong?* (1951); drug use, specifically marijuana, in *The Terrible Truth* (1951); and the self-explanatory *Lunchroom Manners* (1959).

- **Marguerite Higgins** (1920–1966): Female correspondent and journalist who achieved distinction as a war correspondent during the Korean War. At first, she was ordered out of the conflict because the U.S. Army declared "war was no place for a woman." Higgins disregarded the gender discrimination and stayed in Korea. As a result of her journalistic integrity and news coverage, not her gender, she was awarded a Pulitzer Prize for international reporting in 1951. She was so close to the action that while covering the French military in Vietnam in 1953, she was wounded by a land mine explosion that killed a colleague.

- **Martin Luther King** (1929–1968): Minister and a well-known historical American civil rights leader who achieved national prominence in his role during the 1955–1956 Montgomery Bus Boycott. Of Dr. King, Pope Francis said, "I think of the march which Martin Luther King led from Selma to Montgomery fifty years ago [1963] as part of the campaign to fulfill his 'dream' of full civil and political rights for African Americans."

- **Thomas Merton** (1915–1968): Known mainly through his writings on such diverse topics as civil rights, nuclear disarmament, theology, poetry, social justice, and peace. He had a wide following during the 1950s with the autobiographical *The Seven Storey Mountain* (1948) and tales of religious life in *Seeds of Contemplation* (1949). In all he authored more than 70 books. He was praised by Pope Francis in September 2015. The Pontiff said, "Merton was above all a man of prayer, a thinker who challenged the certitudes of his time and opened new horizons for souls and for the Church. He was also a man of dialogue, a promoter of peace between peoples and religions." Similar to Dorothy Day, he was a Catholic convert who became a Trappist monk promoting peace.

- **I.F. "Izzy" Stone** (1907–1989): Known as "a radically liberal journalist in the 1950s when there were not many leftists in any field." At the age of 14, he started his own newspaper, *The Progress*, later working for several newspapers as an investigative journalist. In 1952, he wrote *The Hidden History of the Korean War* that claimed that although the official war was listed as "June 25, 1950–July 27, 1953," American troops had occupied Korea since 1945. (Of note, American troops were still stationed in Korea well into the 21st century.) Also in 1952, Stone published a liberal newspaper *I.F. Stone's Weekly*, which openly criticized the U.S. government. He continued that criticism throughout the decade. Of all the outright suppression of free speech, Stone was never accused of being a Communist, because after a personal visit to the Soviet Union he returned to the United States and published severe criticism of Stalin and Soviet Communism.

- **Norman M. Thomas** (1884–1968): Pacifist, Socialist leader, author, and social critic and an instrumental figure in founding the American Civil Liberties Union (ACLU). His critique of American capitalist society was well respected in numerous media publications including *The World Tomorrow*, which he founded in 1918, and later as an associate editor of *The Nation*. His works include *The Conscientious Objector in America* (1923), *Socialism of Our Time* (1929), *Human Exploitation* (1934), *Appeal to the Nations* (1947), *Socialist's Faith* (1951), *The Test of Freedom* (1954), *The Prerequisite for Peace* (1959), *Great Dissenters* (1961), and *Socialism Reexamined* (1963).

- **Ed Wood** (1924–1978): Film director who made a series of cult films often labeled controversial. He capitalized on the Christine Jorgensen phenomena with his debut as a director with the movie *Glen or Glenda?* (1953). (It was also sometimes titled: *I Changed My Sex*; *I Led Two Lives*; *The Transvestite*; or *He or She.*) Wood starred as the title character, a transvestite named Daniel Davis. The film dealt with a particularly delicate and outright taboo subject of cross-dressing. The film's narrator briefly explained, "Nature makes mistakes, it's proven every day. This person is a transvestite. A man who is more comfortable wearing girl's clothes. The term transvestite is the name given by medical science to those persons who wear the clothing of the opposite sex. Many a transvestite actually wishes to *be* the opposite sex."

HIDDEN WOMEN AND *THE GIRLS WHO WENT AWAY*

During the late 1950s, Buddy Holly achieved widespread fame among teenage fans of Rock 'n' Roll. His musical legacy lived on in many ways including being a major influence for The Beatles and The Rolling Stones. In *Rave On: The Biography of Buddy Holly*, author Phillip Norman provides a truthful and detailed account of the young singer's short but influential life. Yet within the biography is also a grim reality of the acceptable social behavior towards females. In one instance, Norman recounts a typical tale of how violence against women was often an acceptable part of society. A scene is remembered when the young Holly was confronted by a former girlfriend as to paternity of her child. While on a double date at a drive-in movie theater, the unnamed woman told Holly she was pregnant. In the backseat, friend and band mate Niki Sullivan recalled Holly's immediate reaction. Sullivan said, "At that [instant] Buddy hit her. I mean, hit her real hard, so that she jerked forward and hit her head on the windshield. I can still hear the smack it made against the glass." As biographer Norman explained, "But the sad truth is that in the male-dominated late fifties—especially in a place like West Texas—even kindly well-disposed young men saw nothing reprehensible in hitting their girl-friends" (Norman, 134).

Yet unlike later generations when some other options might have been available, the reality during the 1950s was that pregnancy out of wedlock was simply not accepted in society. The usual response for an unmarried pregnancy was to "do the right thing" and get married. Abortion was not discussed and was not readily available. In some cases, the young unwed mother was "sent away" for a time to a so-called "boarding school." The place was one where the young woman could deliver her child and then give the child up for adoption. She would then be allowed to return to her hometown or neighborhood. An excellent recount of this hidden situation is recounted in *The Girls Who Went Away* (Penguin, 2006). Author Ann Fessler makes a compelling argument that the so-called "sexual revolution" of the 1960s actually began during the 1950s. The reason why it was not an overt cultural phenomenon was because of the overly prevalent conformist attitudes of a very conservative acceptable decorum.

Fessler's book does recount the changing dating behavior and rituals from the 1920s, but centers its accounts mainly on the 1950s. Dating rituals began changing in the early 1900s with the widespread commercial use of first, the safety bicycle and shortly thereafter, the automobile. Each offered the freedom for younger individuals to be away from parental chaperoning. Although many instances during the 1920s indicate that the automobile added to the independence of the youth of America, it was not until the 1950s that the "car" allowed true freedom. With the 1950s, the places to park a car such as at a "respectable" drive-in movie theater, burger joint, or even off on dark roads allowed for the complete privacy for a young couple. Within these environments, any sexual encounter could often be kept in secret.

With the unavailability of birth control combined with little or no sex education for females, abstinence was the only safe course. At the time, the society pressures between being labeled a "good girl" or a "bad girl" were dependent upon secrecy. If a pregnancy occurred, discretion was the only option for an unwed young female. Yet the problem of a pregnancy simply had to be erased from all accounts. That erasure in some cases was a dangerous, unsanitary, yet discreet abortion.

It was during the 1950s that abortion as a religious issue came to the forefront. In previous decades such as the early 1940s, abortion was often, as McConnell reminds us, "quietly tolerated." Yet as the proclamation of Christian values was coupled with the fight against Communism, so was the power of religious organizations to shift the repression towards unmarried sexual encounters and contraception. By the late 1940s, McConnell notes, "Safe abortion that had been available, if not always easily so, was suddenly unavailable to the growing numbers of pregnant, unmarried women." And, typical of just about every decade throughout American history, the young men did not suffer any societal consequences. The result for the young man would sometimes include a forced marriage. But in that new acceptable marriage, the man went out to work and was able to engage in many newfound freedoms, while the young woman was confined to the home with the job of rearing the children.

In most of the cases, the only option for any young pregnant girl in that situation was to be "sent away," knowing she would deliver and give up the child for adoption. Of utmost importance, she knew never to speak about the situation. Similar to the fear and paranoia of the Red Scare, the thought of ostracism due to unwed pregnancy was often enough to instill fear in young females to remain abstinent. McConnell writes, "Just so, knowing that disappearance would be their fate if they got pregnant induced sufficient terror to keep most girls in line." Despite the so-called discrete option, usually everyone in the neighborhood or town knew of "something" that had occurred; once again the problem was never openly discussed.

An indication is provided by McConnell's assertion,

Most never recovered from the wrenching loss. In the interviews, woman after woman describes how her personality was forever altered by the experience of giving up a child. The women, many of whom had never told anyone what they had been through until Fessler interviewed them, seem never to have recovered from the shame, the guilt, the secrecy, the inability to achieve intimacy, the sense of being unworthy and forever exiled. Only those who were reunited with their adult children seemed to have achieved some measure of healing. ("The Disappeared," n.p.)

Unmarried, young, pregnant women were not the only individuals hidden from society. Many other women suffered in a hidden situation throughout the growing, affluent, middle-class, American suburban neighborhoods such as Levittown.

KIRCHBERG V. FEENSTRA

Due to carefully enforced segregation, blacks, ethnic minorities, and females had limited access to many of the advantages of a post-war America, including the new suburbia. With hundreds of thousands of new homes in construction the demand for housing was overwhelming. Yet the banks and federal lending agencies sponsored by the FHA and VA refused to provide loans for blacks and women veterans. The economic discrimination also extended to loans and credit of any sort. In fact, females were not legally allowed to obtain credit in their own name until the U.S. Supreme Court decision of *Kirchberg v. Feenstra et al. 450 U.S. 455 (1981)*.

HIDDEN WILLOWBROOK: "AMERICA'S AUSCHWITZ"

During the 1950s, so many of the mentally ill were grossly misdiagnosed. Those who had conditions such as autism, Asperger's, bipolar, dyslexia, cerebral palsy, epilepsy, and schizophrenia, to name a few, were often deemed unsuitable for acceptance into mainstream American society. Many were treated with prescription drugs and almost all were confined to mental institutions, very often by legal decree. Archaic "cures" were often administered, such as electric shock therapy for individuals suffering from depression. That so-called "treatment" was also often cruelly applied to a known homosexual. In the 1950s, it was not uncommon for doctors, often with approval from the legal system, to perform sterilization techniques upon patients suffering from mental retardation. Another common method to "calm down" mentally ill patients was a frontal lobotomy. The archaic procedure involved inserting a metal rod up a patient's nose and severing the frontal lobe portion of the human brain.

Not forgotten, but certainly well hidden, during the 1950s were "the weak, the broken and the mentally crippled." Those individuals were housed at mental institutions such as the infamous Willowbrook State School on Staten Island in New York City. The state-funded "school," which became universally known simply as "Willowbrook," was earmarked during the late 1930s as the "New York State School for Mental Defectives." (The name "Willowbrook" came from the neighborhood of the same name where it was built in the borough of Staten Island in New York City.) Blueprints were completed in January 1940, followed immediately by the start of construction. The opening was curtailed as the onset of the Second World War led to the U.S. government requisitioning the facility for use as a military hospital. With the end of the war, the U.S. military slowly removed its veterans and by April 1951, Willowbrook was restored to the state of New York. Yet, as noted in a published report, "from the start of the post-war years this facility for the retarded was beset with problems, a good deal of it caused by overcrowding and lack of adequate funding, opposition on the part of nearby residents . . . and improper administration" (Greenhouse Consultants, 19–20). The situation of a state facility such as a mental institution built in a local residential neighborhood eventually became known as the NIMBY syndrome, which stood for "Not In My Backyard."

The first of many problems was due to overcrowding; more than 3,600 residents were placed into a facility designed to hold only 2,950. The interred residents ranged in age from infants to adults over the age of 70. Throughout the decade, the overcrowding only worsened. Each month at least 80 to 100 new patients were admitted, all of whom were labeled as "mentally retarded." At least 10 children per week under the age of 5 were part of that monthly number. Many of those children were later found to have been completely misdiagnosed, leading to the institutionalization of children with autism, Asperger's, Down syndrome, dyslexia, and cerebral palsy, among others.

Construction did not outpace, nor did it even begin to alleviate, the problems of which were twofold. First was how to provide adequate facilities and sufficient staff to provide the necessary care. The staff numbered about 2,000, but once again it was not necessarily a problem without a name as much as it was a series of mental afflictions that were both misnamed and misunderstood. It was the second part of the first problem that was insurmountable—acceptance by mainstream American society. In essence, the starting point was naming it the "New York State School for Mental Defectives." The name is certainly indicative of how American society viewed these individuals. The total number of children who were forcibly placed in Willowbrook numbered more than the combined number of children in New York's orphanages. Unlike an orphanage, however, almost all of the infants and children admitted to Willowbrook had known parents. The time period dictated that doctors and administrative professionals recommended that children with mental retardation should not be in a family household, but would be better served while removed from society and placed in an institution. The location of the Willowbrook area of Staten Island turned out to be a perfect "hiding place."

As it was, Staten Island was the perfect hiding place. In 1950, the population among the five boroughs of New York City totaled 7.9 million, making it the largest urban city by a wide margin. Individually, each of the other four boroughs would place on the list of the top ten largest cities by population. Brooklyn was the largest borough (2.6 million); followed by Queens (1.8 million); Manhattan (1.7 million); and Bronx (1.4 million). Staten Island, as a largely suburban borough, counted a mere 192,000 residents (with a marginal increase to 222,000 by 1960). To put those numbers in perspective, in 1950 only five American cities had a population of over one million people and only 20 had over 500,000. Even the paltry population of Staten Island would have placed it at 51st among all cities in America.

But unlike the rest of the city, which had a massive network of interconnected streets and avenues interconnected with a vast metropolitan transportation system of buses and subway system, Staten Island was not physically connected to the rest of the four boroughs. The only connection was by a ferry, which took about 20–30 minutes to reach either Brooklyn or Manhattan. (The Verrazano-Narrows Bridge connection to Brooklyn did not open until 1964.)

Chart 10.1   Population of Largest Urban Places, 1950

Rank	City	Population
1.	New York City	7,891,957
2.	Chicago	3,620,962
3.	Philadelphia	2,071,605
4.	Los Angeles	1,970,358
5.	Detroit	1,849,568
6.	Baltimore	949,708
7.	Cleveland	914,808
8.	St. Louis	856,796
9.	Washington, D.C.	802,178
10.	Boston	801,444

Source: Table 18, Population of the 100 Largest Urban Places 1950, U.S. Bureau of the Census (Internet release date June 15, 1998), www.census.gov/population/www/ documentation/twps0027/tab18.txt. Chart compiled by author.

In addition, the Willowbrook location was within a dense and forested area. Any individual even attempting to drive down what was the main four-lane thoroughfare of Victory Boulevard would be hard-pressed to even see the facility from the road. In addition, as tourism to New York was considered a major attraction throughout all the decades, tourism to Staten Island was virtually non-existent. Willowbrook as both a facility and as a place for children with afflictions thus remained hidden from society.

For the most part, society at large did not care about any individual who was not "normal." As a result, the treatment at Willowbrook was not provided with any sense of decency as the children were living in filth, wallowing in their own feces, and sometimes abused. Nationwide, the U.S. government in collaboration with medical doctors thought it was acceptable to experiment on both disabled people and prison inmates. At Willowbrook, one such experiment included purposely giving the residents hepatitis. Other reports included sterilization as part of a eugenics program. Of the Willowbrook studies such as these, noted vaccine scientist Maurice Hilleman said, "They were the most unethical medical experiments ever performed on children in the United States." Another, bioethicist Art Caplan echoed the outrage, saying, "The Willowbrook studies were a turning point in how we thought about medical experiments in retarded children . . . Children inoculated with hepatitis virus had no chance to benefit from the procedure—only the chance to be harmed" (Offit, 27).

In 1972, however, a photo exposé by TV news journalist Geraldo Rivera brought television cameras into Willowbrook and exposed the deplorable conditions on ABC-TV. (The documentary *Unforgotten: Twenty-Five Years After*

Willowbrook chronicles Rivera's journalistic endeavor.) The result led to a class action lawsuit led by the parents of children housed at Willowbrook. A series of legal actions occurred over a period of years from 1975 to 1980 that became the first federal civil rights laws protecting people with disabilities. Willowbrook was officially closed in 1987, with the former residents placed in small group homes of six to 10 people throughout the city and state. Willowbrook became a prime example as to how television news became involved in social change. The culmination was the Federal American with Disabilities Act (ADA) in 1990. Another offshoot was that the descendants of Robert Kennedy founded the Special Olympics, which integrated the acceptance of athletes of all abilities to compete in activities and recreation. The situation at Willowbrook State School became a "watershed case" for gaining civil rights for Americans with disabilities. Of most importance, it set the groundwork for moral and ethical treatment of those individuals confined to institutions.

A January 2000 *New York Times* magazine exposé documented deplorable conditions at a hospital for the mentally ill in Hidalgo, Mexico. Michael Winerip, in an article titled "Global Willowbrook," wrote of deplorable conditions in a hospital for the mentally ill. He wrote, "Seeing a place like Hidalgo from the inside is like being transported back in time, to the year 1972, to Staten Island . . . into Willowbrook, a state institution for the retarded, and filmed the wards crowded with disabled children, their feces smeared on walls. So horrid were conditions, the American public was moved" (62). In 1993, ABC-TV provided a retrospective on the Willowbrook State School, as it was later known. Newscaster John Johnson called Willowbrook "America's Auschwitz," likening it to the infamous Nazi genocidal camp of the Second World War.

A similar perception was placed against the hundreds of thousands of adults and children afflicted with polio. For those individuals, the derogatory word "crippled" was applied rather than incapacitated or disabled. In either case, those individuals were not viewed favorably in public. Nor were any reasonable accommodations made such as ramp access to public buildings or wheelchair assistance. Considering how American society treated both women and those with disabilities, it does not seem so radical that the United States also had a contentious legal segregation system.

IT'S IN THE TEXTBOOKS

In providing a historical recount of the 1950s, the reader might wonder why the decade of the 1920s was so important. The reason is simple—the Americans who held onto strict racial segregation were taught to accept the racial divide during that time period. Segregationists were often raised with the ideas taught to them not only by their parents, but also, most important, in grade school. In addition, throughout the history of America to that time, political, social, and economic power was held firmly within the control of white males.

The situation of desegregating the public schools was not such a simple matter. In reality, it extended to all walks of life and would require an acceptance by the American public. As historian James Loewen noted in *Teaching What Really Happened*, the support of racial separation was prevalent throughout the nation. Loewen added that white students were taught and passed on to their children "that African Americans are inferior beings . . . kept away, in separate unequal schools, lest they hold white children back. . . . African Americans are a pariah people who cannot even be allowed to eat in white restaurants or rest in white cemeteries" (2009, 73). If anyone thought differently, all that was needed was to look around and see that African Americans lived in undesirable areas, worked inferior jobs, and made much less money than their counterparts. Yet unknown within this cover of ignorance was that the situation was a product of a long history of universally contrived laws by white male legislatures.

Beginning in the 1920s, mandatory public education of all grade-school children throughout the United States swept the nation. (Some states had begun requirements as early as 1905, mandating children belonged in school rather than working in factories.) Therefore, in 1955, a 35-year-old person would have been among the first generation attending mandatory public education. A youth of 5 to 7 years old starting school born to a 20- to 25-year-old parent who was in grade school around 1935 was often provided "factual" information by state issued textbooks.

Regardless of the region, supposed factual information on the inferiority of the non-white races was taught through the use of standard issue textbooks. One example adopted by the New York City Department of Education and also distributed throughout many American schools was: *Geography by Grades, Grade 4B: The Earth, The Continents* (Hinds, Hayden & Eldredge, 1926), authored by Francis Trevelyan Miller and John W. Davis. In the textbook, all references to the "white race" always placed them way above the other "colors." Miller and Davis explained:

> The people of the white race, on the whole, are the most intelligent and progressive of all. . . . They write most of the books in the world, paint most of the pictures, and compose most of the music. . . . They have many schools and universities, at which every kind of knowledge is taught. Most of them make many wise laws for the protection of life and property, and see that these are obeyed. (44)

All throughout the pages of the textbook, the red, brown, yellow, and black races were described with a litany of generalized attributes that could only be described to a 21st-century audience as audacious, prejudicial, and stereotypical. Yet during the 1950s, it was acceptable and understood as truthful among the mainstream American public. The authors also carefully distinguished between the "great" accomplishments of the "white race" and the "progress" of the "black race." The impressionable fourth graders were cautioned:

> But this great race is still uncivilized in parts of native Africa. It is hard for you to picture the life of savages. They have no regular laws or government as we have . . . savages have no cities. They live in mud or wooden huts or in houses made of leaves or thatched grasses. They have no schools, and do not know what it means to read and write. Most of them cannot count beyond ten, the number of their fingers. (45)

If the stereotypical generalizations were not enough, two of the poignant questions asked of the students were quite revealing. One was, "To which race do you belong?" and the second, "Which race has reached the highest state of civilization?" (50–51).

VIRGINIA'S RACIAL INTEGRITY LAWS

The idea of racial segregation by definition was not new. However, the legal definition did not become the official law of the land until after 1910. The precedent began with the 1896 U.S. Supreme Court decision of *Plessy v. Ferguson*. At the time, a growing discontent among mainstream white Americans was wary of immigrants and fearful of race intermingling and worse yet intermarriage that might produce "mongrel" children. In 1910, Tennessee and Louisiana became the first states to make the "one-drop rule" official law. The following year Arkansas and Texas adopted similar legislation, as did the state of Mississippi in 1917. In 1923, North Carolina passed laws defining the "one-drop" law. Yet the most famous was passed by the state of Virginia in 1924.

Virginia was one of the leaders in enacting laws to prevent racial integration, especially through marriage. In 1924, the state passed the Virginia Racial Integrity Act of 1924 and placed administration of the law under the direction of physician Dr. Walter Plecker (1861–1947). (Plecker had been an ardent promoter of enacting the law.) The law provided a strict definition of "white" and "colored." The legal definitions were purposely intended to deny marriages between the races termed as "miscegenation." As part of the definition miscegenation was crudely defined as "the interbreeding of people considered to be of different racial types." In its basic form, a white person could only legally marry another white person as defined by law. The law also prevented any marriage between a white person and someone defined as Asian, Mexican, Hispanic, and of course "colored" (Transcript of The Virginia Racial Integrity Act of 1924).

To provide immediate compliance with the law, the Virginia Department of Health issued a descriptive bulletin in March 1924 outlining the "Instructions on Preserving Racial Integrity." The instructions were mainly intended for any municipal employee that issued marriage licenses. The instructions contained, in part, the following:

> Color is the most important feature of this form of registration. The local registrar must be sure there is no trace of colored blood in anyone offering to register as a white person. ("Virginia Act to Preserve Racial Integrity," n.p.)

The "colored blood" was considered for any person who had even "a single drop of non-white blood as being black." As a result, the law was often known as the "One-Drop Rule." Of interesting note was a special provision known as the "Pocahontas clause." This clause provided for the long-standing wealthy Virginia families to claim exemption as descendants of the famed Indian Pocahontas and her English husband John Rolfe. Therefore, those Virginians could maintain "their all-white status and privileges" (Wolfe, n.p.).

Within a few years, state lawmakers in Alabama, Georgia, Florida, Indiana, Kentucky, Maryland, Missouri, Nebraska, North Dakota, Oklahoma, and Utah joined the cause. Sadly, by the 1950s, every state in America had some kind of similar legislation. Yet the definition of who was "white" and who was "colored" was strictly subjective. In fact, in a letter dated August 9, 1940, Dr. Plecker admitted, "there is no test to determine the race of an individual." He retired in 1946, but his detrimental legacy lived on throughout the 1950s. A telling statistic revealed that prior to 1960, only 4 percent of Americans nationwide believed interracial marriage was acceptable (Loewen, 2009, 70).

The Virginia law preventing interracial marriage remained in effect and was eventually met with a legal challenge. In June 1958, Virginia residents Richard Loving, a white man, and Mildred Jeter, a black woman, were legally married in Washington, D.C. They returned to their home state of Virginia to live as a married couple. In October 1958, they were summoned by a grand jury and eventually found guilty of violating the Virginia marital laws. A one-year jail sentence was imposed for their "illegal marriage." Since their marriage occurred out of state, they were offered a stay of sentence if they agreed to leave the state and not return for a period of 25 years. Instead, they chose legal action, eventually taking the case to the U.S. Supreme Court. In a unanimous decision of *Loving v. Virginia* 388 U.S. 1 (1967), the court ruled that the 1924 Virginia Racial Integrity Act violated the Fourteenth Amendment of the U.S. Constitution. Ultimately, the federal civil rights decision also overturned the ban on interracial marriage in a total of 16 states.

DESEGREGATION: *"THE MOST CONTROVERSIAL QUESTION OF THE CENTURY"*

Prior to 1964, the racial makeup of America was not nearly as diverse as the early 21st century. Throughout the 1950s, and as late as 1980, the U.S. Census counted more than 80 percent of the total population as white. (That number declined to 66 percent by 2015.) The "colored" population was a little over 12 percent and the Hispanic population accounted for 6 percent. The remaining 2 percent of the population was composed of Asians and "Others." The country was also strictly segregated by race in all places of public accommodation.

In 1954, the *Brown v. The Board of Education of Topeka Kansas* Supreme Court decision was a landmark case that officially ended the legal practice of school segregation. The U.S. Supreme Court decision was carried as major news all across the country. On May 18, 1954, *The New York Times*, for example, ran a two-line banner headline as follows:

HIGH COURT BANS SCHOOL SEGREGATION:
9-TO-0 DECISION GRANTS TIME TO COMPLY

In a unanimous decision, the Court ruled school segregation illegal and that all public schools throughout the nation should "proceed with deliberate speed" to desegregate. In reading the ruling Chief Justice Earl Warren said that segregation was "permissive or mandatory" in 21 states and the District of Columbia. In speaking for the court, Warren cited sociological causes rather legal precedent. He said, "To separate them from others of similar age and qualifications solely because of their race generates a feeling of inferiority as to their status in the community that may affect their hearts and minds in a way unlikely ever to be undone." In the summation the ruling declared segregation as unconstitutional. Thus, as journalist James Reston writing in *The New York Times* on the announcement said, "The principal court of the land managed to agree unanimously on what heretofore had been one of the most controversial questions of the century." One quirk in the court mandate did not apply to private schools, nor require the municipalities to continue funding their public school system (14).

THE MURDER OF EMMETT TILL

During the summer of 1955, a 14-year-old named Emmett Till was sent from Chicago by his mother to spend the school break with his uncle Mose Wright in the small southern town of Money, Mississippi. At one point he was in a local store with some other young African Americans. Supposedly upon leaving the store, Till was prompted by his friends to say "Bye, Baby" to a white woman. Till did not know about the strict segregation laws, thereby insulting her "honor." Three days later, the woman's husband and brother-in-law kidnapped, brutally beat, and killed Till. Juan Williams in *Eyes on The Prize* described the horrific scene: "Till's body was found three days later. The barbed wire holding the cotton-gin fan around his neck had become snagged on a tangled river root. There was a bullet in the boy's skull, one eye was gouged out, and his forehead was crushed on one side" (43).

His mother Mamie Till Bradley issued a public statement that was carried in hundreds of newspapers across the country. She asked, "Have you ever sent a loved son on vacation and had him returned to you in a pine box, so horribly battered and water-logged that someone needs to tell you that sickening sight is your son—lynched?" (Williams, 44). Till's mother also made the courageous decision to have an open-casket funeral, so that the brutal reality of segregation could be seen by all. *Jet* magazine, which was primarily read by African Americans, printed the photo of the brutally disfigured Emmett Till. The story was soon picked up and published on the front page of all the major northern newspapers across the country. As she had insisted upon the open coffin for all the world to see, Mamie Till Bradley also had the courage to explain what she saw up close what was done to "her baby." She described the brutality involved in the murder as she first saw him before he was placed in the coffin:

> I saw that his tongue was choked out. I noticed that the right eye was lying midway on his cheek. I noticed that his nose had been broken like somebody took a meat chopper and chopped his nose in several places. As I kept looking, I saw a hole, which I presumed was a bullet hole, and I could look through that hole and see daylight on the other side. And I wondered: Was it necessary to shoot him? (Blow, n.p.)

The sensationalism attached to the murder could not just pass away as did so many other murders of the time.

Mose Wright identified the two kidnappers as Roy Bryant and J.W. Milam, who were later charged with the murder. During the short trial, the all-white jury barely deliberated at all and returned an innocent verdict. A few months later, both Bryant and Milam bragged about the killing in an admission to a reporter for the national publication *Look* magazine. Since they were already acquitted, they could not be tried, despite their own admission of guilt. The Till story did bring the grim reality of the segregation laws in vivid pictures to the American public, yet very little sympathy came from the southern states. The reality for the entire century to date was that segregation was an ugly monster that interfered with the daily life of many Americans, whether going on vacation or even attempting to eat lunch in a public facility.

BROWN II AND "THE LITTLE ROCK NINE"

Despite the federal mandate by the U.S. Supreme Court, the southern states steadfastly refused integration, especially in the public schools. Attempts to enter schools legally were met with violence, and school districts flat out refused to provide any plans on how to implement the process. As a result, the U.S. Supreme Court issued a second ruling in 1955, which became known as *Brown II*. It was that second ruling that mandated the schools proceed, "with all deliberate speed," to desegregate the schools. The "deliberate speed" to integrate was often very slow, or did not happen at all. Many of the southern states either refused or others planned organized resistance. In Little Rock, Arkansas, for example, two all-white, pro-segregation groups were formed to organize resistance to any integration plans called the Capital Citizens Council and the Mother's League of Central High School.

The first test came in 1957, as nine African-American students enrolled at Central High School in Little Rock, Arkansas. Daisy Bates (1914–1999), president of the Arkansas NAACP, had carefully selected a group of exemplary academic students ranging in age from 14 to 17, who became known as the "Little Rock Nine." Each of the nine—Minnijean Brown, Elizabeth Eckford, Ernest Green, Thelma Mothershed, Melba Patillo, Gloria Ray, Terrence Roberts, Jefferson Thomas, and Carlotta Walls—were also selected based on their ability to have "possessed the strength and determination to face the resistance they would encounter." During the late summer the group attended training sessions on how to "respond to anticipated hostile situations." That training was fully put to the test beginning on the very first day of classes scheduled for September 4, 1957.

As the nine students attempted to enter Central High School, they were refused entry. That refusal came from the Arkansas State National Guard, which was ordered to prevent the nine black students from entering the building. Governor Orval Faubus, who was a known strict segregationist, had issued that order. (Faubus actually ordered the Arkansas National Guard to form a complete ring around the entire school to prevent any integration.) The story was covered as headline news by many local and national newspapers. One headline story in *The New York Times* of September 16, 1957, carried a picture of angry, white, male students taunting two of the nine. The caption read:

> Students Resist Integration: A white youth dares one of the Negro students to try to enter the North Little Rock High School. The Negroes, who were among six students turned away from school yesterday, were pushed down steps and onto [the] sidewalk. ("Little Rock: 40 Years Later," n.p.)

The students were not the only ones met with taunts and jeers. The incident attracted nationwide media attention. As a result, journalists and photographers covering the event were also met with resistance. As the situation worsened, it was the news reports, and especially the visual imagery, that provided stark reality to the rest of the nation. The images clearly showed the outright hate and violent resistance to deny the basic human rights of American citizens protected by the United States Constitution.

It was during this incident that one of the most famous photographs of the 20th century was taken. As one of the students, 15-year-old Elizabeth Eckford, tried to enter the school, photographers Johnny Jenkins of UPI and Will

The resistance to school integration continued for years. In this photograph, a rally against school integration protesting the admission of the "Little Rock Nine" to Central High School took place on the steps of the Arkansas State Capitol building. The prominent display of the American flag was a purported attempt to somehow indicate that integration supported Communism and was "un-American." (Library of Congress)

Counts each captured the tension in a singular telling image. (Jenkins image was awarded a Pulitzer Prize for Photography.) Eight of the students had previously arrived together in a car driven by Daisy Bates. Eckford did not arrive with the others, therefore she was alone as the photograph was taken. The photograph clearly shows Eckford maintaining her composure. She is holding a binder in her left arm, while behind her, angry and vicious white students taunted her. To her side were two white parents who also shouted racial taunts over her attempted entry. The girl directly behind Eckford shouting with such virulent hate was later identified as Hazel Massery. The teenage Eckford later recalled that the taunts and jeers also came with one woman spitting on her.

The situation at Little Rock was not isolated. Other attempts to enter school legally happened all across the nation. On that same front page of *The New York Times* on September 10, 1957, two similar incidents were reported in Birmingham, Alabama, and Nashville, Tennessee:

- Alabama Negro Clergyman Beaten While Trying to Enroll Students
- Nashville Holds 5 In School Strife: Violence Mars Integration—Many Pupils Taken Out

Some instances such as in Philadelphia reported three schools integrated without incident. In the Philadelphia Coatesville school district, two elementary schools, one "all-Negro" school and another "all-white" each integrated. A third in the Kennett Square area was also integrated.

Despite some peaceful reports, the situation at Little Rock worsened. In order to end the siege, the U.S. federal government prepared to intercede and overrule Governor Faubus. A *New York Times* headline of September 10, 1957, read:

U.S. TO SEEK WRIT TO FORCE FAUBUS
AND GUARD TO PERMIT INTEGRATION;
EXTENDED COURT BATTLE EXPECTED

A small article appeared at the bottom of that same issue as a reminder that on the same date, during the American Civil War on September 10, 1863, Union forces overtook the city of Little Rock, Arkansas. *The New York Times* noted, "Now the Federal Government is coming back. It seeks to enjoin the Arkansas Governor, who has defied the United States on the issue of integration" (24). The "coming back" was by the U.S. Military 101st Airborne Division.

On September 20, the National Guard was removed by a judicial decree. The situation was briefly taken over by local police who escorted the students into the school on the 23rd of September. Yet the violent protests continued outside, resulting in the students being removed from the building. The following day, over 1,200 members of the U.S. Army's 101st Airborne Division were dispatched from Fort Campbell in Kentucky. By order of President Dwight D. Eisenhower, the Army was to escort the "Little Rock Nine" into the school. The entire Arkansas National Guard was also ordered by the president to be placed under direct orders issued only by the U.S. Army and not by Governor Faubus. As a result, the first official "full day" of school was on September 25, 1957. However, the troubles did not end, as many newspapers reported that once inside the school the harassment and verbal taunts continued throughout the entire school year.

As it turned out, the end of the school year did not bring an end to the resistance to integration. Rather than continue desegregation, Governor Faubus ordered all the high schools in Little Rock closed. His reasoning was that the residents of Little Rock should have a "democratic" vote on the issue. The citizens of Little Rock overwhelming voted against school integration by a tally of 19,470 to 7,561. The public schools therefore remained closed for an entire academic year. In late 1959, all the Little Rock public schools eventually reopened. Yet violence towards blacks continued for decades, as did resistance to desegregate the public schools.

PRINCE EDWARD COUNTY IN VIRGINIA SAYS "NO TO INTEGRATION"

Rather than comply with integration, many other cities also decided to close their public schools. Prince Edward County in Virginia was one example. In *Something Must Be Done About Prince Edward County*, author Kristen Green revealed that rather than desegregate, the county officials mandated a closing of all the public schools. In place of public schools, funding was authorized for a private charter known as the "Prince Edward Academy." As a "private" facility, the county did not have to comply with the Supreme Court decision. In turn, Prince Edward Academy was able to remain exclusively white. But rather than leave the public schools as an option, county officials with the help of "white volunteers, stripped classrooms of desks, books, and supplies." All of the items removed from the public schools were reused at the new private academy. The situation also applied to the local high school, as the football goal posts were also relocated to the private school, which fielded a "whites only" football team (Sugrue, "Shut Out," 14).

Although the school, as many others throughout the nation, was listed as "private," it relied on a significant amount of public money and land grants. In Prince Edward, residents "earmarked" 25 percent of their property taxes to fund the newly segregated school. In addition, the "all white" schools were often stocked with pilfered furniture and supplies from the public schools. The response by whites, as Sugrue noted, was often that blacks should "get a group together and open up a school." Without the equal financial resources, either privately or politically, that option was almost always impossible. One of the few "resources" came if a southern black family had relatives living in northern cities that maintained desegregated school districts. In such a situation, a painful decision was often made to send school-age sons and daughters to live with far-away relatives (Sugrue, "Shut Out," 14).

THE KU KLUX KLAN AND THE JOHN BIRCH SOCIETY

As historian David Halberstam pointed out, organizations such as the "White Citizens Council" that were formed to resist integration were just a thinly veiled front by white supremacist groups such as the Ku Klux Klan and the John Birch Society (43). The John Birch Society was formed under the precept of defending the Constitution, being "anti-Communist," and staunchly supporting the dead Senator Joseph McCarthy. Yet by the time of its founding in 1959, the falsehoods of Communist infiltration had been debunked. Any study of their members showed them to be just another group in opposition to desegregation. The most notorious and often violent suppressor of court-mandated desegregation was the Ku Klux Klan (KKK). At the time, the KKK was notorious throughout the south (and many northern states). By the 1950s, the Klan was a secret organization, but just 25 years earlier it was the single-largest open fraternal organization in the United States. Noted American historian Eric Foner, in *The Story of American Freedom* reminds us:

> Perhaps the most menacing reflection of the renewed association between racialism, citizenship, and ideas of freedom was the spectacular resurgence of the Ku Klux Klan in the early 1920s. By mid-decade the Klan claimed over 3 million members, nearly all white native-born Protestants, mostly respectable members of their communities. (188)

THE *SOUTHERN MANIFESTO* SAYS "NO TO INTEGRATION"

The Supreme Court decision of *Brown v. Board of Education* actually prompted a vicious backlash from Congress—not in support of desegregation, but rather in *opposition* to the decision and in continued support of legal segregation. On March 12, 1956, Congressman Howard Smith of Virginia, presiding chair of the House Rules Committee, introduced to Congress the "Declaration of Constitutional Principles." The resolution officially "condemned" the *Brown* decision as "a clear abuse of judicial power" by the Supreme Court. In fact, as a response to the decision, more than 100 U.S. congressmen signed the Southern Manifesto in staunch *opposition* of the Supreme Court ruling. The document, which was more commonly known as the "Southern Manifesto," had the endorsement of 19 U.S. senators and 77 members of the House of Representatives.

In presenting the well-orchestrated Southern Manifesto, Congressman Smith was not alone. He co-opted with Senator Walter F. George of Georgia who introduced the measure on the Senate floor. The tale is well documented in a PBS.org documentary and a companion history page titled "Southern Manifesto on Integration (March 12, 1956)." The documentary provides further reference to Smith's role as the chairman of the Rules Committee who left a notorious decade-long trail of disallowing any type of civil rights legislation out of committee. The southern members of Congress applauded Smith's presentation to the House of Representatives. Although all of the supporters of the Southern Manifesto were from the southern states, not one member of Congress spoke out publicly against the proposal.

AN EXCERPT FROM THE TRANSCRIPT OF
THE SOUTHERN MANIFESTO

The unwarranted decision of the Supreme Court in the public school cases is now bearing the fruit always produced when men substitute naked power for established law. . . .

We regard the decision of the Supreme Court in the school cases as clear abuse of judicial power. It climaxes a trend in the Federal judiciary undertaking to legislate, in derogation of the authority of Congress, and to encroach upon the reserved rights of the states and the people.

The original Constitutional does not mention education. Neither does the Fourteenth Amendment nor any other amendment. The debates preceding the submission of the Fourteenth Amendment clearly show that there was no intent that it should affect the systems of education maintained by the states. . . .

As admitted by the Supreme Court in the public school case (Brown v. Board of Education), the doctrine of separate but equal schools "apparently originated in Roberts v. City of Boston (1849), upholding school segregation against attack as being violative of a state constitutional guarantee of equality." This constitutional doctrine began in the North-not in the South-and it was followed not only in Massachusetts but in Connecticut, New York, Illinois, Indiana, Michigan, Minnesota, New Jersey, Ohio, Pennsylvania and other northern states until they, exercising their rights as states through the constitutional processes of local self-government, changed their school systems. . . .

Though there has been no constitutional amendment or act of Congress changing this established legal principle almost a century old, the Supreme Court of the United States, with no legal basis for such action, undertook to exercise their naked judicial power and substituted their personal political and social ideas for the established law of the land.

This unwarranted exercise of power by the court, contrary to the Constitution, is creating chaos and confusion in the states principally affected. It is destroying the amicable relations between the white and Negro races that have been created through ninety years of patient effort by the good people of both races. It has planted hatred and suspicion where there has been heretofore friendship and understanding.

Without regard to the consent of the governed, outside agitators are threatening immediate and revolutionary changes in our public school systems. If done, this is certain to destroy the system of public education in some of the states. . . .

We decry the Supreme Court's encroachments on rights reserved to the states and to the people, contrary to established law and to the Constitution.

We commend the motives of those states which have declared the intention to resist forced integration by any lawful means. . . .

We pledge ourselves to use all lawful means to bring about a reversal of this decision which is contrary to the Constitution and to prevent the use of force in its implementation.

In this trying period, as we all seek to right this wrong, we appeal to our people not to be provoked by the agitators and troublemakers invading our states and to scrupulously refrain from disorder and lawless acts.

Source: From Congressional Record, 84th Congress Second Session. Vol. 102, part 4. Washington, D.C.: Governmental Printing Office, 1956. 4459–4460.

This formidable political opposition led to a 1958 U.S. Supreme Court challenge. In the case of *Cooper v. Aaron* 358 U.S. 1 (1958), an argument was based upon the decision to remain solely on an individual state-by-state basis to either implement or maintain school segregation. The appeal was rejected as the U.S. Supreme Court upheld the *Brown* decision. A brief summary referenced that a state-by-state basis would violate the Tenth Amendment. The Court affirmed "that the states were bound by the ruling and affirming that its interpretation of the Constitution was the supreme law of the land." Nonetheless, the southern states did not abide by the Court's decision.

ROSA PARKS AND THE MONTGOMERY BUS BOYCOTT

Oftentimes the 1950s are viewed as the time when the legal racial segregation that existed throughout much of the nation ended. That reference is usually associated with the Montgomery Bus Boycott that began with Rosa Parks' refusal to give up her seat on a municipal bus. As a point of reference, Ms. Parks was not the first to refuse giving up her seat to a white passenger. By 1955, the black community of Montgomery was ready to enact action in protest of the discriminatory bus practice. They were just waiting for the right time and place. One prior incident occurred in early March 1955, as a 15-year-old high school student named Claudette Colvin boarded a bus and sat way in the back. As the bus became overcrowded, the driver, as he was legally authorized, demanded that seats be vacated to accommodate the additional white passengers. The young Colvin refused so the bus driver summoned a local police officer. She resisted, supposedly "kicking and screaming" as she was handcuffed and taken off in a police vehicle. She was later released pending a court appearance. As local civil rights leaders planned to use the incident as a test case to propel a citywide boycott, they became aware that the unmarried Colvin was pregnant. Thinking that the moral scandal would lessen the validity of a boycott, the leaders withdrew their plans. A few months later, on December 1, 1955, a similar situation happened with Rosa Parks' refusal to give up her seat.

For Rosa Parks, it was not her first encounter with the bus driver James Blake, nor was he an unfamiliar perpetrator of racial indignity. Historian Douglas Brinkley once described Blake as a "vicious bigot who spat tobacco juice out of his bus window and cursed at 'n*****' just for the fun of it" (201). Blake was known as always acting particularly spiteful when it came to black passengers on his bus. Brinkley added, "[Blake's] favorite sport was making African-Americans pay in front and walk back to board in the rear, then leaving them with a face full of exhaust as he gunned the bus away before they could get on" (58, 201). With the Parks incident, the time and person were enough to start a planned citywide boycott. (Parks' refusal was also sparked by her disgust of the well-publicized murder of Emmett Till only a few months earlier.)

The refusal by Parks sparked a long bus boycott. A little over one year later, the 381-day bus boycott effectively ended after the U.S. Supreme Court upheld a decision made by a lower U.S. district court. In June 1956, the lower court in *Browder v. Gayle* had ruled the Alabama segregation bus ban as unconstitutional. The verdict did cite the *Brown v. Board of Education* decision as a precedent. But the actual boycott continued until the U.S. Supreme Court provided affirmation on November 13, 1956. The following day, journalist Bob Ingram of the *Montgomery Advertiser* wrote:

> Laws requiring racial segregation on buses in Montgomery and throughout Alabama were declared unconstitutional yesterday in another historic decision by the U. S. Supreme Court. And while the decision dealt specifically with Alabama statutes and ordinances of the City of Montgomery, in effect it also outlawed similar segregation laws throughout the South since this ruling sets the precedent for all similar cases in the future. ("Montgomery Bus Boycott," n.p.)

One local leader of the white Montgomery Citizens' Council, Luther Ingalls, warned, "[A]ny attempt to enforce this decision will inevitably lead to riot and bloodshed." Another white citizen leader of the Alabama Public Service Commission was quoted as saying that segregation was necessary "to keep down violence and bloodshed" (Williams, 157). According to Juan Williams writing in *Eyes on the Prize*, "Since the bus boycott, racial tension had intensified in Montgomery. The city had recently closed all its public parks and its zoo rather than allow blacks to visit them" (157).

VIOLENCE, RAPE, AND THE "SIMPLISTIC IDEA OF CIVIL RIGHTS"

Rosa Park's refusal was not the first time that an African American refused to give up her seat on a public bus. Ten years before, a 27-year-old mother of two by the name of Irene Morgan had also refused to give up her seat on a bus. On July 14, 1944, Morgan boarded a Greyhound bus in Gloucester County, Virginia, intending to go to Baltimore, Maryland, to see a doctor. Once onboard she moved to the back and sat in the prescribed "Colored Section." Later, as a white couple boarded the bus, the driver ordered Morgan to relinquish her seat. She refused and was arrested as the driver called for a local sheriff. Morgan defied the sheriff, supposedly tearing up a citation and fighting and kicking the officer. As a result, she was jailed for resisting arrest and in violation of Virginia's segregation laws. She pleaded guilty only to resisting arrest and paid a $100 fine. Morgan, however, refused to accept guilt for violation of the segregation laws and appealed all the way to the U.S. Supreme Court. In her case, *Irene Morgan v. Commonwealth of Virginia*, 328 U.S. 373 (1946), the court issued a 6–1 decision in favor of Morgan declaring "enforcing segregation on interstate buses was illegal." The decision applied only to interstate travel and therefore was not applicable to the municipal bus travel segregation law that was challenged by Rosa Parks on December 1, 1955 ("Irene Morgan," n.p.).

So many history textbooks for American high schools and colleges often include only the Rosa Parks incident. The tale is often told that Parks was a "tired seamstress" who one day decided enough was enough. In reality, Parks was not an unknown within either her own community or to the NAACP. Yet the history books make the historical turning point as a matter of seat preference, rather than providing the true brutal and violent background of the story. In fact, at the time of her 1955 arrest, Rosa Parks was "a seasoned activist" and also served as a long-time field investigator for the NAACP. Her work included providing documentation of a long-standing policy of sexual violence and rape against black women in the south. In one instance in 1944, Parks was assigned the task of looking into the brutal rape of a black woman by a group of white men. In all the irony that can ever be placed before an individual, the rape had occurred on a similar Montgomery, Alabama, bus stop where the Rosa Parks legacy ignited a mass movement for civil rights in the United States (Steinem, 2015, 43–44).

That 1944 incident involved a 24-year-old mother named Recy Taylor, who recounted her terrible incident on February 28, 2011, in a National Public Radio (NPR) interview with host Michel Martin. Martin asked of Taylor: "I know this is hard to talk about, but if you could, I'd like it if you could tell us what happened back in 1944 when you were walking home that day." Taylor replied:

> I was—went to my friend's house. . . . A car running around outside of us, six young men jumped out with a gun and said that—you're the one that cut a white boy in Clarkton. And the police got us out looking for you. You get in the car and we will take you uptown to the police station. And they got me in the car and carried me straight through the woods, but before they go where they was going, they blindfolded me. After they messed over and did what they were going to do me, say, we're going to take you back. We're going to put you out. But if you tell it, we're going to kill you. (Martin, "Hidden Pattern of Rape Helped Stir Civil Rights Movement," n.p.)

A few days later, she recalled meeting with Rosa Parks who documented the case. Needless to say, the NAACP was powerless to bring forth action and Taylor was fearful to go out at night in fear of being attacked.

As part of that same NPR radio interview, host Michel Martin spoke with Professor Danielle L. McGuire, author of *At the Dark End of the Street: Black Women, Rape, and Resistance* (Vintage Press, 2011). McGuire added a very poignant fact often overlooked by researchers and by the authors of the history books:

> I think that historians have always been focused on civil rights, voting rights, desegregation, access to public accommodations, and they've left out some of the larger things that people were worried about, particularly human rights. And they ignored some of these stories. I mean, black women have been testifying about his crimes for years. They're on the front pages of black newspaper throughout the 1940s and the early 1950s, but mainstream historians never really

picked it up, because I think they were really just focused on major leaders, major campaigns, and the very simplistic idea of civil rights. (Martin, "Hidden Pattern of Rape Helped Stir Civil Rights Movement," n.p.)

As it turned out, the incident was not isolated as a series of similar rapes had occurred over many years. As with all similar incidents involving brutal attacks against black females by white men, nothing was done to either investigate or seek an arrest. As McGuire also reminded us, the 1950s was a time of complete female subjugation. She told the NPR radio audience:

It really sits at the volatile core of the modern civil rights struggle, and interracial sexual violence is really the point here. And so white men, I think, projected their own deviant behavior onto black men and accused black men of attacking white women when the truth was that white men were in the habit of attacking black women. So black men had to be very careful and they could be charged with eye rape. I mean there's a case in the 1950s of a black man who looked at a white girl from a distance of 75 feet and was literally charged with eye rape. I mean, it was preposterous. (Martin, "Hidden Pattern of Rape Helped Stir Civil Rights Movement," n.p.)

"OPERATION WETBACK"

The racial hatred was not confined solely to African Americans. In July 1954, a U.S. government deportation program of Mexican workers under the derogatory name of "Operation Wetback" began. Officially it was listed as a "repatriation project of the United States Immigration and Naturalization Service to remove undocumented Mexican immigrants from the Southwest." The deportation program under the command of U.S. Army General Joseph M. Swing began on July 15. During the first day, more than 4,800 supposed "illegal immigrants" were escorted across the Rio Grande Valley into Mexico. The next day resulted in another 1,100 escorted over the border. Thereafter, the U.S. military tracked down about 1,000 per day. In all, about 80,000 were deported in a few short months. The program was put in place under the ploy to make jobs available for the thousands of American servicemen being acclimated back into society. The irony was that the United States had once recruited those same immigrants during the height of labor shortages during the Second World War. To meet the labor demand created by the millions of Americans drafted into military service, the U.S. Congress, authorized by Public Law 78, enacted a "Bracero Program" in the southwest portion of the United States. The program allowed about 4.6 million Mexicans to legally cross the border and work in place of the labor vacancies. In fact, most of the general American public was not even aware of the Mexican-American situation (Koch, 2A).

The short-lived deportation process was not handled with decorum. In fact, brutal transportation conditions resulted in numerous deaths. In 2015, Eyder Peralta, speaking for NPR.org, claimed at least 88 deportees "died of sun stroke as a result of a round-up that had taken place in 112-degree heat." Other reports indicate that Mexicans "were brought [into Mexico] like cows on trucks and

unloaded fifteen miles down the highway from the border, in the desert."
When the program ended in the fall of 1954, the U.S. government claimed the
program a success and that "the border had been secured." With the border
"secured" American officials were free to act against other perceived threats
such as teenage juvenile delinquency.

TEENAGERS, JUVENILE DELINQUENCY, AND MORALITY

The post-war period saw the emergence of a new distinct demographic—the
"teenager." Unlike the pre-war years, a large number of teenagers had money
of their own and bought products specific to their own age group. By 1956,
estimates placed the number of teenagers at more than 13 million with a
total disposable income equal to that of an entire American family in 1940 (Halberstam, 473). In turn, businesses catered to selling items specifically for teenagers such as clothing and Rock 'n' Roll music, among others. Most of the
mainstream American public viewed the trend in teenage independence as a
threat to the moral fabric of society. Those fears were echoed with growing
concern over juvenile delinquency, going steady, and Rock 'n' Roll, to name a
few. In reality, adults were scared of change, scared of non-conformity, scared
of heightened sexuality, scared of rebellion, and mostly were scared of the
weakening of segregation. The Hollywood movie industry portrayed the
teenage juvenile delinquent in such movies as *The Wild One* (1954); *Blackboard
Jungle* (1955); *Rebel Without a Cause* (1955); *Crime in the Streets* (1956); and *High
School Confidential* (1958), among others. The movie poster for *High School Confidential* claimed "behind these 'nice' school walls A TEACHER'S NIGHT-
MARE A TEEN-AGE JUNGLE!" The ad for *Crime in The Streets* asked: "How
can you tell them to be good when their girlfriends like them better when
they're bad?" Parents and municipal and religious leaders placed all the blame
upon juvenile delinquency, teenage gangs, and Rock 'n' Roll ("Rock & Roll
Generation," 122–123).

The morality of Elvis Presley was also put into question. In separate instances
in San Diego and Florida, Presley was threatened with arrest if he moved on
stage in an "obscene way." Rock 'n' Roll concerts were routinely cancelled in
cities all throughout the nation. The most common reason was to prevent the
perceived increase in rioting and juvenile delinquency. However, the real reason was to prevent the intermingling of black and white teenagers, especially
by dancing with each other. Teenage dancing did occur, but inside areas such
as local high school gymnasiums, where the music and behavior could be carefully monitored, and segregated, by adult chaperones. Morality regarding
dancing also held sway over municipal regulations. In 1956, the city of Atlanta
banned teenagers from dancing in public "without the written consent of their
parents." That same year, the Los Angeles County Board of Supervisors resurrected a progressive era law that prohibited public dancing in parks and public open spaces. One political official claimed that it "would lead to a lot of
dancing in the darkness [and] might contribute to increased juvenile delinquency" (Macías-Rojas, 709).

A simple, no-cost method of gathering with other teenage friends that also added cause for adult concern was "hanging out." (The term was from a pre-war leisure pursuit, which simply meant gathering with friends on a street corner, local park, or rural area.) Some did get together at a soda shop, roller skating rink, or even a record store. Yet just the idea of teens doing anything on their own without adult supervision was viewed as a cause for inviting trouble and likened them all as "juvenile delinquents." To combat the problem, Houston, Texas, as just one example, formed "The Juvenile Delinquency and Crime Commission." A constant reason for adult concern always seemed to be linked to Rock 'n' Roll (Time-Life Books,"Rock & Roll Generation," 122–123).

Some did not hide their outright disdain of the music for promoting "race-mixing." The executive secretary of the Alabama White Citizens Council claimed, "The obscenity and vulgarity of the Rock and Roll music is obviously a means by which the white man and his children can be driven to the level of the nigra [sic]. . . . [I]t is Communist ideology." The chairman of the Alabama White Citizens Council proudly displayed a sign reading, "We serve WHITE customers Only." He also publicly announced, "We set up a twenty-man committee to do away with this vulgar and cannibalistic nigger rock and roll bop" (*Rock and Roll: The Early Days,* video).

ALGER HISS AND JULIUS AND ETHEL ROSENBERG

One of the fundamental problems facing Americans was the fear of subversive infiltration by the Communists. The concern was heightened by the media-sensationalized trials of Alger Hiss and Julius and Ethel Rosenberg. In 1948, Alger Hiss (1904–1996), a former high-ranking member of the U.S. State Department, was placed on trial for espionage. The evidence against Hiss was minimal and provided mainly by one person, a former member of the American Communist Party named Whittaker Chambers (1901–1961). At the time, the Hiss trail was considered as one of "the most sensational trials in U.S. history," as it grabbed a large share of media attention. Hiss was convicted on January 21, 1950, and eventually served almost two years in prison.

The conviction of Hiss swayed a large majority of American popular opinion to believe that Communist infiltration "existed" in high levels of the U.S. government. Looking back, the evidence was circumstantial at best and Hiss spent the remainder of his life promoting his innocence, yet no one would listen. One member of the HUAC Committee who gained national recognition due to the Hiss conviction was Richard M. Nixon, a first-term congressional representative from California. (Nixon would later go on to serve as the 37th president of the United States.) Within a few weeks after the conviction, on February 9, 1950, Senator Joseph McCarthy delivered what became known as his "Enemies Within" speech in Wheeling, West Virginia. McCarthy was able to seize on a simmering panic and turn it into a full-blown mass hysteria. It was within that hysteria that another situation arose, providing the American public with "truth" about the extent of Communist infiltration in America.

Not long after the highly publicized Hiss trial, the media had another opportunity as the married couple Julius and Ethel Rosenberg was accused of espionage. The actual accusations involved "conspiracy to commit espionage" by providing atomic energy secrets to the Soviet Union. (*Conspiracy* is defined as "a secret plan by a group to do something unlawful or harmful." *Espionage* is defined as "the practice of spying or of using spies, typically by governments to obtain political and military information.") No proof existed that the Rosenberg's actually "committed" any espionage, rather the accusation upon the "conspiracy" they were planning to commit espionage.

The Rosenbergs were soon convicted for conspiracy to commit espionage. The highly publicized conviction on March 29, 1951, came with the news that both had received the death sentence. On June 19, 1953, the Rosenbergs were put to death in the electric chair in the infamous Sing Sing prison in Ossining, New York. Julius died first around 8:00 p.m.; a few minutes later Ethel was electrocuted in the same chair and died around 8:16 p.m. At the time, there was very little public sympathy for the Rosenbergs. At the trial it was revealed that during the pre-war years they had been members of the American Communist Party.

On the morning of the execution, Ethel Rosenberg wrote a farewell letter to her two young children, Michael, age ten, and Robby, age six. (The children would later be adopted by Abel Meeropol.) A significant statement to them read in part as follows:

> Eventually, too you must come to believe that life is worth the living. Be comforted that even now, with the end of ours slowly approaching, that we know this with a conviction that defeats the executioner! Your lives must teach you, too, that good cannot really flourish in the midst of evil; that freedom and all the things that go to make up a truly satisfying and worthwhile life, must sometimes be purchased very dearly. Be comforted then that we were serene and understood with the deepest kind of understanding, that civilization had not as yet progressed to the point where life did not have to be lost for the sake of life; and that we were comforted in the sure knowledge that others would carry on after us. (Meeropol, n.p.)

The death of the Rosenbergs did not end the controversy surrounding their conviction. All of the historical information pointed to the fact that Julius was probably guilty of only conspiring to enter into an espionage ring with his brother-in-law and sister-in-law, but he never did follow through and actually commit espionage. In addition, all indications were that Ethel was completely innocent. That information came to light in a 46-page, August 7, 1950, grand jury transcript of testimony provided by Ethel's brother David Greenglass. As the Meeropol brothers wrote in their request, the transcript that was made public in 2015 revealed that Greenglass had no doubts that Ethel was not involved. In 1950, Greenglass said to the grand jury, "My sister has never spoken to me about this subject. And, I said before, and say it again, honestly, this is a fact: I never spoke to my sister about this at all." The Meeropols claimed that this was one of numerous instances within the testimony that "demonstrates conclusively that our mother was prosecuted primarily for refusing to turn on our father." The evidence showed that Ethel was never in attendance when conspiracy was discussed. Yet later testimony by Greenglass showed that he reversed his previous sworn testimony to protect both himself and his own wife from prosecution (Meeropol, n.p.).

"ARE YOU NOW, OR HAVE YOU EVER BEEN, A MEMBER OF THE COMMUNIST PARTY?"

With the media attention given to the convictions of Alger Hiss and the Rosenbergs, the flames of hysteria were being fanned. There was no more dominant controversy or major issue more prevalent during than the 1950s than the Red Scare perpetuated by the HUAC and Senator Joseph McCarthy. During the height of the Red Scare, the HUAC reached its zenith and also its most xenophobic intensity from 1947 to 1954. The HUAC was an official congressional committee staffed by members of the U.S. House of Representatives and Senate. Its most prominent member and virulent voice was U.S. Senator Joseph McCarthy, a Republican from Wisconsin. (In 1969, it was renamed the Committee on Internal Security and remained as a standing committee until 1975 ("HUAC," n.p.).)

Senator McCarthy's accusations were delivered to the American public through widely read newspapers, magazines, and radio broadcasts. His picture was often prominently placed in all the national newspapers and magazines. His vibrato voice proclaiming internal subversion was often heard over the radio, as no American was unaware of his presence. McCarthy was able to seize the headlines promoting a new "Red Scare." (The first Red Scare in America occurred during 1919 to 1920 as a young J. Edgar Hoover, who served as FBI director throughout the 1950s, claimed Communists had infiltrated trade unions. He also claimed that Communists were involved with placing a series of bombs and assassination attempts upon American dignitaries.)

The full power of the HUAC was fully understood as Congress voted to override President Truman's veto of the McCarran Internal Security Act in 1950. The law stated in part that all "subversives" in the United States were required to submit to government supervision. The law also enabled McCarthy and the HUAC to basically accuse anyone of being a Communist without any factual evidence. As a result, from 1951 to 1954, a new "Red Scare" was at its zenith. The accusations falsely warned that Americans were endangered by Communist infiltration by way of Hollywood movies and also subversives had infiltrated the U.S. government, among other wild claims. The power of both the HUAC and McCarthy was so rampant and widespread that the federal government, state agencies and most businesses required employees to take an oath of loyalty to the United States of America. The question "Are you now, or have you ever been, a member of the Communist Party?" became as routine as asking a person "What time is it?" Yet, despite a lack of any proof of subversion, more than 2,000 government employees lost their jobs as a result of the mere accusation that McCarthy would launch an investigation.

Any individual who refused to take the oath was routinely fired and unofficially "blacklisted." Historian Stephen Whitfield recalled that the requirement was so ridiculous that "[a] loyalty oath was imposed on [New York state] applicants who wanted to fish in municipal reservoirs." An early 1950s Gallup Poll puts it into context: the Red Scare was indeed both real and rampant, as more than 53 percent of Americans believed that a nuclear war and invasion by the Soviets were imminent. The scare was so pervasive that for the first time the distinction between politics, culture, and leisure lifestyles was almost completely obliterated (44–45).

SENATOR MCCARTHY: "CAN YOU *SEE IT NOW*"

On March 9, 1954, the truth about McCarthy was exposed by journalist Edward R. Murrow on his *See It Now* television program. At the time, the program was among the highest-rated national programs attracting millions of trusted viewers. McCarthy refused to be interviewed for the show; nonetheless, during the half-hour show, Murrow played various recorded news clips of McCarthy. The clips aired by Murrow and his staff provided the viewing public with a sense of "how shallow" the Wisconsin senator was. The exposé also revealed the true intent of McCarthy's self-serving interests as a ploy to gain one-party control of the U.S. government.

McCarthy's first grasp at public fame came at the 1950 "Enemies Within" speech in Wheeling, West Virginia. But no cameras were available for that speech to record his statements about one-party control. As it was presented on *See It Now*, McCarthy tried to cover up his claim from that Wheeling speech in late 1952, during a recorded speech in Milwaukee:

> The American people realize that this cannot be made a fight between America's two great political parties. If this fight against communism is made a fight between America's two great political parties, the American people know that one of those parties will be destroyed, and the Republic can't endure very long as a one-party system. (Transcript: Murrow, "A Report on Senator Joseph R. McCarthy," n.p.)

On February 4, 1954, Senator McCarthy accused the Democrats who served under Roosevelt and Truman of "treason" against the American people. This was the speech in Charleston, West Virginia, where there were no cameras running. There might not have been cameras, but the wild accusations of "treason" were recorded on tape. As Murrow rolled tape, the audience heard the all-too familiar McCarthy voice bellow the words:

> The issue between Republicans and Democrats is clearly drawn. It has been deliberately drawn by those who have been in charge of twenty years of treason. Now the hard fact is—the hard fact is that those who wear the label—those who wear the label "Democrat" wear it with the stain of a historic betrayal. (Transcript: Murrow, "A Report on Senator Joseph R. McCarthy," n.p.)

Murrow continued to provide factual evidence and recorded statements of McCarthy's vicious methods of blatantly spewing lie after lie to promote his own agenda. The program certainly revealed to the viewing audience an understanding of the shallow, self-serving, demagoguery of Senator Joseph McCarthy. Murrow's closing statement carefully reminded the American public:

> It is necessary to investigate before legislating, but the line between investigating and persecuting is a very fine one, and the Junior Senator from Wisconsin has stepped over it repeatedly. His primary achievement has been in confusing the public mind as between the internal and the external threats of communism. (Transcript: Murrow, "A Report on Senator Joseph R. McCarthy," n.p.)

Murrow closed the show with his trademark statement of "Good night and good luck."

Two days after the program aired, Jack Gould, writing in *The New York Times* on March 11, 1954, said of the exposé:

> Edward R. Murrow's television program on Senator Joseph R. McCarthy was an exciting and provocative examination of the man and his methods. It was crusading journalism of high responsibility and genuine courage. For TV, so often plagued by timidity and hesitation, the program was a milestone that reflected enlightened citizenship on the part of the Columbia Broadcasting System . . . who paid the bill to make it possible. (Simon, "See It Now," n.p.)

The *See It Now* CBS-TV news program was the very first "autonomous news unit" that did not have to answer for its editorial content to either advertisers or outside political influence (Simon, "See It Now," n.p.).

Murrow's show angered some of the top executives at CBS-TV. The corporate executives of CBS suggested that Murrow had overstepped the boundaries of editorial objectivity. Yet during the 1954–1955 television season, Murrow continued a series of interviews with other controversial figures. They included:

- J. Robert Oppenheimer, the physicist accused as a Soviet spy who was removed as advisor to the Atomic Energy Commission.
- The effects of the *Brown v. Board of Education* desegregation decision.
- The link between cigarettes and lung cancer. (Murrow himself was a heavy smoker.)
- A Texas land scandal that implicated his own sponsor Alcoa (the result was a sponsorship withdrawal by the aluminum company).

Murrow's legacy has remained among the highest integrity of any news journalist in American history. In complete contrast, the decline of Senator McCarthy was about to come crashing down and be forever linked with one of the lowest points in American history.

THE ARMY-McCARTHY HEARINGS: "HAVE YOU NO SENSE OF DECENCY, SIR!"

Coming directly off of Murrow's televised exposé, the Wisconsin senator just continued on the attack with more false accusations. By April 1954, Senator

McCarthy still claimed to see Communist infiltration everywhere and any-where within the country and he was at the peak of his popularity. His growing demagoguery (an appeal to people that plays on their emotions and preju-dices rather than on their rational side) of wild accusations and outright fear mongering decrying the "growing infiltration of Communists within America" not only captivated but also swayed millions of Americans to believe his word as the ultimate truth.

Undeterred by Murrow's exposé, McCarthy decided to take on a larger fac-tion of the U.S. government, specifically the U.S. Army. Over the course of 36 days from April to June of 1954, live televised hearings captured the event. On one side was a gathering of elected representatives of both the Democratic and Republican parties; representatives from the Eisenhower Administration; mem-bers of the media; federal attorneys; and high-ranking officials of the U.S. Army. In staunch opposition was the Wisconsin senator and his small staff of G. David Shine and Roy Cohn that was described as "rag tag." In essence the battle lines were drawn between "McCarthyism" and millions of American citizens who believed his lies against the U.S. government. Eventually, the entire proceedings became known simply as "The Army-McCarthy Hearings."

In June 1954, television cameras were in the midst of over 36 days of live cov-erage from the Senate office building in Washington, D.C.; a drama unfolded as Senator McCarthy brought accusations of Communist infiltration against the U.S. Army. The news cameras kept focused on the hearings as McCarthy and his staff tried to browbeat the wide contingent of elected representatives as well as high-ranking members of the military. Those accusations claimed that the officials knowingly knew of Communists infiltrators within the U.S. Army. The tensions unfolded as McCarthy squarely placed direct accusations against the U.S. Army and high ranking officers including former General George C. Marshall.

In his relentless pursuit, McCarthy's arrogance got the best of him. With the television cameras focused on the disheveled Wisconsin senator (who by 1954, as later facts revealed, was a compulsive alcoholic), he quickly became undone. At one point, during the hearings on June 9, 1954, McCarthy actually accused the United States military of treasonous actions. Realizing that McCarthy's demagoguery had crossed the line, Senator Joseph Welch, who was serving as chief legal counsel for the U.S. Army, uttered the now famous phrase, "Have you no sense of decency, sir!" That simple phrase summed up everything about McCarthy and his staff—they had "no sense of decency."

One month after the end of the proceedings, a resolution was introduced into the U.S. Senate calling for a vote to censure McCarthy. "Censure" is defined by the U.S. Senate as:

> Less severe than expulsion, a censure (sometimes referred to as condemnation or denouncement) does not remove a senator from office. It is a formal statement of disapproval, however, that can have a powerful psychological effect on a mem-ber and his/her relationships in the Senate.

On July 30, 1954, Republican Senator Ralph Flanders of Vermont introduced a resolution calling for the censure of his colleague. In part, the resolution stated that McCarthy's actions were "contrary to senatorial traditions." Other senators added 46 specific charges of misconduct to the original censure resolution that his actions were: "inexcusable," "reprehensible," "vulgar and insulting," and "unbecoming a senator," among others.

The end of the proceedings came on December 2, 1954, as a call for a vote was proposed. By this time, the Wisconsin senator had lost many of his allies as well as public support. His colleagues in the U.S. Senate soon censured him by a vote of 67 to 22. In typical McCarthy fashion, he did not go quietly. He called the censure proceedings a "lynch party" and actually accused his fellow Republican senators as an "unwitting handmaiden of the Communist Party." Despite the vote, the Wisconsin senator did not lose his senate seat, but he did lose all his luster and power. In May 1957, he died due to his severe alcoholism at the age of 48 (History.com, "Joseph R. McCarthy," n.p.).

THE HUAC AND PAUL ROBESON

Joe McCarthy might have been finished, but not the HUAC. On June 12, 1956, the great African-American entertainer and social activist Paul Robeson (1898–1976) was called before the HUAC. He was just one of many African Americans (including baseball legend Jackie Robinson) subpoenaed to appear before the HUAC. Robeson was an extremely talented, diversified athlete, actor, singer, and performer. As a student at Rutgers University he was a Phi Beta Kappa as well as an all-American football player who lettered 12 times in four sports. He earned a law degree from Columbia University, but faced severe segregation in an attempt to work with any New York law firms. He eventually pursued an internationally known career as an accomplished Shakespearean stage actor as well as starred on Broadway and in Hollywood movies. Throughout it all he was an outspoken social activist for civil rights.

The HUAC hearings resulted in Robeson's attempt to retain a passport that was revoked in 1950. In July 1954, he reapplied for a passport. To obtain the document, federal regulations required each citizen to sign a non-Communist affidavit. He refused and was subsequently denied. In turn, Robeson was called before the congressional committee as an example "on the vital issue of the use of American passports as travel documents in furtherance of the objectives of the Communist conspiracy." Although he was continually pestered by committee members to publicly state his political affiliations, Robeson defiantly stated, "Under no conditions would I think of signing any such affidavit, that it is a complete contradiction of the rights of American citizens."

Towards the end of the hearing, Robeson accused the HUAC as the "un-Americans." After a long arduous interrogation, Robeson added, "You gentlemen belong with the Alien and Sedition Acts, and you are the nonpatriots, and you are the un-Americans, and you ought to be ashamed of yourselves." Immediately after that statement the HUAC chairman quickly interceded and declared, "The hearing is now adjourned." Despite the fact that Robeson wanted to read and enter a rebuttal into the record, the chairman once again replied, "No, you cannot read it. The meeting is adjourned." Two years after the hearing, the U.S. Supreme Court ruled that a citizen's right to travel could not be taken away without "constitutional due process." As a result, Robeson has his passport returned ("Testimony of Paul Robeson before the HUAC").

FURTHER READING

Michael Barson and Steven Heller. *Red Scared: The Commie Menace in Propaganda and Popular Culture*. San Francisco: Chronicle Books, 2001.

Douglas Brinkley. *Rosa Parks*. New York: Viking Press, 2000.

Ann Fessler. *The Girls Who Went Away: The Hidden Story of Women Who Surrendered Children for Adoption in the decades Before Roe v. Wade*. New York: Penguin, 2006.

Eric Foner. *The Story of American Freedom*. New York: W. W. Norton & Company, 1998.

James W. Loewen. *Lies My Teacher Told Me*. New York: Touchstone Books, Simon & Schuster, Inc, 2007.

James W. Loewen. *Teaching What Really Happened*, New York: Teachers College Press 2009.

Danielle McGuire. *At the Dark End of the Street: Black Women, Rape, and Resistance*. New York: Vintage Books, 2011.

Francis Trevelyan Miller and John W. Davis. *Geography By Grades, Grade 4B: The Earth, The Continents*. New York: Hinds, Hayden & Eldredge, Inc., 1926.

Juan Williams. *Eyes on the Prize: America's Civil Rights Years 1954—1965*. New York: Penguin Books, 1987.

Howard Zinn. *A People's History of the United States*. New York: Harper Perennial, 2005.

CHAPTER 11

Game Changers

Weapons employed by the United States in the ideological fight against the Soviets were God and patriotism. Both were used to battle the so-called "godless Communists." (The term *godless* was applied because the Soviet Union adopted atheism as a state belief.) Any non-religious American, or worse yet, a self-proclaimed atheist, was deemed suspicious. By the mid-1950s, American patriotism was fostered by various fraternal organizations such as the American Legion with more than three million members, the Knights of Columbus at 920,000 members, and the Catholic War Veterans with more than 200,000 members. (Their membership was almost exclusively white and male.) All of those organizations held onto a strong belief in mandatory patriotic loyalty and religion (Whitfield, 92).

A significant number of Americans claimed a religious affiliation as church membership reached an all-time high. The U.S. Census Bureau indicated that 96 percent of the nation's population cited a religious affiliation. The overwhelming majority of the population, at more than 66 percent, was Christian Protestant. (The more common Protestant denominations included Anglican, Baptist, Calvinist, Lutheran, Methodist, Pentecostal, and Seventh-day Adventist.) More than 26 percent claimed Catholicism. Less than 3 percent were Jewish and about 1 percent claimed "other." Religious leaders such as Catholic Bishop Fulton Sheen (1895–1979), Protestant Reverend Norman Vincent Peale (1898–1993), and Evangelist Billy Graham (1918–) rose to national prominence as anti-Communist crusaders. Each had syndicated newspaper columns, best-selling books, and television programs.

The fiercest anti-Communist crusader was Billy Graham, whose weekly column was carried in more than 125 newspapers. An estimated 50 million people regularly watched his television show. Cultural historian Stephen Whitfield said that Graham promoted regular church attendance preaching a message against not only Communism, but also the "sins of drinking, smoking, card playing, dancing, swearing, [and] reading salacious magazines." Graham received overwhelming support as he received more than 10,000 weekly letters praising his mission. That "support" often came with significant monetary donations, which made Graham a wealthy individual (Whitfield, 77–79, 83).

GOD, THE PLEDGE OF ALLEGIANCE: "AND JUSTICE FOR ALL?"

All of the fraternal organizations and religious leaders held a firm belief to affirm patriotism with a mandatory reciting of the American Pledge of Allegiance. In 2003, an article in *Smithsonian Magazine* titled "The Man Who Wrote the Pledge of Allegiance" noted, "The schoolroom staple didn't originally include 'under God,' even though it was created by an ordained minister." The minister was Francis Bellamy (1855–1931) who was also a self-proclaimed socialist. In fact, the "Pledge" does not even date to colonial times. It was first written in 1892 and as a simple 23-word statement, as follows:

> I PLEDGE ALLEGIANCE TO MY FLAG,
> AND TO THE REPUBLIC FOR WHICH IT STANDS:
> ONE NATION INDIVISIBLE,
> WITH LIBERTY AND JUSTICE FOR ALL.
> (Written by Francis Bellamy, October 1892)

Bellamy, the son of a minister, continued his father's tradition preaching as an ordained minister in both Boston and New York. Around 1891, Bellamy left the pulpit because his sermons leaned too heavily upon his socialist creed. He accepted a position to write for a Boston magazine called *The Youth's Companion* (published from 1827 to 1929). The magazine had a substantial mail-order subscription of more than 500,000. At the time, the 37-year-old Bellamy was assigned by editor Daniel Ford to work with a department "arranging a patriotic program for schools around the country to coincide with opening ceremonies for the Columbian Exposition in October 1892." The Columbian Exposition coincided with the 400th anniversary of Christopher Columbus's voyages to the New World.

Bellamy's Pledge of Allegiance was published on September 8, 1892, in *The Youth's Companion* with a detailed description for the proper observance of the forthcoming Columbus Day celebration. One source suggested that Bellamy wished to write in the word "equality" for the final line to read as, "with Liberty, Equality, and Justice for All." However, Bellamy was fully aware that "equality" was not available at the time for either women or blacks. Therefore, he omitted the word rather than face the problem of either being forced to remove it, or have it rejected outright by his editor. Bellamy did provide his own account of why he chose the specific wording of his Pledge:

> It began as an intensive communing with salient points of our national history, from the Declaration of Independence onwards; with the makings of the Constitution . . . with the meaning of the Civil War; with the aspiration of the people. . . .

> The true reason for allegiance to the Flag is the republic for which it stands. . . . And what does that vast thing, the Republic mean? It is the concise political word for the Nation—the One Nation that the Civil War was fought to prove. To make that One Nation idea clear, we must specify that it is indivisible, as Webster and Lincoln used to repeat in their great speeches. And its future? (Baer, n.p.)

In later years, Bellamy recalled that as the publishing deadline neared, his editor said, "You write it. You have a knack at words." Bellamy produced the pledge in about two hours as "a succinct and rhythmic tribute" (Baer, n.p.).

One key element proposed by Bellamy was a unified salute to the American flag. One notion was that a unified salute to one flag might heal some of the wounds from the catastrophic divisive Civil War. The request proved fruitful. President Benjamin Harrison issued by a joint resolution on July 21, 1892, of the Senate and House of Representatives a proclamation that read in part:

> That the President of the United States be authorized and directed to issue a proclamation recommending to the people the observance in all their localities of the four hundredth anniversary of the discovery of America, on the 21st of October, 1892, by public demonstrations and by suitable exercises in their schools and other places of assembly. ("Proclamation 335: 400th Anniversary of the Discovery of America by Columbus")

In the earlier September 8, 1892, issue of *The Youth's Companion*, Bellamy described the proper salute during the recital of the pledge upon a signal from the school principal. In response, all the students would face the flag with their hands at their sides "in ordered ranks." They would begin "with a military salute." ("Right hand lifted, palm downward, to a line with the forehead and close to it hand held at forehead.") After the words "to the flag" (and as signaled by the principal) he proposed that the arm be "extended toward the flag." He noted "till the end of the affirmation; whereupon all hands immediately drop to the side" (Bellamy, 446).

During the 1920s, a "National Flag Conference" was organized jointly by the American Legion and the Daughters of the American Revolution. Their mission was to change the words of the pledge (without consultation or approval by Bellamy, who was still alive) from "my flag" to "the flag of the United States." The reason cited was so that "immigrant children" would know exactly "which flag they were saluting." The 1923 revision took out the arbitrary term of "my flag" and clarified it to read:

I PLEDGE ALLEGIANCE TO **THE** FLAG
OF THE UNITED STATES,
AND TO THE REPUBLIC FOR WHICH IT STANDS:
ONE NATION INDIVISIBLE,
WITH LIBERTY AND JUSTICE FOR ALL.
(*Revised*: June 14, 1923)

In 1924, it was revised again. The National Flag Conference met to add the words "of America" to complete the full phrase "the flag of the United States of America." The new official revision adopted by the U.S. Congress for Flag Day observance of 1924 read as:

I PLEDGE ALLEGIANCE TO THE FLAG
OF THE UNITED STATES **OF AMERICA**,
AND TO THE REPUBLIC FOR WHICH IT STANDS,
ONE NATION INDIVISIBLE
WITH LIBERTY AND JUSTICE FOR ALL.
(*Revised*: June 14, 1924)

The Pledge went through revisions, but the flag salute remained consistent. It was a raised right arm, fingers close together and palm down, known as the "Olympic Salute."

Controversy over the Pledge salute arose during the 1936 Olympics in Berlin, Germany. The raised right hand of the "Olympic Salute" was similar to the American Pledge of Allegiance, yet it was also the official salute of the Nazi Party under Adolf Hitler. Many of the athletes were aware of what Hitler was doing in Europe and refused to salute in the same manner. In one instance, American athlete Jesse Owens chose a military salute. On the stand alongside Owens for his acceptance of a gold medal for the long jump, German silver medalist Luz Long provided the "Heil Hitler" salute. Later in 1942, as the United States was involved in World War II, Congress rejected the American Nazi-style salute and replaced it with a hand over the heart.

In 1954, the right hand over the heart became official by a Congressional decree, as did an affirmation to God. A well-orchestrated lobbying campaign led by the Catholic Fraternal organization Knights of Columbus demanded the insertion of the words "one nation under God" into the Pledge of Allegiance. Their desire to provide an overriding proclamation of religion into politics was disguised under the declaration of "fighting Communism." They claimed, "The phrase 'under God' recognizes only the guidance of God in our national affairs" (Whitfield, 124).

The resolution for adding "under God" as part of "one nation indivisible" passed both houses of Congress. The Congressional resolution adding Section 4 of the Flag Code that was signed into law by President Dwight D. Eisenhower states:

The Pledge of Allegiance to the Flag: "I pledge allegiance to the Flag of the United States of America, and to the Republic for which it stands, one Nation under God, indivisible, with liberty and justice for all" should be rendered by standing at attention facing the flag with the right hand over the heart. When not in uniform men should remove any non-religious headdress with their right hand and hold it at the left shoulder, the hand being over the heart. Persons in uniform should remain silent, face the flag, and render the military salute.

Eisenhower signed the law into effect on Flag Day of June 14, 1954. He said, "In this way we are reaffirming the transcendence of religious faith in America's heritage and future; in this way we shall constantly strengthen those spiritual weapons which forever will be our country's most powerful resource in peace and war." The revised official Pledge of Allegiance that has remained in place to the current day reads as follows:

> I PLEDGE ALLEGIANCE TO THE FLAG
> OF THE UNITED STATES OF AMERICA,
> AND TO THE REPUBLIC FOR WHICH IT STANDS,
> ONE NATION **UNDER GOD** INDIVISIBLE,
> WITH LIBERTY AND JUSTICE FOR ALL.
> (*Revised*: June 14, 1954)

Francis Bellamy was never consulted for any of the revisions to his Pledge of Allegiance. As the revisions were made while he was alive, he never made a public statement. After his death, his granddaughter objected to the phrase "under God." In a 2003 article for *Smithsonian Magazine*, Jeffrey Owen Jones (1944–2007) speculated, "But it's ironic that the debate centers on a reference to God that an ordained minister left out. And we can be sure that Bellamy, if he was like most writers, would have balked at anyone tinkering with his prose" ("The Man Who Wrote the Pledge of Allegiance").

A SUBURBAN SHIFT OF THE POPULATION

The massive American population shift to suburbia was the most visible example of social change after the war. In 1940, less than 10 percent of Americans lived in suburbs. During the post-war period, spurred by FHA and VA supported loans, more than 40 million Americans moved to the suburbs. Millions of new homes were built and over 85 percent of the new homes were single-family detached homes in suburban developments. By 1964, the population of the country was almost evenly divided in thirds among the suburbs, cities, and rural areas. More significant was that for the first time more Americans owned homes rather than rented.

It was the sheer amount of homes that were built during the post-World War II period that greatly changed the face of American home dwelling. In the pre-war years, the suburban houses almost universally had a front porch and orientated family life towards the front of the house. The front porch was eliminated on most of the new homes as a way of reducing building costs. The outside life was shifted towards the backyard, which was often closed in with a perimeter fence. As social interaction was limited, activity was promoted such as caring for the lawn, gardening, or relaxing in a hammock, among other simple pursuits. Almost as quickly as the new homes were built, so was the need for an immaculate front lawn as the ultimate prestige symbol of the new suburbia. Yet the lawn was nothing more than a well-maintained area of green grass often without having to add any flowers or tress. Mowing the lawn and keeping an immaculate garden became a symbol of suburban civic pride.

The media often promoted an idealized version of a backyard barbeque for a family cookout. The thought of owning a suburban home and being able to buy items that were in either short supply or non-existent during the war quickly became a new craze. An overwhelming amount of consumer products for the home such as washing machines, clothes dryers, automobiles, and, of course, television sets, permeated society. Television sitcoms and commercials aided the cause with a continuous promotion of consumerism and the idea that a "woman's place was in the home." In contrast, the man's place was in the garage or workshop. For the suburban male, the converted garages or basements served as a substitute for the pre-war urban saloon as a meeting place. Magazines and television advertisements illustrated this phenomenon as an almost exclusive male environment (Giordano, 2003, 148–149).

THE BIG THREE, THE V8 ENGINE, AND AUTO VACATIONS

During the war, Americans were often besieged by images of the "Big Three" of the Allied leaders: Winston Churchill, Franklin D. Roosevelt, and Josef Stalin. After the war, a new "Big Three" emerged that changed the production facilities which had churned out massive amounts of war material to produce the most desired and visible of all the post-war consumer products—the American automobile. The new "Big Three" included the American automakers of Ford Motor Company, Chrysler Corporation, and General Motors. By the mid-1950s, the "Big Three" automakers accounted for more than 94 percent of all the cars sold in the United States. At the time, almost all of the production came out of midwestern American factories.

In 1945, the country had 25.6 million registered automobiles. Most were more than 10 years old, as new production was virtually non-existent due to wartime needs. As peacetime prosperity increased, a significant number of new car purchases were made. By 1950, the number of registered vehicles numbered 40.1 million. By mid-decade it was 52 million, and by 1960 more than 74 million automobiles were registered in the United States. New purchases amounted to over 68 million as more than 4.5 million old cars were scrapped each year. The numbers of used cars being bought and sold also increased dramatically. The number of auto sales continued spiraling upward with over 91 million by 1965. By the year 1970, as suburbia was firmly entrenched within American society, the number of registered automobiles was 111.2 million (Halberstam, 486–487).

The boom in the production of automobiles can often be paralleled with the massive construction of interstate highways, which came about on June 29, 1956, as President Dwight Eisenhower signed the Federal-Aid Highway Act of 1956. The official name was "The National System of Interstate and Defense Highways." The act was declared "essential to the national interest" to build paved roads to interconnect all the towns and cities with a population in excess of 50,000 people. The proponents of the bill claimed the roads were an absolute necessity for national defense "in case of atomic attack on our key cities, the road net [would] permit quick evacuation of target areas." According to Eisenhower, the new plan would eliminate unsafe roads, inefficient routes, traffic jams, and all that got in the way of "speedy, safe transcontinental travel."

The highways interconnected a seemingly endless open road, allowing Americans to travel at their own leisure with amenities never before imagined. The highways also provided access to the new suburban developments such as Levittown in Long Island and Levittown in Pennsylvania, among dozens of

Chart 11.1   Total Number of U.S. Automobiles,
1940–2015

Year	In Millions
1940	27.3
1945	25.6
1950	40.1
1955	51.9
1960	74.3
1965	91.7
1970	111.2
1975	137.9
1980	161.5
1985	177.1
1990	193.1
1995	205.4
2000	225.8
2005	247.5
2010	250.1
2015	257.8

Source: U.S. Department of Transportation. Chart
compiled by author.

others. Unlike the pre-war highways, the interstates were wider, averaging two
to three lanes in each direction. One aspect of achieving the allocation of the
large federal budget was a claim that the long, wide, straight highways could
double as landing fields for the strategic air command. They could also provide easier evacuation from the cities in case of a nuclear attack. Many, however, believed that aspect was just a Cold War ploy.

With the massive amount of auto production came a concentration on styling rather than convenience. Advertisers continually stressed the idea of trading in the old model every couple of years to buy a "new and improved model."
As for the styling initiatives, consumer advocate Ralph Nader would later call
it "stylistic pornography over engineering integrity." For the auto manufacturers, the technology was rapidly advancing not for safety and convenience, but
rather speed and power. The constant push was for advanced technology for
engines with more horsepower. As historian Karal Ann Marling,wrote, "Arguably the most influential change in automotive history was the overhead-valve
V8 engine" (160–161).

In 1954, V8 automobile engines pushed out 250 horsepower (hp), a significant increase from the 6-cylinder 100hp to 160hp engines of previous years.
The 6-cylinder engines were usually in a straight line and therefore known as
an "inline engine." The designation of a "V8" indicated that the engine was an
8-cylinder "vee shape." It had two sets of four cylinders with spark plugs on

either side of the engine block igniting the pistons. The cylinders drove a common crankshaft connected to the driveshaft mounted to a differential transmission to turn the rear wheels. (Most powered only one of the rear wheels.) The extra power provided by the V8 allowed for new, extra-cost features such as air conditioning, but the main output for the engine was speed (Halberstam, 495).

THE AUTO VACATION

During the post-war period, vacationing became available as a permanent way of life for middle-class Americans. A 1954 Department of Commerce survey indicated more than 83 percent of the middle class and 47 percent of the working class took a yearly vacation. More than 62 percent vacationed at least twice a year with an average combined stay of 18 days. Many modes of transportation existed, yet 80 percent of all pleasure trips were by automobile. By mid-decade, the U.S. Bureau of Public Roads estimated that for a specific trip for outdoor recreation, more than 93 percent favored getting to their destination by automobile. One 1952 Michigan Travel Bureau survey and a 1953 Colorado survey indicated similar destination results for automobile travelers. Over 70 percent of the combined respondents drove on a sightseeing adventure. Over 55 percent of the auto travelers went on fishing excursions, mostly to lakes. Another 40 percent went to the beaches and lakes, and 13 percent camped. The lodgings for these types of activities were usually in roadside motels (Jakle, 186–87; Kaplan, 212).

In 1951, more than 26,000 independent roadside motels existed across the country. Very few were alike and conditions varied from excellent to barely acceptable. Room rates varied, as did unadvertised extra costs, such as for children. The construction of the new interstate highway system actually eliminated many the former surprises of the bygone eras. All along the new highways came the construction of new gas stations and repair shops with familiar names such as Texaco, which was a sponsor of the popular Milton Berle television show. Along the highways, new standardized motels, hotels, and restaurant chains that included Holiday Inn and Howard Johnson's appeared.

In 1952, Kemmons Wilson opened the first Holiday Inn outside Memphis, Tennessee. With his new hotel, Wilson sought to standardize and create a friendly environment for the traveler and family. The Holiday Inn sign came to represent a clean room, an available restaurant, no surprises, and children always free of charge. By 1970, Wilson eventually expanded his franchise to include more than 1,500 motels along the nation's highways. Howard Johnson's had existed prior to the war, operating as a small chain of restaurants offering inexpensive meals and numerous flavors of ice cream. In response to the ongoing suburban building boom, the chain expanded by 1954 to include more than 400 restaurants operating in 32 states. Their trademark high-peaked, orange roof was instantly recognizable and motoring families knew immediately what to expect. In 1959, Howard Johnson's opened their first motor lodge, which was a combined motel and restaurant. The chain expanded rapidly and within 20 years operated more than 1,000 restaurants and 520 motor lodges (Halberstam, 177–179).

AUTOMOBILE DEATHS, SAFETY, AND SEATBELTS

The automobile increased the mobility of many Americans. Yet the benefit of the new freedom was accompanied by deadly new risks. The power of the V8 engines, for example, did in fact produce more speed, which in turn produced more accidents and fatalities. Therefore, the average car placed a significant amount of power and speed in the hands of millions of people. With the abundance of cars on the American roads, the number of accidents and deaths increased. The causes and effective solutions were soon being researched and debated by physicians, safety advocates, engineers, journalists, and others. No common consensus was agreed upon as differing opinions about the causes of accidents, injuries, and fatalities were numerous.

A sad attachment to the growing number of automobiles was the rising death toll from auto accidents. By 1950, the accumulative total of those killed in accidents since the inception of the automobile for the previous 50 years or so claimed about one million lives. The figures are estimated, since the National Highway Traffic Safety Administration NHTSA only began accurately tracking traffic fatalities in 1950. Yet, just during the 10-year period of the 1950s, more than 385,000 individuals were killed in auto accidents on the American roads and millions more were injured. By 2010, the American population was about twice that of 1950 (152.3 million to 308.7 million), yet with more than 250 million cars the traffic fatalities numbered 33,808. In addition, the NHTSA reported traffic deaths in 2010 to 2015 were much lower statistically than the 1950s. The reason why the fatalities did not keep pace with the population growth was a result of federally mandated safety restrictions placed upon the auto manufacturers.

The NHTSA stated that the leading cause of death for those between the ages of 3 and 34 was automobile accidents. Another factor not included within the statistics is how many of the deaths were alcohol-related. Technically, driving while drunk was against the law, but at the time, it was very often overlooked.

Chart 11.2   U.S. Automobile Traffic Deaths, 1950–1960

Year	Total Deaths
1950	33,186
1951	35,309
1952	36,088
1953	36,190
1954	33,890
1955	36,688
1956	37,965
1957	36,932
1958	35,331
1959	36,223
1960	36,399

Source: Federal Statistics at SafeRoad.org. Chart compiled by author.

The NHTSA noted that alcohol-related traffic deaths were one of the leading causes of traffic accidents, amounting to one-third of all fatalities.

Alcohol was not the only reason for traffic deaths and accidents, as there were many causes. During the decade, some notable automobile tragic accidents garnered headlines, including:

1949

- *August 16:* Margaret Mitchell, author of *Gone with the Wind*, died at the age of 48 in Atlanta, Georgia, after being hit by a drunken taxicab driver.

1955

- *September 30:* Movie actor James Dean was killed while driving on a California highway. (See Film chapter.)

1956

- *March 21:* Singer Carl Perkins was seriously injured in a car crash on his way to a performance. His brother Jay Perkins was killed. The injury seriously curtailed Perkins' career as he was skyrocketing to fame with his hit "Blue Suede Shoes."
- *August 11:* Famed pop artist Jackson Pollock (see Art and Architecture chapter) died at the age of 44. He lost control of his car near East Hampton, New York, and hit an oak tree. He apparently died instantly of a skull fracture.

1957

- *July 3:* Actress Judy Tyler who played opposite Elvis Presley in *Jailhouse Rock* died at the age of 24 in a car crash in Wyoming. Her husband Gregory was also killed, as they were driving home to New York after completing the movie. She was well known to a legion of young children as Princess Summerfall Winterspring on *The Howdy Doody Show* from 1950 to 1953. (See Television chapter.)

As concerns arose over traffic safety, so did the scientific study of auto safety. Independent testing labs began researching both the causes of automobile accidents and the impact upon humans involved in a collision. One idea to eliminate injury and fatalities was the simple suggestion to provide a padded dashboard. By 1956, most of the auto manufacturers installed a padded dashboard—but only at additional cost. By the mid-1960s, the U.S. government responded with legislation requiring mandatory padded dashboards as a standard feature. One specific item that proved without a doubt to save lives was the seat belt. In 1948, auto pioneer Preston Tucker (1903–1956) had offered both seat belts and a padded dashboard in an experimental concept car. In 1949, the Nash Motors Company was the first car manufacturer to offer a safety type of seat belt, but as an extra cost option on some limited models. Yet, by the mid-1950s, with more than 90 percent of the market controlled by the Chrysler

Corporation, the Ford Motor Company, and General Motors, seat belts were almost non-existent. The extra cost was resisted, as the Big Three lobbied Congress to forestall them as mandatory. By 1955, only the Ford Motor Company offered seat belts as an extra cost option on limited models. Yet only 2 percent of the Ford buyers purchased the seatbelt option ("Starting to Click: A History of Automotive Seatbelts," n.p.).

The first three-point restraint seat belt (which by the 21st century was mandated by federal law) was patented in 1955 by two Americans, Roger W. Griswold and Hugh DeHaven. It was improved by another Swedish car company, Volvo, which provided it as standard equipment in 1959. Volvo had tested the three-point device in a study of more than 28,000 accidents below an average speed of 60 mph. In all cases, when the three-point seat belt was used, fatalities amounted to zero, whereas no seat belt restraint proved fatal in many cases. Despite the significant statistical evidence, the Big Three were slow to react, but by 1964, in advance of a forthcoming federal mandate, most of their models had three-point front seat belts as standard equipment. The response was due mainly to the media sensation created by a young consumer advocate ("Starting to Click: A History of Automotive Seatbelts," n.p.).

UNSAFE AT ANY SPEED

"For over half a century the automobile has brought death, injury and the most inestimable sorrow and deprivation to millions of people."

Ralph Nader, *Unsafe at Any Speed*

For many years Congress, aided by lobbying efforts by the Big Three, did not respond to the inherent danger of the automobile. In fact, the congressional response was only prompted by the sensation provided in a nationwide bestseller by a young consumer advocate named Ralph Nader. In 1956, as a second-year law student at Harvard University, Nader first began researching the automobile industry for inherent safety violations. Throughout the years, he kept coming back to his research as he decided upon applying his law skills to protect the American consumer. Nader cited a 1959 Department of Commerce report projecting a death total of 51,000 persons would be killed by automobiles in 1975. Yet, at the current rate of automobile purchases and access to new interstate highways, some forecasted that number of deaths on the roads would happen within half that time. Nader's work led to a public outcry for the automakers to be responsible to add safety measures in their products to reduce the amount of fatalities.

On April 11, 1959, Nader provided a preview of what was to come in his later publication. In "The *Safe* Car You Can't Buy" (italics in original title) for *The Nation*, Nader claimed, "It is clear that Detroit today is designing automobiles for style, cost, performance and calculated obsolescence, but not for safety" (Nader, "The Article That Launched the Consumer-Rights Movement" n.p.). He noted instances of doors that became unhinged during an accident, that would "fly open on impact." He reported other instances of seats that were not secured properly to the frame, causing occupants to be flung from the vehicle during an impact. He also provided evidence on the inadequacy of windshield glass. During a car crash, passengers were often thrown forward, with their heads crashing into a broken windshield with sufficient force to "chisel one's head into fractions." He also included other dangers such as glove compartment doors that loosened and "were known to guillotine a child." He noted that previous years' accident investigations had focused on driver error without concern for a major factor in accidents and deaths, which was the product itself (Nader, "The *Safe* Car You Can't Buy," n.p.).

In 1965, as a 32-year-old experienced lawyer, Nader explained, "I aspired to the level of getting a law through, getting an agency to implement it." In November 1965, Nader's publication *Unsafe at Any Speed: The Designed-in Dangers of the American Automobile* provided the public with startling evidence on the inherent danger of the American automobile. His opening sentence said it all: "For over half a century the automobile has brought death, injury and the most inestimable sorrow and deprivation to millions of people." Nader's bestseller caused shock, revelation, reality, and concern for safety by the American consumer. The staff at History.com added:

> Nader's book popularized some harsh truths about cars and car companies that auto-safety advocates had known for some time. In 1956, at a series of Congressional hearings on traffic safety, doctors and other experts lamented the "wholesale slaughter" on American highways. ("Unsafe at any Speed Hits Bookstores," n.p.)

As an assault upon the "human body," all businesses were soon obligated by law to fully examine the risk before launching an advertising campaign to the consumer. They were required to define any new product laden with risks. In 1953, the post-war courts placed the burden upon the manufacturer "to produce a safe product." In *Dalehite v. United States*, Supreme Court Justice Robert H. Jackson (1892–1954) defined the duty of the manufacturers by saying,

> Where experiment or research is necessary to determine the presence or the degree of danger, the product must not be tried out on the public, nor must the public be expected to possess the facilities or the technical knowledge to learn for itself of inherent but latent dangers. The claim that a hazard was not foreseen is not available to one who did not use foresight appropriate to his enterprise.

At the time, the law was aimed at protecting the consumer and the public concerning safety.

Nader noted that when it came to money the auto manufacturers as well as other makers of consumer products placed the emphasis on profit rather than safety of the people. He said, "A great problem of contemporary life is how to control the power of economic interests, which ignore the harmful effects of their applied science and technology." That statement was aimed directly at the Big Three auto manufacturers, yet it could easily have been applied to just about every American industry at the time. One aspect of American society that completely ignored the harmful effects was the U.S. Atomic Energy

Commission. Yet the application of technology, science, the automobile, and suburbia came together in suburban amusement parks.

DISNEYLAND

On July 17, 1955, the idea of an amusement park was forever changed with the opening of a theme park in California. The idea of Disneyland came directly from Walt Disney. Unlike the earlier amusement parks that were easily accessible by public transportation, the Disney theme park was located in suburban Anaheim, California. It was far from the inner urban areas and only accessible by automobile or excursion bus. The Disney focus was on "a clean family atmosphere" and a return to a fantasy idea of yesteryear. Similar to the suburban housing developments, its remote location provided an atmosphere that appeared free of any social, political, or economical conflicts of the time (Giordano, 2003, 157–158).

During the 1950s, the Disney studios had produced some of the highest-grossing movies that included *Cinderella* (1950); *Peter Pan* (1953); *Sleeping Beauty* (1959); and the top film for the entire decade, *Lady and the Tramp* (1955). As the popularity of his studio grew, Disney was often besieged with regular requests to tour the studio grounds. Those requests are often credited with providing the initial idea for a central location that the public could visit.

Shortly after the war, he purchased 160 acres of land in suburban Anaheim. The acquisition of the land coincided with the new Federal Aid Highway Act of 1956. The roads to and around the Anaheim park were rebuilt from a smaller U.S. route into a larger and wider interstate highway. The new highway allowed easy access to the park, but was limited to either an automobile or an excursion bus. The land purchase was not unusual as thousands of acres in suburbia were being purchased for new home development. Disney was not buying the land to build houses; he had another idea.

During the 1950s, ABC-TV had a hit afternoon lineup that featured the teenage dance show *American Bandstand* followed by the *Mickey Mouse Club*. The *Mickey Mouse Club* quickly became a perennial

Walt Disney conceived of the idea for Disneyland, which opened on July 17, 1955, in California. (Library of Congress)

favorite among the United States' children. Its popularity was soon paired with a nighttime show *Walt Disney Presents*, that was later renamed *The Wonderful World of Disney*. In 1960, it aired weekly on Sunday nights and ran for 21 years. Prior to his death in 1964, Disney was the on-air host of the weekly series. The TV show was developed as a way of securing the financial means to build the Disney amusement park. In 1954, ABC-TV and Walt Disney reached a common agreement to provide programming for three years. In exchange the payment for those programs would be used for construction of Disneyland (The Disney empire would get so big it eventually purchased the ABC-TV station in 1995 for $19 billion.) (Polsson, "Chronology of Disneyland Theme Park," n.p.).

The original Disneyland was credited as being designed and built under the direct supervision of Walt Disney. According to the Walt Disney Family Museum, the concept began when he visited Griffith Park, an amusement park in Los Angeles, with his daughters. Supposedly, as he stood and watched his children enjoying the rides, he envisioned a singular place where adults and children could enjoy attractions together as a family. Yet as he sat on a bench watching his daughters play, he noticed that the small amusement park was dirty and unkempt. He also observed how people reacted to the different types of rides. Of special notice was that adults had very little to do other than watch the children have fun. He thought about a new type of amusement park, one that would always be immaculately clean and also provide attractions for both parents and children: Disney explained his concept as:

> What this country really needs is an amusement park that families can take their children to. They've gotten so honky tonk with a lot of questionable characters running around, and they're not so safe. They're not well kept. I want to have a place that's as clean as anything could ever be, and all the people in it [his park] are first-class citizens, and treated like guests.

Credit for the overall planning of the park is given directly to Walt Disney down "to every detail" ("Walt Disney's Disneyland," n.p.).

Disney's pride and joy was in the design and construction of "Main Street, U.S.A." Along this route was where all visitors would enter the park before branching out into four different themed areas: For the design of the theme park, he said:

> For those of us who remember the carefree time it recreates, Main Street will bring back happy memories. For younger visitors, it is an adventure in turning back the calendar to the days of grandfather's youth.

The design does serve as a good reminder that the ideological nostalgia of a misguided historical past presented Americans with just as much a fantasy as the theme park.

On July 17, 1955, visitors were greeted by a proclamation which read:

> To all who come to this happy place: Welcome. Disneyland is your land. Here age relives fond memories of the past, and here youth may savor the challenge

and promise of the future. Disneyland is dedicated to the ideals, the dreams, and the hard facts that have created America, with the hope that it will be a source of joy and inspiration to all the world.

The first-day gala event was "invitation only" with the opening for the general public scheduled for the following day. The grand opening ceremonies were televised to a nationwide audience on ABC-TV, hosted by celebrities and friends of Walt Disney that included Art Linkletter, Bob Cummings, and Ronald Reagan (Cotter, 17).

Unfortunately, the day had many problems, which included temperatures in excess of 100°F. (One account listed the temperature at 110°F.) Other problems included broken drinking fountains, traffic jams, limited food supply, unfinished construction, and the unexpected closure of some rides due to malfunction. Three of the theme park areas, Adventureland, Frontierland, and Fantasyland, closed early due to a gas leak. By all accounts, the day was considered "a terrible disaster." Later Disney and his staff called the event "Black Sunday." Despite the initial setbacks, Disneyland was an immediate success. In the first six months, more than one million customers entered the park. (Visitation would soon reach over 16 million per year.) Through the years Disneyland expanded and renovated. In 1971, another larger and more expansive theme park was opened as Walt Disney World in Orlando, Florida. By the late 1970s, Walt Disney World Resort became the world's best-known destination vacation resort ("Disneyland History," n.p.).

BUCKMINSTER FULLER AND "SPACESHIP EARTH"

With the opening of EPCOT Center as the second of four theme parks of Disney World in Florida, the most recognizable of all Disney buildings, other than the iconic Cinderella's Castle, was Spaceship Earth that opened on October 1, 1982. Disney advertised it as "the iconic and symbolic structure of Epcot." The unique design of the world's first "geodesic sphere" is credited to Richard Buckminster "Bucky" Fuller (1895–1983), first designed during the 1950s. Fuller was a world-renowned 20th-century inventor, architect, engineer, systems theorist, designer, and humanitarian. The Buckminster Fuller Institute described him as a "comprehensive anticipatory design scientist," adding, "Fuller's true impact on the world today can be found in his continued influence upon generations of designers, architects, scientists and artists working to create a more sustainable planet." During his lifetime, he received 28 patents, wrote 28 books, and received 47 honorary degrees. The most famous of all of his innovations was the geodesic dome, which from time to time was applied in an attempt to solve some of the previously mentioned world problems.

Fuller spent his entire life striving to make the earth a better place "to help humanity better understand, benefit from, and more efficiently utilize the world's resources for humanity." He later provided a follow-up publication titled *Operating Manual for Spaceship Earth* (1968), in which he described all the inhabitants of Earth as "astronauts" living on the Spaceship Earth.

Around 1951, he developed the basis for an easy-to-assemble, lightweight dome capable of spanning distances without any interior support columns. Fuller's dome applied a mathematical engineering concept of using metal tubing in the simplest, yet strongest of all geometric forms: the triangle. The result was a structure able to withstand severe climatic conditions. He termed the concept "synergetic geometry," providing a balance between the tension and compression forces of a structure. Fuller conceived a similar idea of a "geodesic dome" that received a U.S. patent on June 29, 1954. The fascination with the geodesic dome was that it required very little actual structural members, providing a lightweight, strong structure. In 1953, his first commercial dome was at the Ford Motor Company headquarters in Dearborn, Michigan. A short time later, the U.S. military contracted Fuller to build geodesic domes for remote radar stations in the Artic. More than 300,000 geodesic

Chart 11.3

domes were eventually constructed throughout the world. Some of the smallest and simplest were on children's playgrounds, serving as climbers. During the late 1950s he became a professor at Southern Illinois University, where he and his wife lived in a geodesic dome when he was in residence ("About Fuller," n.p.).

UFOs AND FRISBEES

On January 23, 1957, the WHAM-O toy company capitalized on the public's fascination with unidentified flying objects (UFOs) with the "frisbee." The frisbee was actually an accidental discovery dating to the late 19th century. In 1871, William Frisbie opened the Frisbie Baking Company in Bridgeport, Connecticut, making pies on a tin plate pie holder. (The company continued making pies until 1958, which coincidentally was the same year that the frisbee was a mass market toy.) Supposedly, students at local colleges around the Bridgeport area took to tossing the pie tins in the air and playing catch with them. Wham-O's official website claimed the students "yelled 'Frisbee!' to warn passersby of the spinning discs flying through the air."

The idea for a similar aerodynamic dish that could be tossed from person to person came about in 1948, when partners Walter F. Morrison and Warren Franscioni created a plastic disc they called the "flying saucer." It was named in response to the recent numerous public sightings of UFOs in 1947 by a private pilot named Kenneth Arnold and later that same year, near a secret military base in Roswell, New Mexico. In 1955, Morrison improved on the disc, selling the rights to Wham-O as the renamed "Pluto Platter." In 1957, it was available to the consumer market as the Pluto Platter.™ Wham-O's original packaging listed it as:

> Wham-O Pluto-Platter
> Flying Saucers
> Are Here
> It Boomerangs
> It Sails
> It Flies

In 1958, the disc was modified and renamed the "FRISBEE disc." The disc was thrown in backyards, on urban streets, in city parks, and at beaches, among many others. By the early 1960s, millions of the plastic disc were sold. Frisbee games were popular on college campuses and it was viewed as a "counterculture" sport to the more traditional conservative sports of football and basketball. Organized tournaments arose in California and "ultimate frisbee" (a cross between football, soccer and basketball) began among high school students in New Jersey. Many offshoots of the games included frisbee golf, frisbee football, and freestyle frisbee, among many others. And many a dog has been seen jumping high to snatch a frisbee out of the air. By the end of the century, Wham-O claimed to have sold more than 100 million frisbees ("Wham-O's History," n.p.).

THE HULA HOOP AND BUBBLE GUM CARDS

In 1958, Wham-O created the biggest fad of the century—the hula hoop. In two short months, more than 25 million were sold and, within a few more years, over 100 million. The device, a circular lightweight plastic hoop about 42 inches in diameter, was intended to be spun around a person's waist in a fashion similar to a Hawaiian hula dance. Yet in reality it had nothing to do with the Hawaiian dance. Unlike spontaneous dance, the Hawaiian hula is an intricate, interpretative dance. The dance tells a complete story through the specific use of fluid hand and body movements. Without knowledge of Hawaiian culture, non-natives misunderstood the dance and created simplified versions. With Hawaii achieving statehood, many Americans on the continent held "Welcome Hawaii" themed parties. They encouraged Hawaiian attire, such as wearing a lei and pseudo hula dancing; some even danced with a hula hoop (Panati, 264).

The actual idea for the hula hoop came from a different area of the South Pacific. Arthur Melin and Richard Knerr developed the idea from an Australian schoolyard method of encouraging children to exercise while using a bamboo ring. In the United States, Merlin and Knerr often demonstrated their new hula hoops to children on California playgrounds and gave away free samples. The fad soon swept the nation as millions were sold.

TOPPS BUBBLEGUM CARDS

Another lasting legacy that began as children's fascination in the early 1950s was collecting baseball cards. By the 21st century, "baseball cards" and all sorts of other trading cards branched out into an adult hobby (sometimes termed "hobbyist culture"). In the words of Topps, "What humbly began as a family gum business in Brooklyn has evolved into a classic American sports company." In 1938, the company transformed its former tobacco business into Topps Chewing Gum, Inc. By the early 1950s, various types of collectable cards, including those of professional baseball players, had been around for quite a few years. In the past, distribution was limited and often part of a promotion for a specific consumer product, such as tobacco. In 1949, that all changed as Topps introduced an age-old campaign that spun off into a new industry.

In 1951, Topps advertised a series of baseball cards packaged with taffy rather than bubblegum. Those cards were intended to let children play a card game variation of baseball. The following year, as a way of selling more gum and outpacing competitors, Topps packaged a single stick of gum with five different cards featuring current major league baseball players. The 1952 set which packaged five cards with a single stick of gum is officially known as when the "modern baseball card era begins." The five cards were part of two different sets of 52 cards each. The idea soon spread that kids, mostly boys, would try and collect entire sets. The cards were randomly packed and additional purchases often produced duplicates of the same card. In order to obtain a complete set, kids had to buy more packages.

Without much prompting, a ritual developed as young boys would hustle to a local candy store, buy a package, unwrap it, put the gum in their mouth, and sort through the cards. The idea was to look for either their favorite player or for specific cards to make a complete set. All sorts of other rituals and games arose such as trading with friends or flipping the cards to match face-up or facedown. Some realized that the cardboard card could be fastened to a bicycle wheel, thereby making a clicking noise as they pedaled along. In 1954, the card collection was expanded to include a National Hockey League (NHL) set of 60 cards. Those cards only included players from the four American-based teams—the Boston Bruins, Chicago Blackhawks, Detroit Red Wings, and New York Rangers. In later years, other sports including basketball and football were added. By the mid 1950s, other companies issued trading cards for baseball, football, popular culture, and even Elvis Presley, among others. About the only common factor was the material, which was thin cardboard. Size often varied, but most soon conformed to the Topps standard that were rectangular at 2 ½ inches by 3 ½ inches.

THE BARBIE DOLL AND BOARD GAMES

Gender separation was very distinct during the 1950s; young girls were drawn not to the trading cards, but rather to the Barbie doll. First introduced in 1959 by the Mattel Toy Company, it became the doll by which all others were judged. The doll, at 11 ½ inches high, was advertised as "the only anatomically similar" doll manufactured to date. The Barbie doll not only sold millions, but Mattel also sold millions of clothes and accessories and spurned fan clubs and a *Barbie* magazine (Whitfield, 71).

New board games included the preschool-age Candyland; school-age Chutes and Ladders; and for teenagers and adults Scrabble and Clue. In 1954, Scrabble, which had been around since the 1930s, experienced a market resurgence as over 4.5 million sets were sold. (Only 58,000 sets were sold in the previous two years.) Most of the board games were advertised to encourage family togetherness. Another lasting item from the time was the Slinky. As one of the United States' most recognizable toys, the lightweight steel coil sold at a rate of at least one million each year for the remainder of the century. Another such fad was Silly Putty, introduced in 1949. It was a new synthetic product that when rolled on newspaper comics could pick up the image. They were packaged in brightly colored plastic eggs (to prevent the "putty" from drying out). From 1950 to 1955 more than 32 million Silly Putty eggs were sold (Panati, 262–265).

FURTHER READING

Cindy S. Aron. *Working at Play: A History of Vacations in the United States.* New York: Oxford University Press, 1999.

Bill Cotter. *The Wonderful World of Disney Television.* New York: Hyperion Books, 1997.

Vince Gargiulo. *Palisade Amusement Park: A Century of Fond Memories.* New Brunswick, NJ: Rutgers University Press, 1995.

Ralph Nader. *Unsafe at Any Speed: The Designed-In Dangers of the American Automobile.* New York: Grossman Publishers, 1965.

Charles Panati. *Panati's Parade of Fads, Follies, and Manias.* New York: Harper Collins, 1991.

CHAPTER 12

Legacy

Many items mentioned throughout this book have lived on well into the 21st century. They include:

- Civil rights equality
- Comic books
- Federal Aviation Administration (FAA)
- Jet engines
- Independent filmmaking
- National Film Registry of 1950s movies
- Peace symbol
- Polio vaccine
- Rock 'n' Roll
- Satellites
- Frank Sinatra
- Suburbia
- Solid body electric guitar
- Television
- Thermonuclear weapons
- West Coast baseball
- Wide-screen feature films

Some noteworthy developments in the United States that either occurred or were introduced during the time period included:

- **Alaska and Hawaii:** Both Alaska and Hawaii as territorial possessions of the United States became the 49th and 50th states. Alaska was admitted on

January 3, 1959, and Hawaii was admitted on March 18, 1959. The addition of the two states also brought cultures distinct from the continental 48 states. The introduction of the jet aircraft and civilian air transportation opened up the Hawaiian Islands for many mainland tourists. On the most populous island of Oahu, Waikiki Beach, for example, was featured as an exotic get-away for vacationing, relaxing, and surfing. Alaska, sometimes termed the last frontier, promoted more rugged activities such as dogsledding, sport fishing, and kayaking.

- **Fiberglass "Glasspar" Boats:** In 1950, Bill Tritt introduced the Glasspar small motorboat. Previously, small pleasure craft were often expensive and made of wood. The Glasspar, made of inexpensive lightweight fiberglass, were easier to maintain, and could be easily loaded from a trailer towed by an automobile. The boat and trailer could also be easily stored on a suburban driveway. By 1953, sales increased with the addition of outboard motors such as the Kiekhaefer Corporation Mercury Mark 5 and Mercury Mark 15. The motors were removable and could easily be replaced and stored in a garage during the winter months. Before the Glasspar, about 300,000 pleasure boats existed; by 1953, recreational boats numbered more than eight million. With increased recreational boat use also was a comparative increase in fishing, water skiing, snorkeling, and scuba diving.

- **Las Vegas:** In 1931, Nevada had become the first state to legalize gambling. Prior to the war, Las Vegas was nothing more than a small town with a total population of around two thousand. During the war, a significant number of workers flooded the area as the U.S. government set up wartime production and research facilities nearby. In their free time, workers discovered that within Las Vegas, a few smaller hotels such as the Golden Nugget, Pioneer, and the Mint, among others, offered gambling in the form of table games and slot machines. In 1946, The Flamingo opened as the first legalized hotel and gambling casino in the country. Apparently, the hotel was financed by a consortium of mobsters including Benjamin "Bugsy" Siegel (1906–1947) and Meyer Lansky (1902–1983). Others added that the mob connection provided The Flamingo the ability to book such top-name entertainers as singer Frank Sinatra to attract more people to Las Vegas. The Flamingo soon flourished, leading to the construction of other large and lavish gambling casinos. By 1955, gambling income in Las Vegas totaled more than $20 billion.

- **Vacation Travel:** Prior to the war, vacation travel was limited to wealthier individuals. In the post-war years, more working-class and middle-class individuals had the availability of disposable income and time for a vacation. Some of those were promoted as "family vacations" in an automobile, driving to various locations throughout the country. In 1951, Liberty Travel introduced the idea of a travel agency promoting exotic locations. The first offices in New York City marketed the idea of a "vacation package plan" to middle- and working-class Americans. A "package plan" vacation offered a total price that included airfare, hotel booking, food, and other amenities. The total cost was less than if each portion was purchased individually. Package plans varied from long weekends, an airplane trip to a Caribbean island, or even a luxury cruise, among others. Other travel agencies offering competitive rates soon copied the idea.

- **Veterans Day:** In 1919, the 11th day of November was proclaimed by President Woodrow Wilson as "Armistice Day." The day was recognized to honor "the heroism of those who died in the country's service and with gratitude for the victory." Across the nation and throughout Europe, it was honored as a day of peace that ended "The War to End All Wars." In 1938, the day was recognized as a legal national holiday. The outbreak of a second world war and a new conflict in Korea prompted the U.S. Congress to amend the title of Armistice Day. In June 1954, the word "armistice" was removed and officially replaced with "Veterans Day." For the first observance of the newly renamed Veterans Day, President Eisenhower issued a proclamation on October 8, 1954, that stated, in part, "In order to ensure proper and widespread observance of this anniversary, all veterans, all veterans' organizations, and the entire citizenry will wish to join hands in the common purpose" ("History of Veterans Day," n.p.).

Some other notable "legacies" that began in the 1950s and continued into the 21st century are well known, such as Disneyland, while others, such as Malcom McLean, are not.

MALCOM McLEAN AND THE $4 TRILLION SHIPPING CONTAINER

For the most part, public interest in sea-going travel was often associated with luxury ocean liners and an emerging travel industry offering cruise destinations for the middle class to exotic destinations such as Hawaii and the Caribbean islands. Other nautical aficionados studied the paddlewheel boats of the Mississippi River, battleships and aircraft carriers of the world wars, submarines, tales of pirate ship adventures and the like. In fact, a popular activity during the 1950s was building plastic scale models popularized by companies such as Aurora and Revell who issued historical kits of the aforementioned ship types. Hardly anyone was aware of the importance and impact of the cargo and merchant ships.

The least known, but probably the singular most important legacy of the 1950s was the "shipping container." The shipping container is a rectangular steel or aluminum packing box that completely changed global trade in the modern world. Manufactured consumer goods and products were placed within a shipping container and loaded onto a cargo ship. In essence, the "box" became the central component to a $4 trillion industry, with incalculable ancillary economic profits. The credit for inventing the modern-day shipping container belongs to Malcom McLean (1913/14–2001). Writing in "The Containership Revolution" for *TR News*, Brian J. Cudahy explained:

> The value of this utilitarian object lies not in what it is, but in how it is used. The container is at the core of a highly automated system for moving goods from anywhere to anywhere, with a minimum of cost and complication. The container made shipping cheap and changed the shape of the world economy. (5)

McLean, a North Carolina native who changed his birth name from "Malcolm" to "Malcom," was a trucking entrepreneur. During the war his military assignment oversaw the loading of trucks and other vehicles onto ships for transport to the war zones. After the war, he sought to provide a similar situation of loading transport trucks onto cargo ships for worldwide distribution of consumer goods. By the mid-1950s, his McLean Trucking Company generated $12 million in business with more than 1,700 company-owned trucks. Prior to that time, port cities in the United States were limited. Dock laborers known as "longshoremen" performed the loading and unloading of cargo.

Prior to McLean, many businesses did not seek to import goods from other countries simply because the shipping cost was too high. In some cases, shipping was as high as 25 percent of the total cost. The loading and unloading was also labor intensive and slow, often performed by singular individuals each carrying an item such as large canvas bags of coffee or a crate of consumer goods. Dozens of similar items would be physically carried off the ship (sometimes aided by a dockside crane lifting a cargo net of crates) and handloaded onto trucks for distribution to stores. McLean envisioned a fully loaded truck placed upon a ship at the point of origin and taken off the ship without the intermediary process of human labor loading and unloading for sea transport. He once wrote, "There has to be a better way than loading cargo aboard ship piece by piece. Why couldn't an entire truck be hoisted aboard ship, for instance, and then used for delivery purposes at the other end of the line?" In pursuit of a better solution, McLean secured a large bank loan in order to purchase two large ships and dock privileges. He immediately retrofitted the ships and dockside loading techniques according to his new vision. His new company, Pan Atlantic (renamed to "Sea-Land Service" in 1960), was in business.

McLean's attained the solution after many different designs had been tried. At first, McLean thought of detaching the storage portion of the trailer trucks separating the engine cab and wheels, in essence just loading the "container" portion. He settled upon a solution of a rectangular box that could be lifted off and on a flatbed trailer. The final result, patented in 1958, standardized the length at 25 feet and was "theft resistant, stackable, easy to load, unload, truck, rail, ship, and certainly store." Each unit was fully stackable and could bear the weight of eight to 10 fully loaded containers placed atop each other. In a short time, the cost of loading freight was reduced by more than 90 percent. (In 1956, it cost $5.86 to load one ton of cargo. After the introduction and use of McLean's containers that cost was drastically reduced to only 0.16¢ cents per ton of cargo.) Marc Levinson, writing in *The Box: How the Shipping Container Made the World Smaller and the World Economy Bigger,* summed it up as follows: "It is better to assume that moving goods is essentially costless than to assume that moving goods is an important component of the production process. Before the container, such a statement was unimaginable" (n.p.).

On April 26, 1956, McLean's first ship, the *Ideal X* with 58 containers, sailed from Port Newark in New Jersey in transport to the port of Houston in Texas. On hand were invited dignitaries, as well as union officials representing the International Longshoremen's Association. One top-level representative for the longshoremen named Freddy Fields obviously foresaw the lessened need for the physical presence of laborers. Supposedly, he said, "I'd like to sink that son of a bitch." The prophetic animosity was in response to the reduced need of human labor. Cudahy explained the economic savings:

One steamship executive suggested that it cost his company more to move cargo 1,000 feet from the street in front of a pier into the hold of a moored ship than it did to transport the cargo thousands of miles across a hostile ocean. ("The Containership Revolution," 5)

The container ships greatly reduced the labor and amount of time required in the transportation of goods, thereby greatly reducing cost. In addition, the individual sealed containers added to a significant reduction in stolen cargo. Although McLean's first ships, including the *Ideal X*, are often cited as the "world's first successful containerships," they were actually conversions and retrofits of ships designed for other types of seafaring service. Many of them were war surplus cargo ships that were retrofitted as container ships. The first ships designed and built from the keel up for the specific purpose of carrying containers occurred in 1957. Thereafter all container ships were built from the keel up with the specific purpose of providing "a deck house located well to the stern of the ship, a large open area with container-carrying holds between the deck house and bow, and room for additional containers aft of the deck house." The basic design feature remained the same since its inception to the present day. The sealed containers also eliminated the need to build large warehouses to protect cargo. In its place were large open tracts of land where the containers could be stacked without concern of weather or pilferage (Cudahy, "The Containership Revolution," 5–9).

Within a decade after McLean's container went international, the volume of seafaring trade goods grew at an amazing rate. Due to the reliability of containers, new production plants opened in cheap labor markets, many in Asia. By the year 2000, very few manufactured items or products were produced within the United States. In a reversal from the 1950s, almost 90 percent of everything in America was brought into the country. All of it was connected by a vast global trade network all wholly dependent upon container ships. The drastic change on reliance on importation of goods led to the geographical shift of new port cities in locations where ports had never existed such as Busan in South Korea and Tanjun Pelepas in Malaysia (Levinson, *The Box*, n.p.).

Upon his death in 2001, McLean was for the most part a forgotten footnote to the history of the United States. However, his contributions were not forgotten among those in the maritime industry. A statement released by U.S. Transportation Secretary Norman Y. Mineta read as follows:

A true giant, Malcom revolutionized the maritime industry in the 20th century. His idea for modernizing the loading and unloading of ships, which was previously conducted in much the same way the ancient Phoenicians did 3,000 years ago, has resulted in much safer and less-expensive transport of goods, faster delivery, and better service. We owe so much to a man of vision, the father of containerization, Malcom P. McLean. (n.p.)

The shipping container allowed for a global economy that led to the formation of the World Trade Organization (WTO) as an international cooperative of nations to regulate international trade. In 2004, the WTO attributed McLean's container as a major contributor "in increasing the integration of the global economy" (Levinson, 114–29). Granted, McLean's contributions to a trillion-dollar industry are often overlooked by the American public. In contrast, a major legacy from the 1950s that has not been forgotten in the 21st century was the King of Rock 'n' Roll.

ELVIS IMPERSONATORS

The popularity of Elvis Presley and Rock 'n' Roll cannot be underestimated. More than any other artist of the time, Presley defined the image of Rock 'n' Roll (see Music chapter). Often overlooked was that he was a musical pioneer. As he was about to make his first record, he supposedly told his producer Sam Phillips, "I don't sound like nobody." As a young white man growing up in the highly segregated south, his music crossed the cultural barrier between black and white. As a pioneer, Elvis moved and danced onstage and in his movies in a way that no other white entertainer had done before. Elvis's dancing style was not new, but for the first time white audiences saw a performer move his pelvic and hip area that in the past were strictly confined to segregated jook joints and honky tonks. In 1955, at separate performances in San Diego and Florida, authorities warned Presley that if he moved at all during his show "he would be arrested on obscenity charges" (Johnson, n.p.).

Despite it all, the "Elvis" legacy has lived on. His popularity has continued to grow among new generations of fans who were born long after the singer died in 1977. An uncanny phenomenon in American culture was the rapid rise of Elvis impersonators available for all sorts of entertainment venues. In 2015, one talent agency, GigMasters.com, as an example, listed 27 Elvis impersonators available within New York City and another 106 in the immediate metropolitan area. They also advertised a choice of multiple Elvis impersonators in all of the 50 states, including the District of Columbia and Canada. In the Las Vegas area, the talent agency managed 82 regular performers of Presley songs. On their website, GigMasters.com said the variety of choice was up to the customer. They wrote,

> We're all shook up over our top-rated Elvis Impersonators. From tribute performances to tradeshow appearances, these professional impersonators can play the part of The King at just about any event. You can book one straight out of Graceland or closer to you in the New York City area.

GigMasters.com was one of only dozens of talent agencies offering the services of an Elvis impersonator. The "Elvis" performers were not limited to talent agencies as others could also be found working independently. Many worked in casinos such as Las Vegas, Atlantic City in New Jersey, and Foxwoods Casino in Connecticut, to name a few. Others could often be found entertaining at vacation resorts.

Each year since his death, a weeklong tribute is held at his home known as Graceland in Memphis, Tennessee. The tribute includes musical performances, full-length concerts, and the sale of all sorts of memorabilia. The highlight is an annual "Ultimate Elvis Tribute Artist Contest" that awards a hefty cash prize to the winner. A similar Elvis festival and contest is held annually in Las Vegas. The amount of Elvis memorabilia and tributes are too numerous to recollect. In 2016, a search of the online retailer Amazon.com produced more than 70,000 items related to Elvis. A similar search on the popular auction site Ebay .com turned up almost 130,000 listings. Not only had the 1950s legacy of Elvis Presley remained relevant, so had the iconic movie starlet Marilyn Monroe.

MARILYN MONROE MEMORABILIA

"I knew I belonged to the public and to the world, not because I was talented or even beautiful but because I had never belonged to anything or anyone else."

—From the unfinished biography of Marilyn Monroe

And belong to the public she did. At the time she was alive, many types of memorabilia of Marilyn Monroe were available such as posters and photographs. The most popular was a wall calendar. Yet as the years continued past her death in August 1962, it seemed that Marilyn Monroe became even more iconic in death than when she was alive. The public clamored for all sorts of memorabilia such as t-shirts, posters, photos, movies, magazines, newspaper articles, and lifesize cardboard stand-ups. During the 21st century, many popular retail outlets such as K-Mart, Target, and Wal-Mart sold posters and prints, as did online sources such as Art.com, among hundreds of other retail outlets. One prominent example by the international retail furniture giant IKEA was a large 35 ½" by 35 ½" canvas poster picture that carried the title "Marilyn Monroe EGERSTA series."

The ultimate confirmation of Monroe's lasting legacy might well have come during a 2016 Super Bowl commercial. The Super Bowl was often the single-most watched television event of the entire year. In response, advertisers responded with multi-million-dollar advertising campaigns in the form of highly stylized commercials. In turn, a public fascination grew to simply watch the commercials. For Marilyn Monroe, that honor came during the 2016 Super Bowl, which was the 50th anniversary of the game. The actual commercial for the Snickers candy bar from Mars, Inc., played off of the famous wind-blown dress scene from *The Seven Year Itch* (see Film chapter). The commercial began with Monroe standing over the subway grill in her famous white halter dress. As her dress is blowing upward, the scene switches to male actor Willem Dafoe in the same dress. (At the time Dafoe was 60 years old.) The scene was described as the "actor mustered up as much femininity he possibly can as he channels Marilyn Monroe." In a later interview in *AdWeek*, Dafoe said, "I have to admit playing a Hollywood bombshell is a new challenge for me. But as a huge fan of Marilyn Monroe, I just couldn't resist the opportunity to take a walk in her shoes and famous white dress."

One website, GiftaPolis.com listed more than 300 different items in a link titled the "Marilyn Monroe Store." The online store was devoted entirely to: "Marilyn Monroe Gifts, Merchandise, and Collectibles" of license plates, mugs, sippy cups, auto chargers, air fresheners, lunch boxes, Christmas ornaments, key chains, and the list went on. The Mattel Toy Company produced a limited series of Barbie doll figures (most of them released in 1997) of Marilyn in some of her most notable dresses. The most popular figure was of her in the famous white halter dress from the movie *The Seven Year Itch* (1955). Two other Barbie dolls included her character from *Gentlemen Prefer Blondes* (1953) and in the glittery gown she wore at John F. Kennedy's 1961 inauguration ball.

Some of the most popular Marilyn Monroe memorabilia items continued as yearly wall calendars that often reproduced the 1953 *Playboy* photograph. On the other hand, most of the yearly calendars, and also the best selling, were 12-month types featuring her in different non-nude glamour images. One example of a 2016 calendar advertisement listed on the online retail giant Amazon .com proclaimed:

> Spend the year with Marilyn Monroe, a symbol of beauty in the 50's and 60's. Featuring black and white imagery with contemporary pops of color. Features a mid-sized planning grid. Printed on a glossy paper stock suitable for pen and pencil note taking. This calendar is 12″ wide × 12″ tall when closed and 12″ wide × 24″ tall when open.

This one particular wall calendar was just one item among more than 800,000 offered for sale by Amazon.com. A comparative search of the popular auction site of Ebay.com listed more than 170,000 items, for a combined total of almost one million items just from those two searches. She easily outpaced all other comparable notable figures from the 1950s.

Elvis Presley was the only other popular culture figure that had impressive memorabilia numbers of more than 70,000 items on Amazon and almost 130,000 on Ebay. A comparative Frank Sinatra search turned up over 65,000 combined memorabilia items. James Dean also proved popular with more than

Chart 12.1   Comparative Memorabilia of 1950s Popular Figures

Name	Amazon.com	Ebay.com	Total
Marilyn Monroe	803,807	174,898	978,705
Elvis Presley	70,503	129,859	200,362
Frank Sinatra	34,271	31,406	65,677
James Dean	10,968	22,892	33,860
Bettie Page	4,411	20,843	25,254
Dwight D. Eisenhower	5,493	4,394	9,887
Rosa Parks	3,087	2,805	5,892
Senator Joseph McCarthy	1,602	466	2,068
Emmett Till	288	209	497

Source: Online search of Amazon.com and ebay.com. Chart and statistics compiled by author.

33,500 combined memorabilia items. The iconic pin-up Bettie Page listed over 4,000 Amazon items and more than 20,000 items on Ebay. Unlike the others, a significant amount of Bettie Page items included clothing such as dresses and bathing suits. On the political end, President Dwight D. Eisenhower turned up over 9,900 combined items that far outdistanced Senator Joseph McCarthy at a little over 2,000 items. The civil rights icon Rosa Parks produced almost 6,000 search items and Emmett Till a little over 500 items.

In all fairness to Till, Parks, and McCarthy, most of those search items were book publications and not necessarily items such as music, movies, t-shirts, posters, holiday ornaments, or coffee cups, among others. Similarly, with Sinatra, a significant amount of his popularity could be attributed to the fact that many of his items did encompass a career well beyond the 1950s as he continued as a popular entertainer from the 1960s through the 1990s. As for the American fascination with celebrity memorabilia, an often-overlooked fact is that fiction far outweighs the reality. The legacy and influence of stars such as James Dean, Marilyn Monroe, Elvis Presley, and Frank Sinatra have certainly contributed profoundly to the American culture and also the economy. Yet, the reality is that individuals such as Rosa Parks and Emmett Till are still relevant.

EMMETT TILL STILL MATTERS

Looking forward from the murder of Emmett Till in 1955, he was not forgotten. In 2015, the Southern Poverty Law Center (SPLC) provided an update titled, "60 Years Later Emmett Till Still Vital." The story was in response to the ongoing nationwide killings of innocent young black teens and children without any criminal action brought against the killers. The statement issued by the SPLC on social media explained:

> What we come to see with the loss of Emmett is just what racism has cost us in this country. What it costs us still, in the loss of so many bright, gifted kids. When we begin to see the Emmett Till story in this context, we realize that we all lose something to racism. Emmett Till is a vital American story. ("SPLC.org," n.p.)

The "vital American story" came to life in social movements such as the much-heralded Black Lives Matter campaign of the 21st century. It was created in 2012 after a series of murders involving innocent young black teenagers and children. The organizers at #BlackLivesMatter state the movement "is a call to action and a response to the virulent anti-Black racism that permeates our society." During the 21st century many Americans seemed to ignore the inherent problem of racism. The Black Lives Matter organizers explained, "We are talking about the ways in which Black lives are deprived of our basic human rights and dignity." The platform echoed Emmett Till, reminding the social media world of the 21st century to look back to "a savage beating of a 14-year-old Chicago boy . . . sadly familiar to today's young black people."

In an opinion piece written by Charles M. Blow in *The New York Times* in 2016, two celebrities, Will Smith and Jay-Z, announced their sponsorship of an HBO-TV mini-series production based on the life and death of Emmett Till. The story, projected for a 2017 release, was the first in-depth production of the

civil rights moment. Up to that time, one of the only nationally televised stories of the incident was a 2003 PBS documentary titled *The Murder of Emmett
Till*. Another documentary in 2005 was *The Untold Story of Emmett Till* directed
by Keith Beauchamp. Each documentary provided in-depth interviews with
some of the few remaining survivors. The PBS crew did claim to uncover new
evidence that led to Till's body being exhumed for a new autopsy. On July 31,
2005, a 4,500-word story appeared in the Sunday magazine section of *The New
York Times* under the title, "The Ghosts of Emmett Till." Journalist Richard
Rubin explained why the story just never went away:

> We've known his story forever, it seems. Maybe that's because it's a tale so stark
> and powerful that it has assumed an air of timelessness, something almost myth-
> ical. Yes, we know this story very well—perhaps even too well. It has been like a
> burr in our national consciousness for 50 years now. From time to time it has
> flared up, inspiring commemorative outbursts of sorrow, anger and outrage, all
> of which ran their course quickly and then died down.

The story did not go away and continued to garner national media attention.
In 2007, evidence was presented to a grand jury to indict Carolyn Bryant as an
accessory to the 1955 murder. She was the woman whom Till had either whistled at or said "Bye Baby." Her husband Roy Bryant (1931–1994) and J.W.
Milam (d. 1980) were tried for the Till murder and were quickly acquitted.
However, in 2007, the grand jury decided against an indictment for the then
70-year-old Carolyn Bryant.

Many of the racially motivated murder cases from the 1960s and 1970s went
unsolved. The reason for lack of prosecution was due to state-sponsored segregation. With many of the "cold cases" still on the books, U.S. House Representative John Lewis (D-Georgia) introduced and later presided over the passage of
the "Emmett Till Unsolved Civil Rights Crime Act of 2007." In 2008, an office
was set up within the U.S. Justice Department "to investigate unsolved murders
from the civil rights era." The law was not overly wordy or detailed. It stated:

> It is the sense of Congress that all authorities with jurisdiction, including the
> Federal Bureau of Investigation and other entities within the Department of Jus-
> tice, should—
>
> 1. Expeditiously investigate unsolved civil rights murders, due to the amount
>   of time that has passed since the murders and the age of potential witnesses;
>   and
> 2. Provide all the resources necessary to ensure timely and thorough investiga-
>   tions in the cases involved.

In 2008, the new evidence led the CBS-TV show *60 Minutes* to investigate.
As a preview to the report of October 2008, the producers released the following statement:

> One of the reasons Rosa Parks refused to move to the back of the bus in 1955 was
> because a black teenager was tortured and murdered in Mississippi for whistling

at a white woman a few months before. No one ever paid for the crime, but 60 MINUTES has confirmed that the recently reopened investigation into the torture-murder of 14-year-old Emmett Till is focused on at least two people: the woman he whistled at and a man who witnesses say they saw on a truck with Till after his abduction. Ed Bradley's report on the case that helped galvanize the civil rights movement in America will be broadcast on 60 MINUTES Sunday, Oct. 24 (7:00–8:00 PM, ET/PT) on the CBS Television Network. Journalist Ed Bradley did in fact locate the former Mrs. Bryant living in Greenville, Mississippi, under her remarried name of Carolyn Donham. The *60 Minutes* camera crew did get some footage of her. Yet when Bradley approached her front door and knocked, he said, "She refused to open the door." A few moments later her son Frank Bryant drove up, who also refused to talk. At one point he told Bradley to leave and appeared ready to use physical force, until he realized the scene was on camera. The new information prompted the U.S. Justice Department to seek a new trial, but nothing came of it.

On August 31, 2015, *New York Times* journalist Charles M. Blow reminded readers, "Friday was the 60th anniversary of the savage killing of Emmett Till." Like so many other instances, Blow retold the story of Till's 1955 murder. He connected the piece to a June 2015 incident when a white man by the name of Dylann Roof shot and killed nine black people during church services in Charleston, South Carolina. Roof echoed the sentiment that was supposed to be lost to the 1950s. He claimed that he was protecting the purity of southern white women against the black people who are "raping our women." Blow tried to make a 21st-century audience aware that the cultural attitudes of the 1950s had not gone away:

> There is the thread of couching his [Roof's] cowardice as chivalry, framing his selfish hatred as noble altruism in defense of white femininity from the black brute. So much black blood has been spilled and so many black necks noosed in the name of protecting white femininity, and by extension, white purity. That thread seems altered but unbroken from Emmett's time to ours. (n.p.)

In that same month of August 2015, author Devery S. Anderson published *Emmett Till: The Murder That Shocked the World and Propelled the Civil Rights Movement*. The book promised "the first truly comprehensive account of the 1955 murder and its aftermath." As Anderson explains, "Like no other event in modern history, the death of Emmett Till provoked people all over the United States to seek social change." Ironically, the call for social justice led to a new profitable industry in backyard swimming pools.

PRIVATE AND SUBURBAN SWIMMING POOLS

Recreational swimming was an activity that many Americans pursued with vigor. Some statistics showed that prior to 1950, "Americans went swimming as often as they went to the movies, but they did so in public pools." At the turn of the 20th century, up through the 1920s, public swimming pools were communal and often egalitarian spaces used for leisure, recreation, and also as

---

bathing facilities. During the 1930s, many public swimming pools were constructed as part the New Deal program. However, concerns soon arose over
males and females sharing the same pool facility. One result was some municipalities imposing segregation between the genders by alternating swimming
days. To no surprise, the public facilities had also imposed legal racial segregation. Yet, as desegregation of places of public accommodation was attained
by U.S. Supreme Court decisions, the reaction among whites was outright
resistance to any change.

In one instance in Marshall, Texas, during 1957, it became clear that an
NAACP lawsuit would force the integration of the municipal public pools.
Rather than accept the decision and embrace civil equality, the town not just
closed the public facilities, but sold the land to a private concern. In fact, all of
the public recreation facilities were closed and the land sold to private developers. The decision did not come from local legislation, but rather by a referen-
dum which was voted in favor by a 98 percent margin. (Blacks were prevented
from voting on the matter.) Therefore, the pool facility was sold to a local privately owned fraternal order, the Lions Club. Because they were not a public
entity, they imposed the swimming pool as "a whites-only private facility."

Integration did not come willingly. Many obstacles were put in place such as making swimming pools private membership clubs in order to prevent African Americans from swimming with whites. This photograph, taken around 1963 or 1964, shows several African
American men standing at the entrance to an indoor swimming pool in Cairo, Illinois. Several young white men are standing behind the sign "Private Pool Members Only." (Library
of Congress)

The conflict in Texas was not an isolated incident as many other swimming facilities across the United States were closed. It was not that whites stopped swimming; they merely changed venues. The adverse situation actually created a unique economic opportunity with the rapid rise in the suburban backyard pool industry and of private swimming clubs. Rather than swim in an integrated municipal pool, many built their own private swimming pools. From 1950 to the end of the century, the number of private backyard pools (many in suburban developments) increased from 2,500 to well over 4 million. This increase was aided by technological improvements in low-cost pool construction, both in-ground and above-ground (Applebaum, n.p.).

"THE WORK OF PRESERVING FREEDOM IS NOT YET DONE"

Sadly, many similar instances continued to the present day that create a blockage for social justice. Yet the public call for social justice seems to echo the words of President Eisenhower in 1953:

> The work of preserving freedom is not yet done. We have the disgrace of racial discrimination, or we have prejudice against people because of their religion. We have not had the courage to uproot these things, although we know they are wrong. (Dartmouth College, 1953)

These words were delivered just six months after Eisenhower took the oath of office. Prior to these poignant words, his speech had begun like so many others. His talked about commitment, but soon changed the tone of his speech towards a thoughtful reflection on contemporary society. His aides wondered where the speech came from. Aides found out that Eisenhower had thrown out his prepared speech and spoken from the heart. The peacetime president who had been so instrumental in leading the Allies to a victory over fascism during the war added, "The work of preserving freedom is not yet done."

College students had spent four years besieged by the paranoia created by Senator McCarthy and the Red Scare. In a statement aimed at the red baiters, Eisenhower challenged the students, "Don't join the book burners!" The response came after a *New York Times* reporter named Walter Sullivan had uncovered a "book purge" in Europe during the early 1950s. That purge (removal of certain books from library shelves) "had occurred in libraries run by the United States Information Service in postwar Europe." The decision to remove books by American authors such as Langston Hughes, Dashiell Hammett, Theodore H. White, and Howard Fast, among others, was orchestrated by senatorial aides to McCarthy. They oversaw the removal of more than 30,000 books claiming they were written by Communist sympathizers. Eisenhower did not mention McCarthy by name, but he did not have to; the president's intent was clear as he encouraged the Dartmouth students, "Don't be afraid to go in your library and read every book, as long as that document does not offend your own ideas of decency" (Dwyer, A18).

THE 1950s RECALLED BY A 21st-CENTURY POPE

On September 24, 2015, in a historic speech delivered before a joint session of the U.S. Congress, Pope Francesco ("Francis" in the United States) evoked the "historical memory" of four individuals whom he considered examples of "great Americans." The first was the well-known American president Abraham Lincoln (1809–1865). The Pope reminded listeners that Lincoln had a dream of "liberty." Of the other three, Dr. Martin Luther King was well known; the other two, Dorothy Day and Thomas Merton, were rather obscure. (See Controversies chapter for a brief biography of each.) The Pope briefly outlined that each had dreams for a better United States. For Dr. King, the dream was "liberty in plurality and non-exclusion"; for Dorothy Day, it was "social justice and the rights of persons"; and for Thomas Merton it was "the capacity for dialogue and openness to God."

His words of that day were well received, but seemed forgotten once he returned to Rome. In deference to the 1950s passing into nostalgic amnesia, it might be helpful to read Pope Francesco's words of 2015 with a reminder that the 21st-century social problems sounded very much like those faced during the 1950s. Therefore, I offer his words as both a closing and a reflection piece.

> All of us are quite aware of, and deeply worried by, the disturbing social and political situation of the world today. Our world is increasingly a place of violent conflict, hatred and brutal atrocities, committed even in the name of God and of religion. We know that no religion is immune from forms of individual delusion or ideological extremism. This means that we must be especially attentive to every type of fundamentalism, whether religious or of any other kind. A delicate balance is required to combat violence perpetrated in the name of a religion, an ideology or an economic system, while also safeguarding religious freedom, intellectual freedom and individual freedoms. But there is another temptation which we must especially guard against: the simplistic reductionism which sees only good or evil; or, if you will, the righteous and sinners. The contemporary world, with its open wounds which affect so many of our brothers and sisters, demands that we confront every form of polarization which would divide it into these two camps. We know that in the attempt to be freed of the enemy without, we can be tempted to feed the enemy within. To imitate the hatred and violence of tyrants and murderers is the best way to take their place. That is something which you, as a people, reject"

FURTHER READING

Devery S. Anderson. *Emmett Till: The Murder That Shocked the World and Propelled the Civil Rights Movement.* Jackson, MS: University Press of Mississippi, 2015.

Bill Cotter. *The Wonderful World of Disney Television.* New York: Hyperion Books, 1997.

Brian J. Cudahy. *Box Boats: How Container Ships Changed the World.* New York: Fordham University Press, 2007.

Marc Levinson. *The Box: How the Shipping Container Made the World Smaller and the World Economy Bigger.* Princeton, NJ: Princeton University Press, 2008.

James W. Loewen. *Lies My Teacher Told Me.* New York: Touchstone Books, Simon & Schuster, Inc, 2007.

Howard Zinn. *A People's History of the United States.* New York: Harper Perennial, 2005.

Bibliography

Albrecht, Donald, ed. *World War II and the American Dream: How Wartime Building Changed a Nation.* Cambridge, MA: The MIT Press, 1995.

Aron, Cindy S. *Working at Play: A History of Vacations in the United States.* New York: Oxford University Press, 1999.

Balio, Tino. *United Artists, Volume 2, 1951–1978: The Company That Changed the Film Industry.* Madison, WI: University of Wisconsin Press, 1987.

Barson, Michael and Steven Heller. *Red Scared: The Commie Menace in Propaganda and Popular Culture.* San Francisco: Chronicle Books, 2001.

Bass, Jennifer and Paul Kirkham. *Saul Bass: A Life in Film and Design.* London: Laurence King Publishing, 2011.

Berle, Milton and Haskel Frankel. *Milton Berle: An Autobiography.* New York: Delacorte Press, 1974.

Bilstein, Roger E. *Orders of Magnitude a History of the NACA and NASA, 1915–1990,* "Chapter 3: Going Supersonic," Washington, DC: NASA, 1989. Online book accessed January 23, 2016. history.nasa.gov/SP-4406/chap3.html.

Block, Alex Ben and Lucy Autrey Wilson, eds. *George Lucas's Blockbusting: A Decade-by-Decade Survey of Timeless Movies Including Untold Secrets of Their Financial and Cultural Success.* New York: It Books Harper Collins, 2010.

Bondi, Victor, ed. *American Decades: 1950–1959.* Detroit: Gale Research, 1996.

Boucher, Diane. *The 1950s American Home.* UK: Shire Publications, 2013.

Braden, Donna R. *Leisure and Entertainment in America.* Dearborn, Michigan: Henry Ford Museum & Greenfield Village, 1988.

Brinkley, Douglas. *Rosa Parks.* New York: Penguin, 2005.

Brooks, Tim and Earle Marsh, eds. *The Complete Directory to Prime Time Network TV Shows: 1946–Present,* 5th edition. New York: Ballantine, 1992.

Caldwell, Christopher. "Original Conservative," *The New York Times Book Review,* January 24, 2016, p. 14.

Chafe, William H. *The Unfinished Journey: America Since World War II.* New York: Oxford University Press, 8th Edition, 2014.

Cotter, Bill. *The Wonderful World of Disney Television*. New York: Hyperion Books, 1997.

Cudahy, Brian J. *Box Boats: How Container Ships Changed the World*. New York: Fordham University Press, 2007.

Culbert, David. *Mission to Moscow*. Madison: University of Wisconsin Press, 1980.

Dannett, Sylvia G.L. and Frank R. Rachel. *Down Memory Lane: Arthur Murray's Picture Story of Social Dancing*. New York: Greenberg Publishing, 1954.

D'Emilio, John. *Sexual Politics, Sexual Communities: The Making of a Homosexual Minority in the United States, 1940–1970*. Chicago: University of Chicago Press, 1983.

Driver, Ian. *A Century of Dance: A Hundred Years of Musical Movement, from Waltz to Hip Hop*. London: Octopus Publishing Group Limited, 2000.

Dunning, John. *On the Air: The Encyclopedia of Old-Time Radio*. New York: Oxford University Press, 1998.

Fessler, Ann. *The Girls Who Went Away: The Hidden Story of Women Who Surrendered Children for Adoption in the Decades Before* Roe v. Wade. New York: Penguin, 2006.

Foner, Eric. *The Story of American Freedom*. New York: W.W. Norton & Company, 1998.

Frazier, E. Franklin. *Black Bourgeoisie*, Simon and Schuster, 1957.

Friedan, Betty. *The Feminine Mystique*. New York: W.W. Norton & Company, 1963.

Friskics-Warren, Bill. "Eddy Arnold, 89, Country Singer with Pop Luster, Dies," *The New York Times*, May 9, 2008, C11.

Gargiulo, Vince. *Palisade Amusement Park: A Century of Fond Memories*. New Brunswick, N.J.: Rutgers University Press, 1995.

Giordano, Ralph G. *Country & Western Dancing (American Dance Floor Series)*. Santa Barbara, CA: ABC-CLIO, 2010.

Giordano, Ralph G. *Fun and Games in Twentieth-Century America: A Historical Guide to Leisure*. Westport, CT: Greenwood, 2003.

Giordano, Ralph G. *Satan in the Dance Hall: Rev. John Roach Straton, Social Dancing and Morality in 1920s New York City*. Lanham, MD: Scarecrow Press, 2008.

Giordano, Ralph G. *Social Dancing in America Fair Terpsichore to the Ghost Dance 1607 to 1900* (Vol. 1); and *Lindy Hop to Hip Hop 1901 to 2000* (Vol. 2). Westport, CT: Greenwood Press, 2007.

Green, Victor H. *The Negro Travelers' Green Book*. New York: Victor H. Green & Co., 1956. Digital Library Collection University of South Carolina, Columbia, SC. library.sc.edu/digital/collections/greenbook.html.

Guilbaut, Serge. *How New York Stole the Idea of Modern Art: Abstract Expressionism, Freedom, and the Cold War*. Chicago: University of Chicago Press, 1983.

Hajdu, David. *The Ten-Cent Plague: The Great Comic Book Scare and How It Changed America*. New York: Farrar, Straus and Giroux, 2008.

Handlin, David P. *American Architecture*. New York: Thames and Hudson, Inc., 1985.

Halberstam, David. *The Fifties*. New York: Metro Books, 2001.

Hogan, Michael J. *The End of the Cold War: Its Meaning and Implications*. Cambridge University Press, 1992.

Hollings, Ken. *Welcome to Mars: Politics, Pop Culture, and Weird Science in 1950s America*. Berkeley, CA: North Atlantic Books, 2014.

Jackson, John A. *American Bandstand: Dick Clark and the Making of a Rock 'n' Roll Empire*. New York: Oxford University Press, 1997.

Jakle, John A. *The Motel In America*. John Hopkins University Press, 2002.

Kallen, Stuart A., ed. *The 1950s. America's Decades*. San Diego, CA: Greenhaven Press, 2000.

Kammen, Michael. *American Culture American Tastes: Social Change and the 20th Century*. New York: Basic Books, 1999.

Kaplan, Max. *Leisure in America: A Social Inquiry*. New York: Wiley, 1960.

Kepner, James. *Rough News, Daring Views: 1950's Pioneer Gay Press Journalism.* Binghamton, NY: Harrington Park Press, 1998.

Kifner, John, "No Joke! 37 Years After Death Lenny Bruce Receives Pardon." *The New York Times,* December 24, 2003. Accessed November 14, 2016. http://www.nytimes.com/2003/12/24/nyregion/no-joke-37-years-after-death-lenny-bruce-receives-pardon.html?pagewanted=all&src=pm.

King, Stephen. *11/22/63.* New York: Gallery Books, 2015.

Kirk, Russell. *The Conservative Mind* (1953). Washington D.C.: Regnery Publishing, 7th Revised edition, 2001.

Kostof, Spiro. *America by Design.* New York: Oxford University Press, 1987.

Layman, Richard. *American Decades: 1950–1959.* Detroit: Gale Research, 1994.

Levinson, Marc. *The Box: How the Shipping Container Made the World Smaller and the World Economy Bigger.* Princeton, NJ: Princeton University Press, New York, 2008. Chapter 1: press.princeton.edu/chapters/s9383.html.

Lindop, Edmund and Sarah Decapua. *America in the 1950s.* Minneapolis, MN: Twenty-First Century Books, 2010.

Loewen, James W. *Lies My Teacher Told Me.* New York: Touchstone Books, Simon & Schuster, Inc., 2007.

Loewen, James W. *Teaching What Really Happened.* New York: Teachers College Press 2009.

MacDonald, J. Fred. *One Nation Under Television: The Rise and Decline of Network TV.* New York: Pantheon, 1990.

Macias-Rojas, Patrisia. *From Deportation to Prison: The Politics of Immigration Enforcement in Post-Civil Rights America.* New York: NYU Press, 2016.

Madow, Pauline, ed. *Recreation in America.* Vol. 37: 2, New York: H.W. Wilson Co., 1965.

Marcus, Greil. "Rock Films," in Jim Miller, ed. *The Rolling Stone Illustrated History of Rock & Roll.* New York: Random House, 1980, 390–400.

Marling, Karal Ann. "V-8 Powered Chariots of Fire," in Stuart A. Kallen, ed. *The 1950s. America's Decades.* San Diego, CA: Greenhaven Press, 2000, 159–167.

McCormick, Thomas J. *America's Half-Century: United States Foreign Policy in the Cold War and After.* John Hopkins University Press, 1995. Mies van der Rohe, Ludwig. *Less is More.* New York: Waser Verlag Zurich, 1986.

McQuirter, Marya. "Awkward Moves: Dance Lessons from the 1940s." In Thomas F. De Frantz, ed. *Dancing Many Drums.* Madison, WI: The University of Wisconsin Press, 2002, 81-103.

Mies van der Rohe, Ludwig. *Less is More.* New York: Waser Verlag Zurich, 1986.

Miller, James. *Flowers in the Dustbin: The Rise of Rock and Roll.* New York: Simon & Schuster, 1999.

Mizruchi, Susan L. *Brando's Smile: His Life, Thought, and Work.* New York: W.W. Norton & Company, 2014.

Miller, Francis Trevelyan and John W. Davis. *Geography by Grades, Grade 4B: The Earth the Continents.* New York: Hinds, Hayden & Eldredge, Inc., 1926.

Morthland, John. "The Payola Scandal," in Jim Miller, ed. *The Rolling Stone Illustrated History of Rock & Roll.* New York: Random House, 1980, pp. 101–03.

Moss, George D. *America in the Twentieth Century.* Upper Saddle River, NJ: Prentice Hall, 1993.

Murray, Kathryn. *My Husband, Arthur Murray.* New York: Simon and Schuster, 1960.

Nader, Ralph. *Unsafe at any Speed: The Designed-In Dangers of the American Automobile.* New York: Grossman Publishers, 1965.

Norman, Phillip. *Rave On: The Biography of Buddy Holly.* New York: Simon & Schuster, 1996.

Nyberg, Amy. *Seal of Approval: The History of the Comics Code.* Jackson, MS: University Press of Mississippi, 1998.

Offit, Paul A. *Vaccinated: One Man's Quest to Defeat the World's Deadliest Diseases*. New York: Smithsonian Books/Collins, 2007.

Olson, James S. *Historical Dictionary of the 1950s*. Westport, CT: Greenwood Press.

Panati, Charles. *Panati's Parade of Fads, Follies, and Manias*. New York: Harper Collins, 1991.

Pendergast, Tom and Sara Pendergast. *St. James Encyclopedia of Popular Culture*. Streamwood, IL: St. James Press, 2000.

Phillips, Lisa. *The American Century: Art & Culture, 1950–2000*, 1st edition. New York: Whitney Museum of Art, June 1999.

Reynolds, Quentin. *The F.B.I.* New York: Random House, 1954.

Riesman, David. *The Lonely Crowd*. New Haven: Yale University Press, 2001.

Roberts, John Storm. *The Latin Tinge: The Impact of Latin American Music on the United States*. New York: Oxford University Press, 1999.

Rosenberg, Bernard and David Manning White, eds. *Mass Culture: The Popular Arts in America*. Wilmington, IL: The Free Press, 1957.

Rollin, Lucy. *Twentieth-Century Teen Culture by the Decades*. Westport, CT: Greenwood Press, 1999.

Sanders, Don and Susan. *Drive-in Movie Memories*. Nevada City, CA: Carriage House Publishing, 2000.

Sharp, Dennis. *The Illustrated Encyclopedia of Architects and Architecture*. New York: Quatro Publishing, 1991.

Shore, Michael with Dick Clark. *The History of American Bandstand: It's Got a Great Beat and You Can Dance to It!* New York: Ballantine Books, 1985.

Sklar, Robert. *Movie-Made America: A Cultural History of American Movies*. New York: Vintage Books, 1994.

Steinem, Gloria, with photographs by George Barris. *Marilyn: Norma Jeane*. New York: Signet Classics, 1986.

Steinem, Gloria. *My Life on the Road*. New York: Random House, 2015.

Stitch, Sidra. *Made in USA: An Americanization in Modern Art, The '50s & '60s*. Berkeley, CA: University of California Press, 1987.

Teaford, Jon C. *The Twentieth-Century American City*, 2nd edition. Baltimore: Johns Hopkins University Press, 1993.

Thomas, Bob. *Let's Dance with Marge & Gower Champion*. New York: Grosset & Dunlap, 1954.

Time-Life Books. *Rock & Roll Generation: Teen Life in the '50s*. New York: Time Life Books, 1998.

Time-Life Books. *This Fabulous Century: 1950–1960*. Vol. 6. New York: Time-Life Books, 1970.

U.S. Census Bureau. *Statistical Abstract of the United States*, Washington, D.C., 1986.

Uslan, Michael, and Bruce Solomon. *Dick Clark's the First 25 Years of Rock and Roll*. New York: Dell, 1981.

Walker, Leo. *The Wonderful Era of the Great Dance Bands*. New York: Doubleday, 1972.

Warhol, Andy. *POPism: The Warhol Sixties*. New York: Mariner Books, 2006.

White, Betty. *How to Mambo*. New York: David McKay Company, Inc., 1955.

Whitfield, Stephen J. *The Culture of the Cold War*, 2nd edition. Baltimore, MD: Johns Hopkins University Press, 1996.

Williams, Juan. *Eyes on the Prize: America's Civil Rights Years, 1954—1965*. New York: Penguin Books, 1987.

Wiseman, Carter. *Shaping a Nation: Twentieth-Century American Architecture and Its Makers*. New York: W.W. Norton & Company, 1998.

Wright, Frank Lloyd. *The Natural House*. New York: Horizon Press, 1954.

Young, William H. and Nancy K. Young. *The 1950s.* American Popular Culture Through History Series. Westport, CT: Greenwood Press, 2004.

Zinn, Howard. *A People's History of the United States.* New York: Harper Perennial, 2005.

Zukowsky, John, organizer. *Mies Reconsidered: His Career, Legacy, and Disciples.* New York: Rizzoli, 1986.

PERIODICALS

"The 42 Best Sci-Fi Movies 1950–1965 in 67 Posters," CinemaCom.com. Accessed January 3, 2016. www.cinemacom.com/50s-sci-fi-BEST.html.

"The 100 Best American Films (2015)," ScreenRant.com. Accessed July 25, 2016. screenrant.com/100-best-american-films/.

"About Fuller," *Buckminster Fuller Institute.* Accessed December 5, 2016. https://www .bfi.org/about-fuller/biography.

"Abstract Expressionism." *MoMA Learning.* Museum of Modern Art. Accessed March 18, 2016. www.moma.org/learn/moma_learning/themes/abstract -expressionism.

Adams, Val. "Music Show Bows On ABC-TV Aug. 5," *New York Times*, July 23, 1957, p. 53.

Adler, Margot. "Before Rosa Parks, There Was Claudette Colvin." *NPR.* March 17, 2009. Accessed December 1, 2015. www.NPR.org/templates/story/story.php?storyId =101719889.

Adverting Age. "History 1950s." AdAge.com, September 15, 2003. Accessed December 6, 2016. http://adage.com/article/adage-encyclopedia/history-1950s/98701/.

"AFI's 100 Greatest American Movies of All Time," *American Film Institute (1998).* Accessed July 25, 2016. www.afi.com/100Years/movies.aspx.

African American On Wheels Magazine. www.automag.com/AAOWMagazine/1998 _spring/love3.asp.

"African American Celebrity and the Civil Rights Movement," *The Authentic History Center.* Accessed February 16, 2016. www.authentichistory.com/1946-1960/8 -civilrights/celebrity/.

Akst, Daniel. "One Hundred Years of Freud in America," *The Wall Street Journal* August 6, 2009. Accessed December 10, 2016. http://www.wsj.com/articles/SB 10001424052970204908604574330991380910578.

Allen, Mike. "Kathryn Murray Dies at 92; Coaxed Many to 'Try Dancing,'" *The New York Times*, August 8, 1999, p. 39.

Allen, Steve. "Television in the United States," *Britannica*, February 4, 2014. www .britannica.com/EBchecked/topic/1513870/Television-in-the-United-States# toc283600.

"American Architecture—Twentieth Century, 1950 to 1959." Architecture Week and Artifice, Inc. 1998–2012, GreatBuildings.com. Accessed October 18, 2015. www .greatbuildings.com/types/usa/usa_1950-1959.html.

American Film Institute. "The 100 Best Films," AFI.com. Accessed December 7, 2016. www.afi.com/100years/movies10.aspx.

Anderson, Christopher. "I Love Lucy: U.S. Situation Comedy," *Museum of Broadcast Communications/.* Accessed August 30, 2015. www.museum.tv/eotv/ilovelucy.htm.

"And the Winner Is . . . Marilyn Monroe!" *Newsdesk News Room of the Smithsonian*, December 23, 2015. Accessed July 25, 2016. newsdesk.si.edu/releases/and -winner-marilyn-monroe.

Applebaum, Yoni. "McKinney, Texas, and the Racial History of American Swimming Pools." TheAtlantic.com. www.theatlantic.com/politics/archive/2015/06/troubled-waters-in-mckinney-texas/395150/.

Archibold, Randal C. "Where a Young Actor Died and a Legend Was Born," *The New York Times*, October 2, 2005. Accessed December 28, 2015. www.nytimes.com/2005/10/02/us/where-a-young-actor-died-and-a-legend-wasborn.html.

Army-Technology.com, April 1, 2014. Accessed January 25, 2016 www.army-technology.com/features/featurethe-biggest-and-most-powerfulnuclear-weapons-ever-built-4206787/.

Arnold, Roxanne. "Lucille Ball Dies; TV's Comic Genius Was 77: Death Caused by Ruptured Abdominal Aorta as She Appeared to Be Recovering from Surgery." *The New York Times*, April 27, 1989. articles.latimes.com/1989-04-27/news/mn1618_1_love-lucy-aorta-emergency-heart-surgery.

Asbury, Edith Evans. "Rock 'n' Roll Teen-Agers Tie Up the Times Square Area," *The New York Times*, February 23, 1957, p. 1, 12.

Asbury, Edith Evans."Times Sq. 'Rocks' for Second Day," *The New York Times*, February 24, 1957, 37.

Associated Press. "Victims of Sinister Medical Procedures Included Residents of Staten Island's Infamous Willowbrook State School," Associated Press, March 1, 2011. Accessed November 14, 2015. www.silive.com/northshore/index.ssf/2011/03/victims_of_sinister_medical_pr.html.

Atkinson, Brooks. "First Night at the Theatre," *The New York Times*, December 4, 1947. Accessed December 13. 2015.www.nytimes.com/books/00/12/31/specials/williams-streetcar.html.

"Atoms for Peace." *Dwight D. Eisenhower Presidential Library*. Accessed November 22, 2015. www.eisenhower.archives.gov/research/online_documents/atoms_for_peace.html.

Avery, Ron. "They Began Teen-Show Craze Before 'Bandstand,' Grady, Hurst Reigned." Philly.com. March 20, 1995. Accessed July 28, 2016. articles.philly.com/1995-03-20/news/25701755_1_wpen-today-hurst-teen-ager.

Baer, John W. *The Pledge of Allegiance a Short History*. Annapolis, MD: Free State Press, Inc., 2007, 1992. Accessed November 29, 2015. www.vineyard.net/vineyard/history/pledge.htm.

Baillie, Hugh. "TV Audience Views Atomic Bomb Test for First Time," *The Las Vegas Sun*, April 22, 1952. Accessed July 12, 2015. lasvegassun.com/news/1952/apr/22/tv-audience-views-atomic-bomb-test-first-time/.

BBC. "The 100 Greatest American Films," BBC.com, July 20, 2015. Accessed December 7, 2016. www.bbc.com/culture/story/20150720-the-100-greatest-american-films.

Beanland, Christopher. "Chicago: City of Skyscrapers, Mies Van der Rohe, and Now an Architectural Biennial," *The Independent*. October 5, 2015. Accessed March 12, 2016. www.independent.co.uk/travel/americas/chicago-city-of-skyscrapers-mies-van-der-rohe-and-now-an-architectural-biennial-a6679841.html.

Bellafante, Ginia. "Emily Wilkens, 83, Designer Who Dressed Girls Like Girls," *The New York Times*, December 6, 2000. Accessed December 6, 2016. www.nytimes.com/2000/12/06/nyregion/emily-wilkens-83-designer-who-dressed-girls-like-girls.html.

Bellamy, Francis. *The Youth's Companion*, September 8, 1892, Perry Mason & Co., p. 442.

Bernstein, Adam. "Actor Marlon Brando, 80, Dies," *The Washington Post*, July 2, 2004. Accessed December 28, 2015. www.washingtonpost.com/wp-dyn/articles/A23157-2004Jul2.html.

Berk, Brett. "Car Safety Evolved for the Better, Despite Some Terrible Ideas," *Road & Track.* May 16, 2013. Accessed April 10, 2016. www.roadandtrack.com/car-culture /a4449/the-road-ahead-road-evolution-of-safety/.

Betts, Hannah. "Bettie Page: Look How Far We Haven't Come," *The Telegraph,* December 13, 2008. Accessed January 1, 2016. www.telegraph.co.uk/comment/3741790 /Bettie-Page-Look-how-far-we-havent-come.

Biddle, Sam. "How the CIA Spent Secret Millions Turning Modern Art into a Cold War Arsenal," November 10, 2010. Accessed March 18, 2016. gizmodo.com/5686753 /how-the-cia-spent-secret-millions-turning-modern-art-into-a-cold-war-arsenal.

Bigman, Alex. "Saul Bass: The Man Who Changed Graphic Design," 99Designs.com, June 12, 2012. Accessed March 18, 2016.99designs.com/blog/creative-inspiration /saul-bass-graphic-designer-of-a-century/.

"Billboard Magazine Archives." AmericanRadioHistory.com www.americanradiohistory.com/Billboard-Magazine.htm.

"Bill Haley Biography." *Rock and Roll Hall of Fame and Museum.* rockhall.com/inductees /bill-haley/bio/.

Biography.com Editors. "Marilyn Monroe Biography," Biography.com A&E Television Networks, April 26, 2016. Accessed December 7, 2016. www.biography .com/people/marilyn-monroe-9412123.

Blausen, Whitney. "Elizabeth Hawes," *Fashion Designer Encyclopedia.* Accessed August 14, 2016. www.fashionencyclopedia.com/Ha-Ja/Hawes-Elizabeth.html.

Blow, Charles M. "60 Years Later, Echoes of Emmett Till's Killing," *The New York Times.* August 31, 2015. Accessed April 4, 2016. www.nytimes.com/2015/08/31 /opinion/charles-m-blow-60-years-later-echoes-of-emmett-tills-killing.html ?ref=opinion&_r=0.

Bombay, Scott. "The Day the Supreme Court killed Hollywood's Studio System," *YahooNews,* May 4, 2015. news.yahoo.com/day-supreme-court-killed-hollywood-studio -system-102627410.html.

"Boston Common to Hoot Mon Belt They Rock 'n' Riot Out of This Veldt," *Variety,* May 7, 1958, pp. 1, 58.

Boundless. "Indian Relocation," *Boundless U.S. History.* November 10, 2015. Accessed November 19, 2015. www.boundless.com/u-s-history/textbooks/boundless-u-s -history-textbook/politics-and-culture-of-abundance-1943-1960-28/the-eisen hower-administration-216/indian-relocation-1202-9756/.

Bracker, Milton. "Experts Propose Study of Craze," *The New York Times,* February 23, 1957, p. 12.

Brody, Richard. "Talking with Truffaut," *The New Yorker.* August 15, 2010. Accessed July 23, 2016. www.newyorker.com/culture/richard-brody/talking-with-truffaut

Brohl, Karen. "The 1950s: Pursuing the American Dream," November 12, 2001. *ACHRNEWS.* Accessed July 10, 2015. www.achrnews.com/articles/87033-the -1950s-pursuing-the-american-dream.

"Buddy Holly Biography." *Rock and Roll Hall of Fame and Museum.* rockhall.com /inductees/buddy-holly/bio/.

Burton, Daniel. "Ten Things You Did Not Know About Sputnik," *U.S. News & World Report.* www.usnews.com/news/world/articles/2007/09/28/10-things-you -didnt-know-about-sputnik.

"The Capitol Records Building: The Story of an L.A. Icon," *Discover Los Angeles.* April 14, 2014. Accessed March 7, 2016. www.discoverlosangeles.com/capitol -records-building-hollywood.

Cendón, Sara Fernández. "Pruitt-Igoe 40 Years Later," *The American Institute of Architects.* February 3, 2012. Accessed March 14, 2016.

"Censorship Incidents 1950s." *Parental Advisory: Music Censorship in America*. Accessed July 4, 2004. ericnuzum.com/banned/incidents/50s.html.

Chadwick, Bruce. "The Lost Decade: The 1950s Comes Back with a Roar," HNN *History News Network*. January 9, 2012. Accessed October 23, 2015. historynewsnetwork.org/article/143863.

Charleston, Beth Duncuff. "The Bikini," In *Heilbrunn Timeline of Art History*. Online New York: The Metropolitan Museum of Art, October 2000. Accessed May 4, 2016. www.metmuseum.org/toah/hd/biki/hd_biki.htm.

Christiansen, Richard. "Why Love Lucy? Because Her Humor Never Grows Stale, As Laserdisc Proves 40 Years Later," *The Chicago Tribune*. October 14, 1991. Accessed August 30, 2015. articles.chicagotribune.com/1991-10-14/features/9104020941 _1_love-lucy-redhead-american-television-history.

"Civil Defense Drill Protests: Dorothy Day and Friends Sit in for Peace." *In the Spotlight* April 2009. Marquette University Raynor Libraries. Accessed June 15, 2015. www.marquette.edu/library/archives/News/spotlight/04-2009.shtml.

"Claire McCardell," *Time magazine*, May 2, 1955, Vol. LXV No. 18.

Cogley, John. *Report on Blacklisting: Movies*. San Francisco, CA: The Fund for the Republic, Inc., 1956. pp. 16–17. archive.org/stream/reportonblacklis00coglrich/report onblacklis00coglrich_djvu.txt.

Collins, Glenn. "Jack Gould, Critic, Is Dead at 79; Covered Television for the Times," *The New York Times*. May 23, 1993, p. B6.

Conklin, William R. "Atomic Spy Couple Sentenced to Die: Aide to Get 30 Years," *The New York Times*. April 6, 1951, p. A1.

Cuordileone, K. A. "Politics in an Age of Anxiety," in Cold War Political Culture and the Crisis in American Masculinity, 1949–1960. *The Journal of American History*, Vol. 87, No. 2 (September 2000), pp. 515–545. Published by Organization of American Historians Stable. www.jstor.org/stable/2568762.

Crowther, Bosley. "East of Eden (1955): The Screen: 'East of Eden' Has Debut; Astor Shows Film of Steinbeck Novel," *The New York Times*. March 10, 1955. Accessed December 29, 2015. www.nytimes.com/movie/review?res=9C0DEFD6143EE53 ABC4852DFB566838E649EDE.

Crowther, Bosley. "Forbidden Planet (1956): Screen: Wonderful Trip in Space; 'Forbidden Planet' Is Out of This World," *The New York Times*. May 4, 1956. Accessed January 22, 2016. www.nytimes.com/movie/review?res=9D06E1D7103CE03BB C4C53DFB366838D649EDE.

Crowther, Bosley. "The Man with the Golden Arm" (1955); Narcotics Addict; 'Man with Golden Arm' Opens at Victoria," *The New York Times*. December 16, 1955. www .nytimes.com/movie/review?res=9A06E7DB1E31E73BBC4E52DFB467838E649 EDE.

Crowther, Bosley. "The Screen: 'East of Eden' Has Debut; Astor Shows Film of Steinbeck Novel," *The New York Times*. March 10, 1955. Accessed July 24, 2016. www .nytimes.com/movie/review?res=9C0DEFD6143EE53ABC4852DFB566838E649 EDE.

Crowther, Bosley. "The Screen: Four Newcomers on Local Scene," *The New York Times*. July 21, 1950. Accessed July 24, 2016. www.nytimes.com/movie/review?res=98 00E2D91038E532A25752C2A9619C946192D6CF?.

Crowther, Bosley. "The Screen: Delinquency 'Rebel Without Cause' Has Debut at Astor," *The New York Times*. October 27, 1955. Accessed July 24, 2016. www .nytimes.com/movie/review?res=9F02E0DB1F3AEF34BC4F51DFB667838E649 EDE&pagewanted=print.

Crowther, Bosley. "The Screen in Review: 'Gentlemen Prefer Blondes' at Roxy, With Marilyn Monroe and Jane Russell," *The New York Times*. July 16, 1953. Accessed

July 24, 2016. www.nytimes.com/movie/review?res=9B07E0DC173DE23BBC4E
52DFB1668388649EDE.

Cudahy, Brian J. "The Containership Revolution: Malcom McLean's 1956 Innovation Goes Global," *TR News*. Transportation Research Board, No. 246.—September–October 2006, pp. 5–9. onlinepubs.trb.org/onlinepubs/trnews/trnews246.pdf.

"David Riesman, Sociologist Whose 'Lonely Crowd' Became a Best Seller, Dies at 92," *The New York Times*. May 11, 2002. Accessed November 20, 2015. www.nytimes .com/2002/05/11/books/david-riesman-sociologist-whose-lonely-crowd -became-a-best-seller-dies-at-92.html?pagewanted=all.

Dawidoff, Nicholas. "Hidden America," *The New York Times Magazine*. July 5, 2015, pp 36–48, 51.

"Dick Clark Had Interest in 17 Music Companies." *Philadelphia Daily News* March 4, 1960. Temple University Urban Archives, Philadelphia, n.p.

"Disneyland History," JustDisney.com. Accessed July 3, 2015. justdisney.com /disneyland/history.html.

Doyle, Jack. "Celebrity Gifford: 1950s–2000s," PopHistoryDig.com. January 5, 2014. Accessed June 22, 2015. www.pophistorydig.com/topics/frank-gifford-1950s -2000s/.

Doyle, Jack. "Dinah Shore & Chevrolet, 1956–1963," PopHistoryDig.com. March 22, 2009. Accessed August 6, 2015. www.pophistorydig.com/topics/dinah-shore -chevrolet-1950s-1960s/.

Doyle, Jack. "Moondoog Alan Freed: 1951–1962," Music, Radio & Pop Culture, PopHistoryDig.com. February 28, 2014. Accessed June 22, 2015. www.pophisto-rydig.com/topics/tag/alan-freed-big-beat/.

Dirks, Tim. "History of Sex in Cinema: The Greatest and Most Influential Sexual Films and Scenes, 1950–1954." AMC Film Site *Filmsite.org*. Accessed December 20, 2015. www.filmsite.org/sexinfilms11.html.

Dirks, Tim. "History of Sex in Cinema: The Greatest and Most Influential Sexual Films and Scenes, 1955–1956," AMC Film Site *Filmsite.org*. Accessed December 20, 2015. www.filmsite.org/sexinfilms12.html.

Dirks, Tim. "History of Sex in Cinema: The Greatest and Most Influential Sexual Films and Scenes, 1957–1959," AMC Film Site *Filmsite.org*. Accessed December 20, 2015. www.filmsite.org/sexinfilms13.html.

Druesedow, Jean. "Vera Maxwell - Fashion Designer Encyclopedia," *Encyclopedia of Fashion*, 2016. Accessed December 6, 2016. www.fashionencyclopedia.com/Ma -Mu/Maxwell-Vera.html.

"Edward R. Murrow," Biography.com, A&E Television Networks, Accessed September 27, 2015. www.biography.com/people/edward-r-murrow-9419104.

Dunne, Susan. "Hartford Library to Mark Banned Books Week with Look at Comic-Book Scare," *The Hartford Courant*. September 16, 2014.

Dwyer, Jim. "6 Decades On a Patriotic Plea Still Resonates," *The New York Times*. March 11, 2105, p. A18.

"Elvis '50s Timeline: A Chronicle of Events During the 1950's." www.nachomamascanton .com/elvis_presley_1950.htm.

Ephross, Peter. "How Jews Segregated *and* Integrated Levittown," *New Jersey Jewish News*. February 19, 2009. Accessed July 14, 2015. njjewishnews.com/njjn.com /021909/ltHowJewsSegregated.html.

Erlewine, Stephen Thomas, "Milton Brown, The Other King of Western Swing," *All-Music Guide*. Accessed December 10, 2016. http://elvispelvis.com/miltonbrown.htm.

Eskridge, W.N. "A Jurisprudence of 'Coming Out': Religion, Homosexuality, and Collisions of Liberty and Equality in American Public Law," *Yale Law Journal*. January 1, 1997.

Eisenhower, Dwight D. "Atoms for Peace." *Dwight D. Eisenhower Presidential Library.*
    Accessed November 22, 2015. www.eisenhower.archives.gov/research/online
    _documents/atoms_for_peace.html.

"Elvis Presley: The Milton Berle Show: April 3, 1955," ElvisPresleyPhotos.com. Accessed
    July 27, 2016. www.elvispresleymusic.com.au/pictures/1956-april-3.html.

Everett, Anna. "Golden Age of Television Drama," *Museum of Broadcast Communica-*
    tions. Accessed July 2, 2015. www.museum.tv/eotv/goldenage.htm.

Feaster, Felicia and Scott McGee. "Rebel Without a Cause: The Essentials," Turner Clas-
    sic Movies, TCM.com. Accessed December 29, 2015. www.tcm.com/this-month
    /article/27003%7C0/Rebel-Without-a-Cause.html. www.geaviation.com/company
    /aviation-history.html.

Fong-Torres, Ben. "Biography: Alan Freed." AlanFreed.com. Accessed December 10,
    2016. www.alanfreed.com/wp/biography/.

Franklin, Ruth. "Shirley Jackson's Life Among the Savages," *The New York Times.* May 8,
    2015. Accessed December 10, 2016. Franklin. http://www.nytimes.com/2015/05
    /10/books/review/shirley-jacksons-life-among-the-savages-and-raising-demons
    -reissued.html?_r=0.

Frank, Stanley. "They'd Rather Dance Than Eat," *Saturday Evening Post*, October 12,
    1957, 24-25, 114-120.

"GE Aviation: Powering a Century of Flight," GEAviation.com. Accessed Decem-
    ber 10, 2016. www.geaviation.com/company/aviation-history.html.

Geselbracht, Raymond H. "Harry Truman Speaks," Harry S. Truman Library and
    Museum. Accessed March 21, 2016. www.trumanlibrary.org/speaks.htm.

"GI Bill of Rights," Prentice Hall Documents Library Online. hcl.chass.ncsu.edu/garson
    /dye/docs/gibill.htm.

Gitlin, Todd. "How Our Crowd Got Lonely," The New York Times Bookend, January 9,
    2000. www.nytimes.com/books/00/01/09/bookend/bookend.html.

"Going Steady," Time Magazine, March 11, 1957, No. 10, p. 64.

Gray, Tim. "James Dean: After 60 Years, Still the Coolest Icon of Teen Angst," Variety.
    September 30, 2015. Accessed December 28, 2015. variety.com/2015/film/news
    /james-dean-death-60th-anniversary-cool-1201602001/.

Greenhouse Consultants, Inc. "Phase IA Cultural Resource Survey for The College of
    Staten Island at Willowbrook (CUNY Project No. ST104-084): An Historical and
    Archaeological Evaluation." [Multiple authors], Appendix 21 August 1986.
    Accessed January 10, 2016. s-media.nyc.gov/agencies/lpc/arch_reports/689
    .pdf.

Goldstein, Richard and Frank Weber. "Frank Gifford, 84, Dies; His Celebrity Helped
    Push N.F.L. Into Spotlight," *The New York Times.* August 10, 2015, p. A1, B8.

"Guggenheim," GreatBuildings.com, 1994-2013 Artifice, Inc. Accessed December 7,
    2016. http://greatbuildings.com/buildings/Guggenheim_Museum.

"Hearing Advances Big Housing Plan; Further Action Due May 19 on Metropolitan
    Life Project," *The New York Times.* May 6, 1943. p. 36.

"Highway History: Civil Defense, 1955," U.S. Department of Transportation Federal
    Highway Administration. October 10, 2013. Accessed June 15, 2015. www.fhwa
    .dot.gov/infrastructure/civildef.cfm.

"History: 1950s," Advertising Age. September 15, 2003. Accessed May 1, 2016. adage
    .com/article/adage-encyclopedia/history-1950s/98701/.

"History of the USS Nautilus (SSN 571)," Submarine Force Museum, Accessed Janu-
    ary 25, 2016. www.ussnautilus.org/nautilus/index.shtml.

"History of Veterans Day," U.S. Department of Veteran Affairs. Accessed Novem-
    ber 10, 2015. www.va.gov/opa/vetsday/vetdayhistory.asp.

"Historical Highlights," History, Art & Archives, United States House of Representatives. Accessed July 12, 2015. history.house.gov/Historical-Highlights/1951-2000/The-Southern-Manifesto-of-1956/.

History.com Staff. "HUAC," History.com, A+E Networks 2009. Accessed March 30, 2016. www.history.com/topics/cold-war/huac.

History.com Staff. "Integration of Central High School," History.com, A+E Networks, 2009. Accessed March 27, 2016. www.history.com/topics/black-history/central-high-school-integration.History.com.

History.com Staff. "The Korean War," History.com, A+E Networks 2009. Accessed July 26, 2015. www.history.com/topics/korean-war.

History.com Staff. "Unsafe at Any Speed Hits Bookstores," History.com, A+E Networks, 2009. Accessed August 10, 2016. www.history.com/this-day-in-history/unsafe-at-any-speed-hits-bookstores.

Holden, Stephen. "Back to the 1950s, Days of Innocence and Repression," *New York Times*. July 29, 2016, p. C11.

Hopwood, Jon C. "Marlon Brando." IMDb.com Mini Biography. Accessed December 13, 2015. www.imdb.com/name/nm0000008/bio?ref_=nm_ov_bio_sm.

"Horace Ashenfelter," Ashenfelter 8K Classic. Accessed October 22, 2015. www.ashenfelterclassic.com/horace.shtml.

"Hollywood Ten," History.com, A+E Networks 2009. Accessed May 30, 2015. www.history.com/topics/cold-war/hollywood-ten.

"How Things Fly," Smithsonian National Air and Space Museum. Accessed July 28, 2016. howthingsfly.si.edu/media/speed-sound.

Hyman, Vicki. "How Three Planes Crashed in Three Months in Elizabeth in '50s," NJ Advance Media for NJ.com. May 29, 2015. Accessed July 28, 2016. www.nj.com/entertainment/arts/index.ssf/2015/05/how_three_planes_crashed_in_elizabeth_in_50s.html.

HUAC, House Committee on Un-American Activities, Hearings Regarding the Communist Infiltration of the Motion Picture Industry, 80th Congress, 1st Session, October 23–24, 1947. Washington: Government Printing Office, 1947.

"HUAC," History.com, A+&E Networks 2009, accessed June 14, 2015. www.history.com/topics/cold-war/huac.

"Ike's Warning of Military Expansion, 50 Years Later," NPR Staff, January 17, 2011. Accessed November 26, 2015. www.npr.org/2011/01/17/132942244/ikes-warning-of-military-expansion-50-years-later.

"The Immigration and Nationality Act of 1952 (The McCarran-Walter Act)," US Department of State Office of the Historian. history.state.gov/milestones/1945-1952/immigration-act.

"The Interstate Highway System." www.history.com/topics/interstate-highway-system.

"Irene Morgan," *Richmond Times Dispatch*. February 13, 2004. Accessed January 31, 2016. www.richmond.com/special-section/irene-morgan/article_d7873b66-e5ae-5f42-a399-38aa5548c8f0.html.

"The Jack Benny Program," IMDb.com, February 4, 2005. www.imdb.com/title/tt0042116/.

Jackman, Michael. "Detroit's Turkel House Drips with History," *Metro Times*. Accessed July 10, 2015. www.metrotimes.com/detroit/wright-or-wrong/Content?oid=2184946.

"Jacqueline Cochran, Record Setter," Jackie: The National Aviation Hall of Fame. NationalAviation.org. Accessed February 14, 2016. www.nationalaviation.org/cochran-jacqueline/.

Jarvik, Elaine. "Vestiges of '56 Collision Still Imbedded in Grand Canyon," Deseret News. June 20, 2006. Accessed January 25, 2016. www.deseretnews.com/article/640191166 /Vestiges-of-56-collision-still-imbedded-in-Grand-Canyon.html?pg=all.

Johnson, Troy. "How Dancing in Rock Became Uncool," January 22, 2003, *San Diego City Beat*. Accessed December 5, 2016. http://www.sdcitybeat.com/article.php ?id=473.

Jones, Jeffrey Owen. "The Man Who Wrote the Pledge of Allegiance," Smithsonian Magazine. November 2003. www.smithsonianmag.com/history/the-man-who-wrote-the-pledge-of-allegiance-93907224/.

"Joseph R. McCarthy," History.com, A+E Networks, 2009. Accessed August 19, 2015. www.history.com/topics/cold-war/joseph-mccarthy.

Keys, Kathi. "County Board Bans 'Invisible Man' from School Libraries," The Courier-Tribune. September 16, 2013, Accessed November 19, 2015. courier-tribune.com /sections/news/local/county-board-bans-%E2%80%98invisible-man%E2 %80%99-school-libraries.html.

"The Kennedy-Nixon Debates," www.history.com/topics/us-presidents/kennedy -nixon-debates.

Kimmelman, Michael. "Art of the '50s: When Fortunes Shone," *The New York Times*. December 23, 1988. Accessed March 16, 2016. www.nytimes.com/1988/12/23 /arts/review-art-of-the-50-s-when-fortunes-shone.html?pagewanted=print.

Kiss, Sr., Stephen. "On TV Westerns of the 1950s and '60s," New York Public Library, December 1, 2012. Accessed December 26, 2015. www.nypl.org/blog/2012/12 /01/tv-westerns-1950s-and-60s.

Koch, Wendy, "U.S. Urged to Apologize for 1930s Deportations," *USA Today* April 5, 2006, p. 2A. http://www.amren.com/news/2006/04/us_urged_to_apo/.

Koestler, Fred L. "Operation Wetback," Handbook of Texas Online. Published by the Texas State Historical Association. March 23, 2012. www.tshaonline.org /handbook/online/articles/pqo01.

"Korean War Fast Facts," CNN Library. July 3, 2015. Accessed November 27, 2015. www.cnn.com/2013/06/28/world/asia/korean-war-fast-facts/.

"The Korean War, 1950–1953," US Department of State Office of the Historian. history .state.gov/milestones/1945-1952/korean-war-2.

"Kurt Vonnegut Once Lived in the Shadow of His Brother," Geek's Guide to the Galaxy. January 9, 2016. Accessed January 10, 2016. www.wired.com/2016/01 /geeks-guide-vonnegut-brothers/.

"The 1950s," History.com, A+E Networks 2009. www.history.com/topics/1950s.

Lacy-Pendleton, Stevie. "Racial Identity, Racism and the History of Blood," Staten Island Advance. Friday, February 23, 2007, A22.

LaFrance, Adrienne. "The Site of a 1950s Plane Crash Just Became a National Landmark," The Atlantic. April 24, 2014. Accessed July 25, 2015. www.theatlantic.com /technology/archive/2014/04/the-site-of-a-1950s-plane-crash-just-became-a -national-landmark/361183/.

Lambert, Bruce. "At 50, Levittown Contends with Its Legacy of Bias," *The New York Times*. December 28, 1997. Accessed July 14, 2015. www.nytimes.com/1997/12 /28/nyregion/at-50-levittown-contends-with-its-legacy-of-bias.html?page wanted=print.

Lambie, Ryan. "The Greatest Sci-Fi Movies of the 1950s," Den of Geek. Accessed December 30, 2015. www.denofgeek.us/movies/16511/the-greatest-sci-fi-movies-of-the -1950s.

Le Zotte, Jennifer. "How the Summer of Atomic Bomb Testing Turned the Bikini into a Phenomenon," Smithsonian Magazine. May 21, 2015. Accessed November 20,

2105. www.smithsonianmag.com/smithsonian-institution/how-wake-testing-atomic-bomb-bikini-became-thing-180955346/.

Littlefield, Bill. "The 1951 USF Dons: Uninvited from The Orange Bowl?" NPR and WBUR 90.9 Boston. January 2, 2016. Accessed January 6, 2016. onlyagame.wbur.org/2016/01/02/san-francisco-dons-orange-bowl-undefeated.

"Little Rock: 40 Years Later," *The New York Times*, 1997. Accessed December 5, 2016. http://events.nytimes.com/learning/general/specials/littlerock/little-rock.28.jpg.html.

Litsky, Frank. "Louise Suggs, Golf Pioneer, Dies at 91; Helped Found the Women's Pro Golf Tour," *The New York Times*, p. B8.

Litsky, Frank. "Mal Whitfield, Olympic Gold Medalist and Tuskegee Airman, Dies at 91," *The New York Times*. November 20, 2015, p. B14.

"Local Kids' TV," Pioneers of Television PBS.org. Accessed December 26, 2015. www.pbs.org/wnet/pioneers-of-television/pioneering-programs/local-kids-tv/.

Logan, Michael. "TV Guide Magazine's 60th Anniversary: How Desi Arnaz Jr. Became Our First Cover Star," TVGuide.com. April 3, 2103. Accessed July 19, 2015. www.tvguide.com/news/tv-guide-magazine-60-arnaz-1063463/.

"*Loving v. Virginia.*" U.S. Supreme Court 388 U.S. 1, 1967. *NPS*.gov, Accessed July 19, 2016. www.nps.gov/jame/learn/historyculture/upload/Loving-v-Virginia.pdf.

Lubow, Arthur. "The Triumph of Frank Lloyd Wright," Smithsonian Magazine. June 2009. www.smithsonianmag.com/history/the-triumph-of-frank-lloyd-wright-132535844/?no-ist.

Markel, Howard. "The Day Polio Began Losing Its Grip on America," PBS News Hour. April 12, 2103. www.pbs.org/newshour/rundown/the-day-polio-began-losing-its-grip-on-america/.

Martin, Michel. "Hidden Pattern of Rape Helped Stir Civil Rights Movement," NPR Radio. Transcript, February 28, 2011. Accessed January 31, 2016. www.npr.org/templates/story/story.php?storyId=134131369.

Martin, Richard. "American Ingenuity: Sportswear, 1930s–1970s," Heilbrunn Timeline of Art History. October 2014. Accessed August 14, 2016. www.metmuseum.org/toah/hd/amsp/hd_amsp.htm.

Mattix, Micah. "Did Conservatives Start Creative Writing Programs to Fight the Cold War?" FreeBeacon.com. November 21, 2015. Accessed November 28, 2015. free-beacon.com/culture/did-conservatives-start-creative-writing-programs-to-fight-the-cold-war/.

McConnell, Carolyn. "The Disappeared," The Mother's Movement Online. Spring 2007. Accessed January 9, 2016. www.mothersmovement.org/books/reviews/07/went-away.html.

McLellan, Dennis. "James Dougherty, 84, Was Married to Marilyn Monroe Before She Became a Star," Los Angeles Times. August 18, 2005. Accessed July 24, 2016. articles.latimes.com/2005/aug/18/local/me-dougherty18.

Mead, Julia C. "Memories of Segregation in Levittown," *The New York Times*. May 11, 2003. Accessed July 14, 2015. www.nytimes.com/2003/05/11/nyregion/memories-of-segregation-in-levittown.html?pagewanted=print.

Meeropol, Michael and Robert Meeropol. "Exonerate Ethel Rosenberg," *The New York Times*. August 10, 2015, p. A19.

"Milton Berle on Elvis Presley," EmmyTVLegends.org. Published June 15, 2015. Accessed July 15, 2015. www.youtube.com/watch?v=FjJr5Yimfeo.

Mineta, Norman Y. "Statement of U.S. Transportation Secretary On the Death of Malcom P. McLean," M2 PressWire. M2, May 30, 2001. Accessed August 4, 2016. www.m2.com/m2/web/story.php/2001DBAAB75EC2D8645080256A5C005478F9.

Misra, Tanvi. "These Jim Crow-Era Guides for Black Travelers Are Sadly Still Relevant," CityLab Online, October 30, 2015. www.citylab.com/work/2015/10/these-jim -crow-era-guides-for-black-travelers-are-sadly-still-relevant/413311/.

"Montgomery Bus Boycott," History.com, A+E Networks, 2010. Accessed August 10, 2016. http://www.history.com/topics/black-history/montgomery-bus-boycott.

"Movie Trailer: This is Cinerama," Fandor. Accessed July 23, 2016. www.youtube.com /watch?v=DSndXTOIu98.

Nader, Ralph. "The Article That Launched the Consumer-Rights Movement Innumer-able precedents show that the consumer must be protected from his own indis-cretion and vanity." *The Nation,* March 23, 2015. Accessed December 5, 2016. https://www.thenation.com/article/safe-car-you-cant-buy/.

"National Film Preservation Board (NFP)," Library of Congress (1989). Accessed July 25, 2016. www.loc.gov/programs/national-film-preservation-board/about -this-program.

"National Nielsen, Videodex and Pulse Ratings, April 1950," Television Obscurities. August 16, 2009. Accessed July 11, 2015. www.tvobscurities.com/2009/08/national -nielsen-videodex-and-pulse-ratings-april-1950/.

Nickell, Frank. "The Burning of the Comic Books," *KRCU.org* March 1, 2016. Accessed December 10, 2016. http://krcu.org/post/burning-comic-books#stream/0.

"Nielsen: About Us," Nielsen.com. Accessed July 28, 2016. www.nielsen.com/us/en /about-us.html.

Nixon, Rob. "East of Eden (1955)," Turner Classic Movies, TCM.com. Accessed Decem-ber 29, 2015. www.tcm.com/tcmdb/title/16719/East-of-Eden/articles.html.

"Norman Mattoon Thomas," Encyclopedia of World Biography (2004), The Gale Group Inc. Accessed November 21, 2015. www.encyclopedia.com/topic /Norman_Mattoon_Thomas.aspx.

Novak, Matt. "Nobody Walks in L.A.: The Rise of Cars and the Monorails That Never Were," Smithsonian.com. April 26, 2013. Accessed August 30, 2015. www.smith-sonianmag.com/ist/?next=/history/nobody-walks-in-la-the-rise-of-cars-and -the-monorails-that-never-were-43267593/#rRFhJ8dHkz4pwoE2.01.

"NSC-68." U.S. Department of State Office of the Historian. history.state.gov /milestones/1945-1952/NSC68.

Nyberg, Amy. "Comics Code History: The Seal of Approval," Comic Book Legal Defense Fund (CBLDF), Seton Hall University. Accessed May 26, 2016. cbldf.org /comics-code-history-the-seal-of-approval/.

"Origin of the Peace Symbol," *Campaign for Nuclear Disarmament,* Accessed Decem-ber 10, 2016. www.docspopuli.org/articles/PeaceSymbolArticle.html.

"Oscar Niemeyer and the United Nations Headquarters (1947–1949)," United Nations Archives and Records Management Section. Accessed November 1, 2015. https://archives.un.org/content/oscar-niemeyer-and-united-nations-headquar-ters-1947–1949.

"Oscar Niemeyer Biography," *The* Biography.com, A&E Television Networks. Accessed November 1, 2015. www.biography.com/people/oscar-niemeyer-9423385. Paster-nak, Dan. "Milton Berle Interview," EmmyTVLegends.org. June 11, 1996, Accessed July 27, 2016. www.emmytvlegends.org/interviews/people/milton-berle.

Pennington, Bill. "In 1956, a Racial Law Repelled Harvard's Team," *The New York Times.* March 15, 2012, p. B15.

Peralta, Eyder. "It Came Up in the Debate: Here Are 3 Things to Know About 'Opera-tion Wetback,'" NPR.org. November 11, 2015. Accessed April 2, 2016. www.npr .org/sections/thetwo-way/2015/11/11/455613993/it-came-up-in-the-debate -here-are-3-things-to-know-about-operation-wetback.

Polsson, Ken. "Chronology of Disneyland Theme Park." Accessed July 3, 2015. www
.islandnet.com/~kpolsson/disland/

Pousson, Eli. "Why the West Side Matters: Read's Drugstore and Baltimore's Civil
Rights History," January 7, 2011. Accessed July 12, 2015. https://baltimoreher
itage.org/education/why-the-west-side-matters-reads-drug-store-and-balti-
mores-civil-rights-heritage/#.WK-yA28rLIU.

Proctor, Dr. Robert N. "The History of the Discovery of the Cigarette–Lung Cancer
Link: Evidentiary Traditions, Corporate Denial, Global Toll," History Depart-
ment, Stanford University, Stanford, California, November 22, 2011. Accessed
November 22, 2015. tobaccocontrol.bmj.com/content/21/2/87.full.

"The Quiz Show Scandal," PBS.org The American Experience, 1999. Accessed July 28,
2016. www.pbs.org/wgbh/amex/quizshow/index.html.

Rafferty, Terrence. "Rebel with a Surprising Legacy," *The New York Times*. May 29, 2005.
Accessed December 28, 2015. www.nytimes.com/2005/05/29/movies/rebel
-with-a-surprising-legacy.html.

Radosh, Ronald. "Grasping at Straws to Try and Exonerate Ethel Rosenberg," Wall
Street Journal. July 19, 2015. Accessed August 11, 2016. www.wsj.com/articles
/grasping-at-straws-to-try-to-exonerate-ethel-rosenberg-1437342393.

Rautiolla-Williams, Suzanne. "Howdy Doody," Museum of Broadcast Communications Encyclopedia of Television. www.emmytvlegends.org/interviews/shows
/howdy-doody.

"Rebel Without a Cause," Turner Classic movies, TCM.com. Accessed July 24, 2016.
www.tcm.com/tcmdb/title/16115/Rebel-Without-a-Cause/.

"Red Scare," History.com, A+E Networks 2010. Accessed June 14, 2015. www.history
.com/topics/cold-war/red-scare.

Reston, James. "A Sociological Decision," *The New York Times*. May 18, 1954, p. 14.

Roberts, Sam. "Brother's Secret Grand Jury Testimony Supporting Ethel Rosenberg Is
Released," *The New York Times*. July 16 2015, p. A20.

Roberts, Sam. "Irving Harper, 99, Whimsical Designer," *The New York Times*. September 16, 2015, p. A19.

"Rock-and-Roll Called Communicable Disease," *The New York Times*. March 28, 1956,
p. 33.

Rodden, John. "Dwight and Left," *The American Prospect*. February 20, 2006. prospect
.org/article/dwight-and-left.

Rose, David. "A History of the March of Dimes: The Polio Years," MarchofDimes.org.
August 26, 2010. Accessed February 19, 2016. www.marchofdimes.org/mission
/a-history-of-the-march-of-dimes.aspx.

Ritrosky-Winslow, Madelyn. "Anthology Dramas," Museum of Broadcast Communications. Accessed July 27, 2016. www.museum.tv/eotv/anthologydra.htm.

Ruff, Joshua. "For Sale: The American Dream," *American History*. 42:5, 2007, pp. 42–49.

Rybczynski, Witold. "The Ranch House Anomaly: How America Fell In and Out of
Love with Them," Slate.com. April 17, 2007. Accessed July 10, 2015. www
.slate.com/articles/arts/architecture/2007/04/the_ranch_house_anomaly
.html.

Sahagun, Louis. "Pinup queen Bettie Page dies at 85." *Los Angeles Times*, December 12,
2008. Accessed December 6, 2016. www.latimes.com/local/obituaries/la-me
-page12-2008dec12-story.html.

Samuels, Gertrude. "Why They Rock 'n' Roll—And Should They?" *The New York Times*.
January 12, 1958, Sec. SM, p. 16–20.

Sandow, Greg. "Grand Ole Opry." Microsoft Encarta® Encyclopedia. Microsoft Corporation (1993–2009), CD-ROM.

Scharf, Mike. "Dragon M65 Atomic Annie," *Fine Scale Modeler*. September 2015, p. 59.

Schmidt, Chuck. "The Disney-Welton Becket Connection," *The Staten Island Advance*. January 11, 2012. Accessed March 8, 2016. blog.silive.com/goofy_about_disney /2012/01/post_17.html.

Schulberg, Budd. "The Man Who Would Be King," Vanity Fair. February 28, 2005. Accessed December 28, 2015. www.vanityfair.com/news/2005/03/brando200503.

Schwartz, Dennis. "Little Fugitive, Movie Review," Ozus' World Movie Reviews, December 11, 2003. Accessed July 23, 2016. homepages.sover.net/~ozus /littlefugitive.htm.

Seaman, Margo. "Claire McCardell," Fashion Designer Encyclopedia. Accessed August 14, 2016. www.fashionencyclopedia.com/Ma-Mu/Mccardell-Claire.html.

"The Seven Year Itch," TCM.com. Accessed July 24, 2016. www.tcm.com/tcmdb/title /89662/The-Seven-Year-Itch/.

Sewell, Jessica Elle. "Unpacking the Bachelor Pad," Institute for Advanced Study, Spring 2012. Accessed September 4, 2015. www.ias.edu/about/publications/ias -letter/articles/2012-spring/sewell-bachelor-pad.

Shanley, John P. "Dick Clark—New Rage of the Teenagers," Philadelphia Inquirer. March 16, 1958, Temple University Libraries Urban Archives, Philadelphia, Pennsylvania, n.p.

Shanley, J.P. "Television," America. February 14, 1959, p. 587.

Shanley, J.P. "TV: Teen-Agers Only 'American Bandstand' a Daytime Disk Jockey Show, Bows on Channel 7," *New York Times*. August 6, 1957, p. 42.

"Shirley Jackson, Author of Horror Classic, Dies," *The New York Times*. August 10, 1965. www.nytimes.com/learning/general/onthisday/bday/1214.html.

Sharkey, Lorelei. "Not the Pin-Up We Played Her For." Nerve.com, 1998. Accessed December 6, 2016. www.nerve.com/dispatches/page/pinuplegend.

Simon, Ron. "*See It Now*: U.S. Documentary Series," Museum of Broadcast Communications. Accessed August 19, 2015. www.museum.tv/eotv/seeitnow.htm.

Simmons, Rick. "10 Often-Censored Songs from the Early '50s," Rebeat Magazine. September 4, 2014. www.rebeatmag.com/10-often-censored-songs-from-the -early-50s/.

Sinatra, Frank and Allan Morrison. "The Way I Look at Race," Ebony. July 1958, Vol. 13, Issue 9, p. 34.

Smith, Ken. "Mental Hygiene: The Dos and Don'ts of the Doo-Wop Age," *The New York Times*. January 2, 2000. www.writing.upenn.edu/~afilreis/50s/hygiene-films .html.

"Starting to Click: A History of Automotive Seatbelts," Second Chance Garage. Accessed August 10, 2016. www.secondchancegarage.com/public/seat-belt -history.cfm.

Steinem, Gloria. "The Woman Who Will Not Die," PBS.org. July 19, 2006. Accessed January 1, 2016. www.pbs.org/wnet/americanmasters/marilyn-monroe-marilyn -monroe-still-life/61/.

Stonor Saunders, Frances. "Modern Art was CIA 'Weapon,'" The Independent. 21 October 1995. Accessed March 21, 2016. www.independent.co.uk/news/world /modern-art-was-cia-weapon-1578808.html.

"Southern Manifesto on Integration (March 12, 1956)." From Congressional Record, 84th Congress Second Session. Vol. 102, part 4. Washington, D.C.: Governmental Printing Office, 1956. 4459–4460. PBS.org. Accessed July 12, 2015.www.pbs.org /wnet/supremecourt/rights/sources_document2.html.

Steinem, Gloria. "If Marilyn Had Lived . . . Who Would She Be Today?" Ms. Magazine. August 1986: XV: 2, pp. 40–45, 87–88.

Sugrue, Thomas J. "Motor City: The Story of Detroit," The Gilder Lehrman Institute of American History. October 15, 2012.

Sugrue, Thomas. "Shut Out: After Prince Edward County Closed Its Public Schools, Black Children Had No Access to Education," *New York Times Book Review*. July 5, 2015, p. 14.

Szalai, Jennifer. "Mac the Knife: On Dwight Macdonald," The Nation. November 22, 2011. Accessed July 26, 2015. www.thenation.com/article/mac-knife-dwight -macdonald/.

Taylor, Rich. "A Century of Recreation," Popular Mechanics, EBSCO Publishing, June 7, 2001. www.britannica.com.

"Television," Nielsen.com. Accessed July 11, 2015. www.nielsen.com/us/en/solutions /measurement/television.html.

"Testimony of Paul Robeson before the House Committee on Un-American Activi- ties," Investigation of the Unauthorized Use of U.S. Passports, 84th Congress, Part 3, June 12, 1956; in Thirty Years of Treason: Excerpts from Hearings Before the House Committee on Un-American Activities, 1938–1968, Eric Bentley, ed. New York: Viking Press, 1971, 770.

Tilley, Carol L. "Seducing the Innocent: Fredric Wertham and the Falsifications That Helped Condemn Comics," *A Journal of History*. (47 (4), 2012, 383–413.

Time, March 16, 1953, pp. 23, 29, 42.

Time, June 11, 1951, p. 89;, October 13, 1952, p. 32.

"Timeline of the Nuclear Age," by AtomicArchive.com, AJ Software & Multime- dia1998-2015. Accessed August 6, 2015. www.atomicarchive.com/Timeline /Timeline.shtml.

"Triumph of Frank Lloyd Wright," Smithsonian Magazine. Accessed July 5, 2015. www.smithsonianmag.com/history/the-triumph-of-frank-lloyd-wright-132535 844/#AvL4Z0ZessZAJWQf.99.

"TV History," Archive of American Television. EmmyTVLegends.org. Accessed July 2, 2015. www.emmytvlegends.org/resources/tv-history.

"TV Selling Prices," TVHistory.com. Accessed July 27, 2016. www.tvhistory.tv/tv -prices.htm.

"Twenty-One," Final Van Doren-Stemple Episode. www.youtube.com/watch?v =hMkL4LKb8AU.

Van Gelder, Lawrence. "Milton Berle, TV's First Star as 'Uncle Miltie,' Dies at 93," *The New York Times*. March 28, 2002, p. A29.

Vantoch, Victoria. "The Rise of the Airline Stewardess," Slate Book Review. April 5, 2013. Accessed February 14, 2016. www.slate.com/articles/double_x/books /2013/04/airline_stewardesses_through_history_photos.html.

"Virginia Act to Preserve Racial Integrity of 3/20/1924 (1)," DNA Learning Center. Accessed August 11, 2016. www.dnalc.org/view/11217-Virginia-Act-to -Preserve-Racial-Integrity-of-3-20-1924-1-.html.

"Walt Disney's Disneyland," JustDisney.com. Accessed July 3, 2015. justdisney.com /walt_disney/biography/w_disneyland.html.

Wartts, Adrienne. "Pruitt, Wendell Oliver (1920-1944)," *BlackPast.org* Accessed Decem- ber 7, 2016. www.blackpast.org/aa. h/pruitt-wendell-oliver-1920-1945.

Watson, Margeaux. "Rosa Parks vs. 'Rosa Parks,'" Rolling Stone Magazine. May 13, 1999, p. 22.

Waxer, Lise. "Of Mambo Kings and Songs of Love: Dance Music in Havana and New York from the 1930s to the 1950s," Latin American Music Review. Vol. 15, No. 2 (Autumn-Winter, 1994), 139–176.

Weber, Bruce. "Ronnie Gilbert, Bold-Voiced Singer with the Weavers, Is Dead at 88," *The New York Times*. June 8, 2015, A19.

Weeks, Linton. "4 Hot-Button Kids' Books from The '50s That Sparked Controversy." NPR History Dept. May 7, 2015. www.npr.org/sections/npr-history-dept/2015/05/06/404470968/4-hot-button-kids-books-from-the-50s.

Weiler, A.H. "Niagara Falls Vies with Marilyn Monroe," *The New York Times*. January 22, 1953. Accessed July 24, 2016. www.nytimes.com/movie/review?res=940DE0DF163FE53ABC4A51DFB7668388649EDE.

West, Elliott. *Growing Up in Twentieth-Century America: A History and Reference Guide*. Connecticut: Greenwood Press, 1996.

"Wham-O's History," Wham-O.com. Accessed January 23, 2016. www.wham-o.com/history.html.

"Who Are the Hibakusha," Hibakusha Stories. Accessed January 29, 2016. www.hibakushastories.org/who-are-the-hibakusha/.

"Who Invented the T.V. Dinner." *Library of Congress*, August 23, 2010, *Accessed* December 6, 2016. www.loc.gov/rr/scitech/mysteries/tvdinner.html.

Winerip, Michael. "Global Willowbrook," *The New York Times Magazine*. January 16, 2000, pp. 58–64.

Wirth, Richard. "KTLA & The Atomic Bomb—Live," Pro Video Coalition, August 8, 2013. Accessed February 16, 2016. www.providecoalition.com/ktla-atomic-bomb-live?showall=1.

Wolfe, Brendan. "Racial Integrity Laws (1924–1930)," Encyclopedia Virginia. The University of Virginia. Accessed November 7, 2015. www.encyclopediavirginia.org/Racial_Integrity_Laws_of_the_1920s.

Yahnke, Robert E. "The 1950s—Focus on American Films," University of Minnesota Website. Accessed July 23, 2016. www.tc.umn.edu/~ryahnke/film/cinema4.htm.

Yamazaki, Dr. James N. "Hiroshima and Nagasaki Death Toll," Children of the Atomic Bomb. October 10, 2007. www.aasc.ucla.edu/cab/200708230009.html.

VIDEO/DVD

"Alan Freed on To Tell the Truth," YouTube. Accessed May 31, 2015. www.youtube.com/watch?v=l8j8SECzULw.

"Army-McCarthy Hearings, Have You No Decency Sir," YouTube.www.youtube.com/watch?v=K1eA5bUzVjA. Accessed July 17, 2016.

"Atom Sub. President Officiates at Laying of Keel," Universal Newsreels, June 16, 1952. archive.org/details/1952-06-16_Atom_Sub.

"Atomic Alert: Elementary Version," YouTube. Encyclopedia Britannica Film Division, 1951, www.youtube.com/watch?v=i4k2skbJDm8.

"Atomic/Nuclear Bomb Nevada Test—5/1/1952," YouTube. Accessed July 29, 2016. www.youtube.com/watch?v=d5JsrCPWCl8.

Ballard, Hank. "Rock 'n' Roll: The Early Years." New York: Time-Life Video, 1995.

Bishop, Chris. "No Evil Shall Escape My Sight: Fredric Wertham & The Anti-Comics Crusade," June 20, 2013. Video lecture held in the Archives of the Library of Congress. www.loc.gov/today/cyberlc/feature_wdesc.php?rec=6132.

Braniff Airlines. "The Tantalizing Seductress," YouTube. Accessed February 14, 2016. www.youtube.com/watch?v=3cx7xECjGnU.

Brown, Ruth. "Rock 'n Roll: The Early Years." New York: Time-Life Video, 1995.

"Duck and Cover" (1952). Archer Productions, 9:14 min. Written by Raymond J. Mauer and directed by Anthony Rizzo. Accessed February 20, 2016. www.youtube.com/watch?v=IKqXu-5jw60.

"Edward R. Murrow Addresses Joseph McCarthy," YouTube. First Air Date, March 9, 1954. www.youtube.com/watch?v=-YOIueFbG4g).

"Etta James Live on Alan Freed's Dance Party," YouTube. Accessed May 15, 2015. www.youtube.com/watch?v=jOUDdJn1uec.

Hidden Values: The Movies of the Fifties (2001), Turner Classic Movies, directed by Charlie Coates, 33 min.

"Horace Ashenfelter/Vladimir Kazantsev—Athletics 3000m, 1952," YouTube. Accessed March 7, 2016. www.youtube.com/watch?v=iShrewjO_3o&feature=youtu.be&app=desktop.

"James Dean Warns Kids of Fast Driving on the Highway, 1955," YouTube. Accessed July 24, 2016. www.youtube.com/watch?v=DSiu0z7VcnU.

Jasper Johns: Ideas in Paint, American Masters Film. September 1989. Directed by Rick Tejada-Flores, 53 min.

"Milton Berle Discusses Elvis Presley," EmmyTVLegends.org. June 15, 2015. 4:24 min. Accessed September 5, 2015. www.youtube.com/watch?v=FjJr5Yimfeo.

Murrow, Edward R. "A Report on Senator Joseph R. McCarthy," *See It Now*. (CBS-TV, March 9, 1954). www.otr.com/murrow_mccarthy_see_it_now.html.

Prelinger.com. "Color Footage of Soldiers Being Exposed to High Levels of Radiation," YouTube. Published December 16, 2012. www.youtube.com/watch?v=ZWSMoE3A5DI.

"Presley, Elvis," *The Milton Berle Show*, YouTube. June 5, 1956. Accessed September 5, 2015. www.youtube.com/watch?v=IZSr30yQ8Ts.

Robert Motherwell and the New York School, American Masters Film. August 1991. Directed by Catherine Tatge, 53 min.

"Rock 'n' Roll Explodes," *The History of Rock 'n' Roll Series*. Directed by Andrew Solt Time Life Video & Television and Warner Bros. 1995, videocassette 60 mins.

Rock and Roll: The Early Days, Archive Film Production. Directed by Patrick Montgomery and Pamela Page, TFBI Associates. 1984, videocassette 60 mins.

Trinity and Beyond: The Atomic Bomb Movie, Visual Concept Entertainment. 1995, 93 min.

Twist: A Film by Ron Mann, Home Vision Entertainment. 2002. DVD 74 minutes.

"Unforgotten: Twenty-Five Years After Willowbrook," YouTube. HeartShare Productions. Directed by Jack Fisher. 1997, 57:21 min. www.youtube.com/watch?v=FcjRIZFQcUY.

WJW Aircheck "Alan Freed," YouTube. Accessed May 15, 2015. www.youtube.com/watch?v=GqKRYJS60Rc.

Index

Page numbers in *italic* indicate photographs.

About the Author

Ralph G. Giordano is a professional architect, a full-time teacher at Monsignor Farrell High School on Staten Island, New York, and an adjunct college professor at Kean University in New Jersey. He holds a master's degree from the City University of New York and a bachelor's degree in architecture from the New York Institute of Technology. Giordano has authored six books on American culture and is a member of the Authors Guild. His work has garnered a feature article in *The New York Times*, among many other publications. Giordano has received the prestigious Council of the Arts Humanities Award on Staten Island (COAHSI), recognizing his long commitment to the arts and humanities within New York City; the President's Dolphin Award for Outstanding Service and Contribution at the College of Staten Island; as well as a Faculty Appreciation Award presented by the Student/Athletes of CSI for his excellence in teaching. In 1995, he was inducted into the College of Staten Island Alumni Hall of Fame.